STUDIES

IN

SAIVA-SIDDHANTA

STUDIES

IN

SAIVA-SIDDHANTA

J. M. NALLASVAMI PILLAI B.A., B.L.

WITH AN INTRODUCTION

V. V. RAMANA SASTRIN, Ph. D.

GYAN

Published by

Gyan Publishing House
5, Ansari Road
Daryaganj, New Delhi-110002
Phone: 011-47034999, 9811692060
E-mail: books@gyanbooks.com

Distribution Network
gyanbooks.com
India, USA, Canada, UK, Australia, France

ISBN : 978-81-212-9272-6 (PB)
First Published, 1911

2nd Impression 2023

Printed at: Gyan Press, Delhi.

STUDIES IN SAIVA- SIDDHANTA
Author: J. M. NALLASVAMI PILLAI

STUDIES IN SAIVA-SIDDHANTA

STUDIES

IN

SAIVA-SIDDHANTA

BY

J. M. NALLASVAMI PILLAI B.A., B.L.

DISTRICT MUNSIFF, MADRAS PRESIDENCY

AND PRESIDENT, 3RD & 6TH SAIVA-SIDDHANTA CONFERENCE

WITH AN INTRODUCTION

BY

V. V. RAMANA SASTRIN, Ph. D.

F.Z.S. (LOND) ; O.M.D,S.F.V. (BERLIN) ; M.O.S.M.F. (PARIS) ; ETC., ETC.

MADRAS

AT THE MEYKAṆDĀN PRESS

1911

CONTENTS.

PUBLISHER'S NOTE.

THE following appeared originally in the *Siddhānta Dīpikā*, *Madras Review* and the *New Reformer* and they represent my father's contribution to the study of Siddhānta during the last Fourteen years, besides his translations of *Śivajñāna-bōdham*, *Śivajñāna Siddhiyār*, *Tiruvaruṭpayan* and Tirumūlar's *Tirumantiram* etc. and embody his critical researches and deep learning in the field of Indian Religion and Philosophy. As the earlier volumes of the *Siddhānta Dīpikā* are out of print, these are now published in a collected form for the first time at the pressing request of numerous readers of the *Siddhānta Dīpikā*. I hope to issue as soon as possible the other works of my father. I hope that my father's great labours in the field of South Indian Literature, Philosophy and Religion will be fully appreciated by the ready sale of this edition.

MADRAS
1911

J. N. RAMANATHAN.

INTRODUCTION.

THE assemblage of papers that make up the present volume, records the harvest of twenty-years' ceaseless research in a field of philosophy and mysticism, by one who is acknowledged on all hands to be one of the most well-informed interpreters of the Tamil developments of the great Āgamic school of thought. His translations into English of the Tamil redactions of the *Śivajñānabodha* and the *Śivajñānasiddhi*, and of the *Tiruvaruṭpayan* bring together a mass of explanatory and illustrative material that imparts a freshness and a purity to his performance, elements that we either totally miss, or descry with but exceeding dimness, in the parallel undertakings of the Rev. H. R. Hoisington and the Rev. Dr. G. U. Pope, and more recently of the Rev. H. A. Popley. The claims of Mr. J. M. Nallasvāmi Piḷḷai are thus well established as an excellent student of Tamil letters, and a thoroughly reliable interpreter of the phase of the Āgamānta that is developed and perfected in the magnificent writings of the Tamiḻ mediæval scholastics, divines and saints, among whom Meykaṇḍān was, perhaps, the foremost in point of learning, spirituality and power of suasion. Those mediæval schoolmen were preceded by the earlier Teachers of eminence, like Vāgiśa, Sundara, Sambandha and Maṇivāchaka, men who taught by example, rather than by pounding precepts and arid logomachy, as they took their stand on an actual knowledge of the "mysteries of the Spirit", and never on bare mental brilliance; while mighty spirits like Mūla, combined in them the traits of exemplary ethical observance and compelling spiritual inculcation, which hardly left the ripe Soul without the pabulum that was imperative for its upward growth or unfoldment, and eventual Spiritual Freedom. The object of the present Volume is to open up some of these veins of the purest Āgamic gold, in a style of genial didactics and multi-coloured presentation, veins which, although referred by our author for the most part to the Tamiḷ mines of Śaiva literature, would, on a further following up, yet prove to belong to a system of strata, more ancient in point of time, more remote in point of place, and more precious in point of composition and structure. The gold that is dug out of the veins, is of remarkable quality, be it in the shape of ores, nuggets or ingots, and the reader will be richly repaid for diving into the book, since each paper therein is devoted to a central idea, which is consistently worked out and explained with ample grace and ease of diction, and he may consequently be sure to emerge from its perusal, palpably edified on many of the moot-points of the Hindu Philosophy, as conned with the aid of the search-light of the Āgamic dogmatics that is preserved for us in ancient and mediæval Tamiḷ. It is by no means easy to enter into the genius of the Āgamānta, if one is not conversant with its right traditions which, by the very manner of their preservation and communication in India, are not of easy access to European scholars. A remarkable instance of failure to enter into the spirit of the Āgamic teaching, on account of this disability, is seen in the faulty interpretation put by the Rev. Dr. G. U. Pope on the cardinal doctrine of Āgamic mysticism, *Śakti-nipāta*. The late Oxford professor of Tamil, clever as he was as a skilled translator of the *Kuṟaḷ*, the *Nāladiyār* and the *Tiruvāçagam*, is quite wide of the mark when he explains Śakti-nipāta as "cesssation of energy" in the Introductory Essay prefixed to his edition of the *Tiruvāçagam*. The explanation calls to mind an analogous instance in which a

European Sanskritist, unaware perhaps of the bearings of the expression, rendered the collocation 'Parama-hamsa' into 'great goose'. The strictly pedagogic purist may endeavour to justify such puerile versions on etymological grounds, but they stand self-condemned as mal-interpretations reflecting anything but the sense and soul of the original. Such lapses into unwitting ignorance, need never be expected in any of the essays contained in the present collection, as our author is not only a sturdy and indefatigable researcher in Tamil philosophic literature illuminative of the Āgamic religion, but has also, in his quest after Truth, freely utilised the services of those indigenous *savants*, who represent the highest water-mark of Hindu traditional learning and spiritual associations at the present-day.

It is a remarkable irony of circumstance that, beyond sporadic attempts of uncertain value, no serious endeavour has as yet been made to give to the educated public a connected conspectus of the length and breadth of the teachings contained in the Śaivāgamas. The Rev. Dr. G. U. Pope, the Rev. H. R. Hoisington, the Rev. T. Foulkes and Dr. Karl Graul of an earlier generation, and some English clerics of a more recent date, such as the Rev. H. A. Popley, the Rev. G. E. Phillips, the Rev. W. Goudie, the Rev. A. C. Clayton, and a few others, have now and again tried to expound the Tamil phase of the philosophy to the best of their lights, although unable to fully divest themselves of their Christian leanings and prepossessions. The bed-rock of the Āgamic philosophy and mysticism, has to be delved into, through Sanskrit, and delvers for that purpose have, so far, been few and far between. Even in the otherwise pregnant treatise recently put forth in German by Dr. M. Winternitz on the History of Indian Literature, *Geschichte der indischen Litteratur, Erster Band*, the only mention that is made of the Āgamas is in regard to the Śākta-tantras, which he simply calls 'Tantras'. In other words, he details a few Tantras which are Śāktic, and though Śaivāgamas are not related to the Śākta-tantras by any organic community of thought or descent, such a detailing is, at any rate, indicative of the recent extensions made, by European scholars of light and leading, to the province of Indological research which hitherto has observed a sort of water-tight orthodoxy of scope. It is to be hoped that when a second edition is called for of that German work, Dr. M. Winternitz will not be slow to avail himself of the materials afforded by the Āgamas, and thereby add to the post-Vedic chapters of his book. At the same time, it is clear that Dr. Paul Deussen, another German Sanskritist and metaphysician of superb accomplishments and talents, gives indications of a knowledge of the Śaiva-darśana. In his masterly digest of the Monistic Idealism of Saṅkara, published in German, *Das System des Vedānta, Zweite Auflage*, he refers to the Bhāshya of Śrīkaṇṭha on the Brahma-Sūtras (the related portions were translated by me from German into English for the *Brahmavādin* in 1907-08), and in his more recent work on the post-Vedic Philosophy, issued in the same European language, *Allgemeine Geschichte der Philosophie, Erster Band, Dritte Abteilung, Die nachvedische Philosophie der Inder*, he devotes a chapter to the Śaiva-darśana. There is however nothing to show that Prof. Deussen has dived into the Āgamic literature at first-hand, as he has for instance, done, into the Aupanishadic, in the course of his descent into the wells of the ancient Āryan Monism. Further, the Āgamas have their own interpretations to offer as regards the cardinal precepts and teachings of the archaic Upanishats, and hence a thorough grounding in the Āgamas, and in such of the Purāṇas as have visibly felt the influence of, or been nurtured on the same soil as, the Āgamas, will altogether place the student on a new standpoint, and the Aupanishadic teachings in a new perspective, that is to say, in a setting that will be different to what has till now been considered, by the orthodox school of European orientalists, as the purely Vêdāntic view of the entire arcanum or scheme of Indian metaphysics. Consequently, an independent study of the Āgamas, untrammelled by any prior predilections, will prove of inestimable value to those orientalists who would be glad to investigate *de novo* whether the Aupanishadic teachings will not bear any other philosophic interpretation than the one accorded to it heretofore by the so-called accepted schools of Hindu philosophy. Again, in the last important work that Max Müller published previous to his death, *The Six Systems of Indian Philosophy*, though there are indications that he knew of the existence of the Āgamānta in both Sanskrit and Tamiḷ, there is nothing to show that he went into, or was conversant with, the details of the Śaiva-darśana as developed in the Divyāgamas. Dr. Georg Bühler had, it is said, an idea of making quite a study of the treatises in Sanskrit that were based on the Āgamas, as far as they concerned the Spanda and the Pratyabhijñā phases of the Śaiva-darśana, but his loss came off all too soon in 1898. And so, Dr. L. D. Barnett is perhaps the only extant European orientalist that has for some years past been taking an abiding interest in the study of the literature relative to the Śaiva-darśana in Sanskrit, and it must be said to his lasting credit that he is not only a thoroughgoing Sanskrit scholar, but is also an accomplished student of the Dravidian vernaculars, and his writings bear an unmistakable stamp of very good acquaintance with the works bearing on most of the phases of the Āgamānta, to wit, the Pratyabhijñā, the Vīra-Śaiva and the Suddha Śaiva (the parent of the system developed by Meykaṇḍān in Tamiḷ). He has translated into English the Paramārthasāra of Abhinavagupta (a Pratyabhijñā work), and edited other Śaiva works in Sanskrit. Another Pratyabhijñā work, by name Śivasūtravimarśini, has recently been englished by Mr. P. T. Śrīnivāsa Ayyaṅgār. Dr. Wilhelm Jahn seems to take a lively interest in Āgamic research, (Zeitschrift der Deutschen Morgenländischen Gesellschaft, Band LXV, pp. 380 *et seq.*, *q. v.*), which imports great future possibilities therefor at his hands, and Dr. F. Otto Schrader will not be long in coming out with an edition of the Mahārthamañjarī (a Pratyabhijñā work), to which I have been desired to append an English translation, with critical and exegetical notes. The task of continuing the translation of the Mṛigendra-Āgama from the point where Mr. M. K. Nārāyaṇasvāmi Aiyar left it, has devolved on me as a matter of friendly office, and though I have not been able to make any large progress with the continuation, by interruptions of an unlooked-for description, yet, it is hoped that the entire translation may soon be ready. A totally new translation into English of Nīlakaṇṭha's Brahma-Sutra-Bhāshya, with Appaya's Śivārkamaṇidīpikā which is its elaborate scholium in Sanskrit, has already been undertaken by me, but, it will, in any case, take some time to finish it. That translation will be fortified with rich critical apparatus, illustrative and explanatory notes, and special introductions in which a digest, in English, of the essential portions of most of the Āgamas now available, will, for the first time, be unreservedly incorporated. The above is all that may be said to have been achieved, or to be near within an ace of achievement, in the matter of the elucidation of the Śaiva-darśana.

On the purely expositional side, the doctrines of the Āgamas have found a reverent and apt interpreter in the scholar-sage Mr. P. Rāmanāthan, whose writings it is not possible to surpass either in this peninsula or beyond, for either clarity of thought or directness of appeal. But, unfortunately for scholars, he has not chosen to write on the subject more often or copiously than his writings would lead the reader to expect. On the other hand, the literature and the mysticism of the Āgamas have also had their share of travesty and mockery, in a new-fangled work on Indian Philosophy, recently brought out by Mr. P. T. Śrīnivāsa Ayyaṅgār. The last production is a curious mixture of laborious learning and hoaxing horse-play which will neither appeal to the scholarly philosopher nor the humour-loving general reader. Save for some bibliographical bits of varied character and uncertain authority, the book is a failure as a genuine *résumé* of the factors that enter into the constitution of the many mystic and metaphysical cults that have over run the post-Vedic India; and worst of it all, the chapters of the book, relative to the Āgamas and the Śaiva-darśana, are vitiated, in places, by gross misinterpretations, and, in others, by mistakes of fact begotten of the direst ignorance. As a piece of performance, the book is obviously inspired by a desire to synthetically emulate, in the realm of Hindu philosophic investigation, the divergent achievements of Westerns like Dr. Paul Carus and Prof. David Masson. And how little the author has succeeded in his endeavour, might be transparent to any one who would only care to read with some attention the chapters bearing on the Śaiva dogmatics and the Śaivāgamas. The Christian Literature Society is daily engaged in its storming operations against one phase or another of Indian Thought, so that an occasional devil's advocate from within, certainly fulfils a momentous function in the economy of academic investigation. In that sense, at any rate, such an author as Mr. P. T. Śrīnivāsa Ayyaṅgār ought to be welcomed, instead of being tabooed as unworthy of a piecemeal examination, and sober analysis.

The Āgamas contend that they constitute the truest exegesis of the Vedas, and their origins are certainly as ancient as those of some of the classical Upanishats. If the fire-worship be regarded as the ritual inculcated in the Vedas, as the outer symbolism of spiritual truths, the temple-worship may, on its side, be also said to assume a similar importance in regard to the Āgamas. The Āgamas bring in temple-worship as only a further concomitant of fire-worship, the one being regarded as an ancillary adjunct to the other. The only difference they introduce in the elements of fire-worship is the deletion of animals as objects of sacrifice. The higher interpretations put upon the sacrificial act in many of the Upanishats, are all to be found in the Āgamas, though the latter lead up to those interpretations through the symbolism of fire-worship, as worked out along the channel of temple-worship. For the rest, it will be seen that in India at the present-day, there is hardly a Hindu that does not observe some kind of temple-worship or another, which points to the conclusion that the Āgamas have had, in one form or another, a universal hold upon the continent of Hindu India, and that their influence tells. It may be easy to point to specific passages of the Vedas, and thereby put up a thesis that they do not contemplate temple-worship. Be that as it may, it will be equally easy to demonstrate that the Āgamas are the legitimate outcome of the teachings promulgated by the Vedas, and that the more important portions thereof, that is to say, the purely mystic and philosophical, were in every way anterior to such as deal with the rites of temple-worship and the technique of sacred architecture. Hence, the course of development on Āgamantic lines points to the inception of the Vidyā and the Yoga pādas of the Āgamas, as the next great stride after the stratification of the earlier Upanishats; and the Vidyā and the Yoga pādas did, in their turn, gradually necessitate the outer rites of symbolism, in view of a congregational worship adapted to the needs of the average man with a heart within him. Those liturgic rites were enshrined in the remaining pādas of the Āgamas, and the places for the performance of such rites, became the temples. There are, for instance, Āgamas in which the order of arrangement of the pādas, follows exactly the chronology herein explained; while there are also others in which the arrangement is reversed, due possibly to a later deliberate desire to follow logic of theoretic sequence in preference to the order of natural evolution. Temples are very ancient institutions, though only less ancient than the Upanishats of undoubted antiquity. And there is no doubt that, though the first impulse to temple-worship had come from the Kashmirian Region, the institution flourished in South India with considerable pomp and circumstance. The construction of the sacrificial pavilion for the performance of the Śrauta rites, is, as made out from the Śulba-Sūtras, chiefly astronomical in design and import. And not less so is that of the temple, every part of which has an analogue with either an astronomical phenomenon or a zodiacal convention. And this astronomical significance of the temple-symbolism, runs, in some of the Āgamas, side by side with the spiritual import that we have learnt to associate with the same symbolism. There are also phases of the Śaiva-darśana in which the temple-worship is not regarded with favour, either because it is not considered directly contributory to one's spiritual uplift-ment and eventual Emancipation, or because it proves, at a specific stage, an out-worn and jejune observance unsuited to the spiritual wants of the votary.

The Āgamas have branched out from the same stem of the Vedic tree that produced the earlier Upanishats, and were at one time as wide-spread in India as the Upanishats themselves. Like the Upanishats, the Āgamas also became, in course of centuries, the basis of a number of creeds which, though unanimous in accepting the essentials of the Āgamic teaching, were divergent as regards rituals, observances and minor unessential details. The earliest concretion of the Āgamic doctrines as a code of systematic dogmatics, had its birth in Kashmir, under the name of Spanda and Pratyabijñā darśanas, which gradually swayed the whole of the trans-Vindhyan Upper India. It is not a safe procedure to associate, as some do, the early origins of the Lakuṭiśa-Pāśupata with those of any the phases of the Śaiva-darśana that recognises the Śaivāgamas as its infallible scriptures of authority, since the dividing-line between the two forms of faith, is formed by the circumstance that the Lakuṭiśa-Pāśupata (which, at present, is confined to the upper parts of the Bombay Presidency), does not take its stand on the Śaivāgamas. The stream of the Pratyabhijñā and the Spanda flowed south, and became the parent of the Vīra-Śaiva system that, in its turn, grew influential in and round about the Deccan. An earlier current of the Pratyabhijñā and the Spanda had, in the meantime, found its way into South India, to form the nucleus of what later on, in the days of the mediæval theologians, became the compact system of the Śuddhaśaivadarśana. The philosophy that is at the back of all these three darśanas, is the Āgamānta which is known by various names, the chief of which being the appellation *Saiva-Siddhānta* (= 'the logical conclusion established by the Śaiva-darśana').

The three philosophic Categories which the Āgamānta recognises, are Nature, Soul and Spirit. The entire economy of the present Dispensation is under the active control of the Spirit, and is especially designed by Him in view to the Emancipation of the Soul. Nature is multi-coloured and many-vestured, and is the material cause of not only the outer universe, which hides, within the immensity of its bosom, countless hosts of sidereal systems, but also of our body, with all its grosser and subtler divisions and components, its instruments of knowledge and action, its proclivities and tendencies, in which the Soul lives as in a cottage. The Spirit is immanent in both Nature and Soul, and is in fact their Guiding Principle. He is thus the Soul's Soul. It is not in the power of the Soul to lead an independent existence, either it must remain in unwitting communion with Nature, overpowered by Her blandishments, or in conscious Fellowship with the Spirit, an intermediate state being thus practically denied to it. If it ceases to gravitate towards Nature, it must lean on to the Spirit. The *samsāra-chakra* is the Soul's orbit, which represents the resultant of two forces continually acting upon it. The orbit certainly shrinks up towards the Spirit, when the Soul would not be attracted by Nature. The Soul has the ability to know both Nature and Spirit, as it is possessed of sentiency, an attribute which it only shares in common with the Spirit. But it cannot be cognised by Nature, as She lacks sentiency; and, for the same reason, the senses and the mind, which are fashioned out of insentient Nature, cannot cognise the Soul. Nor has it usually an opportunity to cognise as such, its own true lineaments, because of its ceaseless and indistinguishable communion with either Nature or Spirit, a communion which prevents the Soul from identifying its genuine lineaments. The Soul is possessed, in other words, of the remarkable tendency of ever appearing in the colours of either of the two other Categories that chances to be in association therewith for the nonce, since, as we have shown, it is, for one thing, seldom, if ever, in a state of complete aloofness from both Nature and Spirit, and cannot, for another, associate with either of those Categories, without its being indistinguishably merged in, or its becoming one with it. Consequently, the Soul ordinarily sees in itself either Nature or Spirit, but not its own form. It is beginninglessly entangled in the fascinations of Nature, and the Spirit carries on His five-fold operations with a "body of pure sentient Energy"—the outcome of His own free-will—solely to disentangle it from those ruinous fascinations. The universe that we see around us, has Nature for its material cause, the Spirit for its efficient cause and His "body of pure sentient Energy" for its instrumental cause. Nature is specially superintended by the Spirit, in order that she, albeit insentient, may the more rigorously and consistently exhibit the law of desert and causality, in relation to the Soul. The law of causation is really the inherent and eternal property of Nature. As long as the Soul chooses to enjoy the company of Nature, so long will Her law of causality and desert hold the Soul tight within its meshes. But Her connexion with the Soul is, after all, but temporary, though She is, by Herself, eternal. It is also possessed of an ingrained perversity that is inherited from Nature, and hence eventually eradicable, whereby it mistakes its sensuous or sensual wallowing in the "lap of Nature" for its appointed Goal, and thus converts its Spirit-given instruments of Emancipation, formed out of Nature, into effective engines of its own perdition. The award of Spiritual Freedom is always made by the Spirit to the Soul by an act of Grace, and when the moment for that award (which involves a complete Emancipation from its bondage to Nature) has arrived, the Spirit reveals Himself to the Soul in any manner He pleases, and blesses it with *His Eternal Fellowship* of ineffable power and joy. The above, in short, is the plainest summary of the central truths of the Āgamānta, when shorn of all learned technicalities, and it will not be difficult to see how simple the whole teaching runs.

We shall now look at some of the Āgamic teachings a little more closely. The three categories, Nature, Soul and Spirit, are, as we have already seen, eternal, that is to say, are without either start or finish; but the Soul and Nature are under the control of the Spirit, and have nothing like absolute independence of action which the Spirit alone enjoys to the full. The Spirit is an embodiment of love and compassion, or, as it is sometimes expressed, is nothing but Life, Light and Love. The Souls are infinite in number, but a broad marshalling brings them under three classes, with reference to the varying grades of their bondage to Nature. Nature is governed by ceaseless cycles of periodic manifestation and dissolution, cycles which turn out, however, to be of many sorts and conditions, when regard is had not only to the extent of, or the interval between, the periods, but also to the specific character, phase or grade of the manifestations and dissolutions. Manifestation is simply a process of becoming patent, while Dissolution, that of becoming latent. Nature ever endures, librating between a condition of grossness and ponderability on the one hand, and subtlety and imperceptibility on the other. She is *per se* inert, and every cycle of Her activity is only rendered possible, by the peculiar impact she receives from the Spirit and His immanence in Her. The essential active attribute of the insentient Nature, is Her rigid adherence to the law of causation and desert, both physically and morally, and if the statement be made that She is the Spirit-appointed material instrument of the Soul's Salvation, all we are to understand therefrom is, the Spirit requires the Soul to seek its Emancipation only by wedding Nature, and thereby passing the ordeal of causality. But the elaborate processes which Nature daily employs to bring in more and more Souls as Her suitors, in order that they may be schooled under the law of causation, are indeed very inscrutable, although exceedingly seductive. She first seduces the Soul into Her company by Her irresistible fascinations, and finally tires it by Her inexorable law of causality, which at the same time reveals Her inward gruesomeness to the deceived Soul. The Soul then rates Her at Her proper worth, when She also, in Her turn, becomes a penitent and obedient instrument at its hands, by letting go Her hold of causality on the Soul. And thus Nature proves successively a seducer, a task-master and a servant, in relation to the Soul, in accordance with the degree of spiritual progress attained by it. The Soul is originally stupefied with the darkness of involved or inchoate Nature and, in that condition, remains tossed about in Her unfathomable womb, till the Spirit quickens it, so that it may take its chance towards its permanent Spiritual Freedom, by consciously contacting Nature. At each Dissolution, the unemancipated Soul reverts to the "womb of Nature," and awaits its return to the highway of *samsāra*, with Her next Manifestation. The Salvation of the Soul, when once attained, is permanent and irrevocable, but, the unconscious stupor in which it is primarily plunged, has no beginning. How the Soul comes by that oblivion, or, what amounts to the same thing, how it gets to be beginninglessly entangled in Nature, cannot be satisfactorily explained, and any endeavour to do so, however deftly managed, will be simply landing oneself in a vicious circle of *ad infinitum* regression. In other words, the Soul's state of bondage has no beginning, but has an end, while the Soul's Spiritual Freedom has a definite beginning, but no end. It is at this point the doctrine of the Āgamānta becomes hard of comprehension to those who cannot accept it solely on the testimony of the saints that "know" the "mysteries of the Spirit". Be it remarked however *en passant* that similar difficulties face us when we endeavour to examine other systems of philosophy put forth in India. There is hardly a philosophy or reasoned system without a cornering difficulty that is hydra-headed and protean-shaped, which, if it be deftly eschewed from one part of our discussion, certainly threatens us with paralysis, if not positive extinction, of thought, in another.

The Āgamic mysticism makes quite a speciality of the subjective processes connected with the Soul's Emancipation. On the principle that the " cottage " in which the Soul lives, is a minified copy or replica of the outer Nature, and the active Spirit behind Nature, is again the Soul's Soul, a graduated course of spiritual discipline is prescribed, quite replete with apt methods to suit the Soul in every one of its stages, whereby it is first trained to enter upon a minute examination of the constitution and functions of Nature, through a detailed and searching inspection of its own "cottage", and then taught to slowly and steadily disentangle itself from the enmeshments of Nature, and is finally left in a condition fit for the Grace of Emancipation from the Spirit. The disentanglement from the meshes of Nature, is briefly marshalled as ten-fold (daša-kāryāṇi), the condition of the Soul in its different grades of bondage to Nature, is ear-marked as eighteen-fold (ashṭādaša-avasthāḥ), the course of Nature's manifestation is regarded as six-fold (shaḍ-adhvānaḥ), the mood of Nature is proclaimed as five-fold (pañcha-kalāḥ) and so on, and, in this fashion, many a precious hint is dropped in the Āgamas, not only with reference to the procession of Nature in Her manifestation, and Her precession in Her involution, but also in connexion with Her unsuspected methods of seducing the unwary Soul, and with the only ways of keeping Her at Her proper vocation, to wit, as an obedient handmaiden of the Spiritward-bound Soul. All these, however, but make for a preparation to await the appearance of the Spirit, Who, at the right moment that is only known to Him, suddenly opens the door of His Kingdom (*Šaṅkarapura*) upon the ever-expectant Soul, and admits it to His never-ending Fellowship (*Ananya-sāyujya*).

So much for an imperfect summary of a system of ancient thought, philosophy and mysticism, to an exposition of which, the various papers, now brought together for the first time, in book-form, from the periodicals in which they originally appeared, have addressed themselves. The only mood in which the themes tackled by our author in this book, must be approached, is one of reverence and devotion, that was so eloquently pleaded for, recently, in the stirring address delivered by the Hon. Mr. V. Kṛishṇasvāmi Aiyyar before the Convocation of the Madras University, an address which, though primarily addressed to "boys," has yet graver lessons for "old boys", as these are, in truth, no better than babes in the wide "school of Nature".

MADRAS, V. V. RAMANAN.

13th Dec. 1911.

FLOWER AND FRAGRANCE.

A FLORAL WREATH.

What is there in Nature so full of beauty and so symbolic of the heart's purity, innocence, and love and joy, as the tiniest flower of the field? What reflects the great Divine Beauty and the Divine Loveliness and the Divine Harmony more than the lowliest blossom of the dale? The freshness, the symmetry and the delicate tracery of those flowers, how they appeal to man's inmost nature and how inspiriting they are! Need we wonder therefore that they have attracted, not more than what they are entitled to, we should say, the attention and love of the Oriental; and they enter largely into his enjoyments, his Religion and Philosophy. They hold a considerable place in Oriental symbology, and the Indian has loved to illustrate his great truths from flowers. No ceremonies can be performed without flowers; and he loves to deck with them the Presence of his Heavenly Father and he calls out to his brethern,

சித்தந் தெளிவீர்காள்
அத்தனாரூரனை
பத்திமலர் தூவ
முத்தியாகுமே.

O Ye who wish to attain Peace of mind
If Ye, our Father of Ārūr, worship
With Flowers of Bhakti,
Then will Ye attain Mukti.—(*Devāram*).

The flower in its three-fold character of flower, colour and fragrance appeals to him as the visible presence of That which is Sat, Chit and Ananda.

"பூவண்ணம் பூவின்மணம் போல மெய்ப்போதவின்ப
மாவண்ண மெய்க்கொண்டவன்,"

"Like the flower, its colour and its fragrance
The Lord as Sat, Chit and Ānanda assumes form,"

says the author of "Tiruviḷaiyāḍal Purāṇ," a work, by the way, noted for its charming diction and great powers of clear description.

Our Saint Appar addresses this Divine Form as 'O! Thou cow, the five products of the cow, O! Thou intelligence, Thou agni, Thou sacrificial food, Thou tongue, words proceeding from the tongue, Thou Lord, present in the heart of the four Vedas, *Thou flower, fragrance present in the flower, Thou joy of flower* present in the hearts of the freed, Thou Deva, Deva of of Devas, Thou Effulgent Sun, Lo! Such is Thy Divine Presence".

To the philosophic and highly devout Māṇikkavāchaka, the delicate connection of the flower and its fragrance has appealed in another light and he sings of "His greatness, in filling all inseparably and surpassingly *like the fragrance of the flower*",

"பூவினாற்றம் போன்றுயர்ந்தெங்கு
மொழிவறநிறைந்து மேவியபெருமை."

In another place, he compares this very connection to the connection of body and soul and in comparing both to the connection of the Param, distinguishes them at the same time:

உற்ற வாக்கையி னுறுபொருள் நறுமல
ரெழுதரு நாற்றம்போல்
பற்ற லாவதோர் நிலையிலாப் பரம்பொருள்
அப்பொருள் பாராதே
பெற்றவா பெற்ற பயனது நுகர்ந்திடும்
பித்தர்சொற் றெளியாமே
யத்த னாண்டுதன் னடியரிற் கூட்டிய
அதிசயம் கண்டாமே,

"Like the soul present in the body, and the fragrance in the flower, The Supreme (Param) pervades them and *surpasses* all.

The fools, not perceiving this truth, simply delight in enjoying the fruits of their own Karma. The words of these, my Father has taught me not to listen, by making me his slave and has drawn me to the society of his Bhaktas. This miracle has been permitted to me to see!"

Though God's connection with us is compared to the connection of the soul and the body, yet in this case, the omnipresence of the soul is still confined to the body and the connection yields the soul only a fancied pleasure, and not a real and lasting one, differing thereby from the Supreme who pervades all and surpasses all and who is all Love and all Bliss, ready to impart this Love and Bliss to those who understand him as such; and when this undying love (அயரா அன்பு) is possessed, then, that very moment, "the fragrance of Šivam (Love, Ānanda) will blow out of the flower of Jīva",

"சீவனுக்குள்ளே சிவமணம் பூத்தது."—(*Tirumūlar.*)

That great Yogin, Tirumūlar, is very prolific in the use of the simile of the flower, and amidst a variety of such we select one in which he piles his flowers (of Rhetoric) thick, one over the other, to express the omnipresence of the most Supreme :

"My Lord and my King is present, united in all, like feeling in air, sugar in the cane, butter in milk and the sweet juice in the fruit and *the fragrance in the blossom*",

"காலினூறும் கரும்பினிற் கட்டியும்
பாலினுள் நெய்யும், பழத்து ளிரதமும்
பூவினுள் நாற்றமும் போலுளன் எம்மிறை
காவல னெங்கும் கலந்து நின்றானே."

Our Saint Tāyumānavar, whose felicity in epithets and phrase-making, we will some-day illustrate, uses most happy language in this connection, in invoking that Rock of Love:

"O! Thou support of the devoted who attain to the limitless Yoga-Samādi by the *one word* (of their Divine Guru), when they view this vast world as the Supreme Bliss! O!

Though loving friend of even my lowly self! O! Thou Rock of joy, uniting with and showing in all bodies and the world and the souls, like the *fragrance playing on the half-blown flower* shaped like the half-parted, elegant and sweet-toned tinkling bells on children's feet".

The comparison of the half-opened flower (in the jasmine for instance) in which the fragrance is the sweetest and sharpest, to the sweet bells with half-parted mouths tied round children's feet, is most happy and delicious.

Nakkīrar is a very ancient author said to belong to the last Saṅgham or College of Paṇḍits in Madura and he has,

"Lo! my Lord of Kailāsa, which soars high above all, without any other higher than itself, is present in all, like the meaning in the word, and the soul in the body, *and the fragrance in the flower*".

We will weave into this growing wreath one more flower culled from the garden (Śivabhogasāram) of the founder of the Dharmapura Maṭṭ, inasmuch as it illustrates the meaning of 'Advaita' clearly.

"The *advaita* relation of God and the perfected Soul in Mukti is like the advaita relation existing always between fire and wood, heat and water, sweetness and honey, *fragrance and flower*, ākās and wind".

Mightily diffident as we are of achieving any thing without the Grace (Aruḷ அருள்) of the Most High, and without the spirits of the sanctified filling our inmost soul, we have helped ourselves to these holy flowers of His Bhaktas, to make a wreath and lay at the fragrant Lotus-Feet of Him, Who has never been known to forsake His devotees and pray to Him in all love and in all humility, to crown our humble efforts with success.

THE LIGHT OF TRUTH

OR

UṆMAI VIḶAKKAM

OF

TIRUVADIGAI MANAVĀŠAGAM KAḌANDĀR.

This short treatise consisting of 54 Stanzas is one of the Fourteen Siddhānta Šāstras, and its author is said to be Tiruvadigai Manavāšagam Kaḍandār, one of the 49 disciples of St. Meykaṇḍān. That he was a native of Tiruvadigai and a pupil of St. Meykaṇḍān is certain, but there are no other particulars available about his life-history. That he must have been an advanced sage is evident from the name (காரணப்பெயர்) he bears, which means "he who has passed beyond thought and speech."

The author tries to expound in these few pages, the truth of the Sacred Āgamas, without going into argumentation, just so much as is sufficient for the aspirant after spiritual Truth, to bring the teaching into actual daily practice. They are in the form of questions addressed to the Teacher St. Meykaṇḍān and answers elicited from him. The later part of the treatise explains the truth of the Pañchākshara and Šrī Naṭarāja Symbols. We hope the book will be of use to many.

1. வண்மைதரு மாகமநூல் வைத்தபொருள் வழுவா
வுண்மை விளக்கமுரை செய்யத்—திண்மதஞ்சேர்
அந்திநிறத் தந்திமுகத் தொந்திவயிற் றைங்கரனைப்
பந்தமறப் புந்தியுள் வைப்பாம்.

We place Him, in our heart; the Five-armed God in strong rut, of russet colour, tusked mouth, and pot-belley; so that we may be freed of our ignorance and be enabled without fault to spread the Light of Truth, to be gathered from the Sacred Āgamas.

2. பொய்காட்டிப் பொய்யகற்றிப் போதாந்தப் பொருளா
மெய்காட்டு மெய்கண்டாய் விண்ணப்பம்—பொய்காட்டா
மெய்யா திருவெண்ணெய் வித்தகா சுத்தவிஞ
வைய்யா நீதான் கேட்டருள்.

O Thou, my teacher, that, perceiving the truth, showdst the truth of Supreme Knowledge and Bliss after removing the falsehood, by proving it to be false!

O Thou, Truth, that will not give out false-hood,
O Thou, that residest in Tiruveṇṇainallūr,
Hear, O Thou, my humble petition, and deign to answer my queries!

3. O, my Teacher, explain to me the following!
What are the 36 tatvas? What is Āṇava?
What is that Karma which arose even then?
What am I who seem to differ from these?
Who art Thou? What is the Lord's Sacred Dance and what is the truth of the Pañchākshara?

4. O my son, who is immersed in Bliss-ful Yoga, hear what I am now imparting to you in accordance with the teachings of the Supreme Āgamas, graciously uttered of yore, by the Supreme Śiva.

5. The earth's form is a four-sided figure. The water is of the form of a crescent. The fire is of the form of a triangle always. The air is a six sided-figure. The Ākāś is a circle. And the soul gets a body formed of these.

6. The colour of these is golden, white, red, black, smoky-coloured, respectively and their letters are ல, வ, ர, ய, அ.

7. Their symbols are diamond-sword, the lotus-flower, *svastika*, the six spots, and *Amṛita-bindu* respectively. So the old Āgamas declare, O my Son.

8. The Gods for the elements Earth etc., are Braḥmā, Vishṇu, Rudra, Maheśvara and Sadāśiva; and their functions are respectively Creation, Sustentation, Regeneration, giving Rest, (Tirobhava) and showing Grace (Anugraha).

9. Brahmā creates; The lotus-eyed Vishṇu protects; Rudra destroys, and Īśa gives them rest; and Sadāśiva shows grace always.

10. The Earth is hard, water cool, and fire hot, air flows hither and thither, and Ākāś gives room to all.

11. We have now set forth the number and quality of the elements. If we are to tell you about the five deceitful Perceptions, they are the desire-producing Sound, Touch, Sight, Taste and Smell.

12. Hear the enumeration of the *Jñānendriyas*! Know them to be the ear, the skin, the eye, the tongue and the nose, which perceive the low sensations in this low world.

13 and 14. The ear perceives sound through Ākāś. The body perceives touch through the air. The eye perceives light through fire. The tongue perceives taste through water. And the nose perceives smell through the earth. So the Āgamas declare. They who conquer these senses secure the Bliss-ful Nirvāṇa.

15. The Karmendriyas giving rise to speech etc., are mouth, feet, hands, anus and the genital organs.

16. The mouth speaks through the aid of Ākāś; the feet move through the aid of air; the hands work through the aid of fire; the anus excretes through the aid of water; the genital organs give pleasure through the aid of earth.

17. Hear now the enumeration of the Antaḥkaraṇas! They are Manas, Buddhi, Ahaṅkāra and Chitta. They respectively perceive, reason, linger and reflect.

18. The foregoing 24 tattvas are stated by the ancient Āgamas to be the Ātma-tattvas. Hear, now the Vidyā-tattvas expounded by me.

19. Time, Niyatī, Kalā, Vidyā, Rāga, Purusha, Māyā, this is their order. Hear now their nature with attention.

20. *Time* measures the past, gives enjoyment in the present, and contains new store for the future. *Niyati*-tattva fixes the order and sequence of Karma. *Kalā*-tattva induces action. *Vidyā*-tattva induces intelligence. The Purusha-tattva induces perception of the five senses. And Māyā induces doubt and ignorance.

21. We have now stated the Vidyā-tattvas. Hear now the Śuddha-tattvas! They are Śuddha-Vidyā, Iśvara, Sadāśiva, Śakti and Śiva tatvas.

22. * Śuddha-Vidyā induces more intelligence than action. Iśvara-tattva induces more action than intelligence. Sadāśiva-tattva induces them both in equal proportion. Śakti-tattva induces action, and Śiva-tattva induces Jñāna alone.

23. † We have now fully stated the 36 Tattvas. Hear now about the two kinds of Mala, Āṇava and Karma. Stated, Āṇava induces ignorance; Karma Mala induces you to identify yourself thoroughly with the chain of pleasures and pains.

24. O Thou rare Teacher, Thou hast explained to me the nature of the 36 Tatvas, and Āṇava and Karma. Deign now to show me the nature of myself who seems to differ and not differ from these.

25. Hear well what I state! Achit cannot subsist before Pure Chit. Chit cannot perceive Achit. The Ātmā (Soul) is what distinguishes and perceives both Chit and Achit. So the Vedas declare without doubt.

---

* *Note.*—All these 36 tatvas are component parts of the universe of matter (Māyā), all powerful and all intelligent, in union with which, the soul gets rid of its darkness, and regains its light. This Śiva-tattva and Śakti-tattva etc., forming only matter should not be confounded with the Supreme Śiva and His Śakti.

† *Note.*—This Karma as defined here is exactly what the Buddhists understand by the Individual Ego, or Individuality which of course subsists from moment to moment and is not anything subsisting permanently.

26. Hear now how the 36 Tattvas cannot be conscious of themselves. The six kinds of taste cannot perceive themselves. So also the Tattvas do not know themselves.

27. As a person has to taste these six kinds of taste and then perceive them, so you are the intelligent person who uniting with these Tattvas perceives each and all of them.

28. "Out of thine undiminished grace, hast thou shown me my nature. Explain to me Thy own Imperishable Form." "As the Sun enables the eye to see, so will we enlighten you and your intelligence."

29. Know more. The senses cannot understand without the soul, and cannot understand the soul. So also do we enlighten you without your being able to perceive *us*.

30. "As the Vowel letter 'A' is to the rest of the letters, so do we stand as the Life of all life. When we are not present in any soul, then will there be no light. So the good Āgamās declare."

31. O Meykaṇḍa Nāthā, graciously expound so that I may understand the nature of the Sacred Dance with the sound of the five letters seen by the sages.

32. "O my son, hear; The Supreme Intelligence dances in the soul formed of the letter *ya*, with a Form composed of the five letters *Ši*, *va*, *ya*, *na*, *ma*, for the purpose of removing our sins.

33. Hear now how the Dance is performed! In His feet is *na*; in his Navel is *ma*; in His shoulders is *Ši*; in his face is *va*; in his Head is *ya*.*

34. ‡The Hand holding out protection is *ya*; the hand holding the fire is *na*; the foot holding down *muyalaka* is *ma*.

---

* NOTE.—These letters have to be contemplated in those parts.

‡ NOTE.—This is another form of contemplating the Pañchākshara.

35. The arch (திருவாசி) over Śrī Naṭarājā is *Omkāra* ; and the *akshara* which is never separate from the *omkāra* is the Filling Splendour. This is the Dance of the Lord of Chitambara. They understand this who have lost their self (Ahaṅkāra). Understanding, they leave their births behind.

36. Creation starts from the Drum. Protection proceeds from the Hand of Hope. The Fire produces Destruction. From the Foot holding down proceeds *Tirobhava;* the Foot held aloft gives mukti.

37. By these means, Our Father scatters the darkness of *māyā*, burns the strong *karma*, stamps down *mala* (Āṇava) and showers grace, and lovingly plunges the soul in the Ocean of Bliss. This is the nature of His Dance.

38. The *Silent* Jñānis, destroying the three kinds of *mala* establish themselves where their selves are destroyed. There they witness the Sacred Dance filled with Bliss. This is the Dance of the *Sabhānātha* whose very form is Grace.

39. The One who is past thought and speech assumes graciously the Form composed of the *Pañchākshara* in the Dancing Hall of *Parāśakti*, so as to be seen by His Consort, Umā, Haimavatī. They never see births who see this mystic Dance."

40. O my gracious Guru! Thou hast explained to me beautifully the nature of the *Nadānta* Dance. Let me now know the nature of the Panchākshara. Can they be one with the letters which are perishable?

41. "The Symbols of these letters may be perishable but not their connotation in any language. The meanings of the five letters respectively are God, His grace (Śakti), Soul, Tirobhava, and Mala.

42. God, Grace, Soul, Tirobhava, and Mala are the purport of the five letters (Śivāyanama). If pronounced beginning with *na*, you will not obtain Grace. You will obtain It when you pronounce It begining with *Śi*.

43. If this beautiful *Pañchākshara* is meditated upon, the soul, getting rid of its *Āṇavamala* will land in the Region where there is neither light nor darkness, and there, God's Grace (Šakti), will unite it to Šivam.

44. If the *Pañchākshara* is pronounced with the letters denoting the two *malas*, then will he not get rid of his three *malas*, and obtain Bliss. If pronounced otherwise acccording to law, your *jñāna* will be boundless and you can live in Bliss.

45. In the *Pañchākshara*, are found the Āgamas and the Vedas, given out by the gracious God. In it, are found the *Purāṇas*. In it, is the Blissful Dance. And in it, is found the silent Mukti, which passes beyond all.

46. The Āgamas declare that the nature of the union secured by the Muktas is like that of the fruit and its taste, fire and its heat, the musical composition and its tune.

47. The Vedas with truth declare that as the various Tattvas are found united inseparably in the bound condition, so the souls in the freed condition will dwell as one with God.

48. As the moon's light is indistinguishable in the Light of the Sun, so will the soul unite itself to the foot of the Supreme Lord and plunge itself in Bliss.

49. If it be said that the soul had to go and unite itself to God, then the Omnipresence of Šiva will be destroyed. If God is said to have united Himself to the soul, then they must be different. But what then is the Truth? The position is like that of the Sun which surrounds the man who had lost his blindness."

50. Thou tellest me that the Supreme one, who is past thought and speech, is gracious and suffers no taint, and that like this *Pati*, the *Pašu* and *Pāša* are also eternal. Prove this in *Mukti* also.

51. "O my Son, Hear how they are in *Mukti*! He who enjoys the Supreme Bliss is the soul. He who imparts this

Supreme Bliss is the First Cause. That which increases this happiness is MALA. Understand this in all love."

52. "O my Father, let me know the unfailing means of securing this Mukti?". "Hear me state this! They who regard and worship the *Guru*, *Linga*, and GOD'S DEVOTEES as the incomparable God, will not suffer births and deaths."

53. "Melting in Love, as the cow that had calved recently, the Jīvan-muktas will take strong hold of the *Guru*, *Linga* and *Bhaktas*, and will be possessed of great love to them, which will destroy their sins."

54. வாழ்ந்தேன் அருட்கடலே வற்றாப் பவக்கடலில்
வீழ்ந்தே யலையாமல் மேதினியில்—சூழ்ந்துவிடா
வெண்ணெய் ச்சுவேதவன மெய்கண்ட நாதனே
யுண்மைத் தவப்பயனேயுற்று.

O, Meykaṇḍa-Nāthā, the fruit of True Penance, Who dwellest in both Tiruveṇṇeynallūr and Svetavana, O, Ocean of Grace, I have been saved by thee, saved from being tossed about in the Ocean of Sorrow.

THE HOUSE OF GOD.

"YE ARE THE TEMPLES OF GOD."

" ஆதியாய் நடுவுமாகி யளவிலா அளவுமாகிச்
சோதியாய் உணர்வுமாகித் தோன்றிய பொருளுமாகிப்
பேதியா வேகமாகிப் பெண்ணுமா யாணுமாகிப்
போதியா நிற்குந்தில்லைப் பொதுநடம் போற்றிபோற்றி.

O, Thou, the Beginning, the Middle, the Limitless Limit,
The Light, and the Wisdom, and All Things Manifest,
The Indivisible One, The Female and the Male.
Glory, Glory to Thy Dance in Tillai,
The Intellectual Region of Universalism.

கற்பனை கடந்தசோதி கருணையே யுருவமாகி
அற்புதக் கோலநீடி யருமறை சிரத்தின்மேலாம்
சிற்பர வியோமமாகுந் திருச்சிற்றம் பலத்துள்நின்று
பொற்புட னடஞ்செய்கின்ற பூங்கழல் போற்றிபோற்றி.

O, Thou, the Light from which speech and thought turn back,
The very Form of Grace, The Wonderful Presence,
The Crown resting on the rare Vedaśiras,
In the beautiful Chit-Sabhā of Chit-Para-Vyoma,
Thou dost dance delightedly. Glory, Glory, to Thy tinkling Foot.

குன்றாத மூவுருவாய் அருவாய் ஞானக்
கொழுந்தாகி யறுசமயக் கூத்து மாடி
நின்றாயே மாயையெனுந் திரையை நீக்கி
நின்னையா ரறியவல்லார் நினைப்போர்நெஞ்சம்,
மன்றாக வின்பக்கூத் தாடவல்ல
மணியேயென் கண்ணே மாமருந்தே நால்வர்க்
கன்றாலின் கீழிருந்து மோனஞான
மமைத்த சின்முத்திரைக் கடலே யமரரேறே.

O Thou Imperishable Triple Form, and Formless! O Thou Supreme,
Intelligence working steadfast in the six forms of Religion!
Who could know Thee after raising the curtain of Māyā?
Thou dost dance in the hearts of Those who think of Thee,
Thou art the Priceles Jewel; Thou my eye;
Thou, the Supreme Panacea;
Thou the Ocean of Chinmudrā Wisdom,
Who didst teach the four ancient sons,
Mauna Jñāna from under the Sacred Banyan Tree
Thou, the Deva of Devas.

The first two verses we quote from Saint Šekkiḷār's Periyapurāṇ and the last from Saint Tāyumānavar, in praise of the famous Temple at Chidambaram and the sacred mysteries contained therein. We have elsewhere observed that even if we have lost our books on Veda and Vedānta, we could evolve the whole thing again from the symbols we possess, provided we had the tiny key to unlock these sacred mysteries. The hoariest and most ancient wisdom is thus enshrined in these unmistakable symbols, and when we understand them aright, we are enabled to test and know which is the true Philosophy and which is the true Religion, surrounded as we are to-day by a multitude of Religions and Philosophies conflicting in themselves and yet claiming to be the most ancient and the truest. It is the most unfortunate thing, in India and in Indian Religion, that the same books and the same texts furnish the authority and the sanction for every existing phase of belief and thought, and when this fact is coupled with such a blind ignoring of what is past and what is modern, and when the materials for applying such an historical test are not very considerable, the task of deciding which is the true interpretation and which is false, is rendered very difficult, though not impossible, and the value of a test as indicated above, cannot be lost sight of. In interpreting documents, the rule ought no doubt to be, that where the words are plain and unambiguous, the plain meaning of the words ought to be made to prevail, and no casuistry could be allowed to mar the effects of its plain meaning. It is only when the words are ambiguous, any interpretation as to its real meaning by other evidence is permissible at all. Then, again, when we begin to enquire into the truth of any particular custom and tradition, we find how difficult it is to arrive at an uniform conclusion, when we have to rely on mere oral evidence; and any documentary evidence (we use it in the strictly legal sense) if available, is of the utmost importance, and the older the document, the greater the value thereof. Then, again, consider the difference between the verbal accounts of a dozen people who witnessed a particular scene all at the same time, and the actual scene photographed by an ordinary *Kodak*. We might be sure to discover discrepancies and contradictions in the oral testimony, though it might be perfectly honest. Of course, there might be exceptionally trustworthy witnesses, as there might be untrustworthy cameras. The test we have proposed above, may, as such, be seen to possess all the elements of an old and ancient document, and a trusty camera. And the more so, when we know, as a matter of fact, that the written language of the primitive mankind consisted of pictures only. The most ancient Sumerian, the Chaldean, the Egyptian and the Chinese, were all pictorial languages; and it is well known that these were the people who have tried to leave their highest thoughts on religion and philosophy behind them, in pictures and statues and monuments.

In proceeding therefore to unravel the mysteries connected with our symbolism, we must confess that the task is not one which we can conscientiously think of adequately discharging. In attempting the impossible therefore, we have no other excuse than the one which Sage Šekkiḷār had before him:

> " *அளவு கூட வுரைப் பரிதாயினும்*
> *அளவிலாசை துரப்ப வறைகுவேன்.*"
>
> "Though impossible to reach its limits,
> Insatiate love drives me to the task."

Before we do so however, we have to get clear of two sets of men, who pester us often with their cant. One of such will raise the cry of sectarianism, and the other, with the catch-word, revivalism. There are some very estimable people belonging to both these classes, we admit, as well as their sincerity, but with most it is all mere cant, pure and unmitigated cant. They believe neither in the one nor in the other; they have neither inclination nor wish to study and think, and pause and enquire into the truth of things. They are themselves sectarians, so blind that they will not acknowledge themselves to be such. They start with the inborn conviction that this is trash and they have no patience with those who will honestly differ from them, and they clutch at a word, a phrase, to kick up a dust, with the evident object of besmearing the other side. No doubt, there is a sort of scepticism which we prize much, a scepticism which will lead one to doubt and inquire into the truth of things and not to scorn and scoff at everything. And in our inmost heart, we do not wish to wound the feelings of a single person, of whatever shade of opinion he may belong to. And is not the present enquiry solely devoted to reach 'the region of universalism,' "பொதுமன்று," where, in the words of our Sage Tāyumānavar,

> "பகர்வரிய தில்லை மன்றுட் பார்த்த போதங்கு
> என்மார்க்க மிருக்குதெல்லாம், வெளியேயென்ன
> எச்ச மயத்தவர்களும், வந்திறைஞ் சாநிற்பர்"?

every religionist comes and bows in adoration of the One Supreme, saying they see no symbols of any creed but all *Ākāś*? And he states in the previous lines that he reached this region, after looking in vain in every creed and in every path for that Pure Spirit which seeks to reconcile with the path of noblest knowledge, all the bitter conflicting creeds and religions.

> "சன்மார்க்க ஞானமதின் பொருளாம்வீறு
> சமய சங்கேதப் பொருளுந்தா னொன்றாகப்
> பன்மார்க்க நெறியினிலும் கண்டதில்லை."

And the place is worth a trial visit even to-day, for does not Tāyumānavar record his experience, that his stony heart melted into love and bliss, the moment he saw the Holy Presence?

> "கன்மார்க்க நெஞ்சமுள வெனக்கும் தானே
> கண்டவுட னானந்தம் காண்ட லாகும்."

This has not been his experience only, of believers alone. Ages back, scoffers and atheists have felt the power of this Presence, and it is recorded of the great Atheist Guru, Jaimini, that when he approached, all his unbelief left him, and he composed his song of *Vedapādastava*. And though there are thousands of temples all over the land, the heart of every true believer has always turned, with love and longing, to this *centre-spot*. And it is believed that Chidambaram occupies a central geographical position between the northern and southern extremes of India, including Ceylon. And corresponding to this position in the macrocosm, Ārumukha Nāvalar observes that, in the human microcosm also, the place points to the region of Sushumṇā between Iḍā and Piṅgaḷā *nāḍis*. There is another centre of heat and vitality and light in the human body, and that is the heart. And the heart is the most vital and delicate organ in the whole system. Every other organ requires its help for its nourishment and upkeep. It is saved and protected from many an ill, by its position, which every other organ is exposed to; but that is because that, whereas life can be prolonged even after injury to every other organ, life ebbs away the instant the heart is injured. And then, is not the heart, the seat of love, love pure and undefiled? Pity, kindness, mercy, grace, are all different shades of this one Love, அன்பு, Bhakti, faith. Is there anything else that can compete with this Supreme Principle? Knowledge, you may exclaim, with its seat in the brain. We dare say, 'not.' The slightest injury to the heart completely paralyses the brain. And the pulsation in the brain itself rises and falls with the beat of the heart itself. It is the one organ in the body which is ever active, and knows no rest, when everything else, including the brain, undergoes rest. And in human nature also, what is there which love cannot quicken? It can give life to the despairing and the lifeless, strength to the weak, courage to the coward; and instances have not been wanting to show what extraordinary feats of intellect, love has been the cause of. The whole world is bound by the heart, much more than by the intellect alone. And Mrs. Humphrey Ward has portrayed in glowing words the difference between the man of the intellect and the man of the heart in her *Robert Elsemere*. There, the man of the intellect pines, in secret and in his pride, for that very touch which makes the whole world kin. And it is in this heart, all mankind have liked to build a temple for the Most High. And the only requisite is, that this heart be pure. And the moment this heart is pure, there the light from the Invisible Ākāś will shine, dispelling the darkness that blinds the eye, and enabling it to see.

"வெளியான நெஞ்சனை வெளியூடு விரவினையா
வொளியாரும் கண்ணூறா மிரவியும் போனின்று லாவுவன் காண்!"

"Blessed are the pure in heart, for they shall see God." said the Lord Jesus. And the sage who composed the Taittirīya Upanishat sang long before him: "Satyam jñānam anantam Braḥma, Yo veda nihitam guhāyām Paramevyoman, So'śnute sarvān kāmāntsaha, Braḥmaṇā vipaśchiteti".

"He who knows Braḥman, which is Sat, which is Chit, and which is endless (Bliss), as hidden in the cave (of the heart) in the highest Ākāś, he enjoys all blessings as one with the Omniscient Braḥman." And the most mystical and oldest of the Upanishats, the Chhāndogya, also repeats the same instruction. "Would you like to know what that one thing is, which you have to search for and to know? And when you have to search for it, how to know it? Hear! There is the Braḥmapura (body), and, in it, the Dahara (palace) of the lotus (Puṇḍarīka) of the heart, and, in it, that Antar-Ākāśa. Now, what exists in this Ākāśa. That is to be sought after, That is to be understood.

"As large as this Ākāśa is, so large is that Ākāśa within the heart. Both heaven and earth are contained in it; both

Fire and Air; both Sun and Moon; both Lightning and Stars; and whatever there is of Him in this world, and whatever is not, all that, is contained within it." (VIII, 1. 123) In an earlier chapter, this Supreme Being is called "The Intelligent, Whose body is Prāṇa, Whose form is Light (Jyotis), Whose thoughts are true, Who is like the Ākāśa (omnipresent and invisible), from Whom all works, all desires, all sweet odours, and tastes, proceed; the Ātmā within the heart, smaller than a grain of rice, smaller than a grain of barley, smaller than a mustard-seed, smaller than a canary-seed, or the kernel of a canary-seed; also the Ātmā within the heart, greater than the Earth, greater than the Sky, greater than the Heaven, greater than all these Worlds." (III. 14. 223). In a later passage, the Upanishat says that "He who is called Ākāśa is the revealer of all forms and names; That within which these forms and names are contained, is the Brahman, the Immortal, the Ātmā." (VIII. 13. 1.) The following verse occurs in the Kaṭha (I. 2. 20.), the Svetāśvatara (III. 20.) and the Taittirīya-mahopanishat, and the same is reproduced in the Śivamahāpurāṇa.

"Smaller than small, yet greater than great, in the heart (Guhā) of this creature, Ātmā or Īśa doth repose: That, free from desire, He sees, with His grief gone, the Lord and His might, by His favour." In the Kaivalyopanishat, the same is reproduced, in the following words: "Beyond the heavens, yet shining in the heart (Guhā) of his creatures, Him the sages, free from desire, reach." Śrī Kṛishṇa also imparts this most secret of secrets to his pupil, "that Īśvara dwelleth in the hearts of all beings, O Arjuna, by his māyā, causing all beings to revolve, as though mounted on a potter's wheel," and importunes him to flee to Him to secure Supreme Peace by His Grace. The manner of occupying this seat or dwelling place is elsewhere referred to, in the XIIIth and IXth discourses, 32nd and 6th verses respectively, and these three or four verses bring out the whole of the Upanishat thoughts. "As the Omnipresent *Ākāśa* is not soiled, by reason of its subtlety, so, *seated* everywhere *in the body*, the Self is not soiled." "The support of beings, and not rooted in beings, my Ātmā is their *efficient* cause; as rooted in the *Ākāśa*, the mighty air moves everywhere, so, all things rest, rooted in me." This Supporter, Permitter, Spectator and Enjoyer, is styled Māheśvara, Paramātman and Parama-Purusha, in verse 22, chapter XIII. Another verse in the *Chhāndogya* says that Gāyatri is the body and the heart, because in it all the spirits are established. No wonder, therefore, that in almost every page of the Tamiḻ Veda, and the writings of the later Tamiḻ Saints, God's truest dwelling place, His house, His palace, His seat, is universally referred to as the human heart. "நினைப்பவர் மனமே கோயிலாக்கொண்டவர்." And so it is that the famous Shrine we are speaking of, is, by preëminence called "திருக்கோயில்",* "The beautiful House," inasmuch as it is also called the "Puṇḍarika Viḍu" "புண்டரீகவீடு", "the House of lotus", or "*Dahara* Viḍu" also. And, to-day, we will stop, after identifying this Golden Palace in Chidambaram with the "Human Heart" spoken of in the most ancient writings, and we will speak of the Great King and Lord, Who is the Dweller in this Palace and His characteristics, in a future issue.

[* It is interesting to note that the chief Temple in Mecca is called 'al Caaba,' literally meaning, 'The House' and the Hebrew word for the great Temple at Jerusalem also meant simply, 'The House,' "The House of God."]

LOTUS OF THE HEART.

If the real nature of the Lotus of the Heart is examined, its stalk will be the 24 tattvas, beginning with earth; its petals, vidyā-tattvas and śuddha-vidyā; its pollen, the 64 kalās of Īśvara and Sadāśiva; its ovary, Śakti, the essence of kalās; its seeds, the 51 forms of nādam; and the aruḷ-śakti of the Lord Śiva rests on it (as fragrance).

(Sivajñānabodham IX. 3. c.)

AN ANOTHER SIDE.

We refer to an article entitled 'Wisdom and Worship' in an issue of the *Brahmavādin* dated 5th June 1897. The first paragraph is devoted to the statement and exposition of the two postulates of existence, according to the Sāṅkhyas, namely Nature and Souls, and the next paragraph shows how untenable this theory is, in the view of the Vedāntin, and the article proceeds in its first half to expound the view of the Vedāntin, on the same subject. As the article deals with some of the most fundamental questions connected with Hindu Philosophy, we proceed to-day to examine some of these statements contained in the first part of the article only, leaving the question of worship to be discussed hereafter. According to Sāṅkhya, there is Nature (Pradhāna), which changes and manifests all phenomena, and there are an infinite number of Souls, which being simple cannot change, and must, therefore, be different from Nature. Nature works out all phenomena for the liberation of the Soul, and Liberation consists in the Soul discriminating that it is not nature (Pradhāna). The Soul is omnipresent also. The Vedāntin answers that this is not a perfect sytem. If Nature is simple, and the Soul is also simple, there will be two simples, and the Soul being omnipresent, Nature must be omnipresent also, and then Nature will be beyond time, space and all causation, and no change is possible as such in Nature. There is thus an impossibility of having two simples and two absolutes. How does the Vedāntin solve this problem? His solution is this :—"Because, according to the Sāṅkhyan there must be a Soul apart from Nature, for the reason that Nature in all her modifications, from gross matter up to *chitta*, or the intellect, is simply insentient (even the mind-stuff being insentient), so, there must be some sentient being as the motive-power behind Nature, making the mind think and Nature work. Now, says the Vedāntin, this sentient being, which is behind the whole universe, is what we call God, and consequently this universe is not *wholly* (the italics are ours) different or apart from Him. It is but Himself, Who has *somehow* (the italics are ours) become this universe. He is not only the instrumental cause of the universe, but also the material cause thereof. A cause is never *altogether* different from its effect, and an effect is but its own cause reproduced in another form." All Vedāntins accept these propositions, it is stated, namely first, that God is both the instrumental and material cause of this universe,.and that everything that exists is He; and secondly, that Souls are also part of God, sparks of that Infinite Fire, and an Upanishat Text is quoted in proof of this. No, it is said further down, it is no spark, but the burning log itself, in as much as Braḥman can have no parts. 'Then how can there be so many souls?' We are led into another simile, the oft-repeated simile of the Sun and its myriad reflections in different particles of water: "so all these Souls are but reflections of *Braḥman* and are not real. They are not the real 'I,' the One undivided Being; men, women, brutes are mere reflections of Him, and are unreal." There is but one Infinite Being, and he appears as 'you' and 'me', and the appearance of distinctions, is all a delusion. This apparent division of Him is caused by looking at Him through the net-work of time and space and causation. The Ego is He, the Non-Ego is He. They are not part of Him, but the whole of Him. "It is the Eternal Knower Who stands behind all phenomena; He Himself is the phenomena. He is both the subject and object, He is the Ego and the Non-Ego." Here we might pause, before we proceed to the rest of the paragraphs.

In the first place, we must beg leave to state that the criticism of the Sāṅkhya proceeds on a mere word-quibble; the word that is translated 'simple' is, we believe, 'Avyaktam,' that source of fruitful dispute between a number of learned heads, like the late Mr. T. Subba Rao, the *Light of the East*, the *Thinker* and the *Brahmavādin* itself etc., etc., *i. e.*, where the word occurs in the Gītā. The whole mistake is, no doubt, due to not remembering that this word, and others like Prāṇa, Purusha, Ātmā, Kshetra, etc., are used in the older works in a number of acceptations, and any argument based on such a verbal semblance, is sure to end in fatal error. Now in regard to this word 'Avyakta', it is used in the 10th sūtra of the Sāṅkhya-Kārikā, to distinguish Mūlaprakṛiti from its own products; and the Commentator no doubt says that the distinction might apply to the Soul also. The word might itself be applied to the Soul, but then it only means, 'uncaused' and 'causeless'. And Colebrooke translates it as 'undiscrete'. The 3rd Sūtra makes clear this distinction in the very beginning, "Nature is no production; seven principles are productions and productive; sixteen are productions (unproductive). The Soul is neither a production nor productive." Herein lies all the difference, between the Soul as Avyakta and Nature (Pradhāna) as Avyakta, and the mental and sensory planes. Nature itself occupies a higher position, is more pervasive than the Intellect, and Intellect is more pervasive than the senses, and so on. That is to say, Intellect is omnipresent, and senses are not, when in relation to the senses themselves. But Intellect is not, when in relation to *Pradhāna*, and *Pradhāna* is omnipresent so far as regards its own productions, but its omnipresence is nothing when in the presence of the Soul, since the latter is the superintendent, the enjoyer, and the former ceases to exist when the Soul is in a state of abstraction. As such, the word 'omnipresence' itself is a relative term, as 'space' itself is, and it is absurd to conclude that since both are called simple and omnipresent, ergo, they must be two absolutes, and two such impossible things. We will explain ourselves more fully. Take, for instance, the five senses, the eye, the ear, etc. The eye covers a certain sphere in its operation, but it is limited; it cannot comprehend what the ear can perceive, and the ear cannot do what the nose can feel, and so on. Each sense, in fact, is limited and unpervasive; but take the Intellect in connection with this. The Intellect is omnipresent. It both sees and hears and smells etc. It covers a greater sphere, and all the spheres covered by its own productions, the senses. But take the intellect (Buddhi) itself in its relation to the Soul. The Soul is sentient and *Buddhi* is insentient. The latter is nowhere, when the Soul is in itself. As such, the Soul is more really omnipresent than Pradhāna or Nature. That is to say, there are different planes of existence, and different grades of *Vyāpaka Vyāpya*. The one lowest is *Vyāpya*, and the one higher is *Vyāpaka*, and this higher itself is Vyāpya when compared with something higher than itself, and so on,.till we arrive at a Being, Who is most omnipresent and beyond Whom our thought and mind cannot penetrate. This view of the Sāṅkhyan has no doubt not presented itself to the Vedāntin, and what the latter has however in his mind is the old riddle, how can two things co-exist, and one be omnipresent? Like all such riddles, this is based on a fallacy, in not taking note of the facts above presented, about the essential difference between Pradhāna and the Soul. The riddle supposes that two things are of the same kind, of the same quantity, length, breadth, width and of the same density or tenuity &c. If they are so, no doubt it will be an impossibility. But we contend that things of different densities and tenuities can fill and overlap one over the other, and much more so when one is sentient and *Chit*, and the other is non-sentient and *Achit*. For instance, there can be no two things so contrary in Nature as Light and Darkness. And do they co-exist or not, or are they one and the same? To the objection of the Vedāntin, that darkness is no padārtha, we have only to instance the recent discoveries of our own Hindu Scientist, I mean Dr. Bose, who could demonstrate the presence of invisible rays of light in a pitch-dark room by means of his instrument. What does this mean? The ray of light has been so thin as to be swallowed up in the grosser darkness. When a lamp is brought, it could dispel the darkness itself; but, only within a certain radius. Then a bigger light, a gas-light, an electric light of a vast number of candle powers; but all these pale away before the brilliant light of the Sun. There is, thus, such a merger of one,.the less powerful, in one more tenuous: are not all these summed up in the simple sentence "Nāchichchitsannidhau", 'யாவையும் சூன்யம் சத்தெதிர்', 'In the presence of the Sat, every thing else is *Śūnyam* (non-existent —non-apparent'?

Saint Meykaṇḍa Deva adds 'As before the Perfect and Eternal Intelligence, the imperfect and acquired intelligence (falsehood) is shorn of its light, it is therefore established that in the presence of the Sat, Asat loses its light." And the illustration implied in this, is amplified in the following verse, "Evil (Asat) ceases to exist before Him, as does darkness before the Sun." The term Asat has itself been the parent of many misconceptions, in the East and in the West, and different interpreters of Śaṅkara explain it in different ways. Here is what a critic of Paul Deussen says, "Kant is mostly credited with having proved that there is something behind or beneath the "reality" of our senses, which these cannot fathom. (அசத்தியா). The European scientists say sneeringly: What of that; if we cannot get at it, let us ignore it! And on the other hand, the Neo-Kantian Metaphysicians say: No, this is the only reality; therefore, all the rest is useless rubbish, only fit for momentary amusement: and that is all.

"That is the Western conception of the Indian term Māyā (Asat), indeed a rubbish conception. And mistaken by this illusion, Western philosophers have declared that Eastern philosophy and particularly Vedāntism and Buddhism, are '*Akosmism*' *i.e.*, they deny the existence of the universe altogether. An incredible absurdity! Is not the real meaning of Śaṅkara easy enough to understand? Every one knows that there are different states of consciousness; that of an animal is different from that of a man, that of a savage different from that of a savant, that of a waking man different from that of a dreaming man, and all these are different from that of a sage in Samādhi. Now, it is a matter of course, that the 'reality' of a waking man is different from that 'reality' which he conceives as such when he is dreaming, and both are very different from that 'reality' or those different states of 'reality' of which he becomes conscious when he enters Sushupti and Turiya, and all these are, again, other 'realities' than that as which the Muktā 'realizes' Ātman. Viewed from the standpoint of any of these different states of consciousness, all the other conceptions of 'reality' appear as Māyā, as illusion or as unreal. The material scientist, together with most European philosophers, would even not hesitate a minute to declare the alleged realisation of Ātman an illusion, although he would not deny that this might be some state of consciousness."

And, by the way, he objects to translating Avidyā as ignorance or nescience, but as not-Vidyā or not-yet-wise or other-than-wise. That is, Asat does not mean non-existent, but not-Sat or other-than-Sat. This is Śaṅkara's view according to Dr. Hubbe Schleiden; and this is the view we have taken trouble to expound above, and yet how many followers of Śaṅkara hesitate before reading Māyā as illusion and delusion, and Avidyā as ignorance and nescience. In the very article under review, we read in one sentence that each soul is a spark, a part; in the next sentence, no, it is not a part, but the whole of *Brahman*. In the very next sentence, all these souls are but *reflexions* of *Brahman*, and are *not real*. "Men, women and animals &c., are but reflexions of Him, and are *unreal* in *themselves*." If they are mere reflexions, and unreal, how is it reconcilable with the statement, that each soul is not even apart but the whole of Brahman. The whole argument is made up by the use of similes and by not sticking to one, but by jumping from one into another, to meet the difficulty arising in the former. Either the argument must proceed on simple facts and inferences, and without the use of similes, or, when it is attempted to be proved solely from figures, then no apology should be presented that it is only a figure, and it should not be strained. The simile was expressly used for demonstrating to the ignorant, how the thing is possible and conceivable, and when the ignorant man following the simile, asks if the same antecedents are present in the thing compared, to warrant the conclusion, what answer does the Vedāntin give him? "This apparent division of Him (as 'you' and 'me' and the dog) is caused by looking at Him, through the net-work of time, space and causality." 'Looking at Him' indeed! When? And by whom? How is this 'looking at Him,' and this delusion possible, before the actual division itself? The operation of the division of Him into 'you' and 'me' and animal, must precede the operation of 'you' and 'me' &c., looking upon each other and Him delusively. Does the delusion come in before the evolution of 'Brahman' into 'you' and 'me' and 'animal,' or after such evolution? To any thinking being, it must occur that this delusion must have occurred before, and not after; and the *Brahmavādin* sees this, and states below that there will be in the universe a final duality, Ātman and delusion (mark here and elsewhere the word delusion is simply used as a synonym for Māyā), and this objection is brushed aside on the ground that delusion is no-existence, and that to call it otherwise is idle sophistry! And yet 'you' and 'me' and others, were all this while under a delusion! Were we or were we not? Is that a fact or a delusion itself? Is the evolution of God into men, women and animals, is that a fact or not? If a fact, is the question, 'how is this evolution brought about,' a possible question or an impossible question? If not a fact, why is the statement made in another paragraph, that there are perfect men and imperfect men, men like Christ, Buddha and Kṛishṇa, who have to be worshipped, and men, like ourselves, who have to worship them. This evolution of God into man and animals, is put in one place on a possible and rational basis, in that God wants to know Himself, wants to see Himself and realize Himself by means of His reflexions (why and wherefore it is not stated), in as much He cannot know and see Himself otherwise, in the same way as we on earth cannot see our face, except in a mirror! Again, we ask, is the distinction between a perfect man and an imperfect man real or not? And does our learned brother contemplate the possibility of seeing his beautiful face distorted in a mirror ?* Whose fault was this? It was our brother's fault in not choosing a good mirror. And does he mean to attribute to the Most Intelligent such fault, in not choosing such a vessel in which He can see Himself and know Himself to the best advantage? The Perfect cannot seek to know Himself in the imperfect and the ignorant, the wicked and the sinful, the sorrowing and the suffering. If all this is a play of His and no such distinction, as the imperfect, the wicked and the sinful and the sorrowing and the suffering, exists, and all this is a hallucination, myth, non-existence (we use his own choice words), why should any man aspire to be a good man, a perfect man, a Jīvan-mukta? Why should he *realize his identity* with the Absolute? God, in trying to realize Himself (for His sport or for what?), became man and woman and brute; and look at the bother of this man, woman or brute, doing good acts, acts without attachment, real *tapas, yoga* and *jñāna* to realize his identity with the Absolute! What guarantee is there that, after all this bother, a Jīvan-mukta may not again be differentiated from the Absolute into a man, woman or animal? How senseless and vain all these efforts seem, how ignoble, the purpose of creation and evolution? To the question why does the Perfect become the imperfect, which question our brother states in all its various forms, vulgar and highly philosophic, our brother's answer is that this question is an impossible one, and it should not be put at all! We have already pointed out how inconsequential this question and answer is. But the same question has been put in, and answers, attempted by learned men who are of our brother's ilk; and these answers are various and conflicting in themselves. Of these, Svāmi Vivekānanda gets most glory. His answer is 'I do not know.' Mr. Mukhopādhyāya replies that the Svāmi is wrong, and that the Perfect does not become the imperfect, God does not become man. Man is only a reflexion and as such cannot be God. According to the *Brahmavādin* man is a reflexion, is unreal;

* We have seen in the Bangalore Palace of His Highness, The Mahārājā of Mysore, a number of mirrors in which one's face is distorted in the ugliest and most horrible manner.

but the unreality itself is unreal, and as such man is God. And so no question arises of the Perfect and the imperfect. According to Paul Deussen, the answer is, 'the never ceasing new creation of the world is a moral necessity, connected with the doctrine of samsāra, "A moral necessity for *Ātman*? What a *contradictio in adjecto*!" exclaims his critic*. "*Ātman* as we all agree is that which is beyond all necessity and causality, that is, causality reigns or exists only in our manifested world, of *individual* consciousness of any sort." And the critic's own explanation is that existence is the manifestation of the will to exist, and this will is *trishṇā, tanha*, the desire for enjoyment. Well, whose will, we ask; who desires for enjoyment? The Absolute, the Sachchidānanda, or any other? What, call this hell, an earth, an enjoyment for Him? We leave our learned Doctor to fight out Professor Deussen by himself, and proceed to state another learned lady's opinion. If we remember correctly, she said, Īshwara evolves into man and brute, to gather experience, to improve himself by means of his animal sheaths, and that there could be no perfect Brahman, at any time; It goes on improving Itself, day after day. That if the Veda repeats the cry that there is a Bourne from which there is no return, no return, it is a mere make-believe. And all these are learned expounders of Śaṅkara's school, and who is right? Can we ask this question, or is our question captious? The Siddhāntin's answer is the question itself is based on a fallacy, an assumption. The fact assumed is that the Perfect becomes the imperfect. Is this a fact proved? Does God really become man and brute? What is the proof of this, let alone Vedic texts and the desire to reach a high-sounding philosophic unity? It is this fancied desire to generalize everything into One, that led the Greek philosophers to postulate number and water and fire, as the Final and Ultimate Cause of all things. Why not leave bad, good and evil as they are? Why should you refer the evil to the good, impure to the pure? Will not

---

* Dr. Hubbe Schleiden at page 227, January 1895, 'The Theosophist.'

silence in this respect be golden? Will not *maunam* in this case be real *jñānam* ?

Well, we will here go back to our statement of what the Sāṅkhyan meant when he postulated a Pradhāna and a Soul or souls. The learned Editor of the "*Light of the East*" has evidently fallen into an error when, in his account of the ancient sāṅkhya system, he opines that according to the ancient Sāṅkhya and the Gītā, there is only one Purusha and not many purushas. The mistake is due to the fact that, in the enumeration of the padārthas, the singular only is used; a mere technical usage, as in the phrases, Jīva-Iśvara-Jagat, Chit-Achit-Ishwara, Pati-Paśu-Pāśa. All the words used are in the singular, and it cannot mean that the respective schools mean to postulate only one Jīva, one Chit or one Pāśa. In explaining each, the explanation will be given that the jīva or souls are many. In the same way, in the earlier sūtras of the Sāṅkhya, Purusha in the singular is used, but the subsequent sūtras proceed to state that the purushas are multitudinous. Pradhāna is real and it is the cause, and its effects, the phenomena, are also real, as the effect subsists already in the cause, and as our learned brother approvingly puts it, an effect is its own cause reproduced in another form; and we hope the following sentence from Dr. Brown's lectures, will equally meet with our brother's approval. "That the form of the body is only another name for the relative position of the parts that constitute it, and that the forms of the body are nothing but the body itself." If so, why should the cause be considered real, and the effect unreal, as against the view of Sāṅkhyan by Vedāntins? If the Māyā is phenomenon and effect, why should it be unreal, when the substance and cause is real? The relation of cause and effect has, however, to be kept separate from the relation of substance and phenomenon, and these two, from the questions of reality and delusion. In the second paragraph, however, our brother identifies the Sāṅkhyan's Pradhāna with his own Māyā and the Sāṅkhyan's Purusha with his own God or *Brahman*. If so, why attempt any criticism of the Sāṅkhya? It is all a quibble about words. They practically postulate the same and mean the same things. Then, why is it that the Sāṅkhya is called by Śaṅkara, 'Nirīśvara Sāṅkhya' 'Godless or Atheistic Sāṅkhya', and the Philosophy of the Gītā as Seśvara Sāṅkhya or the Theistic Sāṅkhya. The word Sāṅkhya meaning primarily number, meant with Kapila and Kṛishṇa a theory or philosophy. Compare for instance a similar change in the Tamiḷ word 'எண்' meaning number, and in the verse "எண்ணும் எழுத்தும் கண்ணெனத்தகும்," 'எண்' meaning logic and philosophy. The following quotation from the Gītā itself, will explain the difference between the two schools.

"There are 'two Purushas' in this world, one destructible and the other indestructible, the destructible is sarvabhūtāni (all things), the indestructible is called the Kūṭastha." (Chapter XV. 16.)

Well, look how this verse runs; it mentions only two Purushas, instead of mentioning three, as arising from the next verse; but there is a purpose in so mentioning two Pūrushas; it is seemingly to reiterate the accepted postulate of the pūrvapaksha school, to enable it to state the siddhānta view, in the next verse which is:

"The 'parama Purusha' is verily another, declared as the 'Paramātman', He who pervades and sustaineth the three worlds, the indestructible Īśvara."

Consider again the steps that follow one upon another in the next verse.

"Since I excel the destructible (first Purusha), and am more excellent than the indestructible (second Purusha), in the world and in the Veda, I am proclaimed Purushottama" (third Purusha).

Be it noted here that the word Purusha simply means a category, a padārtha, as when we speak of the Tripadārtha or Tattvatrayam. Note again how in verse 19, chapter 13, the first two Purushas are mentioned as (by its more appropriate names) Prakṛiti and Purusha; and the same definition of these two is given in verses 20 and 21, as by the Śāṅkhya; and a further step beyond Kapila, is taken by Śrī Kṛishṇa in postulating,

"*A spectator and permitter, supporter and enjoyer, Maheśhvara, thus is styled the Paramātman, in this body, the Paramapurusha.*"

And then a most beautiful passage about the distinction of these three Padārthas, and of the different Jñānas, pāśajñāna, Paśujñāna, and patijñāna, occurs. The Lokāyata only knows his body, and has no knowledge of his own self or anything higher. According to the Nirīshvara Sāṅkhyan or the Vedāntin, there are or seem to exist only two things, Prakṛiti and Soul, Māyā and Ātman, and liberation consists in distinguishing his own self as different from a Prakṛiti or Māyā (delusions). This is Paśujñāna or Ātmajñāna. According to the Seśvara Sāṅkhyan, he sees and learns to distinguish Prakṛiti from his self, and his self from the Highest One (verse 29), as Akarta and Karta, and knowing the nature of this One, he reaches Brahman-hood. (verse 30 of Chapter 13). It is also to be remarked particularly that in the whole Gītā, in innumerable passages, as in the one cited above, the knowledge of the Supreme, the devotion wholly to Him, is put forward as the highest path of attaining Liberation, and not the Ātmajñāna doctrine that the knowledge of the individual self, as implied in the phrase 'know Thyself,' is the highest attainment. We beg leave again to quote Dr. Hubbe Schleiden, simply to show how this latter theory is repugnant to the followers of Śaṅkara. "Indeed there can be no more fatal error than to believe with those furthest advanced Western philosophers that *Jñānam*, or *Moksha* means nothing else but the intellectual conception, Monism (Advaita), nothing else but the intellectual enjoyment of a proud theory."

What we have said till now, will convince our readers that there is another side to these questions, and that they do not stand alone where the Sāṅkhyans and the Vedāntins left them. According to this view, the Sāṅkhyans are correct, no doubt, so far as they go, in postulating Prakṛiti and Purusha, and the Vedāntin is quite correct in his identification of these two with his Māyā and *Brahman.* There is but a thin partition between the soul or man of the Sāṅkhya, and the latter's *Brahman.* In fact, man is God. In such identification of man with God, what results is, that man's intelligence does not pass on to the postulating and realizing of a Higher Being than himself; and the Brahman of the Vedāntin is only so in name. The third school postulates this third Padārtha, differing from the soul or Ātman of either school, whom the latter cannot know, except with the grace of the third Padārtha, and though it might be correct to say that man cannot know himself, it will be blasphemous to say that God cannot know himself. This will be attributing a human imperfection to the most High and to limit His nature. How do we know that He cannot know Himself, when we cannot know our own selves, nor Him, without His Grace. Consider the following passage from Saint Meykaṇḍa Deva. "When the soul unites itself to God, and feels His Aruḷ (Love), God covers it with His Supreme Bliss and *becomes one with it. Will He not know Himself, who is understood by the soul, through the intelligence of the soul?*" The next passage we are going to quote will show clearly that God has not manifested His glorious Truth to one people, and in one clime alone. "Why may not the absloute Being be self-conscious?" asks a Christian Divine in almost the same words. "To deny this to Him, would be to deny to Him, one of the perfections which even finite beings may have." * The question reamains, what then is the necessity for all this evolution and resolution. The answer is contained in a simple sentence in the first sūtra of *Śivajñānabodha*, namely, 'மலத் தாதாம்.' The second Padārtha in our categories, and not the third, is imperfect, or more correctly, is shrouded by dross, which has to be removed like the colors on a crystal, so that, its own pristine purity may be apparent, and it can reflect and realize the Glory and Presence of God in all Its brightest effulgence. This existence and resolution is due to the will of

* Rev. J. Iverach's 'Is God knowable?' page 225.

this lower being, Ātman, to perfect itself, and the Will of the Highest comes into play, to enable the soul to work out its own salvation. The *Ichchā*, *Jñāna* and *Kriyā* Śaktis of the Lord induces the *ichchā*, *jñāna* and *kriyā* šaktis of the individual soul, and herein is God's Grace and Love and Omnipotence manifested. The exercise of the Divine Will is not for enabling Itself to exist free from samsāra, not for perfecting Itself, not for knowing, seeing, or realizing Itself, not for Its sport or pleasure, not for no purpose, but it is simply to help and aid the poor soul in its attempt to effect all these things. How well does our Saint Tāyumānavar realize this conception of God's great Beneficence in the following lines:

> " இமையளவும் உபகார மல்லால் வேறொன்று
> இயக்கரிற் குணக்கடலாய் இருந்தவொன்றே."

This view postulates three Padārthas, and it may be called Dualism, or Dvaita or anything of the sort, but how this view is the strict Advaita also, true monism, we will demonstrate in a future article *.

[* See Paper on "Advaita according to Saiva Siddhānta."]

THE TATTVAS AND BEYOND.

"God is not this not this".—*Brihad Ār. Up.*

"Other than the known is God, other than the unknown too."—*Śwetāś. Up.*

We present our readers to-day a table of the 36 tattvas derived from Māyā, together with the other postulates of the Siddhānta school, with which they are connected in *advaita* relation. In Tamiḻ, small tracts called *kaṭṭaḷai* (கட்டளை) exist, which describe and define these tattvas. These tattvas are variously enumerated as 19 or 25 or 36 or 96. Both Siddhāntins and Vedāntins (Idealists) accept the number 36 or 96, but they differ in several particulars. 'Thirty-six' when still more analysed give 'Ninety-six'. The more simpler form of the table is herein given, and this requires to be carefully studied. A careful and precise definition of these tattvas has to follow, but we do not attempt it here for want of space. Rev. Hoisington has translated one of these tracts, as also Rev. Foulkes of Salem. Both these books unfortunately are out of print. We will proceed to explain the table briefly, stating at the same time its points of difference from other Schools. We have to premise first, that the tattvas which are enumerated here are all produced out of and form sub-divisions only of *Māyā* and the term as such does not cover either Āṇava, or Karman or Ātman or God. These tattvas form as it were different coats or vestures, of different texture at different times and at different stages, to the soul undergoing evolution with intent to rid itself of its coil (Āṇava) in strict accordance with the Law of Karma. These form however no vestures for the Supreme Being and He is accordingly addressed as '*Tattvātita*,' 'Beyond the tattvas.' The soul is also sometimes called so, as lying outside the category of the thirty-six tattvas. But a distinction has however to be made between the two. The soul, a subject, when united to the objective (material) body, becomes in a sense objective. But the supreme subject can never become objective. The enumeration of the *tattvas* begins from the lowest and the grossest, which is the earth. And philosophic enquiry also proceeds, and ought to proceed from the lowest, the things known, to the Highest, the Unknown. This is the pure inductive method. And when we come to enquire of the manner in which this enquiry has proceeded, we will find that each school holds on to one or another of the tattvas or something else, as the highest and truest existence, and refuse to recognize that anything else can be real or true. As such we find lokāyatas (materialists) occupy the lowest rung of the ladder. We say lowest from our standpoint, and we beg their pardon for saying so. In their own estimation, they are postulating the Highest possible existence, and every other postulate is only a hoax. The *Lokāyata* will only recognize the first four *tattvas*, earth, water, fire and air, and will not recognize even the Ākāś as a real element. The Buddhists and Jains also recognize only these four elements. If you point to existence of mental powers, the Lokāyatas will refer all of them, as being merely functions of the brain or other organs of the body, and that all these functions are mere phenomena produced out of and caused by the bodily powers. We proceed a step higher, and we come to those who admit the mental powers to be substance, and would reduce all the bodily functions and powers to mere phenomena, and assert that beyond this mind (Buddhi), nothing can there be. If you assert that there is such a thing as an Ātman, they will think you are a fool; and if they want however to take you in, they will only assert that what we have all along believed in, as Ātman and God, cannot be anything but this *Buddhi*, and they will call this by every name you have learned, to apply to what you regard as higher things. Passing beyond this Buddhi, we reach its immediate cause the Mūlaprakṛiti. With most Indian theistic schools, they do not carry their notion of matter beyond this Mūlaprakṛiti, standing at the head of the first twenty-four tattvas. They fail to see that matter can assume even finer and more intelligent forms than these 24 tattvas; and as people, lower down, have mistaken the gross forms as Manas, and Buddhi itself as soul and God, these higher forms of *matter* have also been mistaken for soul and God; and the mistake is made more natural, as the souls whose vestures are formed out of these rarer forms of matter, are more and more advanced spiritually and intellectually. It will be seen that what is called Guṇa (meaning merely quality) is the special essence of Mūlaprakṛiti or matter at this stage, and this Guṇa which divides itself as Sattva, Rajas and Tamas, does not pertain to any higher forms of matter than Mūlaprakṛiti. And this Mūlaprakṛiti forms the special vesture of the lowest classes of souls called *Sa-kala.* And these souls range from the greatest Gods to the minutest living germ; each is clothed with the Guñās, Sattva, Rajas and Tamas. The highest of these classes of souls are clothed with very great powers, and they become the lords of this universe in different manvantras. And these three beings are Rudra, Vishṇu, and Brahmā. And having regard to the greatness of these *jivas* from our own low position, we need not wonder why people have often mistaken these *jivas* to be the Supreme God Himself. And a more grosser mistake was never made than when it is (foolishly) asserted that this Saguṇa-Rudra-*Jiva* is the *Pati* postulated by the Śaiva-Siddhāntins. And some of these latter class of people crow over the former, and say that the worship of this lower Brahm (Saguṇa-Rudra or Iśvara) is all well for a time, but that is no good and cannot secure any *Moksha Sādhana* and that the belief in the *Nirguṇa* Brahm is alone capable of freeing one from one's bonds. But that is making very great stock out of the difference between Saguṇa and Nirguṇa beings. That this is not in fact any very important factor, will be made manifest from the fact that instead of one Nirguṇa Being, as believed in by the Hindu Idealists, there are a host of such Beings, who possess no vestures formed of the three guṇas. The higher orders of *Pralayākalas* and *Vijñānakalas* are all Nirguṇa Beings, and they can never be born again as mortals or human beings.

The Śāṅkhyas and Hindu Idealists postulate Mūlaprakṛiti and the twenty-four tattvas derived therefrom, and for a twenty-fifth they postulate Jīva (souls) or Ātman. When the Ātman (Brahm) otherwise *Nirguṇa*, becomes clothed with a Saguṇa body, it becomes a lower Brahm or Jīva, but when the question is asked how this is possible, some answer honestly that they do not know, and others practice jugglery with words and phrases, and say that there is no such occurrence as the Nirguṇa Brahm becoming a Jīva, and that if it appears so, it is all a delusion. But the other side argue that if this is not a delusion, but that there is a Jīva clothed in darkness, and if the other side would not postulate any being other than the Being who falsely appeared as Jīva, then the Ātmā they believe in, cannot be the highest, but only one of the lower Jīvas; and the same mistaken identity is here manifest as in the positions of those who took matter or mind (Buddhi) or Indra or Brahmā, Vishṇu or Rudra as the Highest Being. Before we pass on, we have to notice one class of *Suguṇa-Vādins*, who would not admit that God is *Nirguṇa* at all, and who seek to explain away all texts which refer to God as a *Nirguṇa* Being by saying that *Nirguṇa* simply means absence of bad qualities, and *Saguṇa*, presence of good qualites, Sattva; and when one is confronted with a text of the Gītā itself, one's highest authority, that God is devoid of all the three *Guṇas*, he does not pause to take the plunge, that absence of the three Guṇas does not negative the presence of the Sattva-Guṇa! There is a whole-sale misreading of the texts, and all this quibbling is made necessary, simply because they would not brook the idea that the Saguṇa Being in whose worship they have become such strong adherents, should turn out after all to be not the Highest. Next above the Sa-kalas (Jīvas) come the Pralayā-kalas who have a special body (Nirguṇa) formed out the tattvas No. 26 to No. 30, and it is so distinctive in kind and form and powers that it has been regarded as a separate *tattva* almost, called *Purusha-tattva* or Ātma-tattva. This will make clear, passages which assert that Avyakta (unmanifested

Prakṛiti) is greater than Ātman and God, is greater than Avyakta. Here Ātman does not mean soul, but this special Purusha-tattva. (What this comparative greatness and smallness mean we have explained in our article on 'An Another Side' in explaining the meaning of Omnipresence, *Vibhutva*). All that constitutes, this *Purusha-tattva*, it will be noticed, proceed from *Aśuddha-Māyā*, and *Aśuddha-Māyā* itself is constituted as the thirty-first tattva. Mūlaprakṛiti issues from the thirtieth, *Kalā*. The next five, the highest tattvas, constitute a different body, highly spiritual, for the highest order of souls, called *Vijñānakalas*, and they proceed from *Suddha-Māyā*. The foremost in rank among these Vijñānakalas become Lords, Iśvaras of the Universe, and they are variously called Maheśvaras, Sadāśivas, Bindu and Nāda. These two latter are so nearest God and so potent in their powers that they are almost called Śiva and Śakti. And yet all these seven Iśvaras, three of which are *Saguṇas* (Brahma, Vishṇu, Rudra) and four *Nirguṇa* (Maheśvara-Brahm, Sadāśiva-Brahm, Bindu-Brahm and Nāda-Brahm) are all souls united to Aśuddha- and Śuddha-Māyā bodies; and in the Vedas and Upanishats, all these Saguṇa and Nirguṇa Gods, are spoken of as the Highest God, and special Upanishats are devoted to the praise of one or other of these Gods. And great confusion arises from the fact that from Rudra (one of the Trinity) upwards, all the different Iśvaras are called by all the names of the most High, Rudra, Śiva, Śaṅkara, Śambhu, Bhava, Sarva, Paśupati etc. The reason for this identity in form and name appears to be that these Iśvaras are in a sense immortal, and are not subject to human re-births as *Sa-kalas*, and that there are no possibilities of reversions among them, and they make a much greater approach to the Majesty of the most High, than other lower Beings. The four Avasthās—Jāgra, Svapna, Sushupti and Turiya are all the conditions attaching to the human soul (Sa-kala), and not to the *Pralayākala* and *Vijñānakala*. These latter classes of souls are not themselves subject to these Avasthās, which mark the varying and diminishing conditions of the soul's intellectuality. To class God, the Param, as being in the Turiya-avasthā condition * is sheer blasphemy. The Siddhāntin argues that the Being postulated by the Pūrvapakshin, if He is really in the *Turiya-avasthā* cannot be the Highest, and that the latter is only mistaking a lower Being for the Highest. But the term Turiya or *Chaturtha* is frequently applied to the Supreme, as in the Text 'Śivam, Advaitam, Śāntam, Chaturtham' but it does not refer there to the avasthā at all, but to the enumeration of the *Padārthas*, (things or person), in special reference to the Trinity, (Brahma, Vishṇu, Rudra). This essential difference and distinction between the Trinity and the 'Fourth' Being, is so much obliterated by the rise of new sects, from time to time, and is so little remembered and understood † now, and much less by European writers, that this has been the cause of a lot of unmerited abuse from the hands of unfriendly critics of Hinduism. In the last number of the *Christian College Magazine*, in noticing the life and writings of the Telugu Poet Vemana, the writer points out that God is there described as beyond the reach of the Trimūrtis, Brahmā, Vishṇu and Rudra themselves, and that Vemana describes the Highest by such terms as Deva, Paramātmā, Brahm and few others, and that he uses the term Śiva to denote the Highest also, and he fails to understand how this can possibly be, when, to-day, the term 'Nārāyaṇa or Vishṇu' is used in the whole of the Telugu country, as the appellation of the most High, and he suggests a probable explanation that it might be due to Liṅgāyit influence. But in the days of the Author of the AtharvaŚikha Upanishat and the Mahimnastotra, not to mention many others, which we have quoted at p. 36, no Liṅgāyit sect had come into being, and yet their belief is exactly similar to that of Vemana. The brief survey we have taken of the tattvas will show what great force and real meaning there is, in the texts we have quoted at the head of our article. The

* *Vide* table at p. 7 in "Theosophy of the Vedas" Vol. I.

† Those who understand it are unwilling to speak it out for fear of offending the feelings of other religious sects.

enquirer as he proceeds from the knowledge of the visible to that of invisible powers in Nature and in man, and ascends to higher and higher knowledge, rejects the lower knowledge as 'not this', 'not this', and transcending the manifested and unmanifested avyakta (both Māyā and Ātmā), knows "The one God, in every *Bhūta* hid, pervading all, the inner *Ātmā* of every *ātmā*, Inspector of all deeds, in Whom everything dwells (the Support), the Witness, Pure Intelligence, and *Nirguṇa* Being,"*

"Him, the *Īśvara* of *Īśvaras*, the *Maheśvara*, the God Supreme of Gods, the King of Kings, the Supreme of the Supreme, the Īsā of the Universe."

"The eternal of eternals, the Intelligence of every intelligence, who, the One, of many, the desires dispenses. Knowing that cause, the God to be approached by Śāṅkhya and Yoga etc., † and 'Him having adored,' the 'Mortal from all Pāsa (bonds) is free ‡

We have referred to Saguṇa and Nirguṇa Beings, and these are often translated as personal and impersonal Beings, but the renderings are not perfectly accurate, and the usage of all these four terms are frequently very loose, and we hope to devote a separate paper for the definition and distinction of these terms.

[* Svetāś. Up. VI. 11. † Śvetāś. Up. VI. 7. ‡ Śvetāś. Up. VI. 13.]

THE NATURE OF THE DIVINE PERSONALITY.

'Satyam Jñānam Anantam Brahma.' Tait. Up. ii. 1

'Bliss is Brahman.' Tait. Up. iii. 6.

'There is one Rudra only,—they do not allow a second—who rules all the words by his powers.'—Atharva Siras.

'God is Love.'

We begin where we left off in our last; and in discussing the nature of Saguṇa and Nirguṇa God, we will discuss the article of the Rev. Father Bartoli on 'God, a Personal Being' which appeared in our last two issues, and the Editorial 'God and the Brahman' of the '*Brahmavādin*' of 16th ultimo, and the lecture of Svāmi Vivekānanda, published in the last November number of the same magazine. These two parties occupy positions which seem almost distant as the poles, and altogether irreconcilable. The Rev. Father asks, 'Why this mockery? Say with the fool that there is no God: that the existence of God is a sham, a bubble, a false show, a cheat, a day dream, a chimera: because an Impersonal God is all this.' The learned Svāmi on the other hand says "The monistic theory has this merit that it is the nearest to a demonstrable truth in theology we can get. The idea that the Impersonal Being is in nature, and that nature is the evolution of that Impersonal, is the nearest that we can get to any truth that is demonstrable, and every conception of God which is partial and little and *Personal* is comparatively not rational." In the editorial note on 'God and Brahman,' a novel and a very presumptuous and misleading distinction in the use of the words God and Brahman is attempted, and the article concludes by saying that the worship of God, in all truth and in all love will never lead one to Moksha. "God is for such, and the Brahman is for those whose goal is perfect rest in perfect freedom." The presumption is in supposing that all other religionists, except those of our learned brother's ilk, do not postulate a Brahman, and that their path, not being the 'Soham' path (Paramahamsa) will not lead one to Moksha; and it is also an unwarranted presumption in trying to restrict the use of the word God to what these people were till now calling the lower Brahman or Saguṇa Brahman or Personal God. The so-called Vedāntists have an insidious way of recommending themselves to the favour of other people by bestowing judiciously, a panegyric here and a panegyric there, and, at the same time, they try to raise themselves above the shoulders of these others, and at the latter's expense. They profess to be full of the milk of human kindness to professors of all creeds and sects, and would willingly take them under their folds, what for? Only, so that these people may see that what they profess to teach is the only true path containing the only truth, and that the other paths are—well—only no paths at all—only it will bring them to the same point of birth and death, containing a so-called—a phenomenal truth. And then what is the truth of these people worth after all? In itself, it is so shaky, or they maul it so badly in their attempt to please every body that their truth (substance) becomes indistinguishable from untruth (phenomena); and this is exactly what the Svāmi's Guru, the Paramahamsa, the Mahātman says. God—the Saguṇa—the Personal God is Māyā or Śakti, indistinguishable as heat from fire and this God or Māyā is as such one with Brahman, and so the distinction of Personal and Impersonal God is a distinction without a difference. *(Prabhudda Bhārata p. 109)*!! It will be seen from a reading of the Rev. Father's article, and from how these words are used in the *Brahmavādin* and the *Prabhudda Bhārata*, that all these parties use the word Saguṇa as fully equivalent to Personal, and Nirguṇa as equivalent to Impersonal Being; and a shade has never crossed these learned people's minds whether such rendering is quite the truth.

In our last we quoted a Śvetāśvatara Mantra in which the One God is called *Nirguṇa*. To-day we quote a Gitā verse in which God is called Nirguṇa. "Beginningless, without qualities (Nirguṇa) the Supreme Self (Paramātman) Imperishable, though seated in the body, O Kaunteya, worketh not, nor is soiled."* And the whole of chapters 13 and 14 have to be read to know the precise meanings of Guṇa, Saguṇa and Nirguṇa. Verses 5 to 18 (chap. 14) define and describe the Guṇas and their varieties—*Sattva, Rajas* and *Tamas*. The three Guṇas are Prakṛiti born. (14. 5., and 13. 19) from which are all action, causes and effects (13. 23) and from where are all bodies produced (14. 20.). Sattva is simply bodily (and mental) purity leading one to the desire of wisdom and bliss, (14.6), wisdom light streameth forth from the *Sattvic* Man; and when he dies, he goes to the worlds of the Gods (Vijñānaloka) and he rises upwards. The *Sattvic* Man is still clothed in the material (Prakṛitic) body, and is not yet released from his bonds, not a Mukta. He is simply what the world esteems as a wise and great man. On the other hand *Rajas* engenders passion, engenders thirst for life and is united to action—greed, out-going energy, undertaking of actions, restlessness, desire—and he is again and again born among people attached to action. *Tamas* engenders ignorance, delusion, sloth, indolence, darkness, negligence &c., and he is born and enveloped in the vilest qualities. From this Prakṛiti and the three Guṇas born of Prakṛiti, is distinguished the Purusha.† Prakṛiti is the cause of causes and effects and instruments; and Purusha is the origin of pleasure and pain *i.e.*, experiences, and is attached to the qualities (guṇa) born of Prakṛiti, and by this attachment or Pāśa undergoes birth and death. So the reason for its undergoing birth and death is its attachment to the Guṇas,

* Chap. XIII. 31.

† In page 582. *Brahmavādin*, Purusha, Brahman, and Spirit are called synonymous terms. In page 247, Mr. Mahādeva Sāstrin's Gitā translation, Śaṅkara says, Purusha, Jīva, Kshetrajña, Bhokta, are all synonymous terms. So Brahman and Jīva are synonymous!!!

Sattva included. And the only way, this Purusha (our *Brahmavādin's Brahman*),the Dweller in the body, can be freed from death unto everlasting life is by crossing over the three Guṇas, (14. 20) and by realizing that all action and change is the result of the three Guṇas, (14. 19), and that he himself (Purusha) is actionless or flawless (13. 29) and that there is One higher than the three Guṇas (Prakriti), (14. 19), other than himself. The Highest Purusha, the Paramātman, He who pervadeth and sustaineth the three worlds, the indestructible Īśvara, (15. 17) the Spectator, and Permitter, Supporter, Enjoyer, the Maheśvara, and this Beginningless, Nirguṇa Paramātman cannot perish though he is also seated in the body, as the Purusha or Ātmā is seated, and is not attached to the three Guṇas of which the bodies are created, and is not tainted nor soiled, as the Purusha was declared to be in verse (19, 20 and 21 of 13th chapter), just as Ākāśa is not soiled, though present in each and every thing. The Purusha (the *Brahmavādin's Brahman*, and our *Jīvātmā*) has also to realize, for effecting his freedom, that he and Prakṛiti are all rooted in this One and proceed from it, (13. 30) and though the One is neither rooted in Prakṛiti nor Purusha, being their efficient cause (9. 5); This one God, the Śvetāśvatara says, (the passage will bear repetition) is "hid in every Bhūta, pervading all, the inner *Ātmā* of every *ātmā*, Inspector of all deeds (spectator) in whom every thing dwells, (the support), the Witness, the Pure Intelligence and Nirguna Being; The Īśvara of Īśvaras, the Maheśvara, the God Supreme of God's; the king of kings, the Supreme of the Supreme, the Īśa of the Universe." "The eternal of Eternals, the consciousness which every being's consciousness contains, who, one, of many, the desires dispenses—The cause." "There shines not the sun nor moon and stars, nor do these lightnings shine, much less this fire. When He shines forth all things shine after Him; By Brahman's shining, shines all here below." This same Being is described below as the all creator and protector, the refuge of all, who created Brahma himself and taught him his craft. This same Being is described by the

Taittiriya Upanishat, as the only true and endless Intelligence, whose head is surely Love, Joy His right wing, Delight his left; Bliss his very self; and Who is other than the *Ātman* whom we know to be also *Sat*, *Chit* and *Ānanda*. The Gītā expressly speaks of God as being other than Purusha and Prakriti. The Śvetāśvatara also does the same. The Vedānta sūtras sum up the teaching of the Upanishats beyond all doubt in sūtras 17 and 21 of first pāda of first chapter; and in the preceding sūtras, God is described as Love, Intelligence, the-inside-of (antas) of everything, the Light, the Person, the Powerful One. It is of Him, it is said by the Muṇḍaka, that He perceives all, knows all, whose penance consists of knowledge; of whom the Śvetāśvatara and Gītā speak of having hands and feet on all sides, eyes and faces on all sides. Now this is the God, Who is described as the creator, protector and destroyer and the refuge, the Truth, the Intelligence, and Love and Bliss, Who is described as the supporter, spectator, seer and person, and Who is declared at the same time to be Nirguṇa, transcending both Prakṛiti and Purusha and Gods and Iśvaras. Now we will ask our Reverend Father Bartoli if he will accept this Nirguṇa Being as the true God or the Saguṇa God or Iśvara (the lower one referred to in Mantra 7, section vi of Śvetāśvatara; whom we showed in our table as forming the Sakala Jivas.) And, in fact, the personal God whom our learned contributor defines and describes is in fact none other than this Nirguṇa Being. The Christian ideal of God is also that He is the Creator of heaven and earth, the only one Truth and Light and Intelligence and changeless Substance who loves and cherishes His creatures and Who is the bridge to immortality and Who is different from His creatures. The Personal God of the Christian Theology does not mean a Being who undergoes change, is clothed in a material body as ourselves, who is born and dies (though they speak of one incarnation for all time to come) ever and anon, who has eyes, hands and senses as we have, and whose intelligence and will and power is finite and limited as ours is. Of course, we have to point out also, that we do not agree with those who falsely suppose that of the Nirguṇa Being, even Sachchidānanda cannot be predicated (if so where is the Being itself and what remains of it at all, and all our Reverend Father's denunciations on the Impersonal God will apply even with greater force), that It is not Knowledge (consciousness) and Power (Jñāna, Kriyā Svarūpam), and that It is not the author of creation and destruction and grace, and that this Nirguṇa God can neither know and love us; nor can we love and know Him either. All these and more are no doubt stated as an article of faith by the so-called Vedāntists but the Editor of the *Light of the East* (a staunch Vedāntist) ranks them as gross materialists and atheists; and we have quoted direct texts to show otherwise. Some of these so-called Vedāntists also claim to have reached the knowledge of the highest by merely learning to speak of God in the neuter, as 'It,' 'That' and '*Brahman*' and by regarding Him as formless and nameless. Nothing can be a greater delusion than this. This 'It' of theirs is nothing but Jiva after all and one with the Universe. Says the Svāmi, "so the whole is the absolute, but within it, every particle is in a constant state of flux and change, unchangeable and changeable at the same time, Impersonal and Personal in one. This is our conception of the Universe, of motion and of God and this is what is meant by 'Thou art That." This may be what the Svāmi holds as true, but this is what we hold to be Pāśa and Paśujñānam, Materialism and Anthropomorphism. The Svāmi glibly enough talks of the *absolute and its particles* and the unchangeable and changeable Brahman. But did he forget the Vedic mantra that God is "partless, actionless and tranquil."? And the Svāmi's guru fitly enough talks of Māyā and Brahman as one. And what is Materialism pray? And then what is this much vaunted attribute of Achala and Niśchala (unchangeability) worth, when its every particle is undergoing change? Man is seated and at perfect rest. Yet so many of his muscles and nerves are in the utmost active condition, and undergoing change and destruction, and the particles of his whole body are also undergoing change, destruction and reconstruction, and his thoughts may wander and wander and create waste in the animal tissues. A pool of water may be at perfect rest but a single breath of wind can cause motion in every particle, and we do not call water a stable element; and we do not aspire ourselves to the condition of rest and freedom described above. This is only a make-believe rest and stability. So, we must rate the Brahman (unchangeable and changing, of the Svāmi as only a being, (every chalana being undergoes rest at short or long intervals, out of sheer exhaustion) wilful, inconstant and unstable, the mere toy of every passing whim, every passing breath. The Infinite and Limitless God whom the *Brahmavādin* pourtrays in such glowing colours to mislead the credulous few, whose throne is Space, and whose queen is Time, and who is limitless and infinite as space and time are limitless, must also share a similar ignoble fate. We never thought that we would have to correct our learned brother in regard to such a simple thing, as that, the very notion of time and space implies both limitation and finiteness. We have no need to turn over big treatises to find authorities for this statement. There is lying before us, a small and well written pamphlet of Dr. Peebles of America, entitled 'The Soul'. In the very opening paragraph, we find the following lines, we quote it only to what a trite notion it has now become. "All beginnings in show, time and space necessarily have their endings. A creature which has its beginning in time is incapable of perpetuating itself or of being perpetuated through eternity. A line projected from a point in space has a further limit which no logic can carry to infinity." We have, on another occasion, pointed out that Infinite space and limitless time are contradictions in words. The absolute can never involve itself in space and time. If it does, there is no use of calling it the absolute and unconditioned. And our brother is quite right in saying that Knowledge of This Brahman is only a misnomer (a myth we should say). Then again (in the same page 587), our brother says that 'the Brahman (It) is formless, for all forms imply a boundary'.

Vainest of delusions! But, does formlessness imply no boundary? So many things in nature are invisible and have no form. If, by formless is meant unextended, such as mind etc., we know mind as a product of Māyā is also limited. But by formless, they generally mean 'Arūpi,' 'invisible'; and invisibility is no great attribute after all, as matter can also be formless and invisible. We have elsewhere pointed out the mistake of taking Form and formless as being respectively equivalent to Personal and Impersonal. To deny to God that he can take form is to deny his Omnipotence and limit his nature. The distinction is from our standpoint. When we begin to identify him with anything we know, from the lowest tattva to ourselves (Ātmā), then this is Anthropomorphic. The distinction does not rest on calling the supreme, as '*Śiva*', or '*Śivāḥ*' or '*Śivam.*' 'He,' 'She' or 'It.' God has form. The Śrutis declare so. God is formless, so also the Śrutis say. He has form and has no form. This is because, His body is not formed of matter, but is pure Chit, or Intelligence. It is when we make God enter a material body, and say that he is born and dies, then it is we blaspheme Him and humanize Him and our conception becomes Anthropomorphic. Some of the so-called Vedāntists who are unable to distinguish between what constitutes God's real nature and Anthropomorphism and Hindu symbolism mistake the ideal of God according to Śaiva Siddhānta. Do they care to understand why when describing God, they say He is neither male nor female nor neuter, neither he, she nor it, neither Rūpi, Arūpi nor Rūpārūpi, and yet when thay address God, He is called Śiva, Śivāḥ or Śivam, 'Rūpam Kṛishṇa Piṅgaḷam,' and worshipped as the invisible air and Ākās. Professor Max Muller points out how with bewildering perplexity the gender varies frequently from the masculine to the neuter in the Śvetāśvatara. Well, in the passage 'it has feet and hands everywhere,' if the neuter Brahman can have feet, why could not the Being with the feet &c. be described as He also. We describe all inanimate creation as it, and when we proceed to call the Supreme as It also, we transcend from

Saguṇa to Nirguṇa !!! We have already cautioned against mistaking the Šakti of Šaiva-Siddhānta to be Māyā. It is this mistake that has been the fruitful source of all the degradation and vice of the northern *Vāmāchārā*. This Šakti is called most frequently in Tamiḷ '*Aruḷ Šakti*' (God's manifestation as Love or Grace) and the greatness of this '*Aruḷ*' is thus beautifully described by Tirumūlar.—

> "அருளெங்குமானவளவையறியார்
> அருளைநுகரமுதானதும்தேரார்
> அருளைங்கருமத்திருக்கமுன்னோர்
> அருளெங்குங்கண்ணானதாரறிவாரே."

" Who knows the Power of this Aruḷ by which Omnipresence is secured?
Who understands that this Love transmuted Herself into tasteful ambrosia?
Who thinks that this Love—permeates subtly the five great operations (Pañchakṛitya)?
Who knows that this Love has eyes on all sides (is Omniscient.)?"

> அருளிற் பிறந்திட் டருளில் வளர்ந்திட்டு
> அருளி லழிந்திளைப் பாறி, மறைந்திட்டு,
> அருளான வானந்தத் தாரமுதூட்டி
> அருளாலென்னந்தி யகம்புகுந்தானே.

> Born in Love, Bred up in Love,
> Changing, and resting in Love,
> Fed in the Supreme ambrosia like Love,
> The Nandi entered me as Love."

He says elsewhere that none knows that Love and God are the same. To go and identify this Supreme Love of God, which, like the emerald, covers everything with Her own Love, and imparts to each and every one its own peculiar beauty and power and grace and will, to Māyā which, like darkness, plunges everything into ignorance and death, is real blasphemy and prostitution indeed. We will stop here the discussion so far as Saguṇa and Nirguṇa is concerned, and glance at the controversy as regards Personal and Impersonal God. It is not very easy to get at the precise definition of these terms, and the quarrel seems to be more often a quarrel over words. One author for instance says that by Personality is implied and involved mortality, corporeality (material,) human volitionality. Another says that personality involves limitation. Is this so, and is this the proper connotation and denotation of the word? If so, nobody need pause that God cannot be personal. But eminent men like Emerson and others say that it does not mean any such thing. To quote again Dr. Peebles, "Personality in its common and outward acceptation is usually associated with appearance and outward character; but to such writers as Emerson, James Freeman Clarke, Frohschammer, Elisha Mulford, Lotze etc., Personality has a far deeper meaning. The Latins used *persona* to signify personating, counterfeiting or wearing a mask. But personality in the sense in which Emerson employes it, signifies true Being, both concrete and spiritual. It alone is original Being. It is not limited. Personality is that universal element that pervades every human soul and which is at once its continent and fount of Being. Distinction from others and Limitation by them results from Individuality, not Personality.

Personality therefore pertains to the substance of the soul and individuality to its form. And the Rev. J. Iverach also controverts very ably in his work, 'Is God knowable' the idea of personality as at first stated, and argues that to say that the absolute and the unconditioned Being is personal, is not a contradiction in terms, such as a round square, but that it will be true, as when we say, a white or crimson square. "When we speak of the absolute, we speak of it as a predicate of pure Being, and what we mean simply is that the absolute is complete in itself, it has no conditions save the conditions contained in itself. When we speak of personality, we ascribe to it, Being, regarded as pure spiritual Being; and we simply mean that absolute personal being is and must be self-conscious, rational and ethical; must answer to the idea of spirit. Why may not the absolute Being be self-conscious? To deny this to Him would be to deny to Him, one of the perfections which even finite beings may have?" And Saint Meykaṇda Deva asked the same question several centuries before. (Šivajñānabotham, XI. Sūtra 1 b.) And our Saint Tirumūlar also staets the question in similar terms.

நானறிந்தன்றே இருக்கின்ற ஈசனை
வானறிந்தா ரறியாது மயங்கினர்
ஊனறிந்துள்ளே உயிர்க்கின்ற வொண்சுடர்
தானறியான் பின்னையாரறிவாரே.

"That day I knew my God ; the same was not nnderstood by the Devas. The Bright Effulgence, lighting inside my body and soul, it is said, does not know. Who else can know them?"

We will stop here for the present. We accept the view of personality as set forth by Emerson and others, in which case we must reject the notion of an impersonal, unintelligent and unconscious, unknown, unknowable, unloveable, and unloving nothing. The Christians and Mahomedans (there are some Saguṇavātis among them also) have no need to fall shy of the Nirguṇa conception, though the Rāmānujas and the Madhwas whose God being identified with Prakṛiti itself (*Vasudeva Para Prakṛiti*) never rise above the Saguṇa Sattvic conception. Some of the Vedāntists halting between two stools contrive to fall most miserably, and their view of a God, both Nirguṇa and Saguṇa, Personal and Impersonal is what, we have no good language to describe. None need be ashamed to proclaim truth, if it is truth. Why undertake the trouble of praising Krishṇa and his teaching to the skies, to say, after all, that Krishṇa (the late Mr. T. Subba Rao stated more plainly that he cannot be the incarnation of the absolute) is only for such who wish to be born again and again, and who consider the service of God as their Highest Felicity, and Brahman is for those whose goal is perfect rest in freedom. These very people will raise a howl, if the Ṡaiva were to state the same truth, which by the way was stated long ago by Ṡrī-Kṛishṇa himself that worship of Ṡiva or Ṡivam alone would secure Sāyujya (Moksha) and the worship of other gods (Īṡvara, Brahma, Vishṇu, Rudra, etc.), would only secure their respective worlds (Pada). There are some more questions which arise out of this discussion, and we reserve them for a future occasion.

VOWELS AND CONSONANTS.

(MIND AND BODY.)

"Of letters, the letter A, I am," Gītā.

"There is an alliance with matter, with the object or extended world; but the thing allied, the mind proper, has itself no extension and cannot be joined in local union. Now, we have a difficulty in providing *any form of language, any familiar analogy*, suited to this unique conjunction; in comparison with all ordinary unions, it is a *paradox* or *contradiction*"—Bain.

The quotation, we give above, is from Dr. Bain's remarkable book 'Mind and Body,' and the several chapters comprising the book are worth close study, even though we are not bound to accept the learned Doctor's conclusions, and share in his hope that the philosophy of the future will be a sort of qualified materialism. The important thing is to get at his facts, as far as they can be arrived at by close observation and experiment, and such inference as are warranted by strict logic, which have been most thoroughly sifted, and about which therefore there can be no doubt. We will enquire, therefore, what are the proved facts concerning the nature of mind and body and their characteristics, and the nature of their connection, so far as they can be ascertained. Now as regards Mind, it is analysed into Feelings (including emotions), Will and Intellect. "These are a trinity in unity; they are characteristic in their several manifestations, yet so dependent among themselves that no one could subsist alone; neither Will nor Intellect could be present in the absence of Feeling; and Feeling manifested in its completeness, carries with it, the germs of the two others." The ultimate analysis of a Feeling, being either a pleasure or a pain, it is seen, however, that volition or thought could not, in any sense, be confounded with Feelings. What Dr. Bain, however, means in the above quotation is that without the acquisition of feelings, no volition or thought could arise first, that feelings are primarily all derived through the sensory organs and centres. And a pleasure is seen to be connected with an activity which tends to promote life (உயிர்க்கிதம்செய்தல்) and a pain, to destroy life (உயிர்க்கேதம்செய்தல்) which determine also in ethics, the nature of right (good) and wrong, *Pāpam* and *Puṇyam.* This principle is stated as the law of self-conservation. But there is a limit to all pleasures; and even a pleasure may become painful, if only carried to excess. Another law exhibited in feelings, which applies also to thought, is what is called the law of relativity, namely that "change of impression is necessary to our being conscious." Either a feeling or a thought, only too long prolonged, becomes feeble and feeble, till it is blotted out altogether, and we are no more conscious of such feeling or thought; and to become conscious again, we soon change this train, and then revert. The Tamiḷ philosophers state this principle in the axiom 'நினைப்புண்டேல், மறப்புண்டாம்' 'If there is thought there is forgetfulness also.' Dr. Bain almost confesses that, both on the mental and physical side, the reason for the exhibition of this law is not very explicable. But Hindu philosophers take this fact as showing that man's intelligence (அறிவு) is weak (சிற்றறிவு) and it can become stronger and stronger, and become all thought by practice (Sādana). In Yogic practice, what comes first is more darkness, oblivion than light, but continuing in the same path, there dawns true light in the last resort, and the nature of the light is so often mistaken in the interval, so many shades of it breaking out. And our volition (இச்சை-Ichcha) determines our actions as impelled by Feeling or Intellect. Intellect is analysed into a sense of difference and sense of similarity, and Retentiveness or Memory. What are called variously as .memory, reason, judgment, imagination, conception and others are all resolvable into these three kinds. And difference lies at the very basis of our intellect. No knowledge and no intellectual operation is possible, if there is no difference in the constituent elements, if there is a mere sameness. If there was only one colour, the art of painting will be an impossibility; if there was only one sound or tune, music, we could never hear. As it is, the law of relativity governs our very being. Sameness could give knowledge, only if there was difference, and hence the sense of similarity is also accounted an intellectual function; and a great function it performs in the field of invention. And no high degree of intellectual power is possible, if we do not possess the power of remembering our past experiences and impressions. And one peculiarity of the human mind, may we call it a defect, may be also noted here, as based on the law of relativity already stated. The mind is not conscious of all the impressions, through all the sense organs, all at once. A man does not become conscious of a sight, a touch, a sound, or a smell, all at once. There must be a transition from one to the other, however momentary it might be. And the case of an *Ashṭāvadāni* is no exception to this. Assisted by a good memory, the more *avadānams* he performs, the more time does he take. It will be noted that, in this analysis of mind, no distinction is drawn between a feeling and a consciousness of a feeling, a volition and a consciousness of a volition, a reasoning and the consciousness of reasoning. Both are taken to be identical and therefore needing no distinction. In Ḥindu philosophy, they are distinguished and a mere feeling or willing or thinking is separated from consciousness of such functions, and the pure consciousness is taken as the soul or Sat, and the rest classed with body and the world as non-soul or Asat (other than Sat). And we will speak of this distinction more further on. From these mental functions, however, are contrasted the body and its functions and the so-called external world. This collectively called matter or the non-ego or the object, possess certain characteristics and properties which are not found in mind at all, such as breadth and length (order in place), extension, hardness and softness (inertia), weight (gravity), colour, heat, light, electricity, organised properties, chemical properties &c., &c.,

and the most important of this is *extension*. Matter is *extended*, Mind is *unextended*. Says Dr. Bain,

"We are in this fix; mental states and bodily states are utterly contrasted; they cannot be compared, they have nothing in common except the most general of all attributes—degree, order in time; when engaged with one we must be oblivious of all that distinguishes the other. When I am studying a brain and nerve communications, I am engrossed with properties exclusively belonging to the object or material world, I am unable at that moment (except by very rapid transitions or alterations) to conceive a truly mental consciousness. Our mental experience, our feelings and thought have *no extension*, no place, no form or outline, no machanical division of parts; and we are incapable of attending to anything mental, until we shut off the view of all that. Walking in the country in spring, our mind is occupied with the foliage, the bloom, and the grassy meads—all purely objective things. We are suddenly and strongly arrested by the odour of the May-blossom; we give way for a moment to the sensation of sweetness; for that moment the objective regards cease; we think of nothing extended, we are in a state, where extension has no footing; there is to us place no longer. Such states are of short duration, mere fits, glimpses; they are constantly shifted and alternated with object states, and while they last and have their full power, we are in a different world; the material world is blotted out, eclipsed, for the instant unthinkable. These subject-movements are studied to advantage in bursts of intense pleasure or intense pain, in fit of engrossed reflection, especially reflection on mental facts; but they are seldom sustained in purity, beyond a very short interval; we are constantly returning to the object side of things—to the world whose basis is extension and place."

However widely these may differ, there is this remarkable fact about them that they are found united together in a sentient being—man or animal. And the exact correlation, correspondence or concomitance in these two sets of phenomena is what Dr. Bain takes very great trouble to show in several chapters. This we need not deny, as Dr. Bain fully admits that this conjunction and correspondence do not warrant us in stating that mind causes body or body causes mind; but his position is that mind-body causes mind-body. There is a duality in the very final resort and ultimate analysis, but a disembodied mind cannot be thought of, and he uses various expressions such as, an 'undivided twin' a 'double faced unity,' 'one substance with two sets of properties.' &c. And we don't see why Dr. Bain should ally himself with materialists if he is not going to call this *one substance*, not as matter altogether, but as only matter-mind or mind-matter; unless it be that he is unable to prove himself the existence of mind except in conjunction with an organized body. This latter circumstance again causes no difficulty to the Siddhānti who postulates 'முத்தியிலும் மும்முதலுளவே,' 'even in Mukti, none of the three *padārthas* are destroyed,' and who no more believes in a disembodied mind than Dr. Bain, unless a body or an organism be taken to be the body composed of all the 25 lower tattvas. From the table given in No. 10 of the first volume of the *Siddhānta Dipikā*, it will be seen, that even the most spiritual beings have a body composed of Asudda or Sudda Māyā, and we have also remarked, cautioning against the common mistake of calling matter dead, that these higher aspects of matter are so potent and active as to be often mistaken for God Himself. Passing from this point however, we now come to the question as to the nature of the union between this mind and body. When we talk of union, the suggestion that it is *union in place* that is most predominant. And Dr. Bain lays great stress on the fact that such a local conjunction is not to be thought of, is impossible. There can be no union in place between an unextended thing (as Chit), and an extended thing (as Achit); and all such expressions external and internal, container and contained are also misleading aud mischievous. The connection is not a causal connection. It is wrong to call such conjunction as one acting on the other, or as one using the other as an instrument. (The theory of occasional causes and of pre-established harmony are also antiquated now). The phenomenon is a most unique one in nature; there is no single similar conjunction in nature, so that we may compare it by analogy, and there is no fitting language to express such conjunction either. The only adequate expression to denote a transition from an object cognition to a subject one is a *change of state.* Language fails, analogy fails, to explain this union, though in itself a fact; and it remains a mystery in a sense, though to seek an explanation for an ultimate fact, can, in no sense, be logical; and all that we can do has been done when we have tried to generalize the various sets of phenomena into the fewest possible number, and if we cannot pass to a higher generalization than two, we can only rest and be thankful.

We are sure that this is a perfectly safe position to hold, and our object in penning this article is in no way to differ from this view; only we fancy, we have an *analogy* in Tamil, which will exactly answear the point and make the union more intelligible, besides bringing out the nature of mind and matter, in a much more favourable light, than from the standpoint of a mere materialist, qualified or otherwise; and we fancy we have been almost every day using language to describe this union, though the name in itself is a *puzzle,* and embodies both a *paradox* and a *contradiction.* Before we state them, however, we will state one or two facts, so far as they bear upon the relation of mind and matter, and which Dr. Bain states more fully in his *Mental Science.* It is that, all objectivity implies the subject-mind at the same time. "All objective states are in a sense also mental." Unless the mind is present, though unconscious, you cannot have object knowledge at all. We cannot have a pure objective condition at all, without the subject supporting it, as it were, though for the time being, it is nonapparent, is entirely blotted out. (*Sūnyam*). Or rather shall we say, though dissimilar, the mind has become thoroughly identified with matter. But mind can ascend to pure subjectivity, and it does not imply the presence of objects, as the object does the subject; and in such a pure subjective state, where is the object? It has become also non-apparent (*Sūnyam*). Regarding the possibility, however, of matter being the primary element, there is this fact. Matter is found both as organic and inorganic, and what a world of difference is there between these conditions of matter? Is the peculiar organization given to it by the presence for the time being of mind in it or is it derived solely by its inherent power. We have admitted that the so-called dead matter might possess potentialities without number. Still, is there any sort of similarity between the inorganic properties exhibited by matter, and the organic or vital properties? However this be, we will now proceed to state our analogy. It is the analogy of vowels and consonants. We have quoted the Gītā verse, but we look in vain even in Śaṅkara's commentary for the meaning we have tried to give it. Possibly Śaṅkara would not give such an explanation, as it would conflict with his preconceived theory. So, if there was truth in it, it remained locked, and the key, altogether, remained with the Siddhānta writers. The most familiar example of the analogy occurs in the sacred Kuṛaḷ, in the very first verse of it.

> "அகரமுதல வெழுத்தெல்லா மாதி
> பகவன் முதற்றே யுலகு."

> "As 'A' is the first of all letters,
> So the ancient Bagavān is the first in this world."

We might fancy an alphabet, in which the letter "A" is not the first, and if the point of comparison is merely to denote God's order in place as the first, so many other analogies might be thought of. And Parimelaḻagar accordingly notes that the order is not order in place, but order in its orgin. It is the most primary and first sound that the human voice can utter, and it is also the one sound which is present in every other sound, vowel or consonant. All other vowels are formed by modifications of this sound. And what are vowels and consonants pray? A vowel is defined as a sound that can be pronounced of itself, without the aid of any other sound. And a consonant is one which cannot be sounded, except with the aid of the vowel. Let us look more carefully into the nature of these sounds. We every day utter these sounds, and yet we fail to recognize the mystery in their connection, solely on account of their familiarity. We try to utter 'A.' It comes pure and simple, by the mere opening of the mouth, without any modification whatever, and requires no other aid. But let us pronounce say 'K.' It is 'Kê in English, in Tamiḷ it is 'Ka', 'க' or 'Ik', 'க்'. There is a vowel sound present in it, 'ê' or 'a' 'i.' Let us eliminate this vowel sound, and try to pronounce the consonant. Well, the task is impossible, you don't get any consonant sound at all. In the consonant, therefore, there is always a vowel sound present, though we never consciously recognize its presence; though in Tamiḷ, the symbolism is so highly philosophical, that we invariably mark its presence, even when we write purely consonants. We dot all our consonants as 'க்,' 'ச்,' &c. and the dot or circle represents in Hindu symbolism the letter 'அ'. This dot or circle begins almost every one of the twelve vowels in the Tamiḷ alphabet, and as to what the other curved and horizontal and perpendicular lines mean we will take another opportunity to explain. When we write 'க்' therefore, the framers of the alphabet meant to represent how the vowel sound underlies the consonant, and supports it, and gives it its very being and existence. Such a mark is unneceesary when we write the vowel-consonant 'Ka', 'க', as we are fuly aware of its presence. In the pure consonant therefore, the vowel is implied and understood, though for the time being its presence is not detected, and it is completely identified with the consonant itself. We have been considering, at learned length, the nature of the union between mind and body, but have we ever paused to consider the nature of the union of the vowel and consonant? Is there any such unique conjunction anywhere else in nature, where one subsists not, except in conjunction with the other. Except the inseparable conjunction, as above stated, we see that the consonant (pure) is no more derived from the vowel than the vowel from the consonant. There is much wider contrast between these, than between any two things in the world. The place of origin is distinct. 'A' is pronounced by the mere opening of the month. The tongue has to be brought into contact with the palate to pronounce 'k' and this same act cannot produce the vowel. So the vowel cannot be said to cause the consonant, nor the consonant the vowel. Nor can we call the consonant and the connection themselves as false, and as a mere illusion or delusion. So neither the principle of Pariṇāma nor Vivartana can apply to this connection. All that we can say of it is, that they are so connected and inseparable, and that no language can be possible, by vowels alone nor by consonants alone, and every consonant is at the same time a vowel-consonant, in which the vowel is apparent or non-apparent; and though we can conceive of the vowels standing alone, to think of consonants as existing by itself is an utter impossibility. Now apply all this to the case of mind and body. Mind is the vowel, and the body (matter) is the consonant. Mind and body are as widely contrasted as vowel and consonants are. One cannot be derived from the other by *Pariṇāma* or *Vivartana*. Yet both are inseparably united, and though the mind occupies an independent position, can be pure subject at times, the body cannot subsist unless it be in conjunction with mind. Mind is always implied in body; mind underlies it, supports it and sustains it, (if all this language derived from material cognition is permissible). When the mind is pure mind, the body is not, it is *asat (Sūnyam)*. When it is pure body, mind is present but non-apparent, it has become one with the body. The mind is there, but it conceals its very self, its very identity, and it is as good as absent. And except at rare intervals, our whole existence is passed in pure objectivity, without recognizing the presence of the true self, the mind. The whole truth of these two analogous cases, the only two, are brought out in Tamiḻ, in the most beautiful manner, by the same words being used to donote vowel and consonant as also mind and body. See what a light bursts when we name 'உயிர்,' 'மெய்' (உடல்). The word 'உயிர்', means both a vowel and mind (soul); and 'மெய்' both body and consonant. Dr. Bain observes that the sense of similarity is the sense of invention and true discovery. The greatest discoveries in science have been made by catching such resemblances at rare intervals. And when the very first Tamiḻ man called his vowels and consonants 'உயிர்' 'மெய்' was he not a born philosopher and had he not comprehended the true nature of the union between mind and body, and vowels and consonants. The simile recieves its best exposition for the first time in the hands of Saint Meykaṇḍa Deva, (*vide* Śivajñānabotham, II. 1. *b.* and notes pp. 12, 19 and 20), and his followers (*vide* Light of Grace pp. 7 and 8); and Saint Meykaṇḍān gives a name in the same verse for denoting this connection. This one word is *Advaita*. This word has been a real puzzle to many; and so many renderings of it have been given. The Tamiḻ Philosopher, however, explains it as meaning "ஒன்றாகாமல், இரண்டாகாமல், ஒன்றுமிரண்டு மின்றாகாமல்," (neither one nor two nor neither), and which fully and beautifully brings out, therefore, the meaning of Dr. Bain's words that the connection is both a *paradox* and a *contradiction*. Very few outside the circle of Siddhānta School could be made to comprehend the truth of this paradox; more so, when their mind is prepossessed with the truth of their own views. But we have always used the analogy of vowels and consonants with very great effect, and it has tended to make the subject much clearer than many a more learned argument. We have confined ourselves in this article to deal with the last two sets of phenomena in Nature, Mind and Matter; and we will reserve to a future article, the Nature of the Higher powers we postulate, and their connection with the lower ones; and a further amplification of the subject, together with the history of the question, in Indian systems of thought.

GOD AND THE WORLD.

THE ADVAITA.

The Vedic Texts *Ekam evādvitiyam Brahma,' 'Ekam Eva Rudro Nadvitiyāya thas teh'* mean that there is only One Supreme Being without a second. And this One is the *Pathi* and not the soul. You, who say ignorantly you are One with the Lord, are the soul, and are bound up with *Pāśa.* As we say without the (primary sound) 'A' all other letters will not sound, so the Vedas say, without the Lord, no' other things will exist." Sivajñānabotham (ii. 1. *b*).

" ஆணவத்தோடத்து விதமானபடி மெய்ஞ்ஞானத்
தாணுவினோ டத்துவித மாகுநாளெந் நாளோ."

"O for the day when I will be in advaita union with the unchangeable True Intellignce, as I am now in union with *Āṇava (Pāśa)*" !

Says Count Tolstoy, "Religion is a certain relation established by man between his separate personality, and the endless universe or its source; morality is the perpetual guiding of life which flows from this relation." And as we have explained in our previous article, even knowledge of a thing means knowledge of its difference and similarity with other things, its relation to things which are dissimilar, and to things which are similar, and from the knowledge of such relation, our further acts are determined. Say, if the object be a new fruit we had not seen before, if we find it related to the edible species, we try to eat it; if not, we throw it away. If one should make however a mistake in the identification, from imperfect experience or knowledge, or misled by the nice and tempting appearance of the fruit, woe befalls him when he partakes thereof. All our good and evil flows accordingly, from our understanding rightly or wrongly, our relation to men and things and society. And the highest philosophy and religion accordingly mean also knowledge and knowledge of the relation of the highest postulates of existence; and different systems arise as different kinds of relationships are postulated. In determining the respective views, imperfect observation and experience, passion and prejudice, trammels created by heredity and society, have all their play; and we have different moral standards followed by men, consciously or unconsiously, as resulting from their already formed convictions.

Proceeding on our own lines of discovering these relationships, we took with us Dr. Bain to help us on to a particular stage. He is a most uncompromising agnostic and materialist (qualified) and yet we were in perfect agreement with him all the way he took us, and if he refuses to go with us further, and sees pitfalls and dangers in such a path and is not willing to brave such, we can quite understand his motives and can only admire his honesty. So far as we went with him also, it was perfect sailing. We were well aware of things we were talking about, there was no mistaking them, the facts were all within our experience, and there was nothing in them which contradicted our experience, and we were not asked to believe things on credit, by appealing to intuition or authority. When reason failed, we were not referred to *Šruti*; and when *Šruti* failed, we were not referred to their own individual yogic experience; and when all these failed, no verbal jugglery was adopted; and nothing was made to look grand by making it a matter of mystery. Our meaning is quite unmistakeable, and we use plain language and if it is not plainer, we shall try to make it so.

We found, accordingly, that our present experiences and facts of cognition resolve themselves into two sets of facts, two grand divisions, totally distinct, and yet in inseparable relation, and we called them respectively mind and matter, ego and non-ego, subject and object, ātmā and pāša, chit and achit, sat and asat. We noted their inter-dependence and inter-relation. As regards the nature of the relation itself, it was in a sense inexplicable. We could say positively that the relation is not one of causation or succession, not mere order in place, and it could not be that of the whole to its part, nor one acting on the other, or using the other as its instrument, nor that of container and contained, nor no relation at all; and we could not thus picture this relation in any one of the modes known to us in our actual experience; and the only analogy available to us in nature, mamely, that of vowels and consonants helped us a good deal to have some idea of this relation. It is not one, it is not two, and our Āchārya asks us to keep us quiet, "சகமிரண்டெள் ஒழற் கம்மாவிரு". But still even this position requires a naming, and for want of a better name too, we use the word 'Advaita' to such relation. The word Advaitam implies the existence of two things and does not negative the reality or the existence of one of the two. It simply postulates a relation between these two. The relation is one in which an identity is perceived, and a difference in substance is also felt. It is this relation which could not easily be postulated in words, but which perhaps may be conceived and which is seen as two (Dvaitam) and at the same time as not two (Na Dvaitam); it is this relation which is called Advaitam (a unity or identity in duality) and the philosophy which postulates such relation is called the Advaita Philosophy; and it being the highest truth also, it is called the *Siddhānta* (The true end). This view has therefore to be distinguished from the monism of the materialist and idealist, and from the dualism of Dr. Reid and Hamilton. But Dr. Bain and others of his school would regard themselves as monists, but in that case, the distinction between this monism, may we call it qualified monism, and the monism of writers before the advent of the present agnostic school must be carefully observed. There is no wrong in using any name for anything, but when particular associations have been already established, it serves no purpose except to confound and confuse to use old words with new meanings introduced into

9

them. In a sense, this view is also the true monistic view. Say from the individual standpoint, when the man is in a pure objective condition, his mind becomes merged in the body; the mind identifies itself thoroughly with the body and is not conscious of its own distinction from the body. By this process of merger and complete identification, the apparent existence is only one, that of the object; when the mind is free from all object consciousness, the object world vanishes as it were, and there is only one fact present, and that is the mind, and nothing else. Without mind, however, nothing else can subsist, and when the mind is in its own place, nothing else is *seen* to subsist. And how appropriate does the interpretation of that oft-quoted and oft-abused Vedic text, '*Ekam evādvitīyam Brahma*' by Saint Meykaṇḍān seem now! When we arrive at the postulate of God, we arrive at the third padārtha, and nobody has yet been found to postulate an existence, higher than these three. And these constitute the tri-padārtha of most of the Hindu schools. They differ, no doubt, in the definition and description of these three entities, as also in the description of their relationships. This third postulate could not be arrived at by direct perception, observation and experiment. We think however it can be proved by strict logical methods, by such proof as is possible, and we are at liberty to postulate it to explain the residuary facts unexplained by the Materialists and Idealists. If this postulate will explain facts, left unexplained by these people, and if it will not contradict any of the facts of human nature and probabilities, there is no harm in having it for a workable hypothesis. We believe also that the Materialists and Idealists leave many facts unexplained and that this third postulate is necessary to explain these facts. We, however, do not propose to go into this wide question now. We only propose to discuss God's relation to mind (soul) and matter just at present. And the relation we postulate is the same as between mind and body which we have already postulated, and we call it by the same name '*advaita*'. And the couplet we have quoted from

Tāyumānavar conveys the idea most beautifully, and the merit of expounding this beautiful view of '*advaita*' must in the first place be accorded to *Saint Meykaṇḍān* whom *Saint Tāyumānavar* himself extols as the பொய்கண்டார் காணாப்புனித மாமத்துவித மெய்கண்டான்," "The Seer of *Advaita* Truth". God is related to the soul, as the soul is related to the world. God is the Pure subject, the Pure Ego, and the Soul is the pure object, non-ego. God is Sat (the true existence); Soul is Asat. As however we have called the world Asat, we are not willing to extend the term to soul also; and it, besides, occupies a peculiar postion between God, and Sat, on the one hand and the word, Asat, on the other hand; and hence, the term *Satasat* has been applied to it. The term means that which is neither God nor the world (māyā) but which, when joined to either, becomes completely identified with each. When united to the body, it is completely identified with the body, and when united to God, it is completely identified with God. We have already observed that when the soul is united to the body, it is completely identified with it, it has not ceased to exist, as the body ceased, when thesoul was in its own plane. The very existence of the body implied the existence of the soul, though for the nonce, the soul was not conscious of its separateness and individuality and distinction from the object or body. Just in the same way when the Jiva is in the Highest union with Śivam, the Jīva is not conscious of its separateness, and individuality and distinction from God. If this consciousness was present, there will be no union; and if the soul was not itself present, to speak of union in Moksha and Anubhava and Ānanda will also be using language without meaning. And this characteristic of the soul is very peculiar. It is named சார்ந்ததன்வண்ணமாதல் or அது அது வாதல், 'becoming one with that to which it is attached.' The Hindu Idealists try to arrive at the postulate of the soul precisely by the same mode of proof as is furnished in sūtras 3 and 4 of Śivajñānabodham, and arriving at this postulate which is found to be above the 24 tattvas, above the elements, above the tanmātras, above the Jñāna and Karmendriyas, above the four antaḥkaraṇa, they have not paused to discover its further nature and characteristics, and have straightway proceeded to identify it with God, whom they have read of, in the Šrutis, and have not tried to learn the relation between these two; and all the absurdities of the Māyāvāda school are clearly traceable to its not understanding the nature of the soul aright. These further aspects of the soul and its relation to God are therefore well brought out in sūtras 7, 6 and 5. And how this Jīva can possibly become Šivam and in what sense, is beautifully brought out in 6. 2. (*e*).

அதுவென்னு மொன்றன்றி அதாவன்றி வேறே
யதுவென்றறி யறிவுமுண்டோ—அதுவென
அறியவிரண்டல்லனுங் கறிவுணிற்றல்
அறியுமறிவே சிவமுமாம்.

"God is not one who can be pointed out as "That." If so, not only will He be an object of knowledge, it will imply a *Jñātā* who understands Him as such. He is not different from the soul, pervading its understanding altogether. The soul so feeling itself is also Šivam."

Chapter II of Light of Grace has also to be read in this connection; and Saint Umāpati Šivāchārya asks a question to bring out the importance of this great characteristic of the soul. "Are there not objects in this world which become dark in darkness and light in light?" he asks, and the answer given by himself elsewhere is "the eye, the mirror and ākāš are such objects." The eye loses its power of seeing in darkness, and recovers it in light; and the others become dark or bright as darkness or light surrounds it. Saint Tāyumānavar also refers to this peculiarity in several places and calls the soul யாதொன்று பற்றின தனியல்பாய் நின்று பந்தமறும் பளிங்கனை யசித்தநீ. 'You who are like the mirror or crystal removed of dust, becoming of the self-same nature of one to which it is joined.' Here the Light is God, darkness is Māyā and the Mirror or Eye or Ākāś is the soul. We all feel that there is a sentience which suffers this change from light to darkness. If this sentience is identified with God himself, surely, the change must descend on His head. We have not yet been able to understand (of course we are ready to confess we do not belong to the superior class of mortals said to possess 'the sharpest intellects, a bold understanding' to which ranks our brother of the *Brahmavādin* elevates himself—*vide* p. 749 current volume) how when they postulate only one padārtha, one self, and no Jīva, how God can be saved from all the impurity and sins and ignorance present in nature. To say that the Śruti says that God cannot be tainted by such contact is only begging the question, and is no answer. To assert that the Infinite God by this false imposition, Avidya, had become divided into millions and millions of finite beings, and without stopping to make good this statement itself by proof except by giving an analogy, (which analogy is found to fail most miserably in most important details) and to assert with the same breath, that this sub-division is false, is a mere myth, a dream, that there is no universe, men or Gods, you or I and then to say further that you and I, Gods and men, and the world are all God seems to be the height of absurdity and not born of 'the sharpest intellect, a bold understanding.' If so, we must have altogether a different definitions of these terms. We will close this paper by quoting two verses from Saint Tirumūlar, and we challenge comparison with them, with anything else found in any writing ancient or modern to express the truth of the double aspect and relation we have been describing above, with the same aptness and richness of illustration.

மரத்தை மறைத்தது மாமதயானை,

மரத்தின் மறைந்தது மாமதயானை,

பரத்தை மறைத்தது பார்முதற்பூதம்,
பரத்தின் மறைந்தது பார்முதற்பூதம்.

The tree was concealed in the mad elephant ;
The tree concealed the mad elephant :
The Supreme was concealed in the world ;
In the Supreme was concealed the world.

(Here tree means a wooden toy elephant).

பொன்னை மறைத்தது பொன்னணிபூஷணம்,
பொன்னின் மறைந்தது பொன்னணிபூஷணம்,
தன்னை மறைத்தது தன்கரணங்களாம்,
தன்னின் மறைந்தது தன்கரணங்களாம்.

The gold was concealed in the golden ornament ;
The gold concealed the golden ornament.
The 'I' was concealed in its own senses ;
In the 'I' were concealed its own senses.

These two verses, though they look similar, are not the same, and we will expound their meaning in our next.

THE TWO GEMS.

(SAT AND SAT-ASAT).

"எவ்வெவர் தன்மையும் தன்வயிற்படுத்தும்
தானேயாகிய தயாபரன் எம்மிறை."

**"To each and every one, His own nature imparting
Our Lord stands alone, Supreme, full of Grace."**

Tiruvāchakam.

We proceed to explain the two verses quoted from Tirumūlar at the close of our last article. The two verses seem so alike that unless they are looked into more closely, their meaning is likely to be lost. These verses explain in fact the *Bhanda* and *Moksha* conditions of the soul, and the soul's ascent through various stages, called *Tattva Darśanam*, *Ātma Darśanam* and *Śiva* or *Parā Darśanam*. The verse, "The gold was concealed in the golden ornament &c." has to be taken first. The object before the seer is a golden ornament. The thing can be looked at from two different points of view, in two different aspects. It can be viewed as merely gold, and then we are solely engaged in looking at its colour, its fineness, specific gravity &c., and while we are so engaged, the other view of it, whether it is a brooch, or medal or a bracelet &c., is altogether lost to view. And in the same manner when we are viewing the object as a mere ornament, then all idea of the gold, its fineness &c. is lost. This happens when the object before us is one and the same, and neither the gold as gold, nor the ornament as ornament can be said to non-exist, in either case, can be said to be unreal or a mere delusion. We merely change our point of view, and we are ourselves under no delusion at either moment. The delusion is neither in the gold nor in the ornament nor in ourselves. The object before us is so made that it possesses this double nature or aspect, so to say, and our own psychological structure is such that we can change from one to the other point. And each point of view has its own vantage ground. A person going to a jeweller's shop cannot afford to lose sight of either point, and if he does, he is sure to make a bad bargain. What would we think of this man, if he goes into the shop with the firm idea, that, of the jewel he is going to buy, the gold is a mere name and delusion, or the ornament is a mere name and delusion. When bargaining, however, after he had once tested the fineness of the gold, and colour, he need trouble himself no more about it, and he can proceed to examine the shape of the ornament, its size &c.

Taking this analogy, Tirumūlar proceeds to point out the same relation between the individual ego, the subject, and its objective senses. The word used is 'தன்,' standing as it does for the individual ego, jīva, soul, paśu, or chit. The phrase 'தன் கரணங்களாம்,' also brings out the meaning of 'தன்,' and it cannot refer to the Supreme Brahman, as was interpreted by a Hindu Idealist. Of course he could not help saying so, as the being which he postulates above 'its senses' (தன்கரணங்கள்) is God, the Supreme. Saint Tirumūlar was prophetic enough to see such a misinterpretation of his words, and it is therefore why he sung the next verse, " மரத்தை மறைத்தது," the tree was concealed &c.' In our article on 'Mind and Body' we have fully discussed the relation which Saint Tirumūlar perceives between the Individual Ego, the soul and its body and senses. When the individual *paśu* lives a purely objective existence, by caring for his body, his comforts, his wealth, his pleasures, &c., his true self, the mind, is altogether identified with the world; and he himself lies buried, concealed. Look at the words, our Saint has selected. He does not cry false, false, delusion, delusion at every turn. He actually uses 'மறைத்தது,' 'மறைந்தது,' "concealed" and "is concealed"! Neither the soul nor the world is a myth, a delusion; but only when the mind was in an objective condition, it was concealed by the object. When the soul regains its own self, by forgetting the world, the world has not become a myth, only it lies concealed, merged in the soul itself. The thoughtless critic is apt to consider such distinctions, as mere wordy warfare, but no student of philosophy can easily afford to ignore the first principles of correct reasoning, by choosing his words, each one to express one particular idea and no other; and many a specious and delusive argument has had its genesis in such ignorant and ambiguous use of words. To proceed, when the soul lies so concealed in the world, this constitutes its *bandha*, bound condition, and the thing so concealing is called *bandha* or *Pāša*. When the soul learns to discriminate between its own nature and the nature of the world, and to rate the lower as its own worth, then it attains to *Tattva Daršanam and Ātma Daršanam*. And the whole field of Ethics is evolved from our perception of these relations aright. When man perceives that the more he is attached to the world, the more his own faculties get clouded and he is led more into sorrow and suffering, and the more he frees himself from such attachment, the more he frees himself from sin and sorrow, and developes in himself his higher spiritual nature, then it is that his moral faculties are developed, and in course of time strengthened by constant practice. But then, there is this peculiarity about the mind of man, which is nowhere noticed in any other system that we know of, and which we have already referred to in our last article, its intermediate nature between *Sat* and *Asat*, and which therefore gives it its name of *Satasat* and which peculiarity *Kaṇṇuḍaiya Vaḷḷalār* (author of Oḷiviloḍukkam) emphasises by using the expressive name of அலி, or hermaphrodite, neither male nor female, neither Sat nor Asat. But the rule in Tamiḷ grammer for determining the sex of the hermaphrodite is "ஆணுறுப்புமிகுந்தால் ஆணாகும், பெண்ணுறுப்புமிகுந்தால் பெண்ணாகும்." 'The sex follows the more predominating organs present,' and so a hermaphrodite person will always be called either he or she and not it. The life of the individual soul is, as such, passed either as Asat or as Sat, and it has no life of its own. That is, it cannot exist by itself, independent of its relation with either Padārtha. If either God or the world did not exist, the existence of the soul would be an impossibility. Saint Meykaṇḍān uses two analogies to illustrate the position. The soul is campared to an object suspended in air, and a flood of water. We cannot imagine an object suspended in air without a support. If the support is removed, the object falls to the ground. Saint Meykaṇḍān had as such distinctly before him the question "why does an apple fall to the ground." The actual example he had before him was a swing attached by a rope to a tree. The tree holds up the object by its own force. When this force is weakened and loosened, another force is brought into place, the force of the earth, gravity. The object was in fact held in between these two forces. The object must either be attached to the tree or to the earth. In spite of the enormous power of gravitation exerted by the earth, the tree was able to hold up the object for a time. Only for a time, for when the fruit matures, the tree cannot hold it up, however it may will to do so. The same act accomplishes the severence from the tree, and the bringing it to the earth. Just so, in the case of the soul. It is bound to Māyā and Mala, so long the soul is not ripe. Before it is ripe, we do not perceive its brightness and sweetness. When the soul perfects itself, fed by the juices from the earth (the Grace of God) it finds its resting place in God. When it so finds itself, united, it becomes one with God, as the fruit itself when left alone becomes one with the earth. The flood again cannot stand still, unless it is held up by an embankment. When this embankment is breached, it will run on and on, till it finds its resting place in the broad arms of the ocean. Without either of these means of support, it will be difficult to restrain the fleeting soul. The embankment or the flood gates are the Māyā support of the soul. The ocean is God. This support is called in Tamiḷ பற்று, a support, a bond of attachment, a rest, desire, love. It is this peculiarity which Saint Tiruvaḷḷuvar expresses in the following couplet,

> பற்றுக பற்றற்றான் பற்றினை, யப்பற்றினைப்
> பற்றுக, பற்றுவிடற்கு,

which again is the mere echo of our Saint Māṇikkavāchakar's words.

> "சுற்றிய சுற்றந் தொடர்வறுப்பான்றொல் புகழே
> பற்றி யிப் பாசத்தைப் பற்றற நாம்பற்றுவான்
> பற்றிய பேரானந்தம் பாடுதும் காணம்மானாய்."

This peculiarity of the soul we have been discussing above, has a tremendous bearing in connection with various philosophical schools. The ancient Buddha and the modern Agnostic would not postulate this other support and resting place of the soul. And we find they are landed in Nihilism accordingly. The moment of perfection is the moment of annihilation to the Buddhist. Nay, with his modern Apostles, Mrs. Annie Besant for example, the cry of the Vedas, 'whence there is no return, there is no return" is merely a vain cry. There is no such thing as final perfection, beatitude or Moksha. The soul must roll on ever and anon, subject to the never-ceasing and ever-recurring evolution due to "the moral necessity connected with the central and most precious doctrine of the exoteric Vedānta, the doctrine of Samsāra." Here of course we see the phenomenon of extremes meeting. The Vedāntist could not deny the possibility of the soul, attaining the so-called moksha, recurring back into the cycle of evolution, as the orginal retrogression of Brahman into Gods and men, brutes and worms is itself not explicable by him. The Agnostic not believing in God, examines into the nature of the mind or soul and perceiving how intimately it is connected with matter, denies of course, its separate personality and independent existence; and hence his denial of the soul's immortality and future existence, when once its mortal coil is broken. In the case of the Vedāntist, however, this peculiarity of the soul will alone furnish the excuse for his theory. And we have heard honest Vedāntists admit this as the only explanation of Śrī Śaṅkara's otherwise untenable position. When in union with God, the soul has lost not merely the consciousness of the world, the Asat, it loses also its self-consciousness, (not be it remarked its self-being) it loses also its consciousness of difference from God &c., and the only perception that remains is the bare perception, the bare enjoyment of God,—the full manifestation and Presence of God, as Love and Bliss, alone is felt; and in such a condition, Śaṅkara could say there is no second thing.

> "சென்று சென்றணுவாய்த் தேய்ந்து
> தேய்ந்தொன்றாம்"

Śaṅkara's experience will therefore by only one-sided one, and the statement cannot stand as a matter of proof. The state of union with God is called Turiya or Para-Avasta, and in this condition, though the conscious perception of the world and soul may not be possible there, be-ness (existence) is not gone. And it is this condition, Saint Tirumūlar expounds in his next verse.

> மரத்தை மறைத்தது மாமதயானை,
> மரத்தின் மறைந்தது மாமதயானை,
> பரத்தை மறைத்தது பார்முதற்பூதம்,
> பரத்தை மறைந்தது பார்முதற்பூதம்.

> The tree was concealed in the mad elephant;
> The tree concealed the mad elephant.
> The world concealed the Supreme,
> In the Supreme was concealed the world.

The Supreme is concealed in the world (not non-existent) the world is concealed in the Supreme (not non-existent). In the sentences, 'I was concealed by the world, the world was concealed in me', note the fact that there are only two names, two categories involved, namely I and the world, soul and māyā. For an intelligent understanding of the proposition, no other category is required. But consider well the propositions, 'the world concealed the Supreme, the world is concealed by the Supreme'. These propositions could not be true as they stand, unless both these stand as objective to the seer, as in the illustration of the wooden-toy itself. The wood of the toy cannot be conscious of its being concealed or not by the elephant form, nor the elephant of the wood. In human language and expression and argument, there is always an ellipsis and the suppression of the middle term. The first two propositions relating to the wooden-toy cannot be true as they stand but is only intelligible, when we supply the factor of the seer. So also, the propositions that follow, though they only contain the two categories Sat and Asat, involve the presence of a third, the Satasat. What we have stated above will explain the Śivajñānabotha Sūtra,

"யாவையுஞ் சூனியம் சத்தெதிராதலின்
சத்தேயறியாது, யசத்திலது அறியாது,
இருதிறனறிவுள திரண்டலா வான்மா."

That we are concealed by our Māyā covering is a fact, the sharpest intellect and the boldest understanding cannot get over it, quibble and juggle as it may, and this being a fact, "that we are here in ignorance, sin, misery, and that we know the way out of them, but the question of a cause for them is senseless." * For nothing can be more senseless to ask for an explanation, when the fact to be explained is itself an ultimate fact. An ounce of fact outweighs a pound of probabilities, say the lawyers. And they only express a logical truth. But the proposition advanced by the Pūrvapakshi is that the jīva, being neither a part nor a different thing, nor a variation of Brahman, must be the Paramātman fully and totally himself, and as such is, clothed with such attributes as all-pervadingness, eternity, almightiness, exemption of time, space and causality, and that this jīva is hidden by the world † (māyā and avidya) as the fire in wood, (or as Saint Tirumūlar would put it, wood in the elephant) and he asks what is the cause of this concealment? Why should the perfect become deluded into the imperfect by avidya and ingorance? Dr. Paul Deussen admits that here all philosophers

* Paul Deussen's *Elements of Metaphysics*, p. 334.

† *Ibid.* p. 334.

of India (of his ilk—Śaṅkara included) and Greece and everywhere have been defective, until Kant came to show us that the whole question is inadmissible. We say 'ditto' also, whatever might be the learned Doctor's understanding of Kant. The whole question is inadmissible, nay the whole proposition of the Pūrvapakshi on which this question is based is inadmissible, it is untrue, is not a fact. The fact is not true that the Supreme Brahman is concealed by Māyā and Avidyā. Dr. Deussen would put his unfortunate Brahman into the dock and arraign him of high crimes and misdemeanours (our friends are never concious of what gross blasphemy they are guilty of—our mind is extremely pained that we should even write so, for argument's sake) and before proving his guilt, with which he charges him, he would indulge in irrelevant and irreverent talk, as to why and wherefore this Brahman committed these crimes. Any ordinary judge would rule his talk as senseless; also, such talk from the accused's counsel, kindly engaged by the crown, would be ruled as senseless, when the accused admits the charge, and there is besides overwhelming testimony as to his guilt, leaving no room for doubt. The case contemplated by the learned Doctor will find a parallel in some of those occasional cases of judicial murder. A greal crime had been committed, there is a great hue and cry, some body ought to be punished, ought to suffer for the unknown criminal. The Police run down some one they have long known, an old offender; witnesses (Pseudo-jñānis, with their Svānubhūti and esoteric experience) only flock in overwhelming numbers to prove the prisoner's guilt; the weight of testimony is only crushing, the poor prisoner at the bar is simply dumb-founded and cannot find speech to exculpate himself, however innocent he might be, and his silence counts for confession and he is condemned to die. Before his bones are whitened however, the real criminal turns up, confesses his crime, and the first conviction is found after all to be based on a case of mistaken identity. We have already shown how liable is the soul to be mistaken for God, to mistake itself for God. Saint Meykaṇḍān even where he teaches the initiate to practice Sohambāvana, cautions him before and after not to mistake himself for God.

'யாவையும் சூனியம் சத்தெதிர்.' In the Presence of the Sat, all else is Sūnyam.' Why, because, 'before the Perfect and Eternal Intelligence, (Truth) the imperfect and acquired intelligence, (the semblance) is shorn of its light,' answers our Saint, and he illustrates it by saying that the Evil Asat ceases to exist before Him, as does darkness before the sun, and explains that Hara cannot know them as objects, as nothing is outside Him. How well this explanation fits in with the vedic text, "There shines not the sun, nor moon, nor stars, neither these lightnings, much less this earthly fire. After Him, the Shining One, all things shine, by His Light is lighted this whole world"* And when before this shining One, even the suns and moons pale, they dare assert that darkness, māyā and avidya can dare lift up their heads and veil and conceal and dim His brightness, and that on account of this veiling, the shining One can become deluded and fancy Himself as Asat, this body and these senses, and this world. Well does the Siddhānti ask, can you show me a sun covered by darkness, for me to believe in a Brahman veiled by Māyā or Upādhi.† No doubt the blind man says, the sun is hid by darkness; he will not confess his own blindness and darkness, and transfers his infirmity to the Effulgent Sun. "After Him, all things shine, by His light is lighted the whole world." Yes, O Lord, we are but broken lights of Thee. The

---

* Svetas vi. 14.

† *c.f.* "இருள்பொதிந்த பானுவுளதேல் உடலையானென்,
மருள்பொதிந்த சித்துளதிம்மன்."

If there is a Sun by darkness veiled
Then may a chit exist by ignorance veiled, mistaking the body for itself

"நின்மலமென்றேயதனை நிகழ்த்திறையதற்குப்
பின்னவித்தை யுண்டென்கைபித்து."

Having called Him Ninmala
It is madness to impute to God, Avidyā.

little light that shines in each one of our souls is simply borrowed from Thee. Without this light, we are but the pieces of diamonds lying in darkness. In bandha, before the diamond is cut and polished, we cannot reflect Thy Glorious Light. We are the diamond crystals, Thou, the light shining in them, வெண்பளிங்கின் உட்பதித்த சோதியானே! As crystal, we become light in light, and dark in darkness. யாதொன்று பற்றின தன் இயல்பாய நின்ற பந்தமறும் பளிங்கனையமாம். Thou art like the Light from the emerald, மரகதம், lighting and colouring everything it touches after itself.

எவ்வெவர் தன்மையும் தன்வயிற் படுத்தும்
தானேயாகிய தயாபரா!

The Diamond crystal (சார்ந்ததன் வண்ணமாகும்) *and the gem Emerland* (சார்ந்ததுதன் வண்ணமாக்கும்), *these are the symbols used by the Siddhāntis for the Soul and Śivam.* Students of Science know the structural difference between those two bodies, as mediums or distributors of light. This Divine Light is Umā, (literally wisdom or light) that Lady wondrous fair, who showed to the astonished immortals, Her Royal Consort, and her colour is green emerald, and we will close this article by invoking her aid and quoting this passage from Kumaragurupara which is poetic and philosophic at the same time.

பண்ணுறு கிளிமொழிப் பாவையின் திருமேனி
  பாசொளிவிரிப்ப வந்தண்,
பவளக் கொடிக் காமர் பச்சிளங் கொடியதாய்,
  பருமுத்தம் மரகதமாய்,
தண்ணுறு மல்லற்றுறை சிறை யனங்களி
  தழைக்குங்கலா மஞ்ஞையாய்
சகலமும் நின்திருச் சொரூபமென் றேலிடும்
  சதுர்மறைப் பொருள் வெளியாகும்.

O Thou parrot-tongued Maid, the emerald Light
  from Thy sacred body spreading,
Converts the red coral reefs into green and the
  big pearls into so many emeralds,
And the winged swans floating on the cool waves
  into so many sporting peacocks
And thus explain the truth which the Vedas proclaim,
  'That after you, all things shine.'

SOME ASPECTS OF THE GOD-HEAD.

"பெண்ணா ணலியெனும் பெற்றியன் காண்க."

"Behold! He is the male, the female and the neuter."!

Tiruvāchakam.

"Šivam šāntam, advaitam chaturtham manyante".

Rāmatapinī Upanishat.

Very often it happens, we have to write upon the same subject over and over again, and nobody need wonder why this should be so. We eat the same kind of rice and dish of vegetables, over and over again, day after day, from the year's end to the year's end, and yet, we never ask why this should be so. The answer is plain that this is the best and safest and most wholesome food we require, every day of our life, for its sustenance and nurture and growth. What applies to the body applies to the mind as well. The mind requires also some wholesome and safe and healthy pabulum for it to feed upon, also, every day, nay, every hour; and you can starve the mind, as well as over-feed it; and you may feed it on unwholesome and unhealthy food; and these are irregularities which we should avoid, as we should avoid irregularities in diet. Wholesome food, however often we may repeat, ought not to tire any body. And this is necessary for another reason also. Man is circumstanced more or less by his environment; all sorts of influences are brought to bear on him; and these create doubts and misgivings even in the most well-regulated minds; and the mind vacillates from one extreme to the other. It is therefore good that the mind is made to face the same truth, ever and anon. And then, indeed, our memory is so weak, we forget what we learnt only yesterday; and what fails to strike our imagination at one time may attract it another time. Besides, errors and fallacies are repeated day after day, and it becomes necessary to repeat what we regard as truths as often. As such, we make no further apology for going fully into a subject which we touched upon in our review of "the Minor Upanishats," in our introduction to the Kaivalya Upanishat, and in our article on the "Personality of God". Very often, a controversy is carried on by means of names and words, and the whole fallacy lies in the different parties to the controversy, understanding the word in as many different ways. We have seen how European writers differed in defining the word "*Personal*" and "Impersonal"; and we have accepted the word "*Personal*" free from all implication of limitation or anthropomorphism and in the manner defined by Emerson, Lotze, Dr. Iverach &c. We have also noted the different ways of interpreting the word *Saguṇa* and *Nirguṇa*. One calls God *Saguṇa*, and interprets *Nirguṇa* in undoubted and authoritative passages as meaning merely "*devoid of bad qualities*". And in this sense *Saguṇa* must mean *full of bad qualities*; and yet this one will only call his God *Saguṇa* and not *Nirguṇa*; and he exhibits a clear prejudice against the word "Nirguṇa," thus clearly making out that his interpretation is, after all, only a doubtful expedient at avoiding an inconvenient corner. We have, however, referred to its technical and original and philosophic acceptation, in that, *Guṇa* means the *Guṇa tattva* which is the name and characteristic of *Mūlaprakṛiti*; and this *Guṇa* comprises the three *Guṇas*, *Sattva*, and *Rajas* and *Tamas*; *Saguṇa* accordingly means clothed with *Sattva* and *Rajas* and *Tamas*, gross material qualities, and *Nirguṇa* means freedom from these three qualities or gross material veilings; and the definition of God as *Nirguṇa*, and not as *Saguṇa*, does not therefore conflict with the literal and consistent acceptation of the two words, or our idea of God's Supreme Nature. By the way, an additional proof that our interpretation is correct is furnished by the fact that the Saguṇa Philosopher actually clothes his God with Sattva-Guṇa. Comparisons are generally odious, but where principles are at stake they cannot be avoided altogether; and we merely invite our readers' attention to the two descriptions of God-head, given in the appendix to Dr. Muir's "Metrical Translations from Sanskrit writers", which are respectively summarised from the Śvetāśvatara Upanishat and Uttara-Rāmāyaṇa. You may omit the names, for they are accidents, due to our ancient religious history, and you may give the bare descriptions to our artist; and we have no doubt he will draw two totally different pictures. No doubt, we admit their Saguṇa conception of God, and as for that, any *bhāvanā* of God serves the purpose of the aspirant after a higher path to a great extent, on the well-known principle laid down by *St. Meykaṇḍān*, "*Choose the form which attracts your love most.*" But as we have pointed out already, we do not remember at times that this is only a form, a symbol and not the truth itself, that truth is beyond one's ordinary ken ("கண்முதற் புலனாற் காட்சியுமில்லோன்—உள்ளத்துணர்ச்சியிற் கொள்ளவும்படான்."), and that yet this vision is possible ("கணனால் யானும் கண்டேன்"), ("புறையற்றிருந்தான் புரிசடையோனே") when leaving our feeling of 'I' and 'Mine', destroying and annihilating our *Paśu* and *Pāśa* nature "ஊன் கெட்டு உயிர் கெட்டு—நான் கெட்டு" and assisted by His Supreme Grace ("அவனருளால்"), we reach the place of peace, Nirvāṇa (Literally non-flowing-as-air) (நிறையற்ற நீர்போற் சிந்தை தெளிவாற்கு) *

What we, therefore, here wish to lay down and impress upon our readers, is that, whatever names we may use, ("ஒருநாமம் ஒருருவம் ஒன்றுமில்லாற்கு, ஆயிரம் திருநாமம்பாடி நாம் தென்னேணம் கொட்டாமோ"—"Let us sing the thousand names of the One who has no name, no form, nothing"), and though we may accept this form and that symbol for worship and practice (Sādhana), yet we hold rigidly to the principle that God is not man, covered by ignorance and matter, and God cannot be born as man, and clothed with Prakṛiti qualities. The rigid acceptance of this one principle alone, that *God* is *Aja*,

* cf., "Be still and know that I am God.—" Book of Psalms.

(*cannot be born*) ought to distinguish and elevate the Siddhānta from all other forms of Religion. And the rigid acceptance of this one principle alone must prevent it from its degenerating into a superstition, and base idolatry, and man and fetish-worship. One great obstacle to the due recognition of the excellence of the Siddhānta is the obstacle thrown by certain names. We use certain names as denoting God and as comprising the characteristic attributes which we clothe Him with. But how can we help it ? We cannot forget our language, and its past traditions; we cannot forget our religious past, however we might try; and we cannot therefore coin new names, simply because some others want us to do so. And what need is there for doing so either ? If we use certain names, they were so used by 90 per cent of the Indian population for the last 30 centuries at least; they were so used in the days of the Purāṇas and Itihāsas, they were so used in the days of the Upanishat writers, and they were so used in the days of the Vedic writers. And some of these Mantras and texts have been used in the daily prayer of everybody. The publishers of "The Theosophy of the Upanishats" recommend to us the following mantra from the Taittirīya Upanishat for our daily prayer:

"Satyam Jñānam Anantam Brahma Ānandarūpam
Amṛitam *yad* vibhūti Śāntam *Śivam*, Advaitam."

And what is there sectarian about the word "*Śivam*" herein? Evan an Upanishat of the Type of Rāmatapinī has this text with the same word, (quoting as it does the above Mantra of course),

"*Śivam*, Śāntam, Advaitam, *Chaturtham* manyante".

There is one thing about the word "*Śivam*". Sanskrit scholars say that the word in this form is not a neuter noun but simply an adjective, and accordingly translate it as *gracious, benignant* &c; but it is remarkable that this word is always used in the Ṛig-Veda and other Vedas and Upanishats in conjunction with the word Rudra, Śaṅkara,

Bhava, &c., and that to denote the same personality and not any other. However this may be, the word (சிவம்) Šivam is used clearly in Tamiḻ as the neuter Form of Šiva or Šivan (சிவன்), as Param (பரம்) of Para or Paran (பரன்), as Brahmam (பிரமம்), of Brahman (பிரமன்), with no change of meaning in either form. That this accounts for the frequent change from one gender to another in describing the Supreme Being, even in the same Mantra, as in the Švetāšvatara, we have already pointed out. That all these names are also declinable in the feminine gender without change of meaning we have also pointed out elsewhere. Whether we say Šiva, Šivam, or Šivā; Šaṅkara, Šaṅkaram, or Šaṅkari; Para, Param, or Parā; we denote the same Supreme Personality. We use these words, and in these forms of gender, as these are all the forms or symbols we perceive in the material universe. To us, therefore, these names are mere names and nothing more; and we affix therefore no greater importance to one form in preference to another. Though Professor Max Muller would prefer to call God, in the neuter, "It" and think it a higher name, we are thoroughly indifferent as to calling the supreme, as *He*, *She* or *It*; and we accordingly with St. Māṇikkavāchaka praise God, as

> பெண்ணாண் அலியெனும் பெற்றியன் காண்க" *
>
> "Behold! He is the male and the female and the neuter."

---

* And yet consider the following lines from the same 'utterence.'

> அச்சன் ஆண்பெண் அலியா காசமாகி
> யாரழலா யந்தமாயப்பால் நின்ற
> செச்சை மாமலர் புரையுமேனி யெங்கள்
> சிவபெருமான் எம்பெருமான் தேவர் கோவே."

"My Father! He became man, woman, and hermaphrodite, the Ākāš, and Fire and this final Cause, and *transcending all these forms*, stands the Supreme Šiva, of the Body glowing like the flame of the forest. He is my Lord and the King of Gods".

> "பெண்ணாகி யாணா யலியாய்ப் பிறங்கொளிசேர்
> விண்ணாகி மண்ணாகி யித்தனையும் வேறாகி
> கண்ணா ரமுதமாய் நின்றான்."

"He became, 'He' and 'She' and 'It' and the Earth and Heaven, and is *different from all these* and stands as my dear Blessedness."

These lines will be found repeated often and often in the Tiruvāchakam, Tevāram and every other sacred writing in Tamil. Can similar lines be quoted from writers of any other school? We dare say, not. But the older Upanishats contain similar thoughts, and that only proves our contention that the Siddhānta school but barely represents to day the oldest traditions, and is the inheritor of the most ancient Philosophy. Of all Indian preachers, it was the late *matakhaṇḍana* Veṅkatagiri Sāstrin that used to dwell on this universal aspect of the Siddhānta in respect of naming Him as 'He', 'She' and 'It', and he used to point out that all names of Śiva are declinable in all the three genders without change of meaning, whereas other names do not admit of this change, and even if they do, the word is meaningless or means something else. We do not know why some people prefer the neuter form to the masculine or feminine, when, in fact, it stands to reason that the male and female represent in each the perfection of organized and organic form, much more so than the neuter forms. If by calling Him,† 'It', we mean to emphasize that God is sexless, we must also insist that God is genderless, and that he cannot be spoken of in the neuter gender. And the phrase, "அவனவளது" "Strīpunnapumsaka," 'He, She, It,' has become a technical phrase with us (see first sūtra of Śivajñānabodham) to mean the whole of the material manifested universe and its various forms; and in naming God with words and forms borrowed from matter, we cannot avoid using these words. But then, the difference between principle and symbol, truth and dogmatism, has to be perceived. We tried to make ourselves clear about this distinction about the "Soham or Tattvamasi" doctrine in our last; and in the subject we have been elucidating above, a similar distinction has to be perceived. One says, 'address God always as He'; and if you call him, 'It,' he says you are addressing a cold abstraction. Another

† The genius of the English Language, reflecting as it does the Christian Religion does not allow us to call God, except in the masculine, though of course we have heard that they do not mean to say that God is a male like a man.

claims to have reached a higher Philosophy by refusing to call Him,* as 'Him' and by calling Him 'It.' Both seem to think that there is something degrading in calling Him as 'She.' But the feeling which induces the European to lift the female to almost divine honors, and the tenderest and most passionate of all our emotions which cling round the word 'mother', ought to enable one to realize our ideal of God as the 'Divine Sakti,' ¶ One who, St Māṇicka Vāchaka says, "is even more loving than my mother." ("தாயிற் பெரிதும் தயாவுடைய தம்பெருமான்"†).

Where, of course, the truth is seen, there will be no more room for ignorant dogmatism, and any and all these modes of address will equally be acceptable to Him, if instead of uttering those bare words, we put into them, such love as will "make our bones melt." and such as is described by our own Saint, in his "போற்றித்திருவகவல்" "Pilgrim's Progress". (p. 101. Siddhānta Dīpikā Vol. I.)

We began our article with the object of quoting from our Lord Māṇikkavāchaka some passages in which he addresses the supreme as "Śivam" in the Superlative Neuter of Prof. Max Müller, and the forgoing remarks will be sufficient to introduce those passages:

"சிந்தனைக்கரிய சிவமே போற்றி."‡ p. 25.
"Praise be to "*Śivam*" beyond reach of thought."

"அன்பருள்ளாம் சிவமே." p. 26,
"O *Śivam*! who dwells in the heart of those who love Him."

---

* In calling God, 'He' and 'Him', we are following only the genius of the English language.

¶ Mrs. Flora Annie Steel speaks of Umā-Haimavatı as the emblem of perfect wife-hood, mother-hood and mystical virginity.

† Consider the following lines also.
"அன்னை யொப்பாய் எனக்கத்தன் ஒப்பாய் என்னரும் பொருளே"
"தாயே யென்றன் ருளடைந்தேன்"

‡ We give the references from the well-printed and neat edition of Kāñchı Nāgalinga Mudaliyār, 45, Bairagimatt Lane, Madras.

"அரிக்கும் பிரமற்குமல்லாத தேவர்கட்கும்
தெரிக்கும்படித்தன்றி நின்ற சிவம்." p. 12.

"*Śivam* which stood unperceived by Hari, and Brahma and other Gods."

"நாமொழிந்து சிவமானவா" Ibid.

"Losing one's 'I'ness became *Śivam*"

"தித்திக்கும் சிவபதம்." p. 119.

"The sweet *Śiva Padam*" (*The Mahat Padam of the Upanishat.*")

"சிவம் வேண்டார்தமை நாளும் தீண்டேன்." p 125.

"I will not touch those who love not *Śivam*."

"சித்தமல மறுவித்துச் சிவமாக்கி யெனையாண்ட அத்தன்." p. 153.

"My Father who took me to His embrace by making me *Śivam*, after cleansing me of my sin."

These are only a few out of a vast number, and this description is found also in the Devāra Hymns and other sacred writings. Probably, if this aspect of Siddhānta had been present to the mind of Prof. Max Muller when he wrote his introduction to the Śvetāśvatara Upanishat, in refuting the argument that the Upanishat was a sectarian one, he need not have gone to the extreme of trying to establish an illusory identity between a Nirguṇa and a Saguṇa God. For, we do not, at any rate, accept the Saguṇa God as God, the Supreme, at all; for the Saguṇa God is only a God in name, but a Paśu or Soul in reality. And we here come to a great fallacy which is the source of a very grievous error. The error consists in interpreting such words as Īśvara, Māheśvara, Parameśvara, Īśā, Īśāna, Maheśa, Deva, Mahādeva, Hara, Rudra, Śiva, Purusha, wherever they occur in the Upanishats, Gītā &c., as meaning the lower or Saguṇa Brahman, and seemingly because these names are also applied to a God who is one of the Trinity or Trimūrtis, Brahma, Vishṇu, and Rudra. But any ordinary student of the Śaiva Siddhānta will perceive that the God they worship is not one of the Trinity, though called by the same name, and that their system speaks of Him, as the *Turiyam* and *Chaturtham*, both meaning fourth, and these thoughts can be picked up from the most ancient and the most recent books in Tamiḷ and in Sanskrit. The typical passage in the Upanishats is the one in the AtharvaŠikhā.

Dhyāyeetesānam pradhyāyithavyam Sarvam idam Brahma Vishṇū Rudrèndrāste sarvè samprasùyantè sarvāni chèndriyā-nicha saha bhutais, nakāranam Kāranānām dhātā dhyātā Karanahtu dhyèyas Sarvaisvarya Sampannas Sarvèsvaras Sambhurākasa madhyè............Šiva éko dhyéya: Śivankara: Šarvam annyat Parityaja Samāpta atharvasikhā.

Taking another book at random, say the Mahimnastotra, which is reputed to be by a very ancient sage, in praise of Šiva, we come upon the following passage also.

"The mystical and immutable One which being composed of the three letters, A. U. M. signify, successively, the three Vedas, the three states of life (awaking, dreaming and sleeping), the three worlds (heaven, earth and hell), the three Gods (Brahma, Vishṇu and Rudra), and by its nasal sound (ardhamātrā) is indicative of thy fourth office as Supreme Lord of All, (ParameŠvara) ever expresses and sets forth thy collective and single Forms."

And we to day only propose to quote similar passages from only one book, and that the Tiruvāchakam.

The first passage is the one occuring on p. 26, which we have already quoted in reviewing the Minor Upanishats. Lest that the 'three' in this verse may be taken to mean Brahma, Vishṇu and some other God than Rudra, our saint himself expressly sets forth his meaning more clearly in the following verse.

தேவர்கோ அறியாத தேவ தேவன்
செழும்பொழில்கள் பயந்துகாத்தழிக்கும் மற்றை
மூவர்கோ னாய்நின்ற முதல்வன் மூர்த்தி
மூதாதை மாதாளும் பாகத்தெந்தை."

"Him the God of Gods not perceived by the king of Gods (Indra)[1] Him the supreme king of the other Triad, who create, sustain and destroy the worlds; The first Mūrti, (the manifest God)[2] the Great Ancestor, my Father who consorts with the Divine Maid.

Consider the following passages also.

முன்னானை மூவர்க்கு முற்றுமாய் முற்றுக்கும்
பின்னானைப் பிஞ்ஞகனைப் பேணுபெருந் துறையின்
மன்னானை வானவனை மாதியலும் பாதியனை."

"Him, *The more ancient than the Triad*, The End (of all things), and yet one who lasts behind all things, the One with the braided hair[3] the King of our loved city Perundurai, The Heavenly God, and the Consort of Umā."

பூவேறு கோனும் புரந்தரனும் பொற்பமைந்த
நாவேறு செல்வியும் நாரணனும் நான்மறையும்
மாவேறு சோதியும் வானவரும் தாமறியாச்
சேவேறு சேவடிக்கே சென்றூதாய்கோத்தும்பீ.

In the following passage, He is identified with the Triad, in the same way as He is often identified with all the works of His creation, Earth, Air, Water &c, though those very passages say at the same time that He is not to be identified with the creature and created things, a doctrine which clearly cannot be mistaken for Pantheism. As a Christian writer points out, the Doctrine of Immanency of God in all nature is quite consistent with our idea of the Transcendency of God.

"யுருமூன்றுமாகி யுணர்வரிதாமொருவன்." p. 79,

"He became the *Triple Form* (of the Triad), and yet remained the one who could not be perceived by the mind."

---

[1] *c.f.*, the story in the Kenopanishat about Indra and other Gods being unable to know Brahman and being taught by Umā Haimavati (God's grace) about the Supreme Brahmam.

[2] Like ghee in butter milk, after churning with knowledge and love.

[3] Kaparidin of the Rig-veda.

முந்துநடுவு முடிவுமாகிய மூவ ரறியாச்
சிந்துரச்சேவடியான்."

"Himself the Beginning, the middle and the end, Him whose beautiful "*Mahat Padam*" could not be perceived by the *Three*." Also the following passages.

யாரூரன்
செம்பெருமான் வெண்மலரான் பாற்கடலான்,
செப்புவபோல் எம்பெருமான் தேவர்பிரானென்று, p. 91.

"He of Ārūr, whom even Rudra, and Brahma and Vishṇu, praised as 'Our King, the King of Gods."

" முந்திய முதல் நடுவிறுதியுமானாய்
மூவருமறிகிலர் யாவர்மற்றறிவார்." p. 95.

"Thou becomest the Foremost, the Beginning, the Middle, and the End and were not understood by the Triad. Who else can know Thee."

" முழுமுதலே, யைம்புலனுக்கும் மூவர்க்குமென்றனக்கும்,
வழிமுதலே." p 97.

The Impartite First, the First Cause or Source of the five senses, (the material universe), the *Three Gods* and myself (Soul)."

" தேவதேவன் மெய்ச்சேவகன் தென்பெருந்துறை நாயகன்
மூவராலு மறியொணா முதலாயவானந்த மூர்த்தியான்
யாவராயினும் அன்பரன்றி யறியொணாமலர்ச் சோதியான்,
தூயமாமலர்ச் சேவடிக்கணஞ் சென்னிமன்னிச் சுடருமே."

("God of Gods, God of Truth, The Lord of South Peruntural
The Lord of Bliss, The first cause whom the Three cannot know,
The Glorious one whom *none can know save those that love.*
His pure bloom-like feet my head does seek and glorify.")

" மூவரு முப்பத்து மூவரு மற்றொழிந்த
தேவருங் காணாச் சிவபெருமான்—மாவேறி
வையகத்தே வந்திழிந்து வார் கழல்கள் வந்திக்க
மெய்யகத்தே யின்ப மிகும்.

("The Lord Šiva, unknown by Devas all,
The Three and Thirty-three—
He that rides the Bull—
His holy feet if here we seek and praise,
Our bliss will sure increase.")

Yes, nothing can be truer than the thought expressed in this verse.

The Highest conception that we can ever reach of God, describing as it does, His inmost nature, and of course the only way we can know Him, is that God is Love and Blessedness, *Šivam.**

And such a great scientist as the late Prof. Romanes has asked with truth:—"What has all the science or all the philosophy of the world done for the thought of mankind to be compared with one doctrine 'God is Love'."

[* The word *Nandi*, a favourite word with St, Tirumūlar and others means also literally the Blissfull; and our readers have to consider why we now call the Great Bull (Pasu) in front of God by the same name Nandi.]

ASHTAMUHURTAM.

"Antarichchanti Tamsena Rudram Promanishayā Krinantī Chikbāḥyā Chacham. (Ṛig-Veda.)"

"Those who meditate with love on the Supreme Rudra which is within all, they eat food."

It is a noteworthy fact that our sages have often compressed a whole philosophy in a single word or phrase. We once before illustrated how pregnant was the naming of vowels and consonants as உயிர் and மெய், Sarīri and Sarīra, in regard to the question of the relation of God to the world. We take up to day another word which is the expansion of the same subject. This word is "Ashta Mūrti" It means Being having Eight Forms and is a synonym of Šiva or Rudra. These Eight Forms are, Earth, Water, Fire, Air, Ākāš, the Sun and the Moon and Soul or Jīva or Pašu.

By these Eight names are comprised the whole universe, both animate and inanimate. The only substance which these terms do not comprise is God; and when therefore God is spoken of by His having these eight forms as His Body, then the relation of God to the world is clearly brought out, namely that of soul and body, which relation, of course, we have fully explained in our article on "Mind and Body." As soul in a body, He is in every thing, and hence called Visvāntaryāmi; and we have quoted a *Rich* verse above in which God (Rudra) is called Antaryāmi; and innumerable passages are also scattered about in the body of the various Upanishats. As having the universe for His Form, God is called Visvasvarūpi

"Visvarūpāya vi Namo Namaḥ."

As giving rise to the whole universe from Himself, He is called Visvakāraṇa or Visvayoniḥ. By the same way, as we often identify our own body with ourselves, God is frequently spoken of as the universe itself, and is accordingly addressed as Earth, Water, Fire, Air, Sky, the Sun and the Moon, and Soul.

But there are clear passages to show that He is none of these. No one could seriously contend to day that where these Upanishats identify God with some of these inanimate forms, that earth or fire or any of these elements, and not the Ruler within or the Puller as He is called in Bṛihadāraṇya, is really God. But the texts identifying the Jīvā with God has caused no amount of confusion, and these texts are quoted as standing authorities by a whole school of Indian philosophers, though texts can be quoted as frequently in which God is spoken of as different from the Jīvā. As being none of these Eight and transcending all, He is called Visvādika.

"Visvādiko Rudra," (Švetāš).

"Who of the Gods is both the source and growth, *the lord of all, the Rudra,* mighty seer; whoever sees the shining germ come into birth— may he with reason pure conjoin us."

"Who of the Gods is over-lord, in whom the worlds are based, who ruleth over his creatures of two feet and four; to God, the "Who," with (our) oblation let us worship give."

These follow naturally the text "That sure is fire, That sun, That air, That surely moon, That verily the Bright, That Brahm, the waters That, That the Creator."

In the previous adhyāya, occurs the passage "What is this all, far, far beyond, That Formless, griefless That." "What God in fire, in water, what doth pervade universe entire, what in the plants, what in the forest lords, to Him, to God, Hail all Hail."

"This God, in sooth, all the quarters is; long, long ago, indeed, he had his birth, he verily (is now) within the germ. He has been born, he will be born; behind all who have birth he stands, with face on every side."

The famous passage in the seventh Brahmana, of the 3rd Adyāya, of the Bṛihadāraṇyaka Upanishat, brings out a full exposition of these Eight forms of God. In the third Mantra, Earth is said to be His body—

Yasyapṛithivī śarīram."

"He who dwells in the earth, and within (or different from) the earth, whom the earth does not know, *whose body the earth is*, and who pulls (rules) the earth within, He is thy Self, the puller (ruler) within, the immortal."

And in Mantrās, 4, 5, 7, 9, 11, 12 and 22 the water, fire, air, sun, moon, Ākāśa and Vijñāna are respectively said to be His bodies.

The passages are all similar to the one relating to the earth and we quote the last, however, in full.

"He who dwells in Vijñāna, and within (or different from) Vijñāna, whom Vijñāna does not know, *whose body Vijñāna is*, and who pulls (rules) Vijñāna within, He is thy Self, the puller (ruler) within, the immortal".

Professor Max Muller translates Vijñāna as knowledge, but he notes at the same time that those of the Madhyāndina school interpret it as meaning the Ātmā or the soul; and according to the text in the *samāna prakaraṇa*—"yasyātma sarīram"—and from the Upa-Brahmanas we will quote below, it will be seen that it is the correct interpretation.

The other text in the Bṛihadāraṇya, makes it much clearer. "God is to be seen, heard and contemplated and enjoyed in the soul. He is beyond the soul. His body is the soul, He penetrates into the recess of the soul." Nothing can be clearer than this text. This Soul and soul, this Ātmā and ātmā, this Self and self (The confusion in thought arises from the name which originally meant the human spirit being applied to the Supreme spirit also), are the two birds which dwell in the tree (human body); these are the two which "enter into the heart, the excellent divine abode" and these are the two which are in the "inside of" of the human eye. The confusion of using the same word to denote and connote two different things is really vicious, and later writings and the present day systems have dropped such uses altogether, and the beginning of such change in nomenclature, and precision in the use of words is seen in the Gītā, and Ātmā is distinguished from Paramātmā, Purusha from Purushottama or Parama Purusha. Verse 22 of Chapter 13, is a characteristic verse in this respect as it gives all these names and the true definition of Sat as distinguished from Sat-asat.

> "Spectator, and Permitter, Supporter, Enjoyer,
> *Mahešvara*, thus is styled *Paramātman*;
> In this body *Parama Purusha*."

We have elsewhere observed how the sole purpose of the Purāṇas and Itihāsas is merely to explain the particular text of the Veda or Upanishat. The passage in the Upa Brahmana embodies the particular text and explains it.

See how this passage, from Parāsara Purāṇa reproduces the words and meaning of the *Rich* text quoted above.

> "Antarichchandiyā Rudram Sadhā Vantayam Manīshyā
> Kruḥnanti Sihvaya tāhirasa pūrno Amṛitodakam
> Antar Nāchchantiyā Rudram Bahvānu Sahitam Šivam
> Purusha Māvagṛiḥnanti Sikvayatānasamšayaḥ."

The following passage from Skānda Purāṇa also says that the Jīva is the body of god.

> "Antaryāmi Sa Avisha Jīvānām Paramešvaraḥ"
> "That same Paramešvara is the Antaryāmi in all jīvas".

Turning to Mahābhārata, the statement that God has these eight objects for His body and that the universe is His Form, that He is different from the universe occurs very frequently.

We cite the following passages from the Anusāsana Parva, P. C. Roy's edition:—

"Him that hath universe for His form" page. 49

"Thou art of the form of all jīvas in the universe" page. 125.

"Thou art the Lord of Jīvas" page 133.

"Thou hast universe for thy form" page 105.

"Thou art He who has the whole universe for His limbs" page 104.

"He pervades all things in the universe and yet is not seen anywhere" page 50.

"Agitating both Prakṛiti and Purusha by means of his energy (Šakti), He created therefrom the universal lord of creatures, Brahma."

"He is both Sat and Asat."

"He transcends both Prakṛiti and Purusha" page 50.

"Thou art He called Sat of Sat" page 127.

"Having created all the worlds beginning with "Bhu" together with all the denizens of heavens, Thou upholdest and cherishest them all, distributing Thyself into the well-known forms numbering eight" page 96.

The poet Kāḷidāsa in his benedictory verse in Sakuntala explains what these eight forms are,

> Iśā preserve you! He who is revealed
> In these eight forms by man perceptible—
> Water, of all creation's works the first;
> The Fire that bears on high the sacrifice
> Presented with solemnity to heaven;
> The Priest, the holy offerer of gifts;
> The Sun and Moon, those two majestic orbs,
> Eternal marshallers of day and night;
> The subtle Ether, vehicle of sound,
> Diffused throughout the boundless universe,
> The Earth, by sages called, 'The place of birth
> Of all material essences and things,'
> And Air, which giveth life to all that breathe.

There is also this verse, for which we cannot find any reference, which gives eight names of God as He dwells in His eight forms.

"Prithivyo Bava, Apach Sarvah, Agne Rudrah, Vāyur Bhimah, Ākāšasya Mahādevah, Sūryas Yograh, Chandrasya Somah, Ātmānah Pašupatih"

Note here that the word Hotri meaning the sacrificer or the Yajamān (master) of the sacrifice, stands for ātmā, Jīva or Pašu. Hence the Lord of the pašu is called Pašupati. (Meda Pati)

We quote a few more passages from Mahābhārata.

"Thou art the eight Prakṛitis; Thou art again above the eight Prakṛitis, everything that exists represents a portion of Thy divine Self". page 99.

The following passage explains why God should multiply Himself, why He should manifest Himself into these eight forms; *i. e.*, why God should bring about the evolution and creation of this world; not of course, from any moral necessity connected with the doctrine of samsāra; not of course, from His Will to exist and desire for enjoyment; not of course, from a desire to see His own reflexion; not, of course, from a necessity to seek His own salvation; but that this evolution is necessitated for the improvement and salvation of the sin-covered soul.

"Know O Kesava, that this all, consisting of animate and inanimate existences, with heaven and other unseen entities, which occurs in these worlds, and which has the All-pervading Lord for its soul, has flowed from Mahešvara, and has been *created* by Him *for the enjoyment of Jīva.*" page 70.

The soul, in its Kevala condition, lies in utter and hopeless oblivion, and helplessness. The Lord Wills (Ichchā šakti) that these souls should reach salvation out of His pure Grace (Aruḷ Šakti); and by means of His own Energy (Kriyā šakti) He agitates and puts motion and life into Prakṛiti (Māyā šakti); and Purusha (souls) and the whole of the manifested universe is brought forth from His womb. The souls in these material bodies act, and gain experience and knowledge, and finally effect freedom from the bondage of birth and death. Thus, the soul passes through its sakala and athītha conditions; and it is the fundamental tenet of every school of Hindu philosophers that unless the soul enters the cycle of samsāra, that wheel of birth and death, the soul cannot reach Mukti.

We close this paper with a few quotations from the Drāviḍa Śruti bearing on the question under discussion. Our saint Tirumūlar says.

(1) ஊனு யுயிரா யுணர்வங்கி யாய்முன்னஞ்
சேணு வானோங்குந் திருவுரு வேயண்டத்
தாணுவு ஞாயிறுந் தண்மதி யுங்கடந்
தான்முழு தண்டமு மாகிநின் றானே.

The body and soul, and fire and far spreading
Air and space, and earth, His form,
The fixed sun, cool moon, transcending these,
Yet stands He as the stupendous world.

(2) எட்டுத் திசையு மடிக்கின்ற காற்றவன்
வட்டத் திரையனல் மாநில மாகாச
மொட்டி யுயிர்நிலை யென்னுமிக் காயப்பை
கட்டியவிழ்க்கின்ற கண்ணுதல் காணுமே.

The wind that blows in eight quarters is He.
The whirling flood and fire, huge earth and space,
The sentient soul with these His bodily frame,
He joins, and leaves, the God with the frontal Eye.

From our Sainted Lady of Kāraikāl, we have the following verse.

(1) அவனே யிருசுடர் தீயாகா சமாவான்
அவனே புவியனல் காற்றாவான்—அவனே
இயமான னாயட்ட மூர்த்தியு மாய்ஞான
மயனாகி நின்றானும் வந்து.

Two Lights, the fire and space is He
The earth and water, air is He
The soul, with these His eight forms
He stands as Intelligence pure.

The text of St. Meykaṇḍa Deva is that

"God is Chit because He is omnipresent" and unless He is pure Intelligence, He cannot be omnipresent. (See for further explanation, 2nd Sūtra Sivajñānabotham, English edition page 11.)

Our Saint Pattinattār gives a most elaborate description in the following Agaval—

இருநிலமடந்தை இயல்பினினுடுத்த
பொருகடன்மேகலை முகமெனப்பொலிந்த
ஒற்றிமாநக ருடையோயுருவின்
பெற்றியொன்றுப் பெற்றோரியாரே
மின்னின்பிறக்கந் துன்னுநின்சடையே
மன்னியவண்டநின் சென்னியின்வடிவே
பாவகன்பரிதி பனிமதிதன்னொடு
மூவகைச்சுடருநின் நுதனேர்நாட்டந்
தண்ணொளியாரந் தாராகணமே
விண்ணவர்முதலா வேறோரிடமாக்
கொண்டுறைவிசும்பே கோலநின்னாகம்
எண்டிசைதிண்டோள் இருங்கடலுடையே
அணியுடையல்கு லவனிமண்டலமே
மணிமுடிப்பாந்தள்நின் தாளிணைவழக்கே
யொழியாதோடிய மாருதமுயிர்ப்பே
வழுவாவோசை முழுதுநின்வாய்மொழி
வானவர்முதலா மன்னுயிர்பரந்த
ஊனமில்ஞானத் தொகுதிநின்னுணர்வே
நெருங்கியவுலகினின் நீர்மையுநிற்றலும்
சுருங்கலும்விரிதலும் தோற்றம்நின்றொழிலே
அமைத்தலுமழித்தலும் ஆங்கதன் பெயர்ச்சியும்
இமைத்தலும்விழித்தலும் ஆகும் நின்னியல்பே
என்றிவைமுதலா இயல்புடைவடி வினொடு
ஒன்றியதுப்புரு இருவகையாகி
முத்திறக்குணத்து நால்வகைப்பிறவி
அத்திறத்தைம்பொறி அறுவகைச் சமயமோடு
எழுலகாகி எண்வகை மூர்த்தியோடு
ஊழியோரேழி யெண்ணிறந்தோங்கி

எவ்வகையளவினிற் கூடிநின்
றவ்வகைப்பொருளுநீ யாகியவிடத்தே.

O Thou Dweller in *Voṟṟi*, which beams
As the face of the sea-girt Earth!
Who owns Thy Form beyond compare?
The Lightning's flash Thy locks do show,
The teeming Earth Thy Head does form.
The Sun and Moon, and Fire, these three,
Are Eyes that light Thy Divine Face.
Thy cool bright wreaths are the countless stars.
The sky where in the gods do dwell
Thy broad Chest forms; The Eight quarters,
Thy shoulders strong. The broad sea Thy Vest.
Thy Organ, Earth; Feet the worlds below.
The flowing wind Thy constant breath,
The flawless sounds are all Thy words.
The faultless wisdom that is together found
In Gods and Men is all Thy own.
The teeming world lives and develops
Vanishes and reappears, These Thy acts.
The world, in life or death, awake,
Or asleep, does show Thy Nature true.
With these Thy Form, Thy one True spirit
Dual becomes; clothed in Gunas three,
Art born as four; Hast senses five,
The six Religions, and seven worlds
Dost become and art the Eight Gods.
And thus for ages and ages progressing
Whatever Thou unitest with
That Thou dost sure become.

The following is the favourite quotation from Tiruvāchakam.

நிலநீர் நெருப்புயிர் நீள்விசும்பு நிலாப்பகலோன்
புலனாய மைந்தனோ டெண்வகையாய்ப் புணர்ந்துநின்றா
னுலகே ழெனத்திசைபத் தெனத்தா னொருவனுமே
பலவாகி நின்றவா தோணோக்க மாடாமோ.

Earth, water, air, fire, sky, the Sun and Moon,
The sentient man, these eight forms He pervades

The seven worlds, ten quarters, He the One,
And Many, He stands, so, let us sing.

Saint Tāyumānavar selects the following verse from St. Appar's Devāram for special praise in his அறிவுருவை.

இருநிலனாய்த் தீயாகி நீருமாகி
இயமான னாயெறியுங் காற்றுமாகி
அருநிலைய திங்களாய் ஞாயிறாகி
ஆகாசமா யட்ட மூர்த்தியாகிப்
பெருநலமுங் குற்றமும் பெண்ணுமாணும்
பிறருருவுந் தம்முருவுந் தாமேயாகி
நெருநலையா யின்றாகி நாளையாகி
நிமிர்புன் சடையடிகள் நின்றவாறே.

As earth, fire, water, air and Ejaman
As moon, the sun and space, as Ashta Murti,
As goodness and evil, as male and female,
Himself the Form of every form,
As yesterday and to-day and to-morrow,
My Lord with the braided hair stands Supreme.

The following verse of St. Appar also explains how this Being who is the greatest of the great is so small also, as to be confined in ourselves.

எட்டுமூர்த்தியாய் நின்றியலுந்தொழில்
எட்டுவான்குணத் தீசனெம்மான்றன்னை
எட்டுமூர்த்தியு மெம்மிறையெம்முளே
எட்டுமூர்த்தியு மெம்முளொடுங்குமே.

As Ashta Murti, He performs functions
He, my Father and God, possessed of eight attributes
He, the Ashta Murti is my Lord and Master
He, the Ashta Murti is confined in me.

Saint Jñāna Sambanda has the following verse.

பாரு நீரொடு பல்கதிரிரவியும் பனிமதி யாகாச
மோரும் வாயுவு மொண்கனல் வேள்வியிற் றலைவனுமாய் நின்றார்
சேருஞ்சந்தன மகிலொடு வந்திழிசெழும்புனற் கோட்டாறு
வாருந் தண்புனல் சூழ்சிரபுரந் தொழுமடியவர் வருந்தாரே.

As Earth, Water, the Sun and Moon and Sky.
The flowing Wind, bright Fire and Hotri' He stands.
Sirapuram, washed by the scented waters of Kôttār
They who praise, they will suffer no pain.

And St. Tāyumānavar himself pertinently asks why when the earth, air &c. are spoken of by the Vedas as God Himself, he should not himself be spoken of as God.

(1) பாராதி நீயாப் பகர்ந்தா லகமெனவும்
ஆராயுஞ் சீவனும் நீயாங்காண் பராபரமே.

(2) வானாதி நீயெனவே வைத்தமறை யென்னையுநீ
தானாகச் சொல்லாதோ சாற்றாய் பராபரமே.

Šiva is also called Digvāsas, Digambara, Nirvāṇi, and He dances in *Chitambara*, and His person and limbs, as we have seen, represent each an element or portion of the universe. And this description of Him, we notice even from the Ṛig Veda downwards. The translator of Mahābhārata frequently remarks that Šiva is identified in those passages as the Supreme Brahman, but this identification has been going on ever since the very beginning. We can speak of an identification only when there is difference orginally. Would it not therefore be more proper to say that the words Šiva and Rudra are merely the names, and His Form, the Form, of the supreme Brahman?

We cannot here omit to note the fact also that there are temples in India in which God (Šiva) is worshipped in one or other of these eight forms.

As Earth, He is worshipped in Kāñchi (Coñjeeveram,) as Water, in Jambukešvaram (Trichinopoly); as Air in Kāḷahasti; as Fire in Tiruvaṇṇāmalai; as Ākāš, in Chidambara; as Sun, when every one performs Sūrya Namaskāram;* as Moon, in Somnāth; as Pašu or Ātmā, in Pašupati Temple in Nepaul.

*My grandmother is even now, in her extreme old age, very regular in her Sūrya Namaskāram but she speaks of Him as 'Šiva Sūrya-Kaṇṇê 'சிவசூரியக்கண்ணே.'

AN UPANISHAT TEXT.

Ātmānam araṇim kritvā, pranavamcha Uttarāraṇim Jñāna nirmathanābhyasāth, pāšam dahatipanditaḥ.

In our Tamiḷ edition was appearing an excellent translation of Kaivalyopanishat by that great Tamiḷ and Sanskrit Scholar of Jaffna, Srimath Senthināthier, who is now staying in Benares. His commentary is a most valuable one, tracing as it does the passages in Kaivalyopanishat to similar passages in various other Upanishats. This Upanishat is by some called a sectarian and a modern one. This we deny, and we will take some other fuller opportunity to expound our views on the age of the Upanishats. At least this is older than the time of Śri Śaṅkara who includes it among the Pañcharudram which he has commented on. The Mantra, "Ātmanam aranim kritva, pranavamcha uttararanim Jñāna nirmathanabhyasath, pāšam dahati pandithah," following as it does Mantra 13 and 14, Part I. Švetāšvatara Upanishat, and with Mantra 11, above would completely demolish the theory of that talented lady Mrs. Besant, that the Išvara evolves, and the sole purpose of His so evolving, is that He make Himself manifest from His unmanifest condition like butter from cream, fire from sticks &c. The passage as it occurs in her last beautiful Adyar lecture is as follows "As salt in the water, in which it is dissolved (Chandogya VI, 14) as fire in the wood before the fire sticks are rubbed together, as butter in the milk that is brought forth by churning, (Švetāš I, 14 to 19) as cream in clarified butter (Ibid IV, 14), so is Brahman concealed as the self of every creature" (Hinduism page 16). No doubt the form in which she has quoted herself has misled her. The passages themselves are these (we quote from Mr. Mead's translation and from no other,)

"By knowledge of God, cessation of all bonds
With sorrows perishing, birth and death's ceasing comes
By contemplating him, with body left behind,
All Lordship Pure Passionless is He".—Mantra II,

How is this knowledge of God to be obtained?

The next verse says,

"This is to be known as ever surely settled in the (self, soul); beyond this surely nought is knowable at all. When one hath dwelt upon what tastes, what is tasted, and what doth ordain, all hath been said. This is the three-fold Brahm (Sat, Chit and Ānanda) (Mantra 12)." The unbelieving may ask, "how do you say God is concealed in our soul, body, we do not see it. No it is not these." The answer is given, illustrating it at the same time and explaining the mode of realization, in the next Mantra No. 13.

"Just as the (outer) form of fire, withdrawn into its source, cannot be seen, yet there is no destruction of its subtle form,—once more indeed out of the upper and lower stick it can be drawn,—so both indeed are to be found, by means of the word's power within the body."

This is more fully explained in the next Mantra.

"One's body taking for the lower stick and for the upper One (the word), by meditation's friction well sustained, let me behold the God, there lurking, as it were."

In the next Mantra, several similes are heaped together to illustrate the same subject.

"As oil in seeds, butter in cream, water in springs, and in the fire sticks fire, so is that Self (Paramātmā) found in the self (jīvātmā) by him who seeks for Him with truth and meditation. The Self pervading all, as butter milk pervades, in meditation and self-knowledge rooted, that Brahman, theme sublime of sacred teaching, of sacred teaching theme sublime".

We will quote again Mantra 16 in part IV, relied on by

Mrs. Besant, as well as the Mantra preceding it, before we finish our comments.

"Surely is He the guardian of all, in every creature hid, in whom the seers of Brahm, powers divine are (all) conjoined. Thus knowing Him, one cuts the bonds of death. Most rare, like as it were that essence rarer far than butter clarified, Him knowing (in his form) benign (Ṣiva) in every creature hid, though One (yet) all embracing, knowing Him, God, from every bond one is free."

Any one reading these verses together as we have read them, will not fail to see that the theory of Mrs. Besant gets no footing here at all. This simply explains the way of Salvation of the bound soul (Jīvātmā), and the nature of the Supreme. The bound soul which cannot see the "the subtler than subtle Ṣiva" (IV. 14), by pursuing the Sādana herein indicated, namely the search after Him with all one's heart and with all one's soul in all love and in all truth, with the aid of the divine Word, will surely behold the Supreme hid in himself, not the Supreme as himself, and then his bonds will be cut-off, and the darkness will vanish as the sun rises in one's horizon. Butter is butter whether it remains in the milk or separately. It itself gains little in one condition or other, but it makes a vast deal of difference to the person who has to eat it. No sane man will think that it matters anything to the Supreme, whether He remains manifest or unmanifest but it matters a great deal to his creatures who are wallowing in the mirky darkness of sin and misery. There are those again who think Pāṡatchaya is alone that occurs in Moksha, and that the freed soul is in itself, and with no knowledge or enjoyment of any sort. No doubt the moment of Pāṡatchaya is also the moment when he recovers his own self (one of the two comprised in 'both',* of Mantra 13, the other being God)

*Mr. Mead absurdly supposes that 'both' refers to the lower Brahman and higher Brahman, that the God of Mantra 14, is the lower Brahman or Iṡvara, the 'self' of Mantra 15 and 16 is the higher Brahman. Reading

and at the same moment is the Divine Effulgence cast full on him, enveloping him on all sides and swallowing him up wholly. "I know the great Purusha, sun-like beyond darkness Him and Him only knowing, one crosseth over death; there is no other path at all to go." Mantra 8, Part III.

Nothing can be clearer than this passage, as to the person seeking salvation, the object of the search, and the mode of attainment, and the only path of securing it. But is one's powers all sufficient? No "smaller than small, yet greater than great in the heart of this creature the Ātmā (God) doth repose: That, free from desire, he (creature) sees, with his grief gone, the mighty Īśa, by His Grace." (Mantra 20 Part III.)

These two mantras are reproduced in the famous verse No. 7 in "House of God" in Tiruvāchakaṁ, a valuable translation of which was printed in Vol. I. p. 49, Siddhānta Dīpikā.

"Light of Truth that entering body and soul has melted all faults, and driven away the false darkness." (Verse 3.)

"O Splendour that rises in my heart, as asking asking I melt." (Verse 6.)

"This day in Thy mercy unto me, thou did'st drive away the darkness and stand in my heart as the Rising Sun,
Of this Thy way of rising—there being not else but Thou—I thought without Thought,
I drew nearer and nearer to Thee wearing away atom by atom
Till I was One with Thee, O Śiva, Dweller in the great holy shrine
Thou art not ought in the universe; Naught is there save Thou.
Who can know Thee." (Verse 7.)

And let the reader ponder well again on the whole verse 7. Every blind man's heart's desire is to regain his eye-sight (His own self-ātmā) but suppose he regained his eye-sight, will the darkness be removed, which formerly pressed on his eye. Not surely, unless the Glorious Sun (God) deigns to show to him

---

again these verses together, could any discover any difference in the nature of Godhead in these Mantras?

in His Supreme Mercy. And the Sun is of course of no use to the blind man, so long as his blindness lasted. So he has to realize himself by being balanced in pleasure and pain (Removal of his Egoism) and to realize His maker, till now hid in his heart. And people have asked and will ask always, whether there is pleasure from this passage from bondage to Freedom. And Saint Meykaṇḍa Deva asks us to consider the case of the blindman passing from darkness to sudden Light. Will there be pleasure or not? Did it ever matter to the Sun, in any whit, when it was hid from the blindman, and now when it shines fully on his newly opened eyes!

> "It was Thyself Thou did'st give and me Thou did'st take,
> Beneficent Lord, who is the gainer?
> Endless bliss I have gained. What hast Thou gained from me?
> O Lord, that hast made my heart Thy temple,
> Šiva, dweller in the great holy shrine,
> O Father, Sovereign, Thou hast made Thy abode in my body.
> For it I have nought to give it in return." *

To remove all doubts that the Being to be sought after is not one's own self, the passage "Ātmānam Araṇim Kṛitvā" refers to the self (Ātmā) itself as the lower piece of firewood. In the Švetāšvatara, it was the body that was the lower piece, in which case both, Soul and God could be realised, but generally the phrases, in my body, in my eye, in my heart, in my mind, and in my soul mean almost the same thing, including soul and all below it. Our Saint Appar puts it in beautiful and unmistakable Tamiḷ the idea conveyed in these Upanishat Texts:—

> விறகிற் றீயினன் பாலிற்படு நெய்போல்
> மறைய நின்றுளன் மாமணிச் சோதியான்
> உறவுகோ னட்டுணர்வு கயிற்றினன்
> முறுக வாங்கிக் கடையமுன் னிற்குமே.

> Like the fire latent in firewood and ghee in milk,
> Non-apparent is the great Light
> With the churner of love and rope of knowledge
> One excites friction, He will become manifest before him.

* Verse 10 of the same Truvāchaka hymn. "The House of God."

THE SVETASVATARA UPANISHAT.

We are glad to say that Professor Max Müller has cleared the ground before us, of many misconceptions and fallacies which were entertained about this Upanishat. He meets in his own way the arguments adduced to show that this is a modern Upanishat and that it is a sectarian Upanishat, an Upanishat of the Sāṅkhya and of Bhakti school and so on, and his conclusions are that "no real argument has ever been brought forward to invalidate the tradition which represents it as belonging to the Taittirīya or Black Yajur Veda," and he points out that it "holds a very high rank among Upanishats" and that its real drift is the same as the Doctrine of the Vedānta Philosophy.

Professor Garbe and Macdonnell however, in their recent works,* speak of this as a *Śivite* compilation, and the latter scholar refers to the Upanishat itself ascribing the authorship to a sage called Śvetāśvatara, unlike other Upanishats. But this is not characteristic of this Upanishat alone. The fifteenth khāṇḍa of the last *Prapāṭhaka* of Chhāndogya Upanishat also traces the line of teachers in a similar way and there is a similar statement in the Māṇḍūkya Upanishat and others. When each Hymn of the Ṛig Veda has its own author, it cannot be any surprise that each particular Upanishat should have an individual author; and we don't suppose the Professor inclines to the orthodox view that the Veda and the Upanishats had no human authors, and were revealed.

---

* Garbe's Philosophy of Ancient India (1897) and Macdonnell's History of Sanskrit Literature (1900).

In regard to the other and deep-rooted fallacy about its being a sectarian Upanishat, we shall speak here atlength.

By taking this objection they mean to imply also that it is modern. And curiously enough we read of scholars ascribing dates for the rise of these sects commencing from the tenth and twelfth centuries. Sir W. W. Hunter seriously contends that Śaṅkara was the great Apostle of Śaivism. But these writers do not see that the History of Hindu Religion is as ancient as the History of the Hindu Philosophy, and that the people must have had a popular religion, even, in the very days, these Upanishats were composed, and that the Purāṇas which embodied the essence of the Upanishat teaching existed in a popular form even in those ancient days, and the words Itihāsa, Purāṇa, occur even in the oldest Upanishats.* These Upanishats are quoted by name in the Purāṇas and particular passages are also commented on.

And it will be an interesting study as to what was the religion of the people in the days of the Upanishats and Mahābhārata and Rāmāyaṇa and of the Purāṇas, and to compare the same with the existing phases of Hindu Religion. We may briefly indicate our own conclusions on the subject, though we could not give our reasons in detail—to wit—that so far as any room for comparisons exist,—the traditions and beliefs and ceremonials and faith of the modern day Śaivas (among whom may be included all Śāktas, Gāṇapatyas and Smārtas), who form now the bulk of the Hindu Race, were exactly the same as those of the people of the days of the oldest Upanishats and Mahābhārata and Rāmāyaṇa. According to the opinions of many old scholars like Lassen, Wilson and Muir and others, the worship of Śiva represented the cult of the Higher castes, Brahmans and Kshatriyas, and a text of Manu mentions that Śiva is the God of the Brahmans, and it is remarkable how the picture of Śiva is exactly the same as that of any ancient

* Bṛihadāraṇyaka-Up. 2-4-10 and 4-1-2 Maittriya-Up. 6-32 and 33, Chhāndogya-Up. VII. 1-2.

Ṛishi (*vide* some of Ravi Varma's pictures). Dr. W. W. Hunter remarks that Šaṅkara in espousing Šaivism combined in the system the highest Philosophy of the ancients and the most popular form of Religion.

Regarding the conception of Šiva and its growth from Vedic times, scholars love to tell us that Rudra was nowhere called Šiva in the Ṛig Veda and that he merely represented the storm God, with his thunder, lightning and the rains, rushing down from the snow-capped hills ; and that this Rudra slowly grew into Šiva of the Hindu Triad, and scholars have not failed to remark about His composite and contradictory aspects.

There is considerable truth in this, and we can clearly trace that in His person is slowly built up the conception of the various Vedic Deities, Indra and Agni, Varuṇa and Vāyu, Sūrya and Soma, Vishṇu and Brahma, and by the time the Vedas were arranged into Ṛig, Yajur, Sāman and Atharvaṇ, Rudra's position as the God of gods had become assured ; and by the time of the earliest Upanishats, when the purely sacrificial Yajñas were being given up, the worship of Rudra-Šiva supplanted the worship of the Vedic Deities, and instead of a blind worship of the elements, a marked distinction was drawn between the Supreme God who dwelt in these elements and gave them special power and glory, and this conception was stereotyped later on by Šiva being called the Ashṭamūrti, the God who had for his body, the five elements, earth, air, water, fire and ākāš, sun and moon and the soul; and Šiva has temples dedicated to him, in which He is worshipped in these eight forms.

Rudra is derived by Sāyana from the roots, Rudrāvāyita, meaning 'he who drives away sorrow.' And consistant with this derivation, Rudra is called in the Ṛig-Veda itself, as the 'bountiful' and the 'Healer' possessed of various remedies (the later Vaidyanāth) 'benign' and 'gracious'. And the term *Šiva* clearly appears in the following text of the Ṛig Veda (X. 92-9.)

"Stomanvā adya Rudrāya śikvase kshyadvirāya namasā didhishṭāna yebhiḥ *Śivaḥ* svavān eva yāvabhirdivaḥ śikshati svāyaśaḥ nikāmabhi." *

Those who are conversant with the actual performing of yajñas will know how the place of the respective priests, Adhvaryu, Hotri, and Udgātri and Brahman are fixed as well as the place of the various gods. And the chief place is assigned to Rudra and apart from other gods. This will clearly explain the force of the epithet of "Medhapatim" in Ṛig Veda, 1-43-4 "Gādhapatim, *Medhapatim* Rudram Jaleshabheshajam, tat samyoḥ sumnam imehi." (We seek from Rudra, the lord of songs, the *lord of Sacrifices* who possesses healing remedies, his auspicious favour), as also "king of sacrifices" (Ṛig. 4-3.) And *Medhapati* is the same word as the more popular word *Paśupati*, Paśu meaning the animal offered in sacrifice, Yajña-Paśu, and symbolically representing the bound soul-jīva. As the Pati of all sacrifices, He is the fulfiller of sacrifices, 'Yajña sādham' (Ṛig. I. 114-4) and 'Rudram yajñānam sa dadhishṭim apasam' (III. 2-5). As the God of gods, He is said to "derive His renown from Himself" 'Rudrāya *Svāyaśase*' His glory is said to be inherent, independent or self-dependant 'Svadhavane' (Ṛig. VII. 46-1.) He is also called *Svapivāta*, which is variously explained as meaning 'readily understanding' 'accessible.' 'gracious,' 'he by whom life is conquered, 'he whose command cannot be transgressed,' 'thou by whom prayers (words) are readily received.' He is called the father of the worlds,' *Bhuvanasya Pitaram*,' VI. 49-10, and the Ṛich story of His becoming the Father of the fatherless Maruts can be recalled in many a Purāṇic story, and local legend, and common folklore.

* With reverence present your Hymn to-day to the mighty Rudra, the ruler of heroes, [and to the Maruts] those rapid and ardent deities with whom the gracious (Śivaḥ) and opulent (Rudra) who derives his renown from himself, protects us from the sky." Sāyana takes 'Śivaḥ' as a substantive and interprets it as meaning Parameśvara; and it seems strange that Muir should take it as an adjective.

He is '*antar ichchanti*'—beyond all thought (VIII. 61-3). His form as described in the Ṛig Veda is almost the same as the Image of later days. He is called the Kapardin, with 'spirally braided hair.' He is of Hiraṇya Rūpam 'golden formed' and brilliant like the sun, and 'shining like gold' "Yaḥ śukra iva Sūryo hiraṇyam iva ro chati" (I. 43-5).* And in Ṛig Veda X. 136-1 to 7, He is the Long haired being who sustains the fire, water and the two worlds; who is to the view the entire sky; and who is called this 'Light' He is *wind clad* (naked) and drinks *Visha* (water or poison) and a Muni is identified with Rudra in this aspect.

When we come to Yajur Veda, His supreme Majesty is fully developed, and He is expressly called Śiva by name 'Śiva nama śi (Yaj. S. 3-63) and the famous mantra, the *Pañchākshara*, is said to be placed in the very heart of the three Vedas, (the name occurs in Tait. S. IV. 5, 1-41 '*namaḥ śambave cha mayobave cha namaḥ Śaṅkarāya cha mayaskārāya cha* NAMAḤ ŚIVĀYA *cha Śivātaraya cha*"). And the famous Śatarudriyam which is praised in the Upanishats and in the Mahābhārat forms also a central portion of this central Veda. And this is a description of God as the all, the all in all, and transcending all, 'Viśvadevo, Viśvasvarūpo, Viśvādhiko'; and any body can see that the famous passage in the Gītā in chapters 10 and 11 merely parodies this other passage. These two chapters are respectively called *Vibhūti Vistāra Yoga* and *Viśvarūpa Sandarśana Yoga* which is exactly the charactor of the Śatarudriya. The Yogi who has reached the highest state "Sees all in God and God in all." In the Śatarudriya and in the whole Veda, *Rudra* is called *Śiva, Śaṅkara Śambhu, Īśāna, Īśa, Bhagavān, Bhava, Sarva, Ugra, Soma, Paśupati, Nīlagrīva, Giriśa, Mahādeva* and *Maheśvara.* And the most famous mantra 'Ekam Eva Rudronadvitīyāya taste' whose very existence in the Vedas and Upanishats scholars doubted at one

* Note how often the Supreme is called the Golden-coloured, and Sunlike in the Upanishats.

time, occurs in the Yajur Samhitā (Tait.) in 1 Canto, 8 Praśna, 6 Anuvāka, 1 Pañchāśat and this very mantra is repeated in our Upanishat, (III 2,) and if the Upanishats did not precede the Vedas, it will be seen how this mantra is the original of the other famous Upanishat mantra, "Ekamevadvitīyam Brahma." In fact, we doubt if the word 'Brahma' occurs even once in the Ṛig-Veda as meaning God, and in the Yajur as meaning the Supreme Being. And Prof. Max Müller is no doubt correct in drawing attention to the fact that the conception of a mere Impersonal Self may be posterior to the conception of God as Śiva, Rudra and Agni. And the texts we have above quoted will for once prove the danger of surmises as to the date of an Upanishat for the sole reason that it uses the words Śiva or Īśa or Īśāna and Rudra.

In the days of the Veda and the Upanishats, these names Rudra, Śiva, Śambhu, Mahādeva, Īśa, Īśāna, Hara and Vishṇu only meant the same as Deva or Brahman or Ātman or Paramātman, and they had no prejudice against the use of the former set of words, as some sectarians of to-day would seem to have. In the Gītā itself, the words Īśvarā, Īśa, Maheśvara and Mahādeva and Parameśvara are freely used, and Śiva is used in the Uttara Gītā, though the modern day Vaishṇava exhibits the greatest prejudice towards these names.

One word about the different aspects of Śiva. As we pointed out before, as the Idea of Rudra, as all the gods or the Powers of Nature, was fully evolved, in Him was also centralized the various aspects of Nature as good and bad, awful and beneficent. Kāḷidāsa playfully brings out this idea in the following lines:

> "The Gods, like clouds, are fierce and gentle too
> Now hurl the bolt, now drop sweet heavenly dew
> In summer heat the streamlet dies away
> Beneath the fury of the God of day,
> Then in due season comes the pleasant rain
> And all is fresh and fair and full again."

However awful the aspect of a fierce storm, with its thunder and lightning, may be, yet no one can appreciate its beneficence more than the dwellers in the Indian soil, the land of so many famines. However fierce the sun may be, yet his existence is absolutely essential to the growth and maturity of all vegetation in the tropics. It will be noted that not only in the case of Rudra but in the case of other gods, their beneficent and malevolent powers are brought out in the Vedas. The Supreme Double Personality of Śiva is thus explained in the Mahābhārata by Lord Krishṇa himself. "Large armed Yudhishtira, understand from me, the greatness of the glorious, *multiform*, many named Rudra. They called Mahādeva, Agni, Sthanu, Maheśvara, one-eyed, Triyambaka, the *Universal formed* and Śiva. Brahmans versed *in the Veda* know two bodies of this God, one awful, one auspicious; and these two bodies have again many forms. 'The dire and awful body is fire, lightning, the sun: the auspicious and beautiful body is virtue, water and the moon. The half of his essence is fire and the other half is called the moon. The one which is his auspicious body practises chastity, while the other which is his most dreadful body, destroys the world. From his being Lord and Great He is called Maheśvara. Since he consumes, since he is fiery, fierce, glorious, an eater of flesh, blood and marrow—he is called Rudra. As He is the greatest of the gods, as His domain is wide and as He preserves the vast Universe,—He is called Mahādeva. From his smoky colour, he is called Dhurjati. Since he constantly prospers all men in all their acts, seeking their welfare (Śiva), He is therefore called Śiva."* And in this, we see Him as not only the destroyer but as the Reproducer and Preserver and as such the conception of Śiva transcends the conception of Rudra as one of the Trinity.

And it can be shown that the picture of God as the fierce and the terrible is not altogether an unchristian idea.

---

* 'Śiva' is derived from 'Vasi' which occurs in Katha-Up. see Lalitā Sahasranāma Commentary under 'Śiva.'

The following paras, we cull from a book called "The Woodlands in Europe" intended for Christian readers; and we could not produce better arguments for the truth of our conception of the Supreme Śiva, the Destroyer and the Creator and the Preserver (*vide* p. 6, Śivajñānabotham, English Edition).

"And how about the dead leaves which season after season, strew the ground beneath the trees? Is their work done because, when their bright summer life is over, they lie softly down to rest under the wintry boughs? Is it only death, and nothing beyond? Nay; if it is death, it is death giving place to life. Let us call it rather change, progress, transformation. It must be progress, when the last year's leaves make the soil for the next year's flowers, and in so doing serve a set purpose and fulfil a given mission. *It must be transformation, when one thing passes into another, and instead of being annihilated, begins life again in a new shape and form.*

"It is interesting to remember that the same snow which weighs down and breaks those fir branches is the nursing mother of the flowers. Softly it comes down upon the tiny seeds and the tender buds and covers them up lovingly, so that from all the stern rigour of the world without, they are safely sheltered. Thus they are getting forward, as it were, and life is already swelling within them; so that when the sun shines and the snow melts, they are ready to burst forth with a rapidity which seems almost miraculous.

"*It is not the only force gifted with both preserving and destroying power, according to the aspect in which we view it.* The fire refines and purifies, but it also destroys; and the same water which rushes down in the cataract with such overwhelming power, falls in the gentlest of drops upon the thirsty flower cup and fills the hollow of the leaf with just the quantity of dew which it needs for its refreshment and sustenance. And in those higher things of which nature is but the type and shadow, the same grand truth holds good; and from our Bibles we learn that *the consuming fire and the love that passeth knowledge are but different sides of the same God:—Just and yet merciful; that will by no means clear the guilty, yet showing mercy unto thousands.*"

Badarāyaṇa also touches upon this subject in I., iii., 40 and we quote below the Pūrvapaksha and Siddhhānta views on this question from the commentary of Śrīkaṇṭha.

"Because of trembling (I, iii, 40). In the Katha-Vallis, in the section treating of the thumb-sized Purusha, it is said as follows:

'Whatever there is, the whole world when gone forth (from the Brahman) trembles in the breath; (it is) a great terror, the thunderbolt uplifted; those who know it become immmortal.' (cit. 6, 2).

Here a doubt arises as to whether the cause of trembling is the Parameśvara or some other being.

(Pūrvapaksha):—Here the Śruti speaks of the trembling of the whole universe by fear caused by the entity denoted by the word "breath." It is not right to say that the Parameśvara, who is so sweet natured as to afford refuge to the whole universe and who is supremely gracious, is the cause of the trembling of the whole universe. Therefore, as the word 'thunderbolt' occurs here, it is the thunderbolt that is the cause of trembling. Or it is the vital air which is the cause of the trembling, because the word 'breath' occurs here. Since the vital air causes the motion of the body, this whole world which is the body as it were, moves on account of the vital air. Then we can explain the passage "whatever there is, the whole world, when gone forth (from the Brahman) trembles in the breath." Then we can also explain the statement that "it is a great terror, the thunderbolt uplifted," inasmuch as like lightning, cloud and rain, the thunderbolt which is the source of great terror is produced by action of the air itself. It is also possible to attain immortality by a knowledge of the air as the following Śruti says:

"Air is everything itself and the air is all things together; he who knows this conquers death" (Bri. Up. 5-3-2).

(Siddhānta):—As against the foregoing, we say that Parameśvara himself is the cause of the trembling. It is possible that, as the Ruler, Parameśvara is the cause of trembling of the whole universe and by the fear of His command all of us abstain from prohibited actions and engage in the prescribed duties; and it is by the fear of His command that Vāyu and others perform their respective duties, as may be learned from such passages as the following:—

"By fear of Him, Vāyu (the wind) blows." (Tait. Up. 2-8).

Though gracious in appearance, Parameśvara becomes awful as the Ruler of all. Hence the Śruti.

'Hence the King's face has to be awful!' (Tait. Brā 3-8-23).

"Wherefore as the Master, Īśvara Himself is the cause of the trembling of the whole universe."

Before we enter into the discussion of the philosophic import of this Upanishat, we have to note the great difficulty felt nearly by all European scholars who are brought up solely in the school of Śaṅkara in interpreting this Upanishat, a difficulty which has equally been felt with regard to the Philosophy of the Gitā. Different scholars have taken it as expounding variously *Sāṅkhya and Yoga, Bhakti and Vedānta, Dualism and non-Dualism*; and Professor Max Müller agrees with Mr. Gough in taking it as fully expounding the Indian idealism school of Vedānta. Professors Garbe and Macdonnell characterise the philosophy as ECLECTIC. Says the latter, (p. 405, History of Sanskrit Literature): "Of the *eclectic* movement combining Śāṅkhya, Yoga and Vedānta doctrines, the oldest literary representative is the *Śvetāśvatara upanishat*. More famous is the Bhagavad Gitā.* "

If ever there was such an eclectic school, have these scholars paused to enquire who their modern representatives are? Or

* Monier Williams was the first to point this out.

is it that there are no such representatives to-day? The real fact is that this was the only true Philosophic creed of the majority of the people, and this philosophy has subsisted untarnished during the last 3000 years or more. During the Upanishat period, the schools whose existence could be distinctly marked are the *Lokāyata or Nāstika, Kapila's Śāṅkhya, Mīmāmsa of Jaimini, Nyāya and Vaiseshika and Yoga*. The first three were Atheistical and the latter Theistic. And of course all these were professed Hindus *, and none would have deviated from the rituals and practices prescribed for the Hindu, though academically speaking, he would have held to this or that view of philosophy. And this inconsistency is what strikes a foreigner even now in the character of the modern Hindu. Mrs. Besant aptly describes this as "the Hindu's principle of rigidity of conduct and freedom of thought". All these schools were based on a certain *number* of *tattvas* or categories. The *Nāstika* postulated four and only four *tattvas*, namely, earth, air, fire and water and would not even believe in *Ākāś* or ether. Kapila increased the *number* of categories he believed in, to 19 which he grouped under *Purusha* and *Pradhāna*. The *Mimāmsaka* believed practically in nothing more, though he laid stress on the authority and eternality of the Vedas. The next three theistic schools believed in 24 or 25 tattvas which they grouped under *Purusha, Pradhāna*, and *Īśvara* or God. As all these schools based their theoretical philosophy on a certain *number* of *tattvas*,† *Śaṅkhya*, the theoretic Philosophy, came to be

* The Majority of every people and nation are virtually atheistic and materialistic, though professing a belief in God and conforming to the usages of society.

† Tirumūlar, a Tamil Saint of about the first century A. C. thus distinguishes the schools existing in his time. "The 96 tattvas or categories are common to all. 36 categories are special to the Śaivas. 28 are the categories of the Vedānti, 24 categories belong to Vaishnavas. 26 categories are those of the Māyāvādi." The particular thing to be noted here is the distinction drawn between Vedānti and Māyāvādi.

called *Sāṅkhya* as distinguished from the practical Religion and code of Morality. And during the Upanishat period and even in the time of the Mahābharāta, the word had not lost its general significance. And it will be noticed when ascertaining what these various categories are, that, with the exception of the Nāstika, all the other five schools believed in almost the same things, though the enumerations were various, except as regards the postulating of God. And even in this idea of God, there was practically very little difference between Kapila and Patañjali. To both of them, the freed *Purusha* was equal to *Išvara*, only Kapila believed that no Išvara was necessary, for the origination and sustenance, &c., of the worlds; but according to Patañjali, there existed an eternally freed Being who created these worlds and resolved them again into their original components. And in the Upanishat period, the Yoga school was the dominant cult and these Upanishats including the *Švetāšvatara* and *Kaivalya &c*, were all books of the yoga school. And the theoretical or argumentative part of the philosophy or creed was called by the name of Šāṅkhya and the practical part, Yoga. As this yoga postulated the highest end achieved by a study of the Vedas, which were set forth in these Upanishats, it was also coming slowly to be called *Vedānta*. That the word *Upanishat* was actually used as a synonym for yoga, we have an example in Chandog, (1-1-10.) "The sacrifice which a man performs with knowledge, faith, and the *Upanishat* is more powerful." Knowledge' or *jñān* here meant the knowledge of the categories and their relation, which according to Kapila was alone sufficient to bring about man's freedom. This, the *Vedānta* held to be insufficient, unless it was accompanied by earnestness and love and by the contemplation of a Supreme Being. This contemplation brought the thinker *nearer* and *nearer* to the *object* of his thoughts, till all distinctions of object and subject were thoroughly merged (distinction of I and Mine) and the *union* or *one-ness* was reached and all bhanda or *pāša* vanished. This is the root-idea in both words 'Upanishat' and 'Yoga.' *Yoga* means union, *union of two things* held apart and brought together, when *the bonds or fetters which separated fell off or perished.* And Upanishat is also derived from *Upa* near, *ni* quite, *sat* to perish. Here also the *nearing of two things*, and the *perishing of something is clearly meant*. Of course, the two things brought together are the Soul and God, and the perishable thing is certainly the *Pāśa*; and the Soul when bound by *Pāśa* is called *Paśu* accordingly

This was the condition of the Philosophic thought down to the days of the Mahābhārat, and we hold this was anterior to the rise of Buddhism and continued for some centuries after Gautama Buddha and till the time of Badarāyana. It was during this time that the philosophy of India spread into and permeated the thought of Europe, and Professor Garbe has lucidly proved in his short History of "The Philosophy of Ancient India," that the influence received by the Greeks down to the neo-Platonic school was almost Śāṅkhyan in its character. It was during this time again, that the blending of the Āryan and Tamilian in art and civilization and Philosophy took place (and we could not here consider how much was common to both, and how much each gained from the other). We have an exactly parallel word in Tamil to the word 'Śāṅkhya' and this word is எண் *eṇ*) which means both 'number' and 'to think', and both *Auvaiyār* and *Tiruvalluvar* use the words to mean *logic* and *mataphysics*: the primary science, on which all thought was built, being mathematics or the science of number. A systematic and historical study of the Tamiḻ works will make good our position; and even to-day the most dominant cult in the Tamiḻ is the Śāṅkhya and Yoga as represented in the Upanishats or Vedānta. This system must have been thoroughly establishad in the Tamiḻ language and literature before the time of Chirist and before Badarāyana's composition of the *Śārīraka Sūtras.* So much so, when Badarāyana's system came into vogue in Southern India, it was recognized as a distinct school. As Badarāyana professed expressly to interpret the Upanishat or Vedānta texts, his school of

Philosophy was stereotyped by the phrase '*Vedānta*' and by collecting all the texts in Tamil down even to the time of Tāyumānavar (16th ceutury) containing references to *Vedānta*, we could prove what the special view of Badarāyana was. This will also show that the exposition of Badarāyana contained in the earliest Bhāshya or commentary we possess in Sanskrit, namely, that of Śrīkaṇṭha, which was later on adopted almost bodily by Rāmānuja, was the true view of Badarāyana. This view we may sum up in Dr. Thibaut's own words:—"If, now, I am shortly to sum up the results of the preceding enquiry as to the teaching of the Sūtras, I must give it as my opinion that they do not set forth the distinction of a higher and lower knowledge of Brahman; that they do not acknowledge the distinction of Brahman and Iśvara in Śaṅkarā's sense; that they do not hold the doctrine of the unreality of the world; and that they do not with Śaṅkara proclaim the absolute identity of the individual and the highest self." (p. 100, Introduction to the Vedānta Sūtras).

And he proves also that this was consistent with the teachings of the Upanishats themselves.

What gave it its special mark, however, is the peculiar relation which Badarāyaṇa postulated between God and the world, the product of *Māyā* or *Prakṛiti*. Though he held on to the distinction of the Supreme and the Human Spirit, he stoutly fought against the old Śāṅkhyan view (comprising nearly all the six schools we enumerated above) that Matter was an independent entity from spirit, though like Leibnitz he never denied its reality. He held God was both the efficient and material cause of the Universe. This doctrine received accordingly its name of *Pariṇāma Vāda or Nimittopadāna-kāraṇa* Vāda, while the Theistic Śāṅkhyan systems stoutly maintained that God was only the efficient cause, though He was immanent in All Nature. As there was nothing inherently vicious and destructive to all true religion and morality in this system of Badarāyaṇa, the Tamil Philosophers welcomed this view also and declared they did not see much difference in the two views and ends postulated by both the old and new school. And both Śrīkaṇṭa and Saint Tirumūlar expressly make this declaration.

But there was one other view which was gaining ground ever since the days of Gautama Buddha, and which was connected with the peculiar theory of *Māyā* or illusion. Buddha declared that all existence was momentary, that there was no world, no mind, no soul and no God, and that what really existed were the *Skandhas,* and when this truth was perceived, all desire and birth and suffering would cease and then there would be cessation of all existence, *Nirvāṇa.* And the Buddhists were accordingly called *Māyāvādis.* But as the Buddhist theory destroyed the very core of the Indian national beliefs, and as it also afforded no stable ground for a national existence based on morality and religion, this was pronounced heterodox, but the seeds sown by him were not in vain, and a Hindu school of Māyāvāda slowly raised its head on the dying embers of this old effete philosophy. And its greatest exponent was Śaṅkara. This Hindu school of Māyāvāda was in existence for several centuries before Śaṅkara, but this was later than the time of St. Māṇickavāchaka and earlier than Tirumūlar though both of them were anterior to Śaṅkara. Śaṅkara's system is referred to as *Māyāvāda* in all the other Hindu prominent schools prevalent since the days of Śaṅkara, and though South Indian followers of Śaṅkara seem to entertain some prejudice against the word, owing to the abuse made of it by their opponents, followers of Śaṅkara in the North even to-day call it the *Māyāvāda.* And in some of its *extreme forms,* it was also called "*Prachchanna Bauddham.*" The great learning and the towering intellect, accompanied by the austere life led by Śaṅkara, created a great following among the Brahmans of the Śaiva faith, and it made great strides in the time of his illustrious follower Sayana or Vidyāraṇya who combined in himself both temporal and spiritual power. And the first interpreters of Hinduism happening to be mostly

Brahmans of this persuasion, during the century when Sanskrit oriental scholarship came into being, this view of Hindu Philosophy has gained most currency among European scholars. But there were not wanting scholars in the past like Colebrook and Wilson, and like Col. Jacob, Prof. Kunte, and Dr. Thibaut in the present generation, who hold that *Māyāvāda* is not the real and true exposition of the Veda or the Vedānta. Prof. Max Muller than whom a more learned or earnest student of Indian Philosophy never existed, though he held very stoutly to the other view, slowly gave in, and has accepted Dr. Thibaut's conclusions as correct. We may add that Professor Macdonnell reiterates the old view, and Prof. Deussen is the greatest adherent of Šaṅkara at the present day.

There is one other great factor in the growth of Indian Religion and Philosophy which we have taken no note of, all this time; and which receives no notice at all in the hands of European scholars. And this is the bearing of the *Āgamas or Tantras*. Such a well informed person as Svāmi Vivekananda has declared, "as to their influence, apart from the Srouta and Smarta rituals, all other forms of ritual observed from the Himalayas to the Comorin have been taken from the Tantras, and they direct the worship of the Šāktas, Šaivas and Vaishṇavas and all others alike." But who were the authors of these works and when did they come into vogue, and what great power had they to monopolize the Religion of the whole of India? The same Svāmi observes. "The Tantras, as we have said, represent the Vedic rituals in a modified form, and before any one jumps into the most absurd conclusions about them, I will advise him to read the *Tantras* in connection with the *Brāhmanas*, especially of the *Adhwaryu* portion. And most of the *Mantras* used in the *Tantras* will be found taken *verbatim* from these *Brāhmanas*." But it could be noted at the same time, that whereas the *Brāhmanas* direct the use of these mantras in connection with the *yajñas* or sacrifices, these Tantras direct their use in connection with the worship of some deity or other. And the object of Vedic sacrifices being well known to be only the first three *Purushārthas*, by the worship of the various Powers of Nature, the object of Tantric or Āgamic worship was the attainment of the fourth *Purushārta* or *Moksha*. By the time we get into the Upanishat period, we could see how a new and spiritual interpretation was put upon the old Vedic sacrifices, and the uselessness of sacrifice as an end in itself was strongly declared. Says M. Barth: "Sacrifice is only an act of preparation. It is the best of acts, but it is an act and its fruit consequently perishable. Accordingly although whole sections of these treatises (Upanishats) are taken up exclusively with speculations on the rites, what they teach may be summed up in the words of Mundaka Upanishat. "Know the Ātman only and away with every thing else; it alone is the bridge to immortality. The Veda itself and the whole cycle of sacred science are quite as sweepingly consigned to the second place. The Veda is not the true Brahman; it is only its reflection; and the science of this imperfect Brahman, this *Sabda Brahman* or Brahman in words is only a science of a lower order. The true science is that which has the true Brahman, the *Parabrahman* for its subject."

As the story in the Kena Upanishat will show, the most powerful of the Ṛig Veda deities, Indra, and Agni and Vāyu and Varuṇa were also relegated to a secondary place; and the worship of the only One, without a second, the Consort of Uma, Haimavati, was commenced. The Kena Upanishat story is repeated in the Purāṇas, the Supreme Brahman is mentioned there as Šiva and Rudra. And the story of Rudra destroying Dakshas's sacrifice, and disgracing the Gods who took part in the sacrifice, with the sequel of His consort, named then *Dākshāyani* (the fruit or spirit of sacrifice) becoming reborn as Uma, (wisdom or Brahmajñān) Haimavati, would seem to go before the story in the Kena Upanishat. The story of the desecration of the sacrifice of the Rishis of Dārukāvana by Šiva and Vishṇu would point to the same moral. So that, by this time, the backbone of the old unmeaning Vedic sacrifices petrified in the Godless school of Mīmāmsa was really broken; and it was here that the Āgamas stepped in and used the same old Mantras again but with a new force and significance, deleting whatever was unmeaning, and preserving only what was useful. It substituted also new symbols though preserving the old names. And from this time, therefore, Modern Hinduism and Hindu system of worship may be said to have commenced. But for these beginnings, we have to go far behind the days of the Mahābhārata and the Purāṇas, for the Āgama doctrines and rituals are fully bound up with these.

A clear advance in the use of symbols was also made, at the same time effectually preserving the distinction between symbols and truth, by the use of proper words. The Sabdha Brahman or the Praṇava was only a symbol and not the truth, as fancied by the Mīmāmsakas, and it was called a mark or Liṅga. And the figured mark of the Praṇava, (*Liṅga* is merely the Praṇava as figured to the eye) the Liṅga, became the universal symbol of God and object of worship, as the *Praṇava* in mantra or sound form was before. In the new system of worship, the Temples that were built were more on the models of the old yajña-sāla; and the yūpa stambha (Dhvaja-stambha) and Balipīṭha, Pašu (Bašava or Naṅdi) and the Gods in their various places were also retained; and a Brahmotsava supplanted virtually the old sacrifice.* In the field of philosophy, it did as much to systematise and build up into a whole what

* In commencing and going through a Brahmotsava, the priests observe technically almost the same rituals as in commencing and going through a great sacrifice. There is a Yajña Sāla in every Šaiva Temple in which the Fire is started by the *Dikshita* and the Dhvaja Ārohaṇa is made by running up a flag with the figure of a bull (Pašu or Bašava) on the Yūpastambha and tying Kusa grass to the Post. The Pašu and the Kusa grass standing merely for the soul or jīva that was bound and offered in sacrifice. After Avarohaṇa, the soul or Pašu becomes freed and is no more called Pašu, but is called God or Naṅdi—the blissful. It will require more space for us to draw out here the parallel between the Yajña Sāla and a Hindu Temple.

was hitherto in scattered form and it did greater service in drawing out more fully the omni-penetrativeness and transcendency of God over both *Chetana* and *Achetana Prapañcha*, the world of souls and the world of matter. The Postulate of God's supreme *Transcendency* is the special effort of the Āgama Philosophy to make out, and as this was the Highest End and Truth, it was called Siddhānta *par excellence* as distinguished from the Vedānta which led up the aspirant only to certain spiritual stages. It divided all philosophy and religion into four paths or Mārgas, called respectively Chariya, Kriya, Yoga and Jñāna; and these were otherwise called Dāsa Mārga, Satputra Mārga, Saha Mārga and San Mārga. In the exposition of these paths, it opened out a thoroughly reasoned system of practical Philosophy, neither contradicting our experience, nor causing violence to the most cherished of our sentiments, both moral and religious; a system of thought which was progressive and built on an adamantine basis, step by step leading to higher knowledge; a system * which by preserving and pointing out the essential difference of God, Soul and Matter, established a true relation between them; which led to the highest monistic knowledge, a system which was at once dualism and non-dualism, Dvaita and Advaita; a system which appealed alike

* Cf. Garbe, *The Philosophy of Ancient India*, p. 30. "As for those who feel inclined to look down slightingly from a monistic point of view upon a dualistic conception of the world, the words of E. Roer in the Introduction of the Bhāshaparichcheda (p. XVI) may be quoted: "Though a higher development of philosophy may destroy the distinctions between soul and matter, " that is, may recognise matter or what is perceived as matter, as the same with the soul (as for instance, Leibnitz did), it is nevertheless certain that no true knowledge of the soul is possible without first drawing a most decided line of demarcation between the phenomena of matter and of the soul". This sharp line of demarcation between the two domains was first drawn by Kapila. The knowledge of the difference between body and soul is one condition, and it is also an indispensable condition, of arriving at a true monism. Every view of the world which confounds this difference can supply at best a one-sided monism, be it a spiritualism or an equally one-sided materialism."

to the peasant and the philosopher. Its system of practical Religion, calculated to secure the Highest End and Bliss, was also progressive, commencing from the simplest rituals in the adoration of God to the highest Yoga, adapted to the means and capacity of the lowest and the highest of human beings. Readers of Svāmi Vivekananda's lectures would have noted how these four paths are essential to any system of thought or religion which claims to be universal; and it is the peculiar boast of the Āgma or Tantra that it was the first to systematise this fourfold teaching. And it is in modern Śaivism and in the Siddhānta Philosophy, this fourfold aspect of Religion and Philosophy is wholly and fully preserved. Śaivism is a ritual mārga, a bhakti mārga, a yoga mārga, a jñāna mārga. And need we wonder that the Siddhānta Philosophy of to-day is as much a puzzle to outsiders, as the Philosophy of our Upanishat and the Gītā? The Siddhānti's definition of *Advaita* as 'neither one nor two nor neither' will bring out the puzzle more prominently. It is a system of dualism, it is also a system of non-dualism, but it differs from the other schools of dualism and nondualism. What was upheld in the Siddhānta as mere paths or mārga, or *Sādhana* or means to reach the Highest End, had come to be each and individually mistaken for the End itself; what was upheld as the mere symbol of the Highest Truth had come to be mistaken for the Truth itself. What was declared as unprovable, indescribable, unknowable and unenjoyable as long as man was in the condition of bondage was held by these sectaries as proved and seen. What was the purest and most transcendent monotheism degenerated into a most crude anthropomorphism and blatant pantheism.

Śaivism is not anthropomorphic, but symbolic. How can it be otherwise, when it draws such minute distinction between God and Soul and Matter? And a system of symbolism is quite consistent with the Highest Transcendental Religion and Philosophy; in fact, all our real knowledge is more truly symbolic than otherwise. In the view of the Siddhānti, the Upanishats, though they deal with all the four paths, are especially the text books of the Yogapāda or Sahamārga, where certain Bhāvanas or Vidyas calculated to create and bring about the Highest Nirvāna and Union, and Freedom from Pāśa, are more fully explained and illustrated.

The above cursory view of the past history of the Indian philosophy will clear the ground a good deal for the proper understanding of our particular Upanishat in question.

We may therefore state that the Śvetāśvatara Upanishat is a genuine Upanishat of the Black Yajur Veda, and is one of the oldest of its kind. It is not a sectarian Upanishat. It more properly belongs to the Yoga Pāda stage of teaching, though the other Pādas are also briefly touched and alluded to. It expounds both a theoretic philosophy and a practical religion, all-comprehensive and all-embracing; a system which was at once Śāṅkhya and Yoga, dualistic and monistic, and appealing to all classes of society.

It lays down the distinction of three padārthas or categories in clear terms. And these are, God, the many souls, and matter or Paśā.

"Two birds, inseparable friends, cling to the same tree. One of them eats the sweet fruits, the other looks on without eating" (iv. 6) which is explained in less figurative language in the next mantra.

"On the same tree, man (Anīśa) sits grieving, immersed, bewildered, by his own impotence. But when he sees the other, Īśa, contented, and knows His glory, then his grief passes away."

That this is the Highest teaching of the Ṛig Veda is pointed out in the next verse.

"He who does not know that indestructible Being (Akshara,) of the Ṛig Veda, that Highest Ether (Parama Vyomam) wherein all the Gods reside, of what use is the Ṛig Veda to him? Those only who know It rest contented."

17

And need it be pointed out that the 6th verse is itself found in the Ṛig-Veda (1, 164-20) and it is repeated in the Atharva Veda and the passage is so popular a one that Katha (iii. 1) and Muṇḍaka (iii. 11) also quote it.

These verses bring out the distinction of God and soul, Īśa and Anīśa, as the spectator and enjoyer respectively. The soul enjoys and performs karma while encased in the body, tree; but though God is immanent in the soul and in the body, yet the works and their fruit do not cling to Him and taint Him. After the due eating of the fruits, the soul knows the greatness of God, and his own insignificance, then his sufferings cease.

The previous mantra (iv. 5) is also a famous and much debated passage, and it is badly translated by Prof. Max Müller. The translation by G. R. S. Mead and Chattopādhyāya is literal and correct. "Aye, that one unborn (Aja-soul) sleeps in the arms of one unborn (nature. Pradhāna), enjoying (her of nature, red, white, and black), who brings forth multitudinous progeny like herself. But when her charms have been enjoyed, he (soul) quits her (prakṛiti) side, the unborn other, Anyata (Lord). "*

There is absolutely no mistaking this plain statement of the three Padārtas as eternal, as well as their relation; and all three are called *Unborn*, *Aja* or uncreated. But the word to be noted here is the word '*other*' '*Anya*' which is almost a technical term or catch word to mean God, the Supreme. And it occurs again in (V. 1).

"In the unperishable, and infinite highest Brahman, wherein the two, Vidya (Vijñāna-Ātma) and Avidya are hidden, the one, Avidya, perishes; the other, Vidya, is immortal; but He who controls both Vidya and Avidya, is *another* (Anyatha)." And in the subsequent verses, this *another*

---

* If we read "he quites her side, for the other" makes the sense complete.

is clearly pointed to be the only One God, without a second, the ruler of all, the generator of all, and the supporter (ripener) of all. This forms the subject of discussion in the hands of Badarāyaṇa in I, ii, 21. And the famous passage in Bṛihadāraṇyaka is referred to. "He who dwells in Ātmā (Vjñāna) and *different from Ātmā*, whom the Ātmā does not know, whose body *Ātmā* is, and who pulls (rules) Ātmā within, He is thy Ātmā, the puller within, the immortal" (iii, 7, 22).

In vi. 6, also God is called the Anya—the other. It occurs again in Gītā, xv. 17. The previous verse postulates two entities of matter and soul, and the next verse proceeds to postulate "*another.*" "But there is *another*, namely, the Supreme Being, called Paramātmā, who being the everlasting Īśvara, and pervading the three worlds, sustains them." That the very use of the word is solely to emphasise God's transcendency over the world of matter and of souls, as against people who only postulated two Padārthas, or would identify God, the supreme Īśvara, with matter or soul, is fully brought out in the next verse.

"As I transcend the perishable (Pradhāna) and as I am higher than even the Imperishable (soul), I am celebrated in the world and sung in the Vedas as *Purushottama.*"

The commonest fallacy that is committed when the eternality of matter and souls is postulated, is in fancying that this, in any way, affects God's transcendency and immanency. Though He pervades all and envelopes all, creates and sustains and takes them back again into Himself, though He is the God in the fire, the God in the water, the God who has entered the whole world, in plants and trees and in every thing else, (ii. 17) yet He stands behind all time and all persons, (vii. 16), and is beyond all *tattvas*. (Verse 15.)

" He is the one God, (Eko Deva), hidden in all beings, all pervading, the Antarātma of all things, watching over all works, dwelling in all beings, the witness, the perceiver, the

Only One, Nirguṇa (Being) vi. 11. And in Verse 16, he is called the first cause, himself uncaused, the all-knower, the master of *Nature and Man*. And by the supreme statement "Ekohi Rudra nadvittiya tasthe, (There is only One Rudra, they do not allow a second) the complete subordination of all other things to Him is clearly postulated. There is nothing else in His presence, as no Asat can subsist in the Presence of the Sat, as no darkness can subsist in the presence of light. And Light, he is called (iii, 12) the Light, by which all other lights, the sun, the moon, and the stars and the lightnings are lighted, (vi. 14) and He is the great Purusha, like the Sun in lustre, beyond darkness. (iii. 8.)

There is only one other passage which we have to quote while we are dealing with the three eternal postulates of this Upanishat. These are the Verses 8 and 9 in the first Adhyāya itself. In these also the distinctions between the Supreme God, and the bound soul, as Īśa and Anīśa, Jña and Ajña, and the third, Pradhāna, Unborn though perishable and ever changing, are finely drawn.

In dealing with the personality of God, who is called in the Upanishats, as Deva, Hara, Vaśi, Śiva, Purusha, Brahman, Paramātmā, Īśa, and Īśvara, &c,. we have to remark that the Upanishat makes no distinction between a Higher and a Lower Brahman; rather, there are no statements made about the Lower God or Gods, except one verse in V. 3, where the Supreme Lord and Mahātmā, is said to have created the *Lords*, and Brahma or Hiranyagarbha is referred to as such a lord. But every statement made to God, by any of the names, we have mentioned above, clearly refers to the one*, without a second, the Highest Brahman, who is also

* Our learned Lord Bishop of Madras complains that the educated Hindu has only to choose one out of the six systems of Philosophy, and that he has no good practical religion and we kindly invite his attention to this paper, and then judge for himself and see if Hindu Philosophy and Religion is, after all, really so poor.

Nirguṇa. And in various passages, this Highest Being is said to create, sustain and destroy the worlds. What some of these people would not believe is, how a Being addressed as Hara and Śiva, Īśa and Īśvara could be the Nirguṇa Absolute Brahman. And they frequently associate this name with the Rudra or Śiva of the Hindu Trinity. But it will be news to these people that even the Rudra of the Trinity is Nirguṇa and not Saguṇa. Absolutely no passage could be found in any of the Upanishats or even in the Purāṇas and the Itihāsas, in which even the trinity Śiva or Rudra is called Saguṇa. Saguṇa means having Bodies (qualities) formed out of Prakṛiti, and when Prakṛiti is itself resolved into its original condition and reproduced by this trinity Rudra, this prakṛiti could not act as his vestment.

But the Rudra and Śiva of our Upanishat is clearly set forth in other Upanishats as the fourth, *chaturtam* and *Turiyam*, transcending the trinity; and the secondless.

> "Satyam Jñānam, Anantam Brahma,
> Ananda Rupam, Amritam Yad Vibhuti,
> Śantam *Śivam Advaitam*."—(*Tait Up.*)
>
> "*Śivam*, Śantam, *Advaitam*
> *Chaturtham*, manyante,"—(*Ramatapini*).
>
> "Dhyāyeteesanam, pradhyāyedavyam,
> Sarvamidam, Brahma Vishṅu Rudrendrasthe,
> Sarve Samprāsuyante, Sarvanichendryanicha;
> Sahabhutaih Nakaranam Karanam Dhāta Dhyāṭa
> Karanantu Dhyeyah Sarvaiswarya Sampannah
> Sarveswsrah Sambhurakasa Madhye.
> Śiva eko Dhyayet: Sivankaṛa, Sarvam
> Anyat Parityaja.—(*Atharva Sikha*).

"Adore the most adorable Īśāna. Brahma, Visṇu, Rudra, Indra and others have an origin. All the senses originate with the elements. The first cause and cause of causes has no origin. The Bestower of all prosperity, the Lord of all, *Sambhu*, He should be contemplated in the middle of the

Ākāsa......Šiva, the one alone, should be contemplated; the Doer of Good; All else should be given up." (Atharva Sikha) "The mystical and immutable one, which being composed of three letters A., U., M., signify successively, the three Vedas, the three states of life (Jāgra, Svapna and Sushupti), the three worlds (heaven, hell and earth) three gods (Brahma, Vishṇu and Rudra) and by its nasal sound (Ardhamātra) is indicative of Thy *fourth* office as the Supreme Lord of all (Paramešvara)* ever expresses and sets forth thy collective forms." (Mahimna Stotra). And the same mistake is committed by outsiders in supposing that the God of the Šaivas is only one of the trinity. Any book in Tamiḻ and Sanskrit taken at random will at once disillusion him, and he will find that the only God held up for the highest worship is the highest Nirguṇa Parama Šiva, and not one of the trinity. Great confusion is caused in the use of the words Nirguṇa† and Saguṇa, by translating them into impersonal and personal respectively. And Europeans themselves are not agreed as to the use of these words. According to Webster, the word 'personal' implies limitation, but other eminent persons like Emerson, Lotze, &c., say there is no such implication. Till the acceptation of these words are therefore settled, we should not make confusion worse confounded, by rendering Nirguṇa and Saguṇa, as Impersonal and Personal.

So far, there can be no doubt on the nature of the God-head described in our Upanishat.

"When there was no darkness, nor day nor night, nor Sat, nor Asat, then Šiva alone existed (Šiva eva Kevalah). That is the absolute, that the adorable (condition) of the Lord. From that too had come forth the wisdom of old—(jñānāšakti). (iv, 18).

---

* A Christian missionary writing to the Christian College Magazine wonders how *Vemana*, the famous Telugu poet, could speak of Šiva as other than the Hindu triad, Brahma, Vishṇu and Rudra. *Cf.*, Bartṛihari's Satakas for the popular conception of Šiva.

† By *Nirguṇa*, we mean 'without Prakritic qualities' and by *Saguṇa* clothed in Prakritic qualities'. And God could therefore be both Nirguṇa and Personal in Emerson's sense.

"He is the eternal and infinite, Unborn Being, partless, action-less, tranquil, without taint, without fault, the Highest Bridge to Immortality (vi. 19). He is the causeless first cause, the all-knower, the all-pervader, the creator, sustainer and liberator of the world, the end and aim of all Religion and of all philosophy, He is the Īśvara of Īśvaras, Maheśvara, the God supreme of Gods, the King of kings, the Supreme of the supreme, the Īśa of the Universe" (vi. 7.)

There is one other matter to be considered in the nature of the Divine Personality. God is spoken of both in masculine and in neuter, and that in the same verse, a peculiarity which is noticeable in modern Śaivaism. And God is addressed in all forms as 'He' 'She' and 'It.' Śivaḥ, Śiva and Śivam.* And the reason is not as stated by Prof. Max Müller, in his note under Ver. 16, Chapter iii, that the gender changes frequently, according as the auther thinks either of the Brahman or its impersonation as "Īśā, Lord." To the Indian whether he addresses his God as Śiva or Śivam, he is addressing the same Supreme Personality who is neither male nor female nor neuter, and there is no jar to him in the sense, as there will be to the Christian, who could only think of and address God in the masculine gender.

The Upanishat does not recognize any difference between the use of 'It' and 'He,' and it does not contemplate that by using 'It' instead of 'He,' a Higher Being is reached.

Coming now to the nature of the soul, as set forth in this Upanishat, the first thing to be noticed is that the Jīva is very often spoken of as *Ātmā* simply and distinguished from God. The other appellation it receives are Purusha, Anīśa, Ajña, the Hamsa, Vidyā, and these are to distinguish it from *the other*, the Paramātma, the Parama Purusha, Īśa and Jña.

This soul is bound, because he is not God (i. 8) because he is ignorant of himself, and of the self within him, (the

*Śivam in Sanskrit, they say, is not the neuter of Śiva. But somewhow this neuter form is quite prevalent in Tamil.

Antarātma). This soul is not selfdependent (i. 2). This soul is confined in the *Pura* (city-body) of nine gates, *i.e.*, is limited and 'flutters about', is changeable, and he enjoys the fruits, pleasures and pains (even pains are a pleasure to him, the ignorant soul) and fondly clings to the body, and performs karma (iii, 18. iv. 5 and 6.)

"But he who is endowed with qualities, and performs Karma that are to bear fruit and enjoys the reward of whatever he has done, migrates through his own works, the lord of life, assuming all forms, led by the three guṇas and the three paths" (vi. 7).

And yet this soul is of the image of God, is infinite and brilliant like the Sun, endowed with Ichcha and Jñāna, and is sinless.

The Supreme One who witnesses all his doings, dwelling within him, without Himself being tainted by the contact, helps to secure the ripening of his mala, and waits till the soul attains to that condition of perfect balancing in good and evil, (v. 5) by the performance of Chariya, Kriya and Yoga (good works, Penance and meditation) with love and knowledge and the syllable Praṇava, he is blessed by the Lord (i. 6,) and God's grace descends on him (vi. 21 and iii, 20) and he knows and sees, with Manas (the supreme grace of God—the spiritual eye) (v. 14) 'The Purusham Mahantam Adityā Varṇam, tamasaḥ parastat,' and his fetters (Pāśa) fall of, and sufferings cease and he enters the Bliss of the Supreme Brahman, and Eternal Peace.

That *Īśvara Prasādam* (iii. 20) or *Anugraham* or grace is necessary is a common belief of the people, and this doctrine is not peculiar to this Upanishat alone. The *Katha* Upanishat puts the same doctrine in much stronger language, "That *Ātmā* (God) cannot be gained by the Veda, nor by understanding, nor by much learning. He whom Ātmā (God) chooses, by him the Ātmā (God) can be gained." (1. 2. 23); but even the supreme Almighty (God) cannot help him, if he had not turned away from wickedness, and is not tranquil, subdued and at rest, dedicating (*Arpaṇam*), all his words, deeds and thoughts to God, (i. 24).

That the doctrine of Bhakti is found well set forth in the oldest Upanishats and the Vedas will be apparent by reading the texts collated by Dr. Muir in his learned "Metrical translations from Sanskrit" under the heading of '*Śraddha and Bhakti.*' By the way, this *Śraddha* and *Bhakti* is not to be understood as a manifestation of feeling only, at one stage of man's spiritual evolution and unnecessary at another stage, but this love is essential to the aspirant whether he is a Dāsamārgi, Satputramārgi, Yogamārgi or Jñānamārgi. That these four paths grow one, out of the other, and are not independent, and each one of these is hardly possible to reach without going through the lower rungs of the ladder, we have already pointed out above.

The Upanishats, all of them, discuss the particular Upāsana or Upāsanas which are required for the salvation of the bound soul, and these Upāsanas are called also Vidyās.

Of these various Vidyās, what is called the Dahara Upāsana or Vidyā is the most favoured of all the Upāsanas in the Śvetāsvatara and Chāndogya, Bṛihadāraṇyaka, Kaṭha, Muṇḍaka and Kaivalya, Atharva Śikha and in the Bhagavad Gitā.

The references to this Highest Yoga practice are most numerous in the Upanishats and the sameness of the various references form the subject of discussion in the Vedānta Sūtras (iii. 3. 23.)

The famous passages are what occur in the Chāndogya Upanishat, commencing with the sentences "There is the city* of Brahman" (viii. 1. 1). "All this is Brahman." (iii. 14. 1 to 4). This worship or Yoga, consists in the aspirant contemplating in his heart, the Supreme one, as the Person of Light and

* This City is exactly reproduced in modern symbolism in the Great Temple of *Chidambaram*.

as Ākāša, as Satchidānanda Paramešvara, with the particular formula that "God is in all beings and all beings are in God." And various synonyms are used to denote this *heart* of man, such as Dahara (subtle) Guha (cave), Puṇḍarīka (lotus), Brahmapura (city), Hridaya (heart).

And the meaning of the words Ākāša, and Vyoma has also to be carefully noted. They are synonymous and do not mean the Bhūta Ākāša, nor the Māyāšakti or Avidyā, but as interpreted by the Purāṇas themselves, they mean Chit or Jñāna, or, Light or Grace, which is the Parāšakti of the Supreme Išvara. That this Ākāša is Chit and not Achit, is further proved by the phrases, *Chitākāša* and *Chidambara*, and this Chit Šakti is the Devātma-Šakti of our Upanishat, which is inherent and concealed in him, (i. 3.) and the supreme Šakti, which is revealed as manifold, *inherent* (Šiva) and manifesting as Kriyā and Jñāna (vi. 8). It is this which is called *Umā* and Light and *Bhargas* † and *Sāvitri* and Gāyatrī. And when we understand therefore, this Ākāša, as light and knowledge, the Supreme Šakti of God, its description as the highest light, the revealer of all forms, the Highest object of adoration, is clear. The description of God also as Ākāša (Šakti) and as dwelling in Ākāša (Šakti) will not be conflicting, as no distinction is made between Sun and his light, much less between God and his Power. ‡

It is this Jñāna Šakti who gives to the Chetana and Achetana Prapañcha its form and shape and life and love and light; but the substance or Upādāna ¶ out of which this

† Cf. Mait. Up. vi. 7, "Rudra is called Bhargas, thus say the Brahman teachers," cf. also vi. 28 last para. "The Shrine (Paramālaya) which consists of the Ākāš in the heart, the blissful, the highest retreat, that is our own, that is our Goal, and that is the heat and brightness of the Fire and Sun."

‡ In the Yajur Veda, this God and Ambika are called *Saha*, which may mean equal or brother and sister.

¶ It is Bādarāyaṇa's view that there is no other Upādāna except God and these worlds arise out of God Himself. When a tree springs out of

Prapañcha is evolved is the Māyā or Pradhāna, which also dwelling in Him is drawn out and drawn in by the Supreme Power (Śakti) with just the ease and dexterity of a spider which spins out or in; or of the magician who draws forth, out of an empty basket, fruits and flowers and sweets. The Māyā (meaning also power) is also a Śakti of His, (Māyāśakti), but differing from the other Śakti, Ichchā Jñāna and Kriyā, just as darkness differs from light. As darkness is necessary for rest and recuperation, so this power of God also works for our rest and recuperation and salvation. And God is called the Lord of Māyā (Māyin) and "beyond" all forms of the tree, as transcending all the "Tattvas, Kalā" &c., and as 'transcending 'Pradhāna.' Why we are required to contemplate God as Ākāśa, Light or Chit is, that by this Light alone we can know Him, and as such Light; and it is as Light, Chit God is immanent in the world, and omnipresent. And this brings out again the reason why this Chit is called Ākāśa, the most subtle and invisible and omnipresent element we have in Nature.

God is present in all nature and pervades it, as oil in seeds, butter in *ghee* and fire in wood (i 15). And this all pervasiveness is thus explained in a text of the Atharva Śiras Upanishat —"Why is it called Sarva Vyāpi? It is so called because like *ghee* diffusing and soaking itself through and through the Rūda (Milk or seed), it pervades every created thing through and through as warp and woof."

And as by reason of this pervasiveness, nothing could be imagined as existing out of Him, the whole is called also Brahman, the whole, with the parts and limbs and bodies (iv. 10) as the Chetana-Achetana Prapañcha, has antaḥkaraṇa as Chit

---

the bare ground, we naturally suppose there was some *seed* imbedded in it without our knowledge, though the earth contained it and is essential for the support and growth of the plant. This is the Aupanishadic view. Bādarāyaṇa would say that no seed is necessary and the earth alone is sufficient.

Śakti, and Himself the *Soul* of this vast whole. And as all of us form but parts of him, we are also enjoined to be kind to one another, for, whatever we do to each other will be also done to His body. We quote the following from Śrīkaṇṭha Śivāchārya's commentary in which this point is discussed.

"All this is Brahman, as beginning, ending, and breathing in Him; and therefore let a man meditate on him."

"This passage may be explained as follows: The origin, existence and end of all this depends on Brahman. All this, both the sentient and insentient existence, is verily Brahman, and therefore let a man meditate on Brahman, tranquil in mind. Just as the water-bubbles which have their origin, existence and end in the ocean, are found to be only forms of that ocean, so too, that which depends for its orign, etc., on Brahman associated with Śakti must be made of Brahman and nothing else. Nothing distinct from him is ever perceived. Accordingly in the Atharva-Śiras, it has been declared by Īśāna as follows:—

> "Alone I was at first, (alone) I am and shall be
> There is none else distinct from Me."

And then was declared by him in the words "I am Brahman," that the whole universe is his own form. And in the words "He entered the more hidden from (or than) the hidden one" &c., his entering into the universe is given as a reason for the whole universe being his own form. Thus this universe having no orign, existence or end outside Brahman, is not a quite distinct thing from Brahman. Accordingly the learned say:—

"His Śaktis or energies (form) the whole world, and the Maheśa or the great lord is the energetic Śaktimān. Never can energy exist distinct from the energetic. Unity of these two is eternal, like that of fire and heat, inasmuch as unseparateness always exists between energy and the energetic. Wherefore supreme energy belongs to the supreme Ātman, since the two are related to each other as substance and attribute. The energy of heat is not conceived to be distinct from fire" and so on.

Vāyu-Samhitā too says: (Parva, 25, ch. 18 and 19).

"From Śakti up to earth, (the whole world) is born of the principle Śiva. By him alone, it is pervaded, as the jar &c., by clay. His variegated Supreme Śakti, whose form is knowledge and bliss, appears as one and many, like the light of the sun."

The following passage of the Śruti speak of Para-Brahman as possessed of infinite powers of creating, ruling and maintaining the world, all inherent in him.

"His Supreme Śakti is spoken of as manifold, inherent, endued with the activity of knowledge and life." (Śvetāś. 6-8).

"One verily is Rudra,—they were not for a second—who rules these worlds with the powers of the ruling." (3-2).

"In short, on the authority of the Śruti, Smṛiti, Itihāsa, Purāṇa, and the saying of the learned, the Supreme Śakti whose manifold manifestation, this whole universe of Chit and Achit is, whose being is composed of Supreme Existence, Intelligence and unlimited by space and time—is inherent in the nature of Śiva, the Supreme Brahman, and constitutes His own essential form and quality. Apart from Śakti, He cannot be the Omniscient, the Omnipotent, the cause of all, the all controlling, the all adorable, the all-gracious, the means of attaining all aspirations, and the omnipresent; and, moreover, such grand designations as "Maheśvara", the *Supreme Lord*, "Mahādeva," the *Supreme Deity*, and Rudra, the *expeller of pain*, cannot apply to him. Thus, it is Brahman whose body is the whole sentient and insentient universe, and who is denoted by all words. Just as the word 'blue' denotes not the blue colour only, but also the lotus which is of a blue colour, so does the word 'universe' also denotes Brahman. Therefore such passages as "All is Rudra verily" teach that Brahman is denoted by all words. Accordingly the passage

"All this, verily, is Brahman" refers to Brahman whose body, the whole of the sentient and unsentient universe is. The universe being thus a form of Brahman and being therefore not an object of hatred &c., let every one be peaceful at heart and worship Brahman. This doctrine is clearly expounded even in the purāṇic texts such as the following:—"The body of the God of Gods is this universe, moving and unmoving. This, the Jīvas (Paśus) do not know, owing to the mighty bondage. They say sentiency is Vidyā, and insentiency Avidyā. The whole universe of Vidyā and Avidyā form no doubt the body of the Lord, the first cause of all; for the whole universe is subject to Him."

"The word "sat" is used by the wise to denote the real and the good, 'asat' is used by Vedic teachers to denote the contrary. The whole universe of the *sat* and the *asat* is the body of Him who is on high. Just as, by the watering of the roots of a tree, its branches are nourished, so by the worship of Śiva, the universe which is His body, is nourished. Ātman is the eighth body, of Śiva the Parameśvara, pervading all other bodies.

"Wherefore the whole universe is ensouled by Śiva. If any embodied being whatsoever be subjected to constraint, it will be quite repugnant to the eight-bodied lord; as to this there is no doubt. Doing good to all, kindness to all, affording shelter to all, this they hold, is the worshipping of Śiva," and so on.

"Brahman being all-Formed, it is but right to say "all is Brahman" and every one be peaceful and worship "Brahman." Wherefore it is Brahman who in the opening passage is stated to be the object of worship, that is also spoken of as *manomāyā*, as partaking of the nature of *manas*, and so on. Neither should it be supposed that the partaking of the nature of manas is a characteristic mark of a samsārin; for Brahman may limit Himself by assuming a shape which can form an object of worship."

"That which," therefore, "eternally rests within the Ātma," (i 12), "dwells in the cave (of the heart) of all beings," (iii 11), "is the greater than the great, smaller than the small, hidden in the heart of the creature" (iii 20), "hidden in all beings; like the subtle film," (iv 16), "and subtler than subtle" (iv 14), the wise should seize in the body (heart) by means of the praṇava, within himself, and by the drill of meditation and penance, (i-14), they should, '*with the mind towards the heart,*' 'love the old Brahman, by the grace of Sāvitrī' (Light or Chit-Šakti) (11-7 and 8), 'grasping by the Manas' (Šakti), (v 14), and perceive 'by the heart, by the soul, by the mind,' (iv 17), in the Highest Turīyātīta plane, where Šiva Dwells alone, the Eternal and the Adorable Light, this most Ancient of Days, Šiva the Blissful and Benign Being, the great Purusha of sunlike brilliancy, dwelling in the Highest *Vyoma*, then their fetters (pāša) fall off, they will cross over to the other shore, after passing through the torrents that cause fear, (ii 8.) their darkness (Ahaṅkāra, Āṇava) will vanish, and all material bodies (Māyā) will fall off, and they will enter into the supreme Bliss and Peace.

The various steps, psychological and spiritual, by which the sanctification of the Soul is accomplished is stated beautifully in i. 10, "From meditating on Him, from joining Him, from becoming one with him, there is further cessation of all Māyā (bodies-births) in the end." In a most beautiful address on the famous text of St. Paul which runs,

"We, all, with unveiled face, reflecting as a mirror, the Glory of the Lord, are transformed into the same image, from Glory to Glory, even as from the Lord the Spirit",

Professor Henry Drummond, who is said to have revolutionized Christian thought in the last few decades, calls these *the laws of reflection, and of assimilation.* He instances the iron which gets magnetized and becomes a magnet, and a mirror, getting rid of its dust, reflects the glorious light and becomes merged with it and lost. And he remarks "All men are mirrors—that is, the first law on which this formula is based. One of the aptest descriptions of a human being is that he is a mirror." And our Upanishat contains fortunately the self-same description and illustration.

"As a metal disk (mirror), tarnished by dust, shines bright again after it has been cleaned, so is the one incarnate person satisfied and freed from grief, after he has seen the real (pure) Nature of himself." "And when by the real nature of his self, he sees as by a lamp, the real nature of the Brahman, then having known the unborn eternal God, who transcends all the tattvas, he is freed from all fetters (pāśa), (ii. 14 & 15). The first text would simply read, in Drummond's language, "see, reflect and become God."

It only remains for us now to point out that the second verse of the first adhyāya is mistranslated by Roer, Max Müller, Mead and others. They contain terms which are not known to the systems they are familiar with, and they are alone preserved in the Siddhānta system. The terms are '*Kalā,*' '*Svabho,*' '*Niyati,*' '*Ichchā,*' '*Bhūta,*' '*Yoni,*' '*Purusha,*' and they are also referred to as '*Yonisvabho*' &c., in v. 4. and in vi. 1 '*Svabho*' and '*Kalā.*'

We stated that the different schools differed in the enumeration of the tattvas or categories but most of them stopped with Prakṛiti or Pradhāna and Purusha, the highest in their list, the 24th and 25th principle (*Vide*, Sentināthaiyar's Table of Tattvas, published in Madras 1899), but the Siddhānta school postulated above this, other tattvas or principles, making up the whole number into 36. These higher tattvas were, Rāgam (Ichchā) Vidyā, Niyati, *Kāla*, Kalā, (constituting what is called the soul's, the purusha's Pañcha Kañchukam), Māyā, Śuddha Vidyā, Maheśvara, Sadāśiva, Bindhu (or Śakti) and Nādam (Śiva). And the terms used in our text is Kāla, Svabho or Kalā, Niyati, Ichcha, or Rāgam, Bhuta or Vidya and Yoni or Suddha Māyā, and Purusha or soul. That our interpretaticn is genuine we could show by quoting the authority of the author of a Purāṇa, who at any rate is anterior to all the commentators whose explanations we now possess. The following occurs in Kailāsa Samhitā of Vāyu Purāṇa and it refers to the Śvetāśvatara text,

" Purushasyatu, Bhoktṛitvam. Pratipamasya, Bhojanecha Prayatnataḥ. Antaraṅgatayātatva pañchakam Prakirtitam. Nirgateḥ kala, rāgaścha Vidyācha Tadanantaram kala Chupañchakamidam Mayotpannam Muniśvara, Mayantu Prakṛitim Vidyān Māyā Śruti etṛitā. Tajjanegetani Tattvāni Śtruti Yuktāni nasamśayaḥ, Katasva bhāvoni yatṛitī Cha Śrutirabravit etat pañchakam evasya pañchakañchuka Muchyate. Ajanan pañcha tatvāni vidvānapi Vimudhadhiḥ. Niyatyadhastat prabrute ruparishṭhaḥ pumanayam Vidyātatvamidam proktam.

The following verse occurs in the Brahmāṇḍa Purāṇa :—

" Purushau Niyati kalarāgaścha kala Vidyecha mayayā "

And this is from Vāyu Samhitā: " Māyā Kālamavasrujat Niyatiñcha Kalām Vidyām Kalāto Rāgapurushau."

A CHAPTER FROM THE KUṞAḶ.

Nobody who has the least insight into the pages of the sacred Kuṟaḷ will fail to endorse the remark of the veteran Tamiḷ scholar, Rev. Dr. G. U. Pope, that this is a work unparalleled in any language. The merits of the work are so apparent that even at its very birth, it received the highest encomiums of the proudest scholars of the day, the Paṇḍits of the far-famed Madura College or Saṅgam. The tradition that the author was of low birth only heightens the value of the appreciations thus showered on him. One of the Collegians compares it to the Veda, and another says, unlike the Veda, Tiruvaḷḷuvar's words do not lose their merit by anybody repeating them. One speaks of it as containing everything worth knowing, and another that there is nothing which is not contained in this work. One says that the words are sweeter than the Heavenly Ambrosia, and unlike the latter, can be partaken of by everybody. And as the poet utters these words even our own mouth begins to water. Another says they are sweet food to the mind, sweet to the ear and sweet to the tongue, and the great panacea for the ills of Karma. One compares it to the sun which dispelling the deep darkness of ignorance, makes the lotus of the heart bloom forth. Another compares it to the lamp dispelling our mental darkness, with the oil-can of *Dharma*, and wick of *Artha*, and ghee of *Kāma*, words of fection—the flame, and the short metres—the lamp-stand. Its brevity, not bordering on unintelligibility or ambiguity as do most of the sūtras in Sanskrit, its perfection of expression and style, its deepness are all matters taken up for praise by these learned Collegians. And what is more, the poet Kallāḍar brings out in his verse its most prominent character, its universality. People wrangle about this or that being the truth, and they range themselves into various schools, but all are agreed about the truth of the words uttered by Tiruvaḷḷuvar. And since his time, all religionists, Buddhists and Jains, Śaivas and Vaishṇavas have all claimed him as their own. And we need not enquire wherefrom he derived his truths. It is enough to acknowledge that it is perfection of Truth, if one can say so, a Perfect Ethical and Religious Code, a perfection of art and thought. Indeed, a close study of the work will bring out its perfect scientific basis and each part, and each chapter, and each verse is placed one after the other in a perfect chain of logical arrangement and argument. And may we hope that some ardent student of the Kuṟaḷ will work out from it a perfect theory of ethics, both private and international.

One more remark, and this will introduce us to the chapter of the book we have taken up for translation and elucidation. It is usually remarked, following the main divisions of the book into Dharma, Artha and Kāma அறம், பொருள், இன்பம், that the author has left out the discussion of the last Purushārtha or Moksha, வீடு, on the ground that religion is a matter which will give room for difference and dispute. But is it true that there are no universal truths of religion and did our author leave them unsaid? His own contemporaries did not understand him as doing so, but have stated in their encomiums that he has explained all the four Purushārtams and that he has shown the path to Moksha. And the Rev. Dr. Pope in his short paper on the Ethics of Kuṟaḷ holds that Tiruvaḷḷuvar bases his ethics on the grand truths of Tripadártha, Pathi, Paśu and Pāśa. In fact, his creed is not a godless creed like that of the Jains or Buddhists. In this respect, there is disparity between the Nālaḍi and this work. Our author's God is the 'first Cause and Lord' 'ஆதிபகவன்,' He is 'Intelligent,' 'வாலறிவன்'; He 'resides in the heart of his creatures' 'மலர்மிசையேகினான்,' He is 'Immaculate, untainted by likes and dislikes', 'வேண்டுதல் வேண்டாமையிலான்,' He is the 'Lord of Lords' and 'king of kings' 'இறைவன்,' He is 'incomparable', 'தனக்குவமையில்லாதான்,' He is the 'source of all Dharma and Beneficent', 'அறவாழி அந்தணன்.' He 'has eight attributes', 'எண்குணத்தான்' (i.e. self-dependent or self-possesed, the Pure, Self-Luminous, the All Knowing, the Ever-Free, the Beneficent, the Infinitely Powerful, and Infinitely Blissful. Parimēlaḷagar rejects all other interpretations of எண்குணம்) and the Eternal Truth மெய்ப்பொருள் and the Perfect and Good Being 'செம்பொருள்.'* No amount of learning is of any good unless a man believes in the existence of God and worships His feet in all love and truth. And without such knowledge and such conduct, the mere attaining of ethical perfection is of no use ("ஐயுணர்வெய்தி" &c.) The true way to get rid of our bonds is to reach the feet of the Ever-Free. And these bonds are not mere myths but they are caused by our own ignorance, Avidyā, Ahaṅkāra or Āṇava which is eternal, *Anādi.* And then, the chain of causation following karma into endless births and suffering is worked out, and the means or Sādana required to get freed from these bonds are fully shown, and of all the means, the greatest Sādana is to reach Him who is past all thought and speech; and unless this is done, it is useless to hope to get our cares destroyed. And as all these principles are fully explained in chapter 36 on 'மெய்யுணர்தல்' 'How to perceive truth,' we have translated the same below, adopting almost the language of Dr. G. U. Pope, together with the famous commentary of Parimēlaḷagar, with some running notes, to show how far this is embodied in the Advaita-Siddhānta. Of course the language of the Kuṛaḷ is the language of the Śaivite writers of the past 2000 years; and no wonder, the truths expounded by all of them should be the same.

How to Perceive Truth?

That is, we know the truth when we know the nature of Birth and Freedom (Moksha) and the causes thereof, free from error and doubt. This the Sanskritists call *Tatvajñāna.* As this knowledge arises after desiring the desire of Him who has

* Paṇḍit Savariroyan derives 'Śivam' from 'செம்' and our Saint uses செம்பொருள் very frequently.

no desire, this chapter is placed in consequence after the chapter on 'துறவு,' 'Sanyāsa.'

1. பொருளல் லவற்றைப் பொருளென் றுணரு
மருளானு மாணாப் பிறப்பு.

The delusion whereby men deem that the truth which is not,
That is the cause of hapless birth.

PARIMELALAGAR'S COMMENTARY.

This delusion consists in believing such books and doctrines which hold that there is no rebirth, no fruits of both kinds of Karma, and that there is no God and such like, to be the true books and doctrines. This delusive belief is same as when one mistakes one thing for another, a block for a man, shell for silver. மருள், delusion, மயக்கம், விபரீத உணர்வு, error, அவிச்சை, Avidyā or ignorance are all synonymous words. As it is only sorrow that is reaped in all the four kinds of birth as Devas, men, animal and astrals, this couplet explains that birth is sorrowful and Avidyā or error is its cause.

NOTE.

By altering only a single letter in the first line an 'அ,' 'a' into 'இ 'e,' (பொருளல்ல into பொருளில்ல) the meaning of the whole passage will be altered, and we will have a new system of philosophy directly opposed to our author's. Instead of it being then the truth, it will become the opposite of it. This is the same question which has arisen in interpreting the negative prefix in the word 'Advaita.' This 'a' or 'na' is interpreted in two ways either as meaning 'அல்ல' 'not' or 'இல்ல' 'no,' though the distinction in the English equivalents will not be very apparent. This is its 'அன்மைப்பொருள்' or 'இன்மைப் பொருள்.' Siddhāntins, of course, accept the former interpretation, and most followers of Śaṅkara prefer the latter one. This latter view involves the negation of one of the two or may be both of the postulates in '*Advaita*.' Over this question, a huge war has raged and volumes have been written by the late Śri-la-Śri Somasundara Nāyagar and his followers on one side, and the late Ratna Cheṭṭiyār and of his ilk on the other side. Anyhow, Saint Tiruvaḷḷuvar's meaning is clear. He does not mean to repudiate anything as unreal or non-existent. To him, delusion or error consists in mistaking one existent thing as the shell, for another existent thing as silver. To him, to know the truth, is to understand the true nature of each one thing. The question of reality or unreality does not come in. Only one must not mistake one thing for the other or doubt its nature. It will be sufficient requirement of the definition, if one understands the true nature of God and man and the world, and one need not beleive any of these to be unreal. One of such truths is that birth is sorrowful. This can be proved to be true. But one's ignorance or delusion comes when one takes this actual sorrow as happiness. You think that with this body, there is an end altogether when in fact there are future births. Believing that there is no future life and future birth, one does not believe that there can be a soul; and if there is one, one thinks the body itself is the soul and believing so, all one's energies in this world are directed solely towards what would procure the greatest pleasure and gratification of one's senses, and one does not care what means one adopts provided one's passions are gratified. As it is, the whole foundation of morality will be undermined and one need have neither fear of men nor of God. All this is the result of want of knowledge of the true nature of his body and himself, and this ignorance is the cause of his birth. This ignorance is a fact, and to believe that this ignorance is itself unreal will be error or false knowledge. It is only when a man knows that he is ignorant, that he will learn and try to remove his ignorance. But can this ignorance be removed? Yes. If so, how? This question is answered in the next couplet.

2. இருணீங்கி யின்பம் பயக்கு மருணீங்கி
மாசறு காட்சி யவர்க்கு.

Darkness departs and rapture springs to men who see
The mystic vision pure from all delusion free.

PARIMELALAGAR'S COMMENTARY.

இருள், darkness is hell. 'The mystic vision pure' is the supreme object of knowledge. By this couplet is explained that by freedom is meant *Niratisayānanda* and the Nimitta *Kāraṇa*, for this, the Supreme Being.

NOTE.

Darkness and ignorance, Light and knowledge have at all times and in all climes been used synonymously and no two things are so analogous in nature as these two pairs of words. When will darkness vanish? When the sun rises. When will the sun rise? After the night is past. When will ignorance cease? When the source of all lights arises in his heart? When will this be? When he has attained to a well balanced mind (இருவினையொப்பு). The Pāsatchayam and Pathijñānam are distinct facts, though the first is not possible without the second. This couplet answers all those who say if the ignorance was eternally attachd to the soul, it cannot be removed, and even if it be removed what follows is only a blank and that no Divine Power is required to give one freedom. This couplet and verse 4 below which gives a most distinct reply to the Buddhist view will remove all doubts as to whether he is a Siddhānti or a Buddhist or a Jain. But some of these truths even when known to a man, doubt often oppresses him, environed by a host of dogmatists who each asserts his own dogma is the only truth. In the next couplet, it is stated that even this doubt is the cause of birth, and the means of getting rid of this doubt is also stated.

3. ஐயத்தினீங் கித்தெளிந் தார்க்கு வையகத்தின்
வான நணிய துடைத்து.

When doubts disperse and clearness is gained,
Nearer is heaven than earth to sage's soul.

PARIMELALAGAR'S COMMENTARY.

Doubt (ஐயம்) is knowing a thing variously. That is doubting if there is or is not God and Karma and Rebirth and without definite belief in anything. This is the same as doubting a thing as water or a mirage, rope or a snake. As it is natural to every system to refute other doctrines and establish its own, the doubts arising from such a multitude of doctrines, those sages well practised in Yoga will remove, by their Svānubhūti or experience, and attain to real knowledge; and hence they are called ஐயத்தின் நீங்கித்தெளிந்தார். As they reach higher and higher Yogic experience, their attachment to the world grows less and less; hence, the author's statement that "heaven is nearer" etc. By this couplet is explained that doubtful knowledge is a cause of birth.

NOTE.

Yoga is a means and not an end. Till Yoga merges into knowledge, no real knowledge is gained. Even the highest Yoga is no good, unless the final goal is reached from whence there is no return. The attainment of Yoga is really difficult, but this is not all. One can subdue his passions and desires, and control his senses, but unless he has the "Vision pure," 'The only Truth,' then this attainment will be only for a time, and the man will again be a prey to his senses. To meet this special Buddhist view that the attainment of mere extinction of all desires is Nirvāṇa, and that there is no such thing as Brahma-Nirvāṇa, is the special object of the next couplet.

4. ஐயுணர் வெய்தியக் கண்ணும் பயமின்றே
மெய்யுணர் வில்லா தவர்க்கு.

Five-fold perception gained, what benefits accrue
To them whose spirit lacks perception of the True.

PARIMELALAGAR'S COMMENTARY.

Five-fold perception is the Manas. By 'gained' is meant, the controlling of the manas and concentrating of it in *Dāraṇa*. As training of this alone is not sufficient, the author says there is no benefit, and he brings out by the 'உம்,' how difficult a feat even this attainment of *Dāraṇa* is. By these two couplets, the greatness of Pathijñāna is explained by pointing out that without this attainment, no Moksha is possible. (And the nature of this Pathijñāna is the subject of the next couplet).

5. எப்பொருள் எத்தன்மைத் தாயினு மப்பொருள்
மெய்ப்பொருள் காண்ப தறிவு.

Whatever thing, of whatsoever kind it be,
'Tis wisdom's part in each the real thing to see.

PARIMELALAGAR'S COMMENTARY.

That is, one must perceive the truth immanent in every thing, after getting rid of our ordinary notions of them. In the phrase "கோச்சேரமான் யானைக்கட் சேய்மாந்தரஞ்சொலிரும்பொறை," the words may mean ordinarily the name of king Seramān of a particular description, but they may mean more particularly the Tattvas from earth to Purusha. When examined and rendered into their final causes, what finally remains is none of this cause and effect, but the Highest Truth, and His knowledge is the true knowledge. By this couplet, is explained the nature of this true knowledge.

NOTE

This is one of the most oft-quoted couplets of Kuraḷ, and is put to more general uses than what is intended here. One has not to go far to discover the Supreme Being and know Him. He is in everything ; but one must lose light of the apparent to gain the real. God is in the earth but the earth is not God ; God is in water but water is not God, and so through every Tattva, and lastly, God is in the soul, but the soul is not God. When one has so learned to discriminate and distinguish, then only will he attain to *Patijñānam*. In the next three couplets, the Sādana required for attaining this *Patijñānam* is given. And the first requisite is hearing or learning.

6. கற்றீண்டு மெய்ப்பொருள் கண்டார் தலைப்படுவர்
மற்றீண்டு வாரா நெறி.

Who learn and here the knowledge of the true obtain,
Shall find the path that cometh not again.

PARIMELALAGAR'S COMMENTARY.

By 'learn,' the author means learning from every body and at all times. By 'here,' the author brings out the greatness of human birth wherefrom alone one can attain Moksha.

"The path that cometh not again" is the path to Moksha. The means or Sādanā for knowing The First cause, the cause of one's attaining Moksha are of three kinds: they are கேள்வி, Hearing or study, விமரிசம், Reflection, பாவனை, Bāvanā or Realising. (In Sanskrit *Śravaṇa, Manana* and *Nidhidyāsana).* This couplet explains *Śravaṇa*.

NOTE.

Though the commentator's idea of what is to be learnt is very large, yet the correction conveyed in the following stanza of Nālaḍiyār is important.

கல்வி கரையில கற்பவர் நாள்சில
மெல்ல நினைக்கிற் பிணிபல—தெள்ளிதின்
ஆராய்ந் தமைவுடைய கற்பவே நீரொழிய
பாலுண் குருகிற் றெரிந்து.

"In this matchless verse," says Dr. Pope, "not a syllable could be spared; while almost every word is common and easy, yet is the very fittest, and is used in its exact meaning. It is somewhat archaic;—has a fascinating air of mystery;—pleasantly exercises and amply rewards the students' ingenuity;—seems dark at first, but once lit up, sparkles for ever.

"This கரை—shore suggests a metaphor: 'learning is a shoreless—infinite—ocean.'

"Then comes the simple antithesis, 'the learner's days are few.' In Tamil the use of the same root twice (in கல்வி and கற்பவர்) and again in the third line (கற்பவே) imports an added charm.

"Into these perfectly (to Tamil ears) harmonious lines is compressed a whole chapter.

"The *subject of study* (கல்வி with a plural verb) is infinitely numerous; but the learner's days are few; and if it be calmly thought out, men are liable to many diseases. [பிணி, natural infirmities or 'bonds' that enfeeble and restrict]. Youthful enthusiasm may lead men to anticipate great and varried triumphs; calm reflection teaches them their natural weakness. So, men should learn with discrimination (தெள்ளிது) examining closely (ஆராய்) things befitting (அமை, suit, satisfy, gladden them) with intelligence, (தெரிந்து) like that of the bird (the semi divine Hamśa, that drinks only the milk and leaves the water, when these mingled are presented to it?"

7. ஓர்த்துள் ளமுள்ள துணரின் ஒருதலையாப்
பேர்த்துள்ள வேண்டா பிறப்பு.

The mind that knows with certitude what is (First-Cause) and ponders well
Its thoughts on birth again to other life need not to dwell.

Commentary.

This explains 'manana.'

8. பிறப்பென்னும் பேதைமைநீங்கச் சிறப்பென்னும்
செம்பொருள் காண்ப தறிவு.

When the folly of desiring birth departs, the soul can view
The *exalted* Home of The Good Being, this is wisdom true.

PARIMELALAGAR'S COMMENTARY.

Birth and ignorance, and Exalted Home and Truth are really related as effect and cause, they are given inversely in this couplet. Of the five faults, as ignorance is the cause of even the other faults, the author has stated this as *the* cause of birth. As Moksha is higher, than all other things, it is spoken of as the 'exalted.' The First Cause is spoken of as the 'Good Being,' inasmuch as He is eternal without birth and death, as all other things are too insignificant to taint Him by their contacts, and as He remains the same without change or taint at all time, though immanent in all things. Hence also, He is spoken of above as the 'True Being' (மெய்ப்பொருள்) and the Existent (உள்ளது). The "viewing" is the soul losing its Mala by constantly realising or practising, (பாவித்தல், Bāvanā) so that it may become one with God (ஒற்றுமையுற). This *Bāvanā* is also called *Samādhi* or *Šukla Dhyāna*. As it is commonly held by all schools of people that the soul when it leaves the body becomes that which it fancied at the time (அதனால் யாதொன்று பாவிக்கப்பட்டது அஃது அதுவாய்த் தோன்றுதலால் *i.e.*, is born assuming that body to which it yearned at the time of death), and so, too, as it is necessary for people who aspire after Moksha to contemplate on the Transcendent Being, so that their thoughts on birth may cease, there is no better means than this Sādana for practice beforehand always. Thus *Bāvanā* is explained in this couplet.

NOTE.

The commentator proves his thesis by taking the common form of belief held by all people. Every one believes that the form he sees, the object he is after, the idea which possesses him at the moment of one's death, will give him a similar form at the future birth, and stories are current about a rishi who was fondling a deer being born a deer etc. But these do not know on what principle this is based; and except in the Siddhānta works, this principle is nowhere expounded. The principle involved regards the nature of the Soul, which is stated briefly and tersely by St. Meykaṇḍān as 'அது அது ஆதல்' 'that, that becomes' as 'சார்ந்ததன் வண்ணமாதல்' 'that becomes that to which it is attached' by St. Aruḷ Nandi, whi.h is paraphrased again by St. Tāyumānavar as

> "யாதொன்று பற்றின் அதன் இயல்பாய்நின்று
> பந்தமறும் பளிங்கனைய சித்தர்."

'Like the dirt-removed crystal which becomes of the nature of that to which it is attached.' St. Tiruvaḷḷuvar himself has clearly expressed this principle in the verse "பற்றுக பற்றற்றான்." &c of the last chapter, and in the second verse of this chapter, and in the next verse "சார்புணர்ந்து &c" and verses 4, 5, 7 and 8 of the first chapter, wherein he shows that unless the soul leaves its clinging to one, it cannot cling to another, from whence is deduced the principle (பற்றுக்கோடின்றி நில்லாமை) that the soul cannot have any independent existence or form unless it is clinging to one thing, (the world or body in Bandha) or the other (God in Moksha), and while so attached, it identifies itself so thoroughly, that it is impossible to discover its separate personality. Hence it was that a Tyndal, an Huxley and a Bain with all their minute anatomical, biological and psychological analysis were not able to discover a mind in the body different from the body, though they could feel that the result was not very satisfactory. The express language used by the commentator "அதனால் யாதொன்று பாவிக்கப் பட்டது அஃது அதுவாய்த் தோன்றும்" "பிறப்பிற்கேதுவாய பாவனை கெடுதற்பொருட்டு மேலைப்பெருமையே பாவித்தல் வேண்டும்" as will appear from the beautiful stanza we quote below from St. Aruḷ Nandi, will show to whom he is indebted for the explantion.

> "கண்டவிவையல்லேனானென்றகன்றுகாணாக்
> கழிபரமுநானல்லேனெனக்கருதிக்கசிந்த
> தொண்டினொடுமுளத்தவன்றானின்றகலப்பாலே
> சோகமெனப்பாவிக்கத்தோன்றுவன்வேறின்றி
> விண்டகலும்மலங்களெல்லாம்கருடத்தியானத்தின்
> விடமழியுமதுபோலவிமலதையுமடையும்
> பண்டைமறைகளுமதுநானானேனென்று
> பாவிக்கச்சொல்லுவதிப்பாவத்தைக்காணே"

The word பாவனை (Bāvanā) is important. Bāvanā, Sādana, Dhyāna, Yoga are all more or less synonymous terms. It means practice by symbolic meditation or realization. You fancy fixedly you are one with that and you become that. And this is the principle which underlies all the *Mahāvākyas* 'Tattvamasi' &c. For fuller treatment, see *Śivajñānabodham*; and *The Siddhānta Dipikā*, Vol. II, the article 'Mind and Body.'

9. சார்புணர்ந்து சார்பு கெடவொழுகின் மற்றழித்துச்
சார்தரா சார்தரு நோய்.

The true support who knows—rejects support he sought before
Sorrow that clings shall cease and cling to him no more.

PARIMELALAGAR'S COMMENTARY.

'ஒழுக்கம்' 'conduct or practice' here means practice of Yoga. This Yoga is of eight kinds; Yama, Niyama, Āsana, Prāṇāyāma, Pratyākāra, Dhāraṇa, Dhyāna, and Samādhi. Their explanations are too long to be given here. See them in the books on Yoga. 'The sorrows that cling to us' are the fruits of Karma which have yet to be experienced, which are the result of infinite Karma performed in births dating from eternity, and which give rise to fruits already eaten in past births and in the present birth. "Shall cease and cling no more," as they will vanish before Yoga and Jñāna like darkness before light. This Jains call 'உவர்ப்பு.' As even Good Karma is the seed of birth, it is called a 'disease.' The author holds that births will cease when the Supreme is perceived by the above-mentioned three means. When the births cease, what can all the ills do, as they cannot cling to these jñānis well practised in Yoga, and there being no support, they will die. This is the purport of the stanza.

NOTE.

The word 'சார்பு' in the verse and 'பற்று' in the previous chapter mean a *support* or *hold*. The soul has two such supports, one in Bandha and one in Moksha and without such supports it cannot stand. This may be compared to a piece of iron held between two magnetic poles, one positive, and one negative, or better still to a fruit growing on a tree. The fruit is held up by the tree, so long and so long only, as it is raw and immature (undeveloped) but so soon as it is ripe, it reaches the ground (Force of gravity); fruit, as such, must be united to the tree or the ground. What happens is, as the fruit grows riper and riper, the sap of the tree does not rise up to the twig and the twig dies, and it falls off. So too as man rises higher, and his desire of the world decreases, and the bonds are sundered, he drops into the Feet of the Lord. "பாசங்கழன்றாற்பசுவுக்கிடம் பதியாம்." The author of திருக்களிற்றுப்படியார் explains 'சார்புணர்வு' as Dhyāna, and 'சார்புகெட ஒழுக்கம்' as Samādhi, the highest Jñāna-Yoga practices. In the next verse this Pāśatchaya is further explained.

10. காமம் வெகுளி மயக்க 'மிவைமூன்ற
னாமங் கெடக்கெடு நோய்.

Parimelalagar's Commentary.

The eternal ignorance, *avidyā*, the consequent *ahaṅkāra*, the feeling of 'I' and 'mine,' the hankering which desires this or that, the eternal desire of this or that object, and dislike or hate arising from unsatisfied desire, these five faults are enumerated by Sanskritists. The author enumerates only three, as 'Ahaṅkāra' can be brought under 'Avidyā', and 'hankering' can be comprised under 'Desire.' As these faults are burnt up before Jñāna-Yoga practices, like cotton before a wildfire, so the author speaks of the disappearance of the very names of these three faults. As those who do not commit these faults, will not commit good or bad Karma caused by them, the author states accordingly in this verse that they suffer no pain therefrom. As a result of the attainment of True Knowledge, the ills of past births and of furture births are destroyed, and thus these two verses find a place in these chapter. We learn from this also, that what remains to those who have perceived the Truth is the present body and ills attaching thereto.

Note.

And the next chapter discusses the means of even getting rid of this bare bodily infirmity and of guarding against what is called *Vāsanā Mala*.

THE ANALOGIES IN THE GĪTĀ.

Analogy is very largely used in the elucidation and explanation of various principles in Oriental philosophy, and with more or less effect. In most cases, they serve a very important function, and many truths there are, which by reason of their dealing with the ultimate existences can alone be demonstrated by such analogies, and not by any other kind of proof. In the use of such analogies there are great dangers also, and the analogy may look so plausible that one is apt to be carried away by it, without noting the inherent flaws in it, and which a little closer investigation will clearly bring out. Care should, however, be taken to distinguish between analogies which are merely similes or metaphors, based on a mere semblance, and intended merely to bring home to our minds, the subject matter in a more impressive and clearer light, and analogies strictly so-called, intended as proof. In the latter case, mere semblance alone will not do, and there must be sameness in the various parts of the illustration and the thing illustrated. Neglect of this rule often leads to great confusion and error in thought. If for the particular inference desired, the antecedents conform to the antecedents in the analogy, the inference will be quite justified, if it conforms to the consequence in the analogy; and it would be simply illogical to strain the illustration to other purposes and to extremes. Analogy at best is but an indifferent kind of proof, and where we do not take the proper precautions in using it, its value in philosophic argument will be almost nothing. Another source of error in the use of analogies by Indian writers is the brevity of expressions which is characteristic of such analogies, as we meet them in some of the most ancient books. Where the analogy is taken literally, without supplying the necessary parts and ellipses, they cannot but lead one astray.

There is one school of philosophers in India, who are inordinately fond of these similes and who at almost every step seek the aid of a simile to help them out of their position; and these similes have now only become too much hackneyed, and they pass from mouth to mouth, and even educated persons repeat them parrot-like, who would easily find out the fallacy, if the matter is only put before them for a moment. We expected at least those learned in the lore of the West to explain their subject instead of building all their argument on the strength of these doubtful similes and in this respect, even European scholars are not without reproach. For what shall we say of a scholar like Dr. Paul Deussen, if he gives expression to the following false analogy? Says he, "And then for him, when death comes, no more *Samsāra*. He enters into Brahman, like streams into the ocean: he leaves behind him *nāma* and *rūpa*, he leaves behind him *individuality*; but he does not leave behind him his Atman, his Self. It is not the falling of the drop into the infinite ocean, it is the whole ocean, becoming free from the fetters of ice, returning from its frozen state to that what it is really and has never ceased to be, to its own all pervading, eternal, almighty nature." In these few lines, he crowds together as may fallacies as there are words in it, and we have neither the time nor patience to indicate all of them. We will however point out the most glaring of them. The soul returning from its migrations to its resting place, its final goal was the stream returning to the bosom of the mighty ocean. When the stream joins the ocean, it loses its name and form? Does it really do so, and if it did what of that, how is it in any way changed? What we generally call a stream is a small body of water flowing between two banks. The water by itself without its local connection cannot be called the stream. The moment the water leaves its local connection, it ceases to be called stream. So it is not really the stream that flows into the ocean but that the water of the stream flowed into and mixed with the water of the ocean. What makes really the difference between the ocean and the stream is the difference in the largeness and smallness of the respective bodies, and the largeness and smallness of the receptacle. The water, in either receptacle, is acted on by the sun and wind, is tempest-tossed and discoloured and made muddy. The juggle by which the learned Doctor converts the stream water, nay a drop, into a mighty *ocean* is not manifest in the illustration. The drop or the stream water is the drop or the stream water in the bosom of the ocean though, for the time being, we are unable to distinguish its *identity*. When the *identity* is lost, its *individuality* is not seen, is lost in a sense also. The water remains as water and has not lost its *nāma* and *rūpa*, though this water gets other names by other accidents. It is the accident that determines the more specific name, and we will have to enquire how the thing acquired this accident or became parted from it. Then we come to the figure of the frozen ocean and the free ocean. Here is a jump from one figure to another. The bound soul was formerly the stream, and the freed soul the ocean. In either case, we observed above, the two bodies of water were subject to the same changeability and disabilities except that one was larger than the other. Now, the bound soul is the frozen ocean and the freed soul is the ocean after it had thawed. And the learned Doctor speaks of the fetters of ice. What does it matter to the ocean whether it was in a frozen condition or otherwise? How does it cease to be almighty, all-pervading and eternal when it is frozen than when it was not? One would think that if the ocean's wishes were to be consulted, it would much better like to be frozen than not, as it would not be subjected to the mercy of the Wind, and the Sun and the Moon. Water is water whether it remains a liquid or a gas or a solid substance. And it would be mere rhetoric to ascribe fetters to it. And this fetter is real or fancied, either an evil or a good. If real and an evil, how did this fetter happen to be put on. If not, why try to get rid of the fetter? The fetter was put on by the ocean's own will or by another will, more powerful still. If the ocean put it on by its own will, it may do so again, and there is no inducement for anybody to try to get rid of this fetter, and "*the strongest support of pure morality, the greatest consolation in the sufferings of life and death,*" would surely be undermined. If by another's will, who is the greater than this Ātman; no doubt the Paramātman, which ends in veritable dualism. In the case of the ocean itself, it did not become frozen by its own will or power. As water, its nature is unstable and changeable, and the change is brought about by other causes. If we apply heat to it, its liquid condition disappears and it becomes a gas. Withdraw the heat, and the more you do it, the water becomes more solid, and in the arctic regions, where the sun, thousands of times more powerful than the ocean water, is altogether absent for several months, the water gets affected by cold and darkness, and gets fettered in ice. The learned Doctor failed to take stock of the antecedent agent, in the frozening or otherwise of the ocean, namely the sun, and hence his error. The Siddhāntins take the water whether it be that of the smallest rill or that of the ocean as analogous to the soul, and the universal *Ākāś* present both in the water of the stream and that of the ocean, as the Parameśvara and Paramātman, the universal Supporter, and all-Pervader; and the Glorious Sun is also God, whose pañcha-kṛitya is also felt on the ocean and stream water, in its making and increasing and dissolving, and under whose powerful Śakti the minor powers of Karma (wind and moon) also find play, and the whole cycle of evolution is set agoing.

And it is this learned Doctor who spoke of the *misinterpreting variations* of Śaṅkara's *advaita*, known under the names of Visishtādvaita, Dvaita, etc, and it is the freqent boast of people of his ilk, that Śaṅkara's Advaita is the most universal and ancient system, whereas all other forms of Indian philosophy are only partial and sectarian and modern; and in the present paper, we propose to deal with this claim, to a certain extent by taking up the Gītā, their most beloved Upanishat, and by merely taking the various analogies used by Lord Kṛishṇa, we will show, whether we find among them or not, any of the favourite and hackneyed similes of this school, and whether the similes actually have any bearing on the special tenets of this school.

The first simile in the book occurs in chapter ii., 13.

"Just as in this body, childhood and youth and old age appertain to the embodied man, so also does it acquire another body."

This is a popular enough simile, and its meaning is plain but it cannot be construed as is done by Śaṅkara, that the soul undergoes no change or is not affected by the change of avastas or change of bodies; for it cannot be contended that the intelligence of Śaṅkara is in the same embryonic stage as that of a new born babe, and the denial of this would also militate against all our ideas of evolutionary progress and the necessity for undergoing many births. In the previous verse, Śrī Kṛishṇa postulated the existence of many souls, by asserting, neither did I not exist, nor thou, nor these rulers of men, and no one of us will ever hereafter cease to exist; "and he reiterates the same fact, in chapter iv, 5, where he alludes to his own former births, which fact is also mentioned by Śrī Kṛishṇa himself again in the Anuśāsana Parva and stated by Vyāsa in the Yuddha Parva. By 'I' and 'thou', and 'these', he clearly does not refer to their bodies as Śaṅkara interprets. The next figure occurs in verse 22 of the same chapter, "just as a man casts off worn-out clothes and puts on others which are new, so the soul casts off worn-out bodies and enters which are new." Similar instances are that of the serpent throwing off its skin, the mind passing from the conscious into the dream condition, and the Yogi into another body, which are given by Saint Meykaṇḍān. The next one occurs in verse 58, where the Sage withdrawing his senses from the objects of sense, is compared to the tortoise withdrawing its limbs, at the approach of anybody. The same simile occurs in *Tiruvaruḷpayan.*

In chapter iii., only one illustration occurs, and this in verse

38, which we have often quoted. "As fire is covered with smoke, as a mirror with dirt, as an embryo is enclosed in a womb, so this is covered with it" Śaṅkara explains, "as a bright fire is covered with a dark smoke *co-existent* with it..... ...so this is covered with desire."! The italics are ours. What 'this' and 'it' are, are seen to be, man and his wisdom-nature, Prakṛiti-guṇa—Rajas and Desire constraining one to the commission of sins. 'Constrained.' Śaṅkara explains as a servant by the King. Man is enslaved by his passion; his wisdom is such that it is deluded by unwisdom, ignorance (verse 40). Śaṅkara leaves these passages quietly enough but when explaining the similar passage (xiv, 5) "Sattva, Rajas, Tamas,—these three Guṇas, O mighty armed, born of Prakṛiti, *bind fast* in the body, the embodied, the indestructible," Śaṅkara says, "now one may ask: It has been said that the embodied is not tainted (xiii, 31). How then, on the contrary, is it said here that the (Guṇas) bind him? We have met this objection by adding '*as it were*'; thus 'they bind him as it were'." It would have been well for his reputation, if he had not raised the objection himself and tried to meet it in the way he has done. Why did not the Omniscient Lord Kṛishṇa himself add this 'as it were,' and leave these passages alone, apparently contradicting each other. In his explanation, he has omitted the force of '*fast*,' and he has forgotten '*Dragged and constrained*' and of the *co-existent darkness and delusion of the former passage and explanation*. There is one other passage relating to the soul and its bound condition namely verse 21 in chapter xiii itself. "Purusha, as seated in Prakṛiti, *experiences the qualities born of Prakṛiti*; "*attachment* to qualities is the cause of his birth in good and evil wombs." Lo, the Supreme Self, attaching itself to qualities born of Prakṛiti, constrained to commit sin, deluded by co-existent darkness, having to undergo births and deaths, and getting fettered and seeking salvation, and all this '*as it were*.'! What a precious excuse would it not prove, this '*as it were*,' to the murderer, the forger, the liar, the thief etc.? Besides, Śaṅkara identifies the *embodied* of verse 5, xiv, with the 'dweller in the body' in xiii, 31. Even so far as forms of expression go, they are not altogether the same thing. It may be noted that the expression 'embodied' is always used in describing the soul, Jīva, and never to denote God. Though God is seated in the hearts of all, He is the Soul of Souls, and Light of Lights. He can never be called the '*embodied*.' The expression '*embodied*' conveys itself the idea of attachment and bondage. Anybody reading verses 36 to 40 of chapter iii, and xiii, 21; xiv, 5, 20; and, verses iv, 14; ix, 9; xiii, 31 together, can fail to observe the utter contrast of the two entities; and we appeal to common sense if Śaṅkara's '*as it were*' will do away with this distinction and contrast. This distinction and contrast is brought out in different chapters, in the same chapter and in contiguous verses, (xv, 16, 17, 18) nay in the same verse (v. 15). The word '*another*' '*Anyatha*' is itself a technical word, as 'the inside of' '*Antas*' &c., and occurs in the Gītā in other places and in a number of Vedic texts to denote God Supreme as distinguished from the souls and the world, the entities admitted by Kapila Sāṅkhyas. Adhikaraṇas 4 to 9 of the Vedānta Sūtra, and the texts quoted therein which appear in Vol. II, *S.D.* pp. 73 to 79, fully bear out our thesis. The apparent confusion caused by both the human spirit and the Supreme Spirit being spoken of as dwelling in the human body is altogether removed by the Mantras which speak of 'the two birds entering into the cave,' 'Rudra, destroyer of pain enters into me,' 'He who abides in the *Vijñāna*,' 'He who abides in the *Ātman*,' 'higher than the high, higher than the imperishable,' (*cf.* xv, 18, Gītā). Leaving this subject for the present, we proceed. Chapter iv contains also only one simile, (37); "As kindled fire reduces fuel to ashes, O Arjuna; so does the wisdom fire reduce all Karma to ashes." The next illustration occurs in chapter v. 16, and is a very familiar one, that of Sun and darkness. "But in those in whom *unwisdom* is destroyed by the Wisdom of the Self, like the Sun the wisdom illuminates That Supreme." We have to read the previous passage together. "The Lord takes neither the evil nor the good deed of any; wisdom is enveloped by unwisdom; thereby mortals are deluded."

Here 'wisdom' clearly means Ātmā, Ātmajñān, Soul, Soul's intelligence. This intelligence is covered by ajñāna, unwisdom. As contrasted with ignorance-covered soul, there stands the Paramēšvara, untouched by evil, though dwelling in the body. How is the Soul's wisdom to get rid of the veil of unwisdom. If it was able to get rid of this wisdom by its own wisdom, it could have got rid of it the moment it wills so, and we will never hear of a soul in bondage. So the illustration explains how this is done. Unwisdom is destroyed not by the soul's wisdom (spoken of merely as wisdom) but by Ātmajñān, Brahmajñān, Šivajñān, leading to the perception and enjoyment of Šivānaṇda, as the darkness covering the individual eye, flees before the Rising Glory of the Effulgent Sun, and the Sun while it dispels the darkness, at the same time enables the eye to exercise its own power of seeing (soul's wisdom) and makes it see the Sun itself. The reader is requested to read the simile as explained, with Šaṅkara's own explanation and form his own conclusions.

"As a lamp in a sheltered spot does not flicker" is the simile of the Yogi in Divine Union. '*திரையற்ற நீர்போல் சிந்தை தெளிவார்.*" "Like the waveless sea-water, the jñāni attains clearness and calm" is another simile. The water and the lamp are by nature changeable, any little gust of wind (karmamala) can make the one flicker and the other form into ripples. But the Sun, or Ākāša (God) can neither flicker nor change. And this is exactly the simile in ix. 6. The simile in vii. 7 demands however our prior attention. "There is naught higher than I, O Dhanañjaya, in me, all this is woven as a row of gems on a string." Here the string is the Išvara, and the gems, other creatures and objects. Neither can the string become the gems, nor the gems the string; it only brings out the distinction of the lower and the higher Padārthas spoken of in verse 5 and how Išvara supports and upholds the whole universe, as a string does support the various gems.

The next simile already alluded to is in chapter ix, 6. "As the mighty wind moving everywhere rests in the Ākāśa, know thou that so do all beings rest in me." And Lord Kṛishṇa states the truth explained by this as the Kingly science, the Kingly secret, immediately comprehensible; and well may he say so, as this explains the true nature of advaita. The verses 4 and 5, have to be stated in full. "By me all this world is pervaded, my form unmanifested. All beings dwell in Me; and I do not dwell in them." "Nor do beings dwell in me, behold my Divine Yoga! Bearing the beings and not dwelling in them is my Self, the cause of beings." With this we might read also the similes in xiii, 32 and 33 "As the all-pervading Ākāśa is, by reason of its subtlety, never soiled, so God seated in the body is not soiled." "As the one Sun illumines all these worlds so does the Kshetri (not Kshetrajña) illumine all Kshetra," and the simile in xv. 8. "When the Lord (the jīva, the lord of the aggregate of the body and the rest—Śaṅkara) acquires a body and when he leaves it, he takes these and goes, as the wind takes scents from their seats." Here Parameśvara is compared to Ākāśa and the soul, jīva is compared to the wind; and the relation between God and Soul is the same relation as between Ākāśa and wind or things contained in Ākāśa. And what is this relation? Logicians and Siddhāntins call this relation as Vyāpaka Vyāpti Sambandam, container and contained. We explained in our article on 'Mind and Body' that this was not a very apt relation as it has reference to quantity, yet it is the best synonym and illustration of the *Advaita* relation, not Bêda (Madhva), not Abêda, not Bêdābêda (Rāmānuja), not Pariṇāma (Vallabha), not Vivarta (Śaṅkara), but Vyāpaka Vyāpti relation. Taking the five elements, and the order of their evolution and involution, it is seen, how all the four evolve from and resolve into Ākāśa. But earth is not water, nor water earth, water is not fire nor fire water, fire is not air, nor air fire, none of these is Ākāśa nor Ākāśa any of these. And yet all solids can be reduced to liquids, and liquids, into gaseous condition and all disappear into Ākāśa. The one lower is contained in the one higher, and all in Ākāśa, but Ākāśa cannot be said to be *contained* in any of these, though present in each. Each one is more subtle and more vast than the lower element, and Ākāśa is the most subtle and vastest and most pervasive and invisible ('my form unmanifested'). Ākāśa is not capable of any change, though the wind and water and fire and earth contained in it, can be contaminated by that to which it becomes attached. Wind carries off scents, and is subjected to all the forces of sun and moon. Water of the ocean becomes saltish, becomes frozen and becomes tempest-tossed. The lamp flickers and becomes smoky or bright, spreads a fragrant smell or otherwise, by the nature of the oil or wood it is burning. The very illustration of sea (space) water and winds, is used by Saint Meykaṇḍān in vii, 3-3 to illustrate ignorance not attaching itself to God but to the Soul. "Ignorance will not arise from God who is the True Intelligence, as it is Asat (like darkness before sun). The soul which is ever united to God is co-eternal with Him. The connection of ignorance with the soul is like the connexion of salt with the water of the sea." The word '*Ākāśa*' by the way is a technical word, like 'another,' 'antas,' 'jyotis' etc. and is a synonym for God (*vide* Vedānta Sūtras I, 1-22 and texts quoted thereunder and in the article 'House of God', 'Chit Ambara' in *The Siddhānta Dipikā*, Vol. I. p. 153.

The simile of streams and the sea occurs in xi, 28, to illustrate not the entering into moksha, but undergoing dissolution and death. The similes in xv, 1 and 2, the Ashvatha rooted above and spreading below, and in xvii, 61, that "the Lord dwells in the hearts of all beings (jīvas) O Arjuna, whirling by Māyā all beings (as if) mounted on a machine,' are the very last to be noted. These are nearly all the similes discovered in the Gītā, and do we not miss here nearly all the favourite similes of the Māyāvāda school, and if so, how was it the omniscient Lord Kṛishṇa failed to use any one of them?

"THE UNION OF INDIAN PHILOSOPHIES."

"All partitions of knowledge should be accepted, rather for lines to mark and distinguish than for sections to divide, and separate, so that the continuance and entirety of knowledge be preserved."—*Bacon.*

This saying of the greatest and wisest man of his age has now greater application in these days and in the land of Bharata, than it was in Bacon's own days. It brings out clearly enough what the purpose and utmost scope of all knowledge can be, and the true principle of toleration and liberalism that ought to guide us in our search after knowledge and the ascertainment of truth. Unless we carefully sift and see what each is, which is placed before us as knowledge and truth and for our acceptance, and mark their lines of similarity and difference, we will gradually emerge into a condition of intellectual colour-blindness; we cease to know what is colour and what is knowledge and what is truth; and the final result is an intellectual and moral atrophy and death. When in, therefore, seeking to avoid such a catastrophe and suicide, we indulge in moral and intellectual disquisitions, the caution has to be borne in mind also that such differences in thought should never divide people in their mutual sympathies and their aspirations in the pursuit of the common good. There is no necessity at all for angry discussions or acrimonious language. Whatever the capabilities of the human mind may be, which may yet remain hidden, yet the human mind is in a sense limited. The laws of thought can be determined positively, and they are as fixed as possible. We can only think on a particular question in a particular number of modes and no more, which in number, in their permutations and combinations, is fully exhibited. Difference in point of time, in clime and in nationality have not affected thought in the least. People have given expression to the same moral sentiments, the same feelings; and the same beauties in nature, and the similarities and the disparities that may exist, have been minutely noted by the poets of all lands. As such, it would not surprise us if the same theories about some of the grand problems of human existence have been discussed and held since man began to ask himself those questions, and for ages to come, also the same theories will endure. The same stories have been told and the same battles have been fought over and over again, but we note also that the honors of the war have often rested and followed the predilections of the people and the eminence of the story teller for the time being. Theories and Schools of Philosophy have had each its own hey-day of life and glory, and each has had its fall, and a subsequent resurrection. Even in the course of a single generation, we see a thinker who is accounted as the greatest Philosopher of the day, as one who has revolutionized all thought and philosophy, discounted very much and pale before the rising stars, whose fads take the popular fancy. By these observations, we do not mean to discourage all theorizing but only to show the uselessness of any dogmatism upon any points, and we, more than ever hold that all partitions of knowledge are useful and should be accepted for consideration. We have ventured upon these observations as in these days, and in this land, what is considered as knowledge and jñānam and philosophy is all seeking a narrow groove and partaking of an one-sided character, and thereby tending to obliterate thought, ignoring the thin and delicate partitions obtaining between different kinds of knowledge and the consequences could not altogether be beneficial. This process of ignorance and obliteration has been going on for some time past, and has been mainly assisted by false or queer notions of what constitutes toleration and universalism. The habit of trying to defend everything and explain away everything from one's own preconceived point of view is clearly a pernicious habit intellectually and morally. The vain search after a fancied unity has ended in a snare often-times; and a similar attempt now a days to reduce every view to one view is purely a procrustean method and fallacious in the extreme. Where is the good of such a procedure? There could neither be profit nor pleasure in seeking such similarities and uniformities in things that are essentially different. Will there be any good in such knowledge and reasoning as this? Black is the same as red, because both are colours. A crow is the same thing as ink, as both are black. Such attempted unification of knowledge is purely delusive and of no moment whatever. When again, commentators say and contend that a certain passage only bears out their interpretation and no other and that each one's own interpretation is the best, yet it must stand to common sense that these views could not all be correct nor could the author have intended all these meanings himself. Our Hindu commentators have often taken the greatest liberties with their author and they have often proved the worst offenders in forcing meanings upon words and passages which they and the context clearly show they do not bear. Yet we are often asked by some very tolerant people to accept every view as truth and to adopt their view as the greatest truth of all. As many of these ancient books are written and commented on in an obsolete tongue and which very few could find time and trouble to master, this delusion has been kept up by a few, and people have often been led by the use of certain charmed names. But the illusions begin to be dispelled, as we get to understand what the real text is, in plain literal language, thanks to the labours of European Scholars, and without encumbering ourselves as to what this commentator and that commentator says. And some of these scholars and translators have been quite honest and outspoken in what they think as the true view as borne out by the text. And no scholar has as yet come forward to controvert the view taken by Dr. Thibaut as to how far Ṣaṅkara's views are borne out by the text of the Vedānta Sūtras. We hope to discuss these, in course of time, as the translation of Śrīkaṇṭa Bhāshya, we are publishing proceeds apace, by comparing and contrasting these; it being only borne in mind now that Śrīkaṇṭha was the elder contemporary of Śaṅkara and the commentary of the former is the oldest of all those on the Vēdāṇta Sūtras now extant. We however propose to discuss in this article the questions in connection with the Bhagavad Gītā which Mr. Charles Johnstone has raised in his valuable paper we extracted in our last, from the *Madras Mail,* "The Union of Indian Philosophies." He puts himself the question to which of the three Schools of Indian Philosophy—Sāṅkhya, Yoga and Vēdāṇta, this book belongs, and says that his off-hand answer would be that it is undoubtedly one of the text books of the Vēdāṇta school, one of the weightiest of them; and yet, for all this, he thinks that there are other aspects of the Gītā, and that there is very much in them which belongs to the Sāṅkhya, and even more that is the property of the Yoga school; and he explains below how the Gītā beginning with a ballad on Kṛishṇa and Arjuna, gradually expanded itself into its present form, incorporating into itself all the teachings of the Upanishats and the teachings of the Sāṅkhya and Yoga schools, together with purāṇic episodes of the transfiguration, which in the opinion of this writer 'reproduces all that grim and gruesome ugliness of many armed Gods, with terrible teeth, which the Purāṇas have preserved most probably from the wild faiths of the dark aboriginals and demon worshippers of Southern India. We will deal with this last statement, which is a pure fiction later on; and the point we wish to draw particular attention to is this, that it has struck the writer as new and he gives it as new to the ignorant world that the Gītā does not represent only Vēdāṇta. To the Indian who knows anything of Indian Philosophy, this could not be news at all, as all the modern Indian schools, including Dvaita and Visishitādvaita and Suddhādvaita, claim the book as an authority and have commented on it too. But the European who has learnt to read the books of one school of philosophy only (all the books translated till now in English are books and commentaries of the Vêdānta School), knows nothing of any other school of philosophy existing in India and what authorities they had, and has gradually come to deny the existence of even such; and young Indians educated in English deriving all their pabulum from such source have also been ignorant of any other phases of Indian Philosophy. We well remember an Indian graduate in arts and law ask us, if there was any such thing as a special school of Śaiva Siddhāṇta Philosophy. Of course, he wears Vibhūti and Rudrāksha and worships Śiva and he knows that the Great Guru Śaṅkara was an avatār of Śiva Himself and all the English books that treated of Hinduism only talked of the Vêdāṇta Philosophy and his surprise and ignorance as such were quite natural. But as a result of the great upheaval that is going on, and the greater attention that is paid to the study of our philosophic and religious literature, even our own people have been slowly waking up to the truth of things. That stoutest adherent of Vêdāṇta, the editor of the *Light of the East* was the first to yield and to point out in his articles on the 'Ancient Śāṅkhya System' that the Gītā expounded also the Śāṅkhya system, though he tries to make an *olla podrida* of it by saying that Vêdāṇta is Śāṅkhya and Śāṅkhya is Vêdāṇta—that the Gītā does not postulate many Purushas (souls). A Madras Professor declared in the Pachaiyappa's Hall that in some of the special doctrines of the Vêdāṇta, such as the doctrine of Māyā, and the identity of the human Soul and the Supreme Soul etc., the Gītā is silent. And our brother of the *Brahmavādin* also affirms in his editorial on 'Māyā,' dated 15th August 1896, after stating that the *word Māyā scarcely occurs in the principal upanishats*, and where it does occur, it seems to be used mostly in the old Vêdic sense of power or creative power, declares, that "on the whole the attitude of the Bhagavad Gītā towards Māyā is similar to that of the Upanishats; and it is rather difficult to evolve out of it the later Vêdāṇtic sense," of illusion, or delusion.

And when it is admitted also that the Buddhists were the first to develope the Māyā theory of illusory nothings, who on that account were called Māyāvādins by the other Hindus, and that Śaṅkara only refined this idea, meaning an illusory nothing, into meaning a phenomenal something, though some of his later followers even went so far as to forget Śaṅkara's teaching as to revert to the Buddhist idea of a blank negation and hence were called cryto-Bhuddhists (Prachchanna Bhaudhas), (*vide* p. 297-Vol. *Brahmavādin* and Max Muller's lectures on Vēdāṇta), and our brother's opinion being merely that in the Vēdas and Upanishats and Gītā, we have merely the germs of the later system of thought out of which was elaborated the Vēdāṇtic theory of Māyā,—a process of double distillation—the point is even worthwhile considering whether Gītā has got anything to do with the Vēdāṇta at all. And it can also be positively proved that it has no such connexion. To day we venture to go no further than what is admitted by the other side that Gītā contains the exposition of other schools of philosophy which according to Mr. Charles Johnstone, postulates the reality and eternality of matter (Prakṛiti) and spirit (Purusha) and that the Purushas are without number and that there is one Supreme Spirit different from the souls.

In understanding the word Śāṅkhya as used in the Gītā our writer falls into a mistake like many others that it means the Philosophy as expounded in the Śāṅkhya School of Philosophy which is attributed to the Sage Kabila. We have shown in our article on 'Another Side' (vide pp. 21 to 34) that it meant no such thing, that it meant merely, a theory or a system or a philosophy or knowledge and that the Gītā instead of having anything to do with Kabila's Śāṅkhya distinctly repudiates it and goes on to postutate its own differences, and this we showed by quoting several passages and that the proper name of the system evolved in the Gītā is 'Sēshvara Śāṅkhya,' as distinguished from Nirēshvara Śāṅkhya of Kabila. To say that this philosophy or the other grew out of this or that is pure fallacy, unless we have real historical evidences about it. We might propound a riddle whether Theism or Atheism was first and which of these rose out of the other. You might argue that Theism was next and grew out of Atheism, as materialists (Lokāyitas) only admit the eternality of matter and would not admit of the existence of any other padārtha. And you might say they came next because they denied the existence of God admitted by Theists. Yet such is the argument covered up in statements frequently made that, of the six systems of Philosophy, one was first and the other arose out of it. They do not at all refer to any historical growth or chronological order. Even in the days of Rig Vēda they believed in Gods and in one God, and we presume there were unbelievers also. Mr. Johnstone is also wrong in saying that the postulate of three powers of nature—we presume he means Satva, Rajas and Tamas—is peculiar to the Śāṅkhya, as also the divisions of Jñātha, Jñēyam and Jñānam. We fail to understand what he means by Śāṅkhya Yōga reconciler. Śāṅkhya, if Kabila's (Pure atheism) postulated no God and Yōga postulated God. And is there any meaning where one talks of a book reconciling Atheism and Theism? And of course, another writer talks similarly of Vēdānta-Śāṅkhya reconciler. In every school there are certain postulates or padārthas which are affirmed and some which are denied. Some postulate only one padārtha, some two, some three and some none, and are we to talk of reconciling these, one with the other, simply because one of the postulates, very often things and their qualities which could not be denied by any one, is common to all or some? This is often the kind of writing that passes for sound knowledge and liberalism and universal philosophy. We dare say the Vēdāṇta as understood by Śaṅkara was not even in existence at the time of the battle of Kurukshetra nor was it probably known to the writer of the Mahābhārata and Gītā, in his days whenever he wrote it. The whole Mahābhārata has to be studied to know what the teaching of Gītā is and in its historical surroundings. The phrase '*Śaṅkhya and Yōga*' is used throughout the Mahābhārata as often as possible and in such conjunctions where the meaning is unmistakeable as referring to the postulate of a Supreme Being.* If Kabila † is praised by Krishṇa as the greatest among sages, it is because the same book Mahābhārata shows elsewhere, how Kabila from being an atheist was afterwards converted to the knowledge of God, and as all such converts, he obtained greater glorification at the hand of his quandom opponents. And as we have shown elsewhere that the Gītā is a clear controversial treatise, he could not do better than cite Kabila himself, who gave up his former faith, in refutation of the school of Atheistic Śāṅkhya. Scholars have observed how the writer of the *Uttara Mīmāmsa Sārīraka Sūtras* spends all his energy and skill in refuting the Śāṅkhya and only casually notices the other schools, it being the reason that in the days of Vyāsa and Krishṇa the Atheistic Śāṅkhya school was the most predominant, in the same way as in later times, Buddhism and Jainism came to have a larger share of

---

* *cf.* The following passages in the Anuśāsana Parva.

"I seek the protection of Him whom the *Śānkhyās describe* and the *Yogins think* of as the Supreme, the foremost, the Purusha, the Pervader of all things and the Master of all existent objects" &c. &c.

"I solicit boons from Him who cannot be comprehended by argument, who represents the object of the *Śāṅkhya* and the *Yoga systems of Philosophy* and who transcends all things, and whom all persons conversant with the topics of enquiry worship and adore."

"The which is Supreme Brahman, that which is the highest entity, that which is the end of both the Śāṅkhyas and the Yogins, is without doubt identical with thee."

† *cf.* The same Parva pp. 140 and 141. P. C. Roy's edition.

"After this, Kabila, who promulgated the doctrines that go by the name of Śāṅkhya, and who is honoured by the gods themselves said—I adored Bhava with great devotion for many lives together. The illustrious deity at last became gratified with me and gave me knowledge that is capable of aiding the acquirer in getting over rebirth."

The Temple at the foot of Tirupati hill is called Kabilêśvara and is the place where tradition says the sage worshipped Bhava or Śiva.

treatment in the hands of Hindu saints and writers. It has also to be noticed that the word Vêdāṇta nowhere occurs in the Gītā or other Upanishats as meaning Śaṅkara's system and the *Brahmavādin* has, as such, taken a broader platform, in properly including under the term, both Advaita of Śaṅkara, the Dvaita and Viśishtādvaita systems and we now hear of Advaita Vêdāṇta, Dvaita Vêdāṇta &c., though the Western habit of calling Śaṅkara's system as Vêdāṇta is still used confusingly enough by people, as in the passage we quoted above from the *Brahmavādin 'the later Vêdāntic sense.'* (The other Indian schools, be it noted, do not indeed call Śaṅkara's system Vêdāṇta or Advaita but have other names for it).

Mr. Johnstone no doubt says that Kṛishṇa quotes directly from many Upanishats (one writer is carried away by his veneration for Gītā to say that the Upanishats quote from the Gītā!) and a number of verses, notably in the second book (we should like to know very much what they are), which have the true ring of the old sacred teachings, and yet art not in them (in which?) as they now stand. And then he airs his theory that Vêdāṇta is the peculiar birth-right of the Kshatriyas and not of Brāhmans. The reason why this unacknowledged quota tions in the Gītā and other similar books are found, is that every Brāhman in the olden days had committed to memory the whole of the Vedas and Vêdāṇta (Upanishats) and as such when they wrote and when they spoke, these old thoughts and verses very naturally flowed from their pen and their mouths,* and it is never the habit of the Indian scholar to quote his authority, chapter and verse. And we come to the fact that the whole of the chapters 9, 10 and 11 of the Gītā is a mere reproduction and a short abstract of that central portion of the whole Vedas, called the *Śatarudriya* of the Yajur Vêda. What is called transfiguration is the *Viśvasvarūpa Darśana,* or the

* We knew a Tamiḻ Scholar who would gossip for hours together, the whole conversation interlarded with quotations from *Kuṟaḷ and Nālaḍiyār* and an ordinary listener could not recognize that he was quoting at all.

vision of the lord as the All, as manifested in the whole universe. One and all, the objects in the whole universe, good, bad, sat, asat, high and low, animate, inanimate are all named in succession and God is identified with all these and it is pointed out that He is not all these and above all these, "the soul of all things, the creator of all things, the pervader of all things" (*Viśvātmanê Viśva sṛijc viśvam avṛitya tishṭhatê.*) This *Śatarudriyam** ought to be known to every Brāhman more or less and it is the portion of the Vêdas which is recited in the temples every day. The praise of the *Śatarudriyam* occurs throughout the Mahābhārata, and most in Droṇa and Anuśāsana Parvas, and these parvas dealing as they do with various visions of God (Viśvasvarūpa Darśana) as granted to Rishis, Upamanyu, Vyāsa, Nārada, Kabila, and Kṛishṇa himself on other occasions, contain the similar reproductions of the *Śatarudriya* as in chapters 9 to 11 of the Gītā. What is more important to be noted is that in the case of Kṛishṇa, he had got the teaching from Upamanyu Maharishi, and after initiation (Dīkshā) into this mystery teaching and performance of tapas, he gets to see the *vision* himself, and he describes it as follows (*vide* page 87 to 91 Anuśāsanaparva. P. C. Roy's translation).

"The hair on my head, O son of Kuṇti, stood on its end, and my eyes expanded with wonder upon beholding Hara, the refuge of all the deities and the dispeller of all their griefs. ....Before me that Lord of all the Gods, *viz.*, Sarva, appeared seated in all his glory. Seeing that Iśāna had showed Himself to me by being seated in glory before my eyes, the whole universe, with Prajāpati to Iṇdra, looked at me. I, however, had not the power to look at Mahādêva. The great Deity then addressed me saying, "Behold, O Krishṇa and speak to me. Thou hast adored me hundreds and thousands of times.

* Śri Kṛishṇa himself says "Hear from me, O King, the *śatarudriya*, which, when risen in the morning, I repeat with joined hands. The great devotee, Prajāpati created that prayer at the end of his austerity." Anuśāsana Parva, chapter V.

There is no one in the three worlds that is dearer to me than thou." And the praise by Kṛishṇa which follows is almost what Arjuna himself hymned about Kṛishṇa. Vyāsa meeting Asvaththāma after his final defeat tells him also that Kṛishṇa and Arjuna had worshipped the Lord hundreds and thousands of times. And does not this explain Krishṇa's own words in the Gītā that he and Arjuna had innumerable births (iv. 5).

What we wish to point out is that this trasfiguration scene with its gruesome description which Mr. Jhonstone wants to trace to *Purāṇic* legends preserved from South Indian aborigines is, by express text and by the authority of Kṛishna himself traced to the second Vēda ; and to say that the Yajur Vēda, the central portion* of this Vēda, should copy the holiest portion of the whole Vēdas, as believed by the contemporaries and predecessors of Kṛishṇa, from the demonology of the South Indians, could only be a parody of truth ; and if this be true, this demonology of the South Indians, instead of a thing being repugnant must have been glorious indeed, to be copied by the *Brahmavādins* of Yajur Vēda days. Western Scholars have only misread and misunderstood the nature of this transfiguration and *Viśvarūpa* mystery, as they have misread the mystic Personality of Rudra or Śiva Himself, whose ideal these scholars say, was also copied from the aborigines. To the credit of Mrs. Besant, be it said, she has understood both these mysteries better than any other European. Śiva's whole personality, with his eight forms, Ashtamuhūrtams (see page 220 of *the Siddhānta*

---

* It is believed and it is a fact that the *Pañchātchara* Mantra of the modern Hinduism is found in the very middle of the three Vēdas, Rig, Yajur and Sāman, which fact is set forth in the following Tamiḻ verse.

> மும்மறையுள் நடுமறையின் முனிவிலெழு காண்டத்தில்
> செம்மைதரும் நடுக்காண்டம் சேர்ந்தஎழு சங்கிதையின்
> அம்மநடுச் சங்கிதையின் ஆதியீ றொழித்திநடுப்
> பொம்மலுற அமர்மனுவின் பொருளாவான் எவன் மைந்தா.

cf. The whole śatarudriya passage quoted in sec. II. chap III. vol. vi. Muir's sanskrit texts.

Dipikā Vol. I, for full description) earth, fire, air etc., and his three eyes, as Sōma, Sūrya and Agni, and His Head as Ākāśa, and his eight arms as the eight cardinal points, his feet as *Padala*, and the sky as his garment, Digambara, and himself, a *Nirvāni* and living in cemeteries and yet with his Śakti, Umā, a Yōgi yet a Bhōgi, all these give a conception of the supreme Majesty of the Supreme Being which, no doubt, nobody can look up in the face. Does any ordinary person dare to look up nature's secrets and nature's ways in the process of destruction and creation and sustentation? If so, he will be a bold man, a great man. Strip nature of its outside smooth and fragrant cloak and what do you see inside? The picture is ugly, dirty and gruesome. Yet the scientist perceives all this with perfect equanimity, nay with very great pleasure. A small drop of water discloses to the microscopic examination multitudes of living germs, and these fight with one another, devour each other with great avidity. We drink the water. Plants drink up the water. Animals eat the plants, insects and animals devour one another. Man, the greatest monster, devours all. There is thus constant struggle of life and death going on in nature. And when this nature is, as thus, exposed to view in the transfiguration, and Arjuna sees before him this havoc, in the Person of the Supreme as the Destroyer, ('Devourer' of Katha Upanishat) (and be it remembered that this Visvasvarūpa Darsan is more gruesome in Gītā no doubt, than similar ones presented in the *Anuśāsana Parva*, as Kṛishṇa's whole burden of advice in the Gītā is simply to force Arjuna to fight and kill his foes, and to conquer his repugnance), a remark that it is derived from Purāṇic legends and aboriginal practices is altogether out of place. We hope to pursue this subject on a future occasion.

THE UNION OF INDIAN PHILOSOPHIES.*

In old India, as elsewhere, the minds of the leading men were of many complexions ; so that we have great idealists, great thinkers of the atomic school, great nihilists, and great preachers of doctrines wholly agnostic. It is the custom to gather a certain group of these teachings together, with the title of the Six Philosophies ; while all others, considered as heterodox, are outside the pale of sympathy, and, therefore, to be ignored. Chiefest among the outcast philosophies is the doctrine of Prince Siddhārta, called also Šākya Muni, and Gautama Buddha. Of the others, it would be hard to find many students of more than three—namely, the Vêdânta, Šākya, and Yōga : while the Vaišēshika, Nyāya, and first Mīmāmsa are little more than a name, even to professed students of Indian thought. They have their followers, doubtless ; but there has not been found one among them of such mental force as to give them a modern expression, or to show that they bear any message to the modern world. We shall speak, here, only of the three most popular among the orthodox schools : and this chiefly in connection with a single noteworthy book,— the Bhagavat Gītā, or "Songs of the Master." If we were asked, off hand, to which of the three schools the Bhagavat Gītā belonged, we should most likely answer, off-hand, that it was, undoubtedly a text-book of the Vêdânta, and indeed one of the weightiest works of the Vêdânta School. For is it not commented on by the Great Šankara, chiefest light of the Vêdânta, and does he not quote from it as of divine authority, a fully inspired scripture ?

Yet, for all this, I think there are other aspects of the Bhagavat Gītā which show that this answer is too simple ; and that, while the Songs of the Master undoubtedly form a bulwark of Vêdântic orthodoxy, there is very much in them which belongs to the Sānkhya, and even more that is the property of the Yōga School. It seems pretty certain that the Bhagavat Gītā has grown up gradually, beginning with a ballad on Kṛishṇa and Arjuna, much of which is preserved in the first book, and which suggests all through, the burden of Kṛishṇa's admonition : Therefore fight, Oh son of Kunti ! It seems likely that the next element in the structure of the Bhagavat Gītā is drawn from the great Upanishats, the Katha Upanishat more especially. And this suggests a very interesting

* Extract from the *Madras Mail*, 23rd December 1897 by Charles Johnston, M.R.A.S., B.C.S., RET.

thought; side by side with many direct quotations from the Upanishats in our possession, there are a number of verses, notably in the second book, which have the true ring of the old sacred teachings, and yet are not in them as they now stand. And this suggests that we have only fragments; that there was once much more, in the form of verses and stories, which made up the mystery teaching of the Rājput Kings,—that secret doctrine spoken of so clearly in the Upanishats themselves as the jealously guarded possession of Kshatriya race. The fourth book of the Bhagavat Gītā fully endorses this idea, since Kṛishṇa traces his doctrine back through the Rajput sages to the solar King, Ikshvāku, to Manu, the Kshatriya, and finally to the sun, the genius of the Rājput race. And this, in connection with that teaching of successive re-births, which, we know from the two greatest Upanishats, was the central point of the royal doctrine. So we are inclined to suggest that we have in many verses of the Bhagavat Gītā, additional portions of the old mystery doctrine, parts of which form the great Upanishats. And it is quite credible that Krishṇa,— whom we believe to be as truly historical as Julius Cæsar,—as an initiate in these doctrines did actually quote to Arjuna a series of verses from the mystery teaching, and that these verses are faithfully preserved for us to the present day. However that may be, there the verses are: a series of verses from the Upanishats, had a second series, entirely resembling these in style and thought. As a third element in the Bhagavat Gītā we have the Purāṇic episode of the transfiguration, and, we must say, it reproduces all that grim and gruesome ugliness of many armed gods, with terrible teeth, which the purāṇas have preserved most probably from the wild faiths of the dark aboriginals and demon worshippers of Southern India.

Finally, there is a very important element, into the midst of which the episode of the transfiguration is forcibly wedged; and of this element we shall more especially speak. It consists of the characteristic Sāṅkhya doctrine of the three potencies of Nature completely developed along physical, mental, and moral lines. A word about this doctrine, which we may, with great likelihood, refer to Kapila himself, the founder of the School. His conception seems to be this; there is the consciousness in us, the spirit, the perceiver: and, over against this there is Nature, the manifested world. This duality of subject and object has great gulf fixed between its two elements, whose characteristics, wholly and irreconcilably opposed. Of the subject, the spirit, consciousness, we can only say that it perceives. To predicate of consciousness any characteristic drawn from our experience of objects, such for instance as mortality, beginning or end, is to be guilty of a cardinal error. Of Nature, the opposite element of existence, Kapila's teaching, it seems, was something like this; Nature may be divided into three elements: the substance of phenomena; the force of phenomena; and thirdly the dark space or void, in which phenomena take place. Take a simple illustration. The observer, with closed eyes, is the spirit or consciousness, not yet involved in Nature. He opens his eyes, and, instead of the dark space, or void, sees the world of visible objects, or substance, and there is perpetual movement among the things thus observed. This is force. Thus we have the three elements of Nature,—the three qualities, as they are generally called,—which make up the central idea of Kapila's cosmic system, and which are not to be found, in that shape, in any of the oldest Upanishats: they are, therefore, no part of the Vêdânta, properly so called, but distinctively Sāṅkhya teachings. Now, these distinctive teachings form a very important part of the Bhagavat Gītā, and are woven into many passages, besides the chief passages already referred to, in the seventeenth and eighteenth books. Thus, as early as the second book, we have a reference to the Sāṅkhya teachings: "The Vêdas have the three Nature-powers as their object; but thou, Arjuna become free from the three powers." It is needless to quote the many passages that refer to the same teaching; to the divisions of the knower, the knowing, the known; thè doer, the doing, the deed; the gift, the giving, the giver; and so forth, according to the three-Nature-powers. All this is carried out with much intellectual skill, and dialectic acumen: but it has nothing in the world to do with the main motive of the book,—Arjuna's action under the calamity of civil war; and Krishṇa's assertion of the soul, as the solution of Arjuna's dilemma.

There is also a very important element in the Bhagavat Gītā, equally characteristic of the Yôga school, whose final exponent, though not, in all probability, its founder, was Patañjali, the author of the commentary on Pāṇini's grammar, who lived, it is believed, some three centuries before our era. We do not regard the directions as to choosing a lonely place, a fawn-skin seat, over sprinkled kusha grass, and the fixing of the attention on the tip of the nose, as necesssrily, or most characteristically belonging to the Yôga school, though they are undoubtedly important elements in that teaching. What seems more vital is the moral concept of action with disinterestedness, of action without atttachment, according to the primary motion of the will; this teaching, it seems to us, is at once characteristic of the Yôga system, and foreign to the spirit of the Upanishats; for the Upanishats, so high is their ideal, are not greatly concerned with fallen man or the means of his redemption. They look on man as an immortal spirit, already free and mighty, anu therefore needing no redemption. Man, needing to be redeemed, is a later thought; one springing from a more self-conscious age.

Now the connection of this thought with the Sāṅkhya philosophy is obvious. It regards man, the spirit, as ensnared by Nature, and consequently as needing release and, for the Sāṅkhya school, this release comes through an effort of intellectual insight. But this concept, man saved by intellect, is essentially untrue to life, where man lives not by intellect alone, or even chiefly, but by the will; and it became necessary, granting our fall, to find a way of salvation, of redemption through the will. This way is the Yōga philosophy. It is the natural counterpart and completion of the Sāṅkhya and has always been so regarded, The pure spirit of the over-intellectual Sāṅkhya becomes Lord of the more religious Yoga;—using religion in the sense of redemption to the will. But, though thus complementary, the two systems might easily come to be considered as opposing each other; and it seems to be part of the mission of the Bhagavat Gītā—or rather, of certain passages forcibly imported into it, to reconcile the Sāṅkhya and the Yoga once for all, and to blend these two with the Vēdānta.

We need only quote two passages, which are obviously due to the Sāṅkhya—Yōga reconciler. The first is dragged into the middle of the following sentence, and evidently has no true place there: "If slain, thou shalt attain to heaven; or conquering, thou shalt inherit the land. Therefore rise, son of Kunti, firmly resolved for the fight. Holding as equal, good and ill-fortune, gain and loss, victory and defeat, gird thyself for the fight, and thou shall not incur sin. And thus there shall be no loss of ground, nor does any defeat exist; a little of this law saves from great fear;"—the law, namely, that the slain in battle go to Paradise. Now into the midst of this complete and continuous passage has been inserted this verse: "This understanding is declared according to Sāṅkhya; hear it now, according to Yoga." Needless to say, the last part of it has as little to do with the Yoga philosophy as the first has with the Sāṅkhya. Then again, in the next book, the third: "Two rules are laid down by me: salvation by intellect for the Sāṅkhya; salvation by works for the followers of Yoga." So that one part of the Bhagavat Gītā is devoted to the reconciliation of these two complementary though rival schools.

TREE OF KNOWLEDGE OF GOOD AND EVIL.

The following passages in the book of Genesis have reference to the subject in hand. " And out of the ground made the Lord God to grow every tree that is pleasant to the sight, and good for food; *the tree of life* also in the midst of the Garden, and *the tree of knowledge of good and evil*" (ii. 9). " And the Lord God commanded the man saying, ' Of every tree of the garden thou mayest freely eat. But of the tree of knowledge of good and evil *thou shalt not eat of it*: for in the day that *thou eatest thereof thou shalt surely die*" (ii. 16 and 17). " And they were both naked, the man and his wife, and were not ashamed" (ii. 25). " And the serpent said unto the woman " Ye shall not surely die. For God doth know that in the day ye eat thereof, your eyes shall be opened and ye shall be as Gods, knowing good and evil. And when the woman *saw the tree was good for food*, that it *was pleasant to the eyes*, *a tree to be desired to make one wise*, she took of the fruit thereof and did eat, and gave also unto her husband with her, and he did eat. And the eyes of them both were opened and they knew that they were naked." (iii. 4 to 7). " Unto the woman he said, I will greatly multiply thy sorrow and thy conception " " In sorrow shalt thou eat of it all the days of thy life." (iii. 16 and 17). " And the Lord God said, Behold the man is become as one of us to know good and evil; and now lest he put forth his hand and take also of the tree of life, and eat and live for ever. Therefore the Lord God sent him from the Garden of Eden (iii. 22 and 23).

And now we ask what are we to understand by this story? Are we to take it literally, as many would suggest, or are we to leave it as a mystery too deep for words to explain? And yet this is the mystery of mysteries, the original mystery by which we came to be born and to die. If we can here get a clue to our birth and death, can we not thereby unravel secrets by which we can surely prevent our death and rebirth, and gain everlasting life. And surely there must be an explanation for the words, Tree of life, and Tree of knowledge of good and evil, cannot be mistaken in their real import, and these cannot be identified with any earthly tree actually in existence. The Tree here is clearly a metaphor signifying the soul's True Being in freedom (moksha) and its false life in Bhaṇda, the light and shadow of our human existence. As bound up in the world the sum of our existence consists in our knowledge of likes and dislikes, of what conduces to our pleasure and what gives us pain, and our memory of both, and as Doctor Bain would define it, the sense of similarity and of difference and retentiveness. That is to say, our human knowledge is built up from our very birth, of a series of acts and experiences which give us pleasure or pain, or make us indifferent, and our sense of them, and Desire and Will are also slowly built up. The greater the pleasure we fancy a certain act or experience gives us, the more do we *desire* its repetition or continuance; the greater the pain we apprehend from an act, the more do we hate its repetition or continuance. But it happens also the greater the pleasure or the pain, the more prolonged its continuance, oftener it is repeated, the pleasure itself palls and we grow callous to the pain. Life may therefore be divided into a series of acts, or a sequence of them, one flowing from another, and close on each, each yielding a certain result or experience or fruit, be it pleasure or pain, good or evil. And God's injunction was that we should not eat the fruit of the knowledge of good and evil or experience the pleasure or pain which will flow from our acts of good and evil, in this tree of wordly life.

And one can ask, why it is we shonld not seek the bent of our inclination, why we should not secure the good in life, and the pleasure and happiness thereof, and avoid the evil, and the pain and suffering thereof, and the best knowledge that will secure to us to attain these ends? And God's injunction appears stranger, when it is seen that there is not only an injunction not to try to know the evil, but that there is also an injunction that we sholud not know the good. And to know the good, if not to know the evil, must at least appear to us to be our duty. And all our moral text books and lessons and sermons are intended to teach us this duty. And the fruits or acts resulting from our knowledge of both good and bad are both forbidden to man, and the punishment for disobeying this Law or Word of God is said to be death itself with the further penalty of being shut out of partaking of the ever lasting Tree of Life.

And of course there may be no wrong in our *knowing* what is good for *us* and what is bad and in our *desiring* to seek the one and avoiding the other, provided we *can know* what is *really* good and what is bad, provided we can get what we *desire* and provided also that we *can know* what it is that we mean by the 'us' or 'I'. Do all persons understand what will *really* bring them good and what will bring them evil? Is every act which gives pleasure at once a good, and every act which gives pain a wrong? When the child cries for sweets, and struggles hard against swallowing a bitter potion, is it really seeking its good and avoiding evil? When the school-boy chafes under school-discipline and desires to sow his own wild oats, is he really avoiding pain and seeking pleasure? Does the man of the world when he seeks power and pelf and resorts to all sorts of ways to gain that end really seek his own good, or when he chafes in a prison as a result of his previous actions, does he think that it is for his good? And then again, when we seek pleasure and beyond our means, does not that really bring us suffering? More than all, how many of us do rightly understand the 'I' and to which we want to minister? To the great majority, the 'I' means nothing more than the bare body, and the external senses, and is not the whole world engaged most strenuously in satisfying their bodily wants and appetites? How many are there who understand that they have a moral nature, how many, that they have a spiritual nature? Even when we do know that we have a moral nature and a spiritual nature, how many do try to act up to the requirements of their moral and spiritual nature, being more or less dragged and constrained by their worldly *desire!* In our ideas of good and bad, don't we confound our several natures, don't we confound what is good for the soul with what is good for the body? To most of us, the world and our belly are our God and nothing more.

Whence therefore this difference in people's likes and dislikes, whence their disability to suit means to ends, and their ignorance of their real selves, and mistaking of one for another? Does it not show that there is an original want of understanding, a want of power, and a want of real knowledge, a serious defect in all sorts and conditions of men? And when, from want of this knowledge, the first wrong step is taken, the first mistake is made, does it not lead to a series of falls, and succession of mistakes, and does not man commit more mistakes in his ignorance when he tries to rectify one error than when he leaves it alone?

We do not propose to answer the question, whence was this defect or ignorance in man, and what is its nature etc., For our present purpose, it is enough to know and recognize that this defect is in us in one and all; that we are all full of faults and liable to err at every step. And these defects were in Eve, the original woman, typical of the lower; man (Adam meaning the Higher life of man, pulled down by the lower part of him.) And when Eve saw the *tree was good for food,* that is to say she only thought of what would give pleasure to her body and satisfy her appetite, regardless of the consequences, just as a child wants to snatch the sweets from a confectioner's shop. She saw that *it was pleasant to the eyes:* that is to say she only mistook what was not good as good * She saw it was

* பொருளல்லவற்றைப் பொருளென்றுணரும்
மருளானாம் மாணாப்பிறப்பு.

The delusion whereby men deem that the truth which is not,
That is the cause of hapless birth.

a tree *to be desired to make one wise*.* And when that most learned of the divines, full of his own knowledge and wisdom, wanted St. Meykaṇḍān to inform him of the nature of Āṇava or Ahankāra or Egoism, what was the reply he had got? The True Seer replied that the Āṇava or Ignorance or Egoism stood before him disclosed. One *desires to be wise*, as Eve desired, then learns much and thinks himself wise, and this is the highest type of Egoism or Ignorance.

So that it is clear that before Eve ate the forbidden fruit, she was ignorant and filled with Egoism or Āṇava. To say that the serpent or the Devil misled her is to carry it one step behind. If she was wise she would not have been misled by the wiles of the tempter. If she knew beforehand what was to befall her, she would not have yielded to the words of the serpent, and disobeyed the word of God. She had as such no knowledge and no forethought. She was weak and ignorant even before the temptation. Being ignorant and weak, the moment the fruits of pleasure and pain were placed before her, she was dazzled, she was attracted, she seized them at once. And the devil, vanishes from the scene. The devil, we take it, merely represents this inherent weakness or ignorance or Āṇava in man and nothing more. Adam and Eve typify the mere babes of human creation. There is something in the merest babe which makes it desire to live, and learn and know. It tries to put everything into its mouth whether a piece of bread or a piece of chalk, and it wants to feel the anotomy of every plaything it handles by pulling it to pieces. Can any amount of warning and advice prevent the baby from touching the flame of a burning candle? The loving parent no doubt gives the warning 'Don't touch, don't touch,' but the advice is all useless and the wise father usually allows it to get a singeing, enough for it to know the good and evil, the pain and pleasure thereof; and he takes care that the baby is not burnt. Throw

* அவா வென்ப வெல்லா உயிர்க்கு மெஞ்ஞான்றும்
தவாப்பிறப்பீனும் வித்து

a brilliantly coloured and glowing fruit of the strychnine tree, the baby will seize it and try to bite it, but the ever watchful father will take care to see that the baby does not swallow it. It is our love that prompts us to give instruction, advice, warning, and even chastisement, but all this will be thrown away if the soil itself is not good. And in our wisdom we recognise that all this is of no use, that the wayward child should be allowed to gain peace by tasting the bitterness "of sorrow in all the days of its life." So too, the All-loving Father in Heaven told Adam and Eve what was not good for them, not to taste or desire the fruits of both good and bad acts, i. e, the pleasures and pains of this world. But they would not bear it in mind nor listen. Did not God know that they would be tempted, and did he try to save them from the Devil ? No; he permitted them to be tempted. Nay, he willed them to taste the fruit as a father would take a child to touch ever so slighty the candle-flame. "He whom the Lord loveth he chasteneth," "நல்லபரமசிவன் நம்மை வருத்துவது கொல்லவல, பொல்லாக்குணம் போக்க". And the misery and suffering that flow from our tasting of the fruit of good and evil acts are merely for our chastening, and purification, and this can only be done in this existence and no other; and the whole purpose and scheme of creation becomes thus evident. (Śivajñānabodha first Sūtra 'மலத்துளதாம்'.) It is for the purpose of removing this defect or weakness or Āṇava or egoism in man that this life is given him, and every means which a loving Father can devise for his betterment is afforded him. But all such means do not influence each individual in the same way. The best of education, the purest of home influence, and the holiest of associations seem, actually thrown away on some people. They have a bent of their own, their own individuality, and this thrusts itself out under all shades and under all cloaks. This contradicts with the theory that human mind is a mere *tabula rasa*. Youth and white paper take impressions as the saying goes. Evolutionists seek heredity to explain it. But it is now acknowledged that heredity does not explain all. The most model of parents have begotten the most vicious of children. Neither the Theologians of the west nor their scientist brethren have explained this aspect of the case, and we must confess this as the only one weak point in modern Christianity which their best defenders have not been able to strengthen. It will not require much thought to see that this story of man's first disobedience, and of his tasting the fruit of that Forbidden tree is nothing more than the Doctrine of Karma as told by all the Indian schools of Philosophy, including the Buddhists.

The knowledge of good and evil is good and bad Karma, நல்வினை and தீவினை and the fruits thereof are the pleasures and pains derived from such acts. There is no harm in performing good and bad acts, but these acts should not be performed for the sake of the fruits, out of selfish desire or dislike. And the moment these are performed with such desire, the thirst (அவா Trishna-Tanha) after such enjoyment increases, and the bonds of wordly existence are more and more made fast. The fruits of both are bad, and are compared to gold and iron-fetters and St. Tiruvaḷḷuvar calls them its இருள்சேர் இருவினை *i. e.*, "the two kinds of Karma, darkness covered." It is significant how in the Indian Philosophic Schools the phrase வினைப்பயன் நுகர்தல் meaning eating the fruits of Karma is the commonest expression and one which exactly corresponds to the eating of the Forbidden fruit of good and evil in the Biblical accounts. More than this, the tree of good and evil fruits, one tree out of which both fruits are produced, is a common figure in the Upanishats and in the Tamiḻ Siddhāṉta works.

The following passages in Muṇḍaka Upanishat iii. 1 to 4 which are repeated in the Katha and Švetāšvatra Upanishats and are derived from the Rigveda, explain the whole fully.

1. Two birds, inseparable friends, cling to the same tree; one of them eats the sweet fruit, and *the other* looks on without eating,

2. On the same tree, man (*anîsa*) sits grieving, immersed by his own impotence. But when he sees *the other* Lord (Īša) contented and knows His glory, then his grief passes away,

3. When the seer sees the brilliant Maker and Lord of the world, and himself as in the womb of God then he is wise, and *shaking off good and evil*, he reaches the Highest oneness, free from passions.

4. Life sure is He who flames through all creation. The wise man knowing Him reaches of naught else. He sports in God, in God finds his delight, yet he doth acts perform (truthfulness, penance, meditation &c.), best of God's universe, he.

5. This God is to be reached by truth alone, and meditation, by knowledge, pure and constant discipline. He is in body's midst, made all of Light, translucent; whom practised men, sins washed away, behold.

6. That heavenly-bright, of thought-transcending nature, shines out both vast and rarer than the rare; far farther than the far, here close at hand that too, just here in all that see nestling within the heart.

7. By eye He is not grasped, nor yet by speech, nor by the other powers, nor by mere meditation, or even holy deeds. By wisdom calm, in essence pure, then not till then does one in ecstacy, Him free from parts, behold.

The second mantra is thus commented on by Śrīkaṇṭhāchārya (vide Siddhānta Dīpikā Vol. 2, p. 74). The traditional interpretation of this passage is given as follows:

"The Jīva, bound by the shackles of beginningless Karma, having entered into many a body made of Māya (Physical matter)—each suited to the enjoying of a particular fruit—is subjected to a lot of incurable misery; and unable to ward it off on account of his impotence, he does not know what to do and grieves. He is thus immersed in the ocean of grief, caused by his great delusion. When, however, by the *Lord's grace*, he intuitively sees Him, who as the Impeller dwells within Himself, who is gracious to all who is ever associated with Umā (Love and Light), then he attains to the unsurpassed greatness of the Lord, free from all grief. Therefore though Śiva, who is independent and who has been free from samsāra from time without beginning, is in contact with the body, he is not subject to its evils, as the Jīva is. Wherefore it is, that Jīva and Parameśvara are said to be in the cave of the heart."

St. Tirumūlar has the following stanza:

வம்பு பழுத்த மலர்பழ மொன்றுண்டு
தம்பாற் பறவை புகுந்துணத் தாவொட்டாது

அம்புகொண் டெய்திட் டகலத் துறந்திடிற்
செம்பொற் சிவகதி சென்றெய்த லாமே."

There is a fruit maturing from flowers of vanity.
One bird partakes of it and another does not.
If aimed with an arrow and driven away,
Sure one can reach the golden seat of Śiva.

St. Māṇickavāchakar calls the tree exactly இருவினை மாமரம், in the following beautiful passage

ஆயிடை வானப் பேரியாற் றகவயிற்
பாய்ந்தெழுந் தின்பப் பெருஞ்சுழி கொழித்துச்
சுழித்தெம் பந்தமாக் கரைபொரு தலைத்திடித்
தூழூழ் ஓங்கிய நங்கள்
இருவினை மாமரம் வேர்பறித் தெழுந்த
உருவ அருணீ ரோட்டா அருவரைச்
சந்தின் வான்சிறை கட்டிமட் டவிழ்
வெறிமலர்க் குளவாய்க் கோலி நிறையகின்
மாப்புகைக் கரைசேர் வண்டுடைக் குளத்தின்
மீக்கொள மேன்மேன் மகிழ்தலி னோக்கி
அருச்சனை வயலுள் அன்புவித் திட்டுத்
தொண்ட உழவர் ஆரத் தந்த
அண்டத் தரும்பெறன் மேகன், வாழ்க!

Meanwhile, the heavenly mighty stream
Rises and rushes, crowned with bubbles of delight,
Eddies around, dashes against the bank of our 'embodiment,'
And twofold deeds of ours growing from age to age,—
Those mighty trees,—roots up and bears away.
It rushes through the cleft of the high hills,
Is imprisoned in the encircling lake,
Where grow the expanded fragrant flowers,—
In tank, where rises smoke of the *agil*, where beetles hum ;
And as it swells with ever-rising joy,
The ploughmen-devotees in the field of worship
Sow in rich abundance seed of love !
Hail, CLOUD-LIKE God,* hard in this universe to reach !

—From Dr. Pope's translation.

* God, 'like clouds is gentle and fierce too,' nourishing both the wicked and good, and in time rooting up the wicked.

25

and St. Paṭṭinattār has a much more elaborate passage, in regard to the uprooting of this (நச்சுமாமரம்) poisonous Mango tree, in Tiruvidai Marudūr Mummaṇik-Kovai (10).

The tree of knowledge of good and evil is the Karmic Life of the individual, made up of the accumulated acts performed by him remaining in a perfect and unchangeable chain of causes and effects, following the man close like his shadow, as distinguished from the tree of life which is the light in him. It is this Karmic existence, this tree of shadow which the Buddhists postulated, and not anything like the tree of Life or the true soul postulated by the theistic Hindu Schools, and they recognized nothing higher than this inpermanent though continuous (as a stream) Karmic Life. To them, all existence seemed only as sorrow and evil, and complete cessation or annihilation of this Karmic existence, by the attainment of mere knowledge, constituted their highest end. To them there was no joy in life, and no means of attaining to such joy, as they would not recognize the all-loving Powers of the Supreme Lord, who could grant them such Joy, out of His immeasurable Grace. The Siddhānta no doubt postulated with the Buddhist that his body (birth and death) must cease, his feelings must cease, his life must cease, his understanding must cease, and that his egoism must cease. But how and whereby could this cessation be brought about? The means are set forth succinctly in the tenth and eleventh Sūtras of Sivajñānabotha.

"அவனே தானே யாகிய அந்நெறி
யேகனாகி இறைபணி நிற்க,
மலமாயை தன்னொடு வல்வினையின்றே."

As the Lord becomes one with the Soul in its human condition, so let the Soul become one with Him, and perceive all its actions to be His. Then will it lose all its *Mala*, *Māya*, and *Karma*.

"காணும் கண்ணுக்குக் காட்டு முளம்போல
காணவுளத்தைக் கண்டு காட்டலின்
அயரா அன்பின் அரன்கழல் செலுமே."

> **As the soul enables the eye to see and itself sees, so Hara enables the soul to know and itself knows. And this *Advaita* knowledge and undying Love will unite it to His Feet.**

They are, becoming one with God, and dedicating one's acts to God, and unceasing Love and devotion to Him. By such dedication, one brings himself in harmony with the divine law, and loses his pride of self-knowledge, and his own ignorance and Karma cease to operate, the man's whole being becoming beauteous by the Flood of His Grace. As clearly distinguished from the Buddhist ethics and psychology, the Siddhāṇti belives that his salvation cannot be secured except by such self-renunciation, and love of the Supreme.

> "இருள்சேர் இருவினையும் சேரா இறைவன்
> பொருள்சேர் புகழ்புரிந்தார் மாட்டு."
>
> "வேண்டுதல் வேண்டாமையிலான் அடிசேர்ந்தார்க்கு
> யாண்டுமிடும்பையில."
>
> "பற்றுக பற்றற்றான் பற்றினையப்பற்றைப்
> பற்றுகபற்றுவிடற்கு."
>
> "பிறப்பென்னும் பேதைமை நீங்கச் சிறப்பென்னும்
> செம்பொருள் காண்ப தறிவு."
>
> "உணர்ந்தமா முனிவரும் பரோடொழிந்தார்
> உணர்வுக்குந் தெரிவரும் பொருளே
> யிணையிலி யெல்லா வுயிர்கட்கு முயிரே
> யெனைப்பிறப்பறுக்கு மெம்மருந்தே
> திணிந்ததோரிருளிற் றெளிந்ததூ வெளியே
> திருப்பெருந் துறையுறை சிவனே
> குணங்கடாமில்லாவின்பமே யுன்னைக்
> குறுகினேற் கினியென்ன குறையே.

He is the one not comprehended by the Gods and the wise. He is the Life of all life. He is the supreme panacea for all the ills of the flesh; and obeying His Law, no one knows death or birth. He is the shining Light of our dark existence. He is the one Joy, but not born of life, not born of Prakriti guṇa, or the world and the transitory; and partaking of this Joy, our highest desires are completely fulfilled, unlike the joys of this world which ever create a flaming desire, a thirst after them, more and more like the unquenchable thirst of the confirmed drunkard. This supreme and resistless Joy as shown in other stanzas of the 'House of God', கோயிற்றிருப்பதிகம் fills our hearts, like the flood brooking not its banks, when, in all humility and love, our body and heart melt in His service.

The contrast between the transient world's joy and the Joy that transcends all states without end, நிலைப்பதங்களி யாவையுங் கடந்த இன்பம், is well brought out in the following stanza by the same Saint Māṇickavāchakar.

> தினைத்தனை யுள்ளதோர் பூவினிற் றேனுண்ணாதே
> நினைத்தொறுங் காண்டொறும் பேசுந்தொறும் எப்போதும்
> அனைத்தெலும் புண்ணெக ஆனந்தத்தேன் சொரியும்
> குனிப்புடையானுக்கே சென்றூதாய் கோத்தும்பீ.

> **Taste not the flower-borne honey drop tiny as a millet seed,**
> **Sing thou of Him who showers honey of bliss**
> **So as to melt one's very marrow-bones,**
> **While thinking, seeing and speaking aye and ever.**

When this joy fills him, then does he sport in God, delight in God as the Muṇḍaka says, then "does he love God, delight in God, revel in God and rejoice in God" as the Chhāṇdogya puts it. In this condition of Svarāj, when he can exclaim 'I am the glorious of the glorious' neither pain, nor pleasures of this world, nor the fruits of the forbidden tree, can touch or attract him, though he desists not from doing his duty, such as truthfulness, meditation, tapas &c., and in this condition, even "if he moves about there, laughing or eating, playing or rejoicing (in his mind), be it with women, carriages, or relatives," (chandog viii. 12. 3) these acts will not affect him, as fire cannot burn a man who is practised in agni-stumbha (see the principle stated in Śivajñāna Siddhiyār. X 5 & 6.)

Compare this with the Christian aspiration to divine joy.

"If to any the tumult of the flesh were hushed, hushed the images of the earth, and water and air, hushed also the ruler of heaven, yea the very soul be hushed to herself, and by not thinking on self surmount self, hushed all dreams and imaginary revelation, every tongue and every sign, and whatsoever exists only in transition, since if we could hear, all these say we made not to ourselves, but He made us that abideth for ever. If then having uttered this, they too should be hushed having roused our ears to him who made them, and He alone speak not by them, but by Himself, that we may hear His word, not through any tongue of flesh, nor angels' voice nor sound of thunder nor in the dark riddle of a similitude, but might hear Whom in these things we love, might hear his very self without these (as we too now strained ourselves and in swift thought touched on the eternal wisdom which abideth over all)—could this be continued on, and other visions of far unlike be withdrawn, and this one ravish and absorb and wrap up its beholder, and these inward joys, so that life might be for ever like that one moment of understanding which we now sighed after, were not this, enter in My Master's joy" (St. Augustine's Confessions Book ix.)

வான்கெட்டு மாருத மாய்ந்தழல் நீர் மண்கெடினும்
தான் கெட்டலின்றிச் சலிப்பறியாத் தன்மையனுக்கு
ஊன்கெட் டுணர்வுகெட் டென்னுள்ளமும்போய்
நான்கெட்ட வாபாடித் தெள்ளேணம் கொட்டாமோ.

While earth and air, water and sky and fire
May change their nature, He changes and wearies not,
In him, I lost my body and sense, my life and mind
I lost my-self, I sing Tellênam.

உரையற்ற தொன்றை உரைசெய்யு மூமர்காள்
கரையற்ற தொன்றைக் கரைகாண லாகுமோ
திரையற்ற நீர்போற் சிந்தை தெளிவார்க்கு
புரையற்றிருந்தான் புரிசடையோனே.

Ye fools! that speak of the unspeakable,
Can ye find the limits of the limitless one?
When as the waveless sea one gains clearness,
To him, will appear the Lord with braided hair.

Compare also,

> தானமழிந்து தனமுமழிந்து
> ஊனுமழிந்து வுயிருமழிந்துடன்
> வானுமழிந்து மனமுமழிந்துபின்
> நானுமழிந்தமை நானறியேனே.

> When deeds perished, and with it wealth,
> When flesh perished, and with it life,
> When mind perished, and its cause Ākās,
> Then my 'I' perished, I did not know.

> பூதங்களற்றுப் பொறியற்றுச் சாரைம்புலன்களற்றுப்
> பேதங்களற்றுப் பேராசை யற்றுப்பின் முன்னற்றுக்
> காதங்கரணங்களுமற்று வானந்தக் காட்சியிலே
> ஏதங்களைந்திருப் பேனிறைவா கச்சியேகம்பனே.

> O, my Lord of Kāñchi, when the elements, senses and sensations,
> The differing guṇas and desires, and sense of time and space,
> When all these are lost in the blissful vision,
> Then am I freed from all evil and rest in peace.

The original fall was brought about by disobeying God's Law, by opposing our will to his Will, and the only way of salvation consists in establishing the harmony of will between His and ours, and completely subordinating our will to His own, and allow His Will to be done as it is in heaven.

When we were first created, we were just like children, fresh and innocent, fully trusting and depending on our loving parents, without caring for the morrow, fully obeying their dictates, and never asserting ourselves nor becoming self-willed. But the child preserves this condition only for a short time; it would not abide by the loving words of wisdom and warning given to it, would know for itself; and slowly its desire and self-will are developed, and in its ignorance and conceit, it accumulates the load of Karma. And unless we become again like children abiding in trust and faith completely on our Beloved Father, we cannot get rid of this sin and sorrow. And unless we become born again, we cannot see the Kingdom of heaven as declared by the same Jesus Christ, whom the world thought he was beside himself *i. e.*, mad. And our St. Tāyumānavar likens the nature of the saintly "பாலரோடு பேயர் பித்தர் பான்மையென நிற்பதுவே சிலமிகுஞானியர் தம் செய்கை பாராபரமே" to the babies, and lunatics and men possessed.

Karma or வினை simply means an act, and this act may give pleasure or pain and if it gives pleasure, it is called good and if it produces pain, it is called evil. Every good act is right and every evil act is wrong, or Puṇyam or pāpam, Virtue or sin. Śivajñāna Siddhiyār defines ***puṇyam*** and ***pāpam*** as உயிர்க்கிதம்செய்தல், doing good to all sensient creatures and உயிர்க்கதம் செய்தல் doing evil to all creatures in the largest and broadest sense of the term, in the same way as any modern utilitarian philosopher would define these terms, and we have no doubt that the definition is quite correct from any point of view. When we interpose conscience in the middle as a judge of good and evil, right and wrong, it is seen how varying the consciences of men are, and so we must necessarily seek a higher authority or test.

Karma therefore signifies acts or series of acts or the aggregate of human experience, acting and reacting on each other; and Law of Karma means the invariable order or Niyati which results, pain or pleasure attaches itself to a doer in accordance with the kind of acts performed by him, in accordance wilh the maxim நன்மை விதைத்தால் நன்மைவிளையும், தீமை விதைத்தால் தீமைவிளையும், "He who sows must reap accordingly".

One result of this law is, that the respective fruits have to be enjoyed in a suitable body and this body is determined by the Karma performed by each, (Vide Śivajñānabotha II. 2. ab) and if his previous Karma is good, he will get a good body, and if it is bad, he will get a bad body. And this accounts for the myriads of physical bodies in every stage of development to the highest, from that of the amœbæ to that of a Christ or Māṇickavāchakar, possessed of every varying mental and spiritual characteristics. The more good a man performs, the better and more developed body does he get, with the accompanying development of mind and heart, and the result of this privilege is, that he is enabled to get a purer and purer body, which, the more it becomes pure, will reflect the Light and Glory of God; so that when man reaches his physical and mental perfection, he reaches the spiritual perfection of complete merger in the supreme Light. And of all bodies, the human body is the one in which a man can work out his salvation, and therefore is he enjoined to take time by the forelock and do good while this body lasts, if not to secure salvation in this birth, atleast to secure a better body in which he can carry on the good work.

> " எண்ணரிய பிறவிதனின் மானிடப் பிறவிதான
> யாதினும் அரிதரிதுகாண்
> இப்பிறவி தப்பினு லெப்பிறவி வாய்க்குமோ
> ஏதுவருமோ வறிகிலேன். &c
>
> **Among births numberless, that of man**
> **Is rare, rare indeed ;**
> **When this birth is lost, what will happen I know not.**
>
> Hence தானந்தவந்தரு மஞ்சந்ததமும் செய்வர்சிவ
> ஞானந்தனையணைய நல்லோர் பராபரமே.
>
> **O thou Supreme of Supreme,**
> **The good desiring to attain Šivajñana, ever perform good deeds and Tapas and make gifts.**

And so this doctrine of Karma instead of leading to quietism and indifference, inculcates a life of active beneficence "desiring the welfare of all" and furnishes as good and sure a basis for perfect ethical conduct as any other system in the world.

But even when doing good works, he is not to have any regard for the result, he is to do it without tasting the fruits thereof, as this tends to bind him to the world still by producing the physical body and will not effect his final release from this body ; and after performing evil and good, he attains to இருவினை யொப்பு, becoming balanced in good and evil, pain and pleasure. This does not mean that he should so perform actions, that all his good actions will weigh as much as his bad actions, or doing as much punyam as pāpam, but it is attaining to a condition of viewing deeds either good or bad without either liking or disliking, a condition of being described as வேண்டுதல் வேண்டாமையிலான். In such a condition, man is not impelled or attracted by any thing which will give him pleasure, he will not be deterred simply because it will cause him pain. Such objects of desire in the world are wealth, health and gratification, and we hate all those acts which will produce the opposite results. To such a person, wealth and poverty, food and poison, praise and blame, will be equally welcome, and one looks on all these as one looks on dust or chaff, without desire or aversion. It is when a man attains to this condition of வேண்டுதல் வேண்டாமை or இருவினை யொப்பு, that he is led in pursuit of the highest Ideals, to do the greatest acts of heroism, and the most magnanimous acts of self-sacrifice, and suffer the greatest martyrdom. The story of the churning of the Ocean is full of this meaning. The gods who were pained at their poverty, and desired wealth, came to reap the fire of the poison, which arose as a result of their own self-seeking, and the Supreme Being who appeared there, not for the sake of any reward, but for the sole purpose of saving the distressed gods, was not affected by the Poison which he swallowed.

So that when God willed to create this earth and the heavens, it was not the result of a mere whim or play, it was not for his own improvement or benefit, it was not for his self-glorification or self-realization, but he willed out of his Infinite Love and Mercy towards the innumerable souls, who were rotting in their bondage, enshrouded in Āṇava mala, without self knowledge and self-action, that they be awakened out of their kêvala (கேவல) condition and move into the cycle or evolution, (சகல), births and deaths, whereby alone they can effect their salvation. One helped on to this, by being given bodies, faculties &c., out of matter, they begin to do, accumulate karma, which has to be eaten fully before the இருவினையொப்பு, the indifference to pain and pleasure, can be gained. In the process of eating the 'bitter fruits' and gaining ஒப்பு (balance), one gathers experience and wisdom and the knowledge of Truth. And unless this Truth be gained, the soul's salvation is a mere myth and nothing more.

THE FOUR PATHS.

RELIGION THEORETICAL AND PRACTICAL.

Good deal of attention has been paid of late to the Theoretical aspects of our Hindu Religion, and most people are familiar with the various systems of Hindu Philosopy—of the Dvaita, Visishtādvaita and Advaita aspects in particular. And in such a study, one is likely to lose sight of the practical aspect of the Religion, and it is to this aspect, I wish to-day to draw your particular attention.

DIFFICULTIES IN UNDERSTANDING HINDU RELIGION.

To the ordinary foreigner, Hinduism appears as a fantastic combination of the grossest superstitions and the most dreamy speculations. Even the sympathetic student of our religion, though he is prepared to admire and appreciate particular aspects of our philosophy, looks down with pity on our so-called errors. And one Christian friend put it to me whether, in Hinduism, we have any real and practical religion. Of course, to the onlooker, the contrast between Temple-worship and its attendant festivals and the austerer practices of the Sanyāsins, the ablutions and pūjah of pious people and the 'Tatvamasi' and 'Ahambrahmasmi' meditations of others, cannot but be bewildering. Even some of us are apt to look upon so much labour and money spent on Temples and in Temple-worship as so much waste, or we are prepared to relegate these practices to the illetirate lower orders, as we are pleased to call them. Can all these various practices have any real meaning and purpose or can they not? Can all these be reduced to certain definite principles or not? These are the questions which I propose to discuss in this paper.

DIFFERENT PATHS AND UPASANAS.

Of course, we have read and heard people talk, about Karma-mārga, Bhakti-mārga and Yōga and Jñāna-mārgas, as though there is little or no bhakti, or bhakti is not wanted in other mārgas, as though there are no actions or duties attached to the others, or all those who do not follow the Jñānamārga are only ignorant people. Does men's smearing themselves with ashes and nā:nams, repeating God's names, constitute bhakti? Does not the relieving of the poor and infirm and the sick constitute part of one's religious duties? Is it the highest duty of the Yōgi and Jñāni that he considers himself superior to others, and thinks that he will be polluted by the mere touch of others, and that he has achieved a great thing if he has injured none?

And then we have heard of different Upāsanas and Vidyās, Sandilya, Dahara, Sakala and Nishkala and Saguṇa and Nirguṇa; and there are people who would advocate the Saguṇa against the Nirguṇa and the Nirguṇa against the Saguṇa.

To begin a statement of my views. Hindus hold as an axiom that no study is of any benefit unless it can lead one to the worship of the supreme One.

"கற்றதனாலாய பயனென்கொல் வாலறிவன்
நற்றாள் தொழாஅ ரெனின்."

And that we cannot be rid of the ills flesh is heir to, and cross the sea of births and deaths, and attain to everlasting joy unless we reach the feet of the Supreme Lord.

"வேண்டுதல் வேண்டாமை யிலானடி சேர்ந்தார்க்
கியாண்டு மிடும்பையில."

"பிறவிப் பெருங்கடல் நீந்துவர் நீந்தார்
இறைவனடி சேராதார்." (*The Kural*).

To get rid of our ills and to attain to His joy is our goal.

That this human birth is given to us to work out our salvation and in this mundane plane, is admitted by all religions, Christianity included.

புவனியிற்போய் பிறவாமை யிருளும்
போக்குகின்றோ மவமேயிந்தப் பூமி
சிவனுய்யக் கொள்கின்ற வாறென்று நோக்கித்
திருப்பெருந் துறையுறைவாய். (*Tiruvāchaka*).

How then can we attain to this end? This is the consideration of the Practical Religion. And our systematic treatises devote considerable space to the treatment of this question. This is the chapter on Sādana in the Vedānta Sūtras and in the Śivajñānabhodha.

As a necessary prelude to this, the nature of the Deity and of the Soul has to be discussed.

NATURE OF GOD.

According to the greatest sage of our Tamiḷ-land, Saint Tiruvaḷḷuvar, He is ஆதி and இறைவன், our Supreme Lord and Master, the author of our being and regeneration, He is the Pure Intelligence and the Transcendent one, வாலறிவன், and தனக்குவமையில்லாதான், He is without likes and dislikes, வேண்டுதல் வேண்டாமையிலான், dwells in our heart மலர்மிசையேகினான் and He is the occean of love and mercy அறவாழி அந்தணன்.

The Upanishats speak of Him as "the Highest great Lord of Lords, God of Gods, King of Kings, the Highest abode, as God, the Lord of the world, the adorable." "He is the one God hidden in all beings, all pervading, the antarātma of all beings, watching over all works, dwelling in all beings, the witness, the perceiver, the only one, the Nirguṇa being. 'His High Power (*Śakti*) is revealed as manifold, as inherent, acting as force and knowledge."

"He is Śiva (the Happy and Blissful). He brings good and removes all evil, the Lord of Bliss, as dwelling within the Ātma the immortal, the support of all."

"No one has grasped Him above or across or in the middle. His form cannot be seen, no one perceives him with the eye."

"That God, the maker of all things, the Paramātma, always

dwelling in the heart of man, is perceived by the heart, the soul, the mind. They who know It become immortal."

"Those who, through heart and mind, know Him thus abiding in the heart, become immortal," "Satyam Jñānam Anantam Brahma Ananda Rūpam Amritam YadVibhuti Shantam Śivam Advaitam." "He is the sat, chit and ānand."

In the Gitā also, He is spoken of as the Lord of Lords, Īshvara and Maheśvara, the spectator and permitter, supporter and enjoyer, the Paramātman, the supporter of elements, as devourer and causer. It is the light of lights and is said to be beyond Tamas. Wisdom knowable, wisdom gainable, centred in every heart.

In the Advaita Siddhānta Śāstras, He is called அர்த்தபாதி one with His Śakti, the 'Śiva Sat.'

> உலகெலாமாகி வேறாய் உடனுமாய் ஒளியாயோங்கி
> அலகிலா வுயிர்கள் கன்மத்து ஆணையினமர்ந்து செல்லத்
> தலைவனாய் இவற்றின் தன்மைதனக் கெய்தலின்றித்தானே
> நிலவுசீர் நின்மலனாகி நின்றனன் நீங்காதெங்கும்.

One with the world, and different, and both, The light transcendent,
The Lord who guides souls innumerable, in obedience to His Will (Ājñā) and each one's karma;
The Nirmala Being, untouched by the defects of His creatures;
Supreme He stands, secondless, pervading all.

> சிவனுரு வருவுமல்லன் சித்தினோடு அசித்துமல்லன்
> பவமுதற்றொழில்கள் பண்ணியொன்று மல்லன்
> தவமுதல் யோகபோகம் தரிப்பவனல்லன்றானே
> இவைபெற வியைந்துமொன்று மியைந்திடா இயல்பினனே.

Śiva is neither a Rūpi nor an Arūpi. He is neither chit nor Achit. He does not create nor sustain nor perform other functions. He was never a Yōgi nor a Bhōgi. Though present in and pervading all these inseparably, yet he is of a nature different from all these.

> சத்திதன் வடிவேதென்னில் தடையிலா ஞானமாகும்
> உய்த்திடு மிச்சைசெய்தி யிவைஞானத் துளவோ வென்னில்

எத்திறஞான முள்ளதத்திற மிச்சைசெய்தி
யைத்திடு மறையின்ஞானமன் மருவிநிச்சயமெல்லாம்.

The form of this Šakti is Pure Intelligence. If asked whether Supreme Will and Power are also found in this Supreme Intelligence, yes. Wherever there is intelligence, there is will and power. As such, the Power and Will will be manifested also by the Supreme Chit Šakti.

அருளது சத்தியாகும் அரன்தனக் கருளையின்றி
தெருள்சிவ மில்லையந்தச் சிவமின்றிச் சத்தியில்லை
மருளினை யருளால்வாட்டி மன்னுயிர்க் களிப்பன்கண்கட்
கிருளினை யொளியாலோட்டும் இரவியைப்போல ஈசன்.

Hara has *Grace* for His Šakti. Except as this Supreme Love and Grace, there is no Šiva. Without Šiva, there is no Šakti. Iša removes the hate of the Souls with his love, and grants them bliss, just as the Sun dispels the darkness, shrouding the eyes, with his light.

This supreme statement was reached in the famous lines of the great Tirumūlar.

அன்பும் சிவமும் இரண்டென்பர் அறிவிலார்
அன்பே சிவமாவதாரு மறிந்திலார்
அன்பே சிவமாவதாரு மறிந்தபின்
அன்பே சிவமா யமர்ந்திருந்தாரே.

"God is Love" and that great agnostic teacher of science who died a sincere believer in God had stated truly, "what has all the science or all the philosophy of the world done for the thought of mankind, to be compared with the one doctrine "God is Love." ?"

God is, as such, all Knowledge and all Love.

NATURE OF THE SOUL.

To talk of the means to attain to this great goal, will be futile if we don't understand the nature of man. From the statements in the first chapter of the Kuṛaḷ, it may be deduced that man is ignorant and subject to births and deaths, and has likes and dislikes, and does sin and suffer, and he could not be compared to God in any way. The following texts bring out the distinction quite plainly enough.

"The knowing one (God) and the non-knowing (soul) are two, both unborn; one is Lord, the other non-Lord (aniša)."

"Patim Vivasy-ātmeswaram (Lord of the soul) Sāsvatam Šivam achyutam."

"He who dwells in the soul and within the soul, whom the soul does not know, whose body the soul is, who rules the soul within, He is thy soul, the ruler within, the immortal."

"But the soul Paramount is *another*. Who is proclaimed as the Paramātma,, who—the infinite king—penetrates all the three worlds and sustains them.

Since I do surpass the kshara, and even do excel the akshara, I am reputed the Purushottama."

A DIFFICULTY IN REACHING THE GOAL.

And here we are met by statements that God is unknowable and imperceptible to our senses. He is past all thought and speech.

> உரையதொன்றை புரைசெய்யு மூடர்கள்
> கரையற்ற தொன்றைக் கரைகாணலாகுமோ. (*Tirumantra*).

And yet the upanishats say that when men should roll up the sky like a hide, then only without knowing Šiva, there could be an end of pain.

And St. Aruḷ Naṇḍi Šivāchāryar states the difficulty thus: "If God is unknowable, then there can be no benefit from Him. He can never pervade us, neither can we unite with him in Moksha. He cannot perform the pañcha-krityas for our benefit. His existence will be like that of the flowers of the sky and of the rope formed of the hairs of the tortoise.

And yet it must stand to reason that we cannot possibly know him if his nature is as we have described above. The moment we assert that we can know him, we assert that he becomes an object of our cognition, and as all Psychologists, Hindu and European, are agreed, all objects of cognition are what is called Achit or Asat or matter. Here is St. Aruḷ Naṇḍi's statement: " If you ask whether God is an object of knowledge or not, then know, if He is an object of knowledge, He will become Achit and Asat. All objects of cognition are achit; all objects of cognition come into being and are destroyed (being bound by time), they divide themselves into the worlds, bodies and organs (being bound by space) and enjoyments. They are identified at one time by the intelligence as itself (bandha) and at another time (in moksha) are seen as separate; and they are all products of Māyā. Hence all such are achit or non-intelligent or Asat (other than sat)."

As God is spoken of as the inner Ruler and Soul of Soul, whose body the Soul is, the knowing Soul is itself in the position of object to the True subject God, and the thinking mind cannot itself think thought, much less can the object perceive or think the subject.

And if he cannot be known, He must be a non-entity, argues St. Aruḷ Naṇḍi. And this exactly is the position which Paul Carus takes in his pamphlet on the "Idea of God." His argument is exactly that of Saint Aruḷ Naṇḍi, that if God is knowable, he can only be known as an object, as matter, which will be absurd. But Paul Carus would however retain God as an idea, or ideal, an abstract thing as redness or whiteness, a beautiful fantasy which will be useful. But as against this view, it is positively asserted by Saint Aruḷ Naṇḍi that He is not a non-entity and that He is Sat and Chit. As He is chit, He is not knowable, and yet He is a positive fact.

How is then this psychological difficulty to be got over?

THE FIRST POSSIBILITY OF OVERCOMING THE DIFFICULTY.

In the first place, it will be futile to think of knowing Him as different from ourselves as an object. Says St. Aruḷ Naṇḍi: " As God is not different from the soul, as He is in the soul, as He is the thinker of all the soul's thoughts, as in Him there is no distinction of I and mine, God cannot be perceived by the soul's intelligence as different." "God is not different from you either as he is inseparably associated with you, and transcend all discriminating intelligence. As He is ever the *inside* of the soul, the soul can be said to be Ṣivam."

The first possibility of our becoming Him will lie, therefore, in the fact that we are inseparably associated with Him, and must think ourselves as one with Him. We must not create distinctions between ourselves and Himself, interpose our will and thought, the feelings of 'I and mine.' Then only will our will and thought come into rapport with Him.

> "ஏகனாகி யிறைபணி நிற்க
> மலமாயை தன்னொடும் வல்வினையின்றே".

> "திரையற்ற நீர்போல் சிந்தை தெளிவார்க்கு
> புரையற்றிருந்தான் புரிசடையோனே".

> மனமே கல்லாலெனக்கன்றோ—தெய்வ
> மௌனகுருவாகி வந்து கைகாட்டி
> எனதாம் பணியறமாற்றி—அவன்
> இன்னருள் வெள்ளத்திருத்தி வைத்தாண்டி.

O mind, was it not for me, that God came under the banyan tree as silent teacher, and with dumb show of hand cured me of acts called *my acts*, and placed me in the blissful ocean of His grace.

> அருளாலெவையும் பாரென்றான்—அத்தை
> அறியாதே சுட்டி யென்னறிவாலே பார்த்தேன்
> இருளான பொருள்கண்டதல்லால்—கண்ட
> என்னையுங் கண்டிலனென்னடி தோழி.

"By grace behold all things," He said. Not understanding, by my intelligence I beheld differentiating. I saw darkness. I saw not even me, the seer. What is this, sister?

> என்னையும் தன்னையும் வேறா—உள்ளத்
> தெண்ணாத வண்ணமிரண்டற நிற்கச்
> சொன்னதுமோ வொருசொல்லே—அந்தச்
> சொல்லால் விளைந்த சுகத்தை யென்சொல்வேன்.

"Of me and thee, think not in thy heart as two. Stand undifferentiating." This one word when He uttered, how can I tell, dear, the Bliss that grew straightaway from that word?

(From Saint Tāyumānavar's ஆனந்தக்களிப்பு 'Revel in Bliss' —translated by P. Aruṇāchalam Esq. M. A., of Colombo.)

THE SECOND POSSIBILITY.

The second possibility lies in the fact that God is not knowledge alone. If He was so, we cannot know Him for certain. But as we have stated above, He is also *all Love*. It is in this Supreme fact that our salvation is based. This Love is in us, surrounds us on all sides, above, below, and all about us. His Love to us passes that of the mother, says Saint Māṇikka-vāçagar.

"சட்டோ நினைக்க மனத்தமுதாம் சங்கரன்"

"உருகிப்பெருகி உளங்குளிர முகந்துகொண்டு
பருகற்கினிய பரங்கருணைத் தடங்கடல்"

"நினைந்தொறும் காண்டொறும் பேசுந்தொறும் எப்போதும் அனைத்
தெலும் புண்ணெக ஆனந்தத்தேன்சொரியும் குனிப்புடையான்"

"தப்பாமே தாளடைந்தார் நெஞ்சுருக்கும் தன்மையினன்"

"அகண்டாகார சிவபோகமெனும் பேரின்பவெள்ளம்,
பொங்கித் ததும்பிப் பூரணமாய் ஏகவுருவாய்க்கிடக்குதையோ
இன்புற்றிட நாமெடுத்ததேகம் விழுமுன் புசிப்பதற்குச்
சேரவாரும் சகத்தீரே."

No selfish want prompts His love. His Love was ever with us from our first beginning to the very end.

"அருளெங்குமான வளையையறியார்
அருளே நகரமுதானதும் தேரார்
அருளான்கருமத்தை நுகக்கமுன்னோர்
அருளெங்கும் கண்ணானதா ரறிவாரே."

Who knows the Power of this Aruḷ by which Omnipresence is secured? Who understands that this Love transmuted Herself into tasteful ambrosia?

Who thinks that this Love—permeates subtly the five great operations (Pañchakṛitya) ?
Who knows that this Love has eyes on all sides (is Omniscient.)? "

" அருளிற்பிறந்திட்டு அருளில் வளர்ந்திட்டு
அருளிலழிந்திளைப்பாற்றி மறைந்திட்டு
அருளானவார முதத்தானந்த மூட்டி
அருளாலென்னந்தி யகம்புகுந்தானே."

Born in Love, Bred up in Love,
Changing, and resting in Love,
Fed in the Supreme ambrosia of Love,
The Naṇdi entered me as Love."

The mother's love will not suffer, even if the child misbehaves and does not deserve it. If we will therefore return His love, then our salvation is secured.

" அயரா அன்பின் அரன்கழல் செலுமே,"

(With undying love, enters the Feet of Hara)

St. Tirumūlar sums up these foregoing facts in a beautiful verse.

ஒன்று மிரண்டு மிலதுமா யொன்றாக
நின்று சமய நிராகார நீங்கியே
நின்று பராபரை நேயத்தைப் பாதத்தால்
சென்று சிவமாதல் சித்தாந்த சித்தியே.

Becoming one, without being one nor two,
Becoming freed of Samaya Nirākāra,
Ascending by the Grace of our Loving mother,
And becoming Śivam is Śiddhāṇta Siddhi.

LOVE, THE GREATEST THING IN THE WORLD.

Now let us realize to ourselves how it is, that to know Him and become one with Him, we must love Him. Let us take our human relations. Is it by birth and caste, wealth and possessions, learning and knowledge, that one is brought nearer to another? Are not all these barriers dividing one from another? By all these means, one regards himself as raised above all other less favoured individuals. It is learning that puffeth up a man. The 'I' ness and 'mine ness' become more and more developed in these men. So these means can never lead one nearer to another. Then what other means have we? It is love, love in all its gradations from pity upwards. This is the greatest Thing in the world, as Prof. Drummond truly said. It is the ideal of both theistic and atheistic systems of the world.

Love is the basis of all human society, the rock on which it is built. This will appear so from the mere heads of the chapters in இல்லறம் in the sacred Kuṟaḷ. It is the one thing which binds man to man, the parent to the child, friend to friend and the woman to the husband. When this prevails, the distinctions created by birth, possessions, and learning, all cease. It is this which impels the servant to engage in his master's service, the mother to sacrifice herself to the child, the friend to give his life for his friend, the lover to forget himself in the loved. All the noblest acts of heroism, philanthropy, and martyrdom, arise from this one source. It is this love which as we have seen, gives rise to the other great fact in Being, namely, Sacrifice. Even naturalists have discovered the connexion of these two facts, Love and Sacrifice, even in the case of lower animals. And should not this law hold good in higher realm than the animal and social? And it is to lead to this end, we have all along been trying.

KNOWLEDGE NECESSARY.

And in this place, the importance of knowledge cannot be ignored. One has to enter a railway platform and watch one of the ever-recurring scenes.

The compartments are crowded more or less. Fresh passengers try to rush into it. The persons, impelled of course by their own comfort, resist the intrusion. Actual fights ensue. Some of them try to get in somehow. They stand for a while.

Those who have comfortable seats are pierced by their own hard heart and they pity and relent. A small space is found for the man who stands. They naturally soon after fall to conversation. They discover soon their mutual friends and relations, and by the time they leave the train, they become the most affectionate of people, and the parting becomes a sorrow. Whereby, was this mutual hate turned into love? It is by knowledge. We are ignorant, all of us, how intimately we are related to each other. We are all god's servants, His children in fact, and may be, we can share in His fellowship. The whole world is ensouled by Him. We are members of His body, says Śrīkaṇṭha.

THE TRUE WORSHIP.

"Wherefore, the whole universe is ensouled by Śiva. If any embodied being whatsoever, be subjected to constraint, it will be quite repugnant to the eight-bodied Lord; as to this, there is no doubt. Doing good to all, kindness to all, affording shelter to all, this they hold as the worshipping of Śiva."

Here, in this last sentence of Śrīkaṇṭha, do we get at the real essence of all religion. What is Śiva? It is Love. What is worship of Him? Loving Him. How can we love Him, whom we do not know? Nay, we can know Him and do know Him though. We do not perceive each other's souls or minds and yet, we love each other. It is the body we know, and it is on each other's body we manifest all our love. We do willing service to the body only of our elders, masters, teachers and parents. It is on that body we love, we lavish all our wealth and labour. So can we worship and love Him by loving His Body which is the whole universe of Chêtana and Achêtana.

பூதங்கள்தோறு நின்றாயெனினல்லாற்
போக்கிலன் வரவிலனென நினைப்புலவோர்
கீதங்கள்பாடு தலாடுதலல்லாற்
கேட்டறியோ முனைக்கண்டறிவாரை—
சீதங்கொள் வயற்றிருப்பெருந்துறை மன்னா

சிந்தனைக்குமரியா யெங்கண்முன் வந்து
ஏதங்களறுத் தெம்மையாண்டருள் புரியும்
எம்பெருமான் பள்ளியெழுந்தருளாயே.

'Thou dwell'st in all the elements," tis said; and yet
'Thou goest not, nor com'st;' the sages thus, have sung
'Their rhythmic songs. Though, neither have we heard, nor learnt
Of those, that Thee by seeing of the eye, have known.
Thou King of *Perun-Turai*, girt with cool rice-fields,
To ponder Thee is hard to human thought. To us
In presence come! Cut off our ills! In mercy make us Thine!
Our mighty Lord, from off Thy couch in grace arise!

As I pointed out above, knowledge is an essential requisite of our love. As knowledge grows, Love will grow. The more and more we understand our nearness to each other and to God, more and more will our love grow. The knowledge and love prevailing between master and servant is weaker than between father and son; between friends it is higher, and in the case of lovers, it is highest.

THE THIRD POSSIBILITY.

I must here point out a Psychological Law which I may state as the basis of this experience and which I may state as the third possibility.

It is the peculiar nature of the soul or mind, whereby it identifies itself with the thing it is united to. This aspect is alone fully discussed in the Siddhānta Śāstras. St. Meykaṇḍān calls it அது அது ஆதல் and in the commentaries as சார்ந்ததன் வண்ணமாதல். St. Tāyumānār paraphrases it as யாதொன்றுபற்றின் அதன் இயல்பாய் நிற்றல். The human soul is a mirror—a crystal. It becomes dark when darkness covers it. A man can be judged by his associates. He can be good or bad as his associates are. With the world in union, the soul has become identified with the world, and lost its individuality. In God, it has become Śivam losing its individuality. In the full glare of mid-day sun, I challenge one to see the mirror. What one will see if he has courage enough to see it, will be, the full radiance of the glorious sun, which will blind him at once.

Says Professor Henry Drummond: "All men are mirrors, that is the first law on which this formula is based. One of the aptest descriptions of a human being is a mirror."

Professor Drummond states this Law as the Law of Reflection and Assimilation, or Law of Influence, or Law of Identity as we may call it, அது அது ஆதல். He instances the iron which gets magnetised and becomes a magnet "இரும்பைக்காந்தம் இழுக்கின்றவாறென்ன"; a mirror, getting rid of its dust, reflects the glorious light and becomes *merged* with it and *lost*.

HOW THE SOUL MERGES AND LOSES ITSELF.

Only one word about the meaning of the words 'merging' and 'losing,' before I continue the thread. I quote from a text-book of science :—

"When a *river* enters the *sea*, it soon *loses* its individuality, it becomes *merged* in the body of the ocean, when it loses its current and when, therefore, it has no power to keep in suspension the sediment which it had brought down from the Higher lands." Please reread the lines in this way and the application will become clear. "When the soul loses its individuality (its feeling of I and mine) Ahaṅkāram or Āṇavam, it becomes merged in God when it loses its karma, and when, therefore, it has no power to keep in suspension its mala, with which it was associated from the beginning. This losing of self is the real sacrifice, brought about by love. It is this sacrifice பலி, we are asked to make as we enter the Temple precincts and the moment we make it, our பசுத்துவம் will leave us and we will become சந்தி the Blissful Śivam.

We likened the soul to the mirror and the following passages from the upanishats may be considered.

"As a metal disc (mirror), tarnished by dust, shines brigth again after it has been cleaned, so is the one incarnate person, satisfied and freed from grief after he has seen the real nature of himself." "And when by the real nature of himself he sees as by a lamp the real nature of the Brahman, then having known the unborn Eternal God, who transcends all tattvas, he is freed from all pāśa."

"From meditating on Him, from joining Him, from becoming one with Him, there is further cessation of all Māyā in the end." In Drummond's language these verses read—"See God, reflect God and become God."

Students of Darwin will have noted how powerful is the law of association and assimilation or identity in the animal and human evolution. Persons who are ever associated with pigs get piggy faces, and with horses horsey faces. In the case of a husband and wife, when they have been perfectly loving, it has been found, to effect a complete assimilation of their facial features சாரூபம். Such is the power of the human mind; it can lower itself to the very depths of the brute or it can raise itself to the very height of Godhood. This law is spoken of in our text-books as the law of 'garuḍadhyānam.'

This brings us to the very end of our subject.

We cannot know God really by all our religious rites and performances, repetition of prayers and formulas by saguṇa or nirguṇa worship, with or without idols, and even by the highest yōga, except when His grace and Love fills us all and we lose ourselves in this Love.

Look at how St. Meykaṇḍān ridicules this idea of the Yogi that he knows God.

"If it can be meditated, then as an object of our senses, it becomes Asat. If you regard it as not conceivable by our organs (internal and external), even then it is of no use. If you contemplate it as beyond contemplation even then it gives you no benefit as it is a mere fiction. If you contemplate it as yourself, this is also fiction. Giving up these fictitious ideas of God, the only way to know Him is by understanding with His Aruḷ or Grace."

THE FOUR PATHS.

So that all our understanding of Him till the final goal is reached will be merely fictitious, or use a better word, symbolical. The conception whether that of the Bhakta or Yogi, Hindu or Christian will only be symbolical. We introduce a real element into it when we introduce love in our conception of God. And this conception naturally divides itself into four forms, that of master and servant, parent and child, friend and friend, and lover and loved. All other conceptions can be reduced into these four. There are love and knowledge in all these different forms of Bāvana or Sādana. As our Lord and master, we do Him and His bhaktās, loving service and obedience and reverence. In the master, we lose our own identity. To the father and mother, obedience and service and reverence and love in a greater degree is exhibited. To the friend we can say 'I am he,' 'he is myself,' 'all mine are his' and 'all his are mine.' In real life, this ideal of friendship is rarely manifested. Our people could hardly appreciate the act of the saint who gave his wife to the bhakta who demanded her of him. How would you like the pourtrayal of Hall Caine of the lowborn and illiterate Manxeman who loved and continued to love more and more the high born and cultured aristocrat who betrayed him, cheated and robbed him of his betrothed, and forfeited all claims to regard and respect? It was because his friendship on his own part was sincere and true.

It is this ideal of the friendship and the Bāvana required under it which reveals the meaning of the formulas of Tatvamasi and Aham Brahmāsmi, given out as the mantras to be practised by the Yōgi. In Yōga, the identity of Bāvana is fully reached. When we understand this fully, we can understand all the episodes in the life of St. Sundara, who was of the very image of Sôma Sundara and whom God chose as his own 'friend.'

ஏழிசையா யிசைப்பயனா யின்னமுதா யென்னுடைய
தோழனுமா யான்செய்யுந் துரிசுகளுக் குடனாகி
மாழையொண்கண் பரவையைத் தந்தாண்டானை மதியிலா
வேழையேன் பிரிந்திருக்கேன் என்னாரூரிறைவனையே.

He, the seven notes, their joy, the sweet ambrosia, my very *friend* who is with me even in my mischiefs, my Lord who gave me my beautiful-eyed Paravai, my Lord of Ārūr, how can I, the poor fool, be separated from Him?

In life, have you felt the hundredth part of this love for your friend, the gnawing pain at heart when you were separated and the boundless joy when you met?

These are then the four paths or mārgas, Charyā, Kriyā Yôga and Jñāna, otherwise called Dāsa, Satputra and Saha and Sanmārga. And the various duties assigned under each, are only such as our love of the master or father or friend or lover will induce us to manifest in tokens of our love. These duties are meaningless except as tokens of our love and as disciplining us to love and love more God and his creatures.

என்பே விறகாயிறைச்சி யறுத்திட்டு
பொன்போற் கனலில் பொரியவறுப்பினும்
அன்போடுருகி யகங்குழைவார்க் கன்றி
என்போல் மணியினை யெய்தவொண்ணாதே.

Even though, with bones for firewood,
The flesh is torn to lines and burnt, like gold in fire,
Except to those who internally melt themselves into Love,
God is not accessible.

These duties are for the Dāsa Mārgi,

எளியன தீபமிடல்மலர் கொய்தல்
அளிதின் மெழுகலதுதூர்த்தல் வாழ்த்தல்
பளிமணி பற்றல் பன்மஞ்சனமாதி
தளிதொழில் செய்வது தான்றாசமார்க்கம்;

The easy duties, lighting lamps, culling flowers, sweeping and washing the temple, praising God and assisting in His service of abhisheka, cooking food, constitute Dāsamārga.

Our christian friends who regard our building temples and spending in ornaments and flowers, will scarcely realize why millions of money are spent on churches and church decorations. The money spent in flowers on Easter and Christmas festivities in churches comes to a million or more each year. Christ rebuked the man who held the joint purse and who objected to Mary's wasting that precious scented-oil on Christ's feet. It was not the value of the oil that was worth anything, but the love that prompted that sacrific was worth all.

But it is not by costly gifts alone, we can manifest our love.

The duties of Satputra-mārgi are as follows,

பூசித்தல் வாசித்தல் போற்றல் சபித்திடல்
ஆசற்ற நற்றவம் வாய்மை யழுக்கின்மை
நேசித்திட்டன்னமுநீ சுத்திசெய்தல் மற்று
ஆசற்ற சற்புத்திர மார்க்கமாகுமே.

Pūja, reading, reciting prayers
Japa, true tapas, and truth,
Purity, loving, offering food
Constitute Satputramārga.

ஆதாரசோதனை யானாடி சுத்திகள்
மேதாதி யீரெண் கலந்து விண்ணொளி
போதாலயத்துட் புலன்கரணம் புந்தி
சாதாரணங்கெடலாஞ் சகமார்க்கமே.

Purifying ourself by Ādhāra and Nāḍi Sōdana, and becoming possessed of 18 Saktis, and entering the Temple of Jñānākāśa (Chidambaram), and getting rid of one's senses and mind is Sahamārga

The eight forms of Yoga referred to are Yama, Niyama, Āsana, Prāṇayāma, Pratyākāra, Dhāraṇa, Dyāna and Samādhi, and we note only here the definition of Yama and Niyama.

Yama is Ahimsa, Satyam, refraining from theft, celebacy or chastity, mercifulness, devoid of deceitfulness, contentedness, courage, taking little food and purity. Niyama is performing tapas, japam, and vratam, believing in God, worshipping Him, reading and meditating on the Śāstras, being cheerful, fearful of evil, and intelligent.

The duties of Sanmārga are stated as follows.

பசுபாசம் நீக்கிப்பதியுடன் கூட்டிக்
கசியாதநெஞ்சம் கசியக் கசிவித்து
தெரியாத உண்மைச் சொரூபோதயத்துற்
றசைவான தில்லாமை யானசன்மார்க்கமே.

Getting rid of one's paśutvam and Pāśa, becoming One with Pati, melting the heart which never melts, in love, entering the True Presence which one can never know, and standing steadfast there, are Sanmārga.

These four sādanas are so arranged that one may lead into the other. And the forms and symbols in each are so chosen that, as one reaches the higher path, fresh meaning and fresh beauty and life burst forth, as his own intelligence and love ripen to receive the fresh life.

The temple built of brick and mortar becomes the very soul and heart of the Yōgi and the Śivaliṅga becomes the Loving Presence and Light of the Supreme. The food பலி offered by the devotee, gradually comes to mean the sacrifice of āṇava or தற்போதம்.

The beauty of such books as the Tiruvāçaga, Dēvāra and Tiruvāimoḷi, consists in this, that it furnishes the required mental and spiritual food to the illiterate and the most cultured minds.

That these four paths are natural divisions, it will be readily perceived. The world's great religions may be ranged under one or other of these heads. Mahomedanism and the ancient Judaism fall under the first division. It was the merit of Jesus Christ that he brought, into greater prominence, the Fatherhood of God. The following quotations from the Bible will show that the other paths are not unrecognized by Jesus Christ.

"Ye call me Master and Lord, and ye say well, for so I am." St. John. xiii. 13.

"Little children, yet awhile, I am with you; a new commandment I give you. That ye love one another; as I have loved you, that ye also love one another." xiii. 33. 34.

"If ye love me, keep my commandments. xiv. 15.

"Greater love hath no man than this, that a man lay down his life for his friends." xv. 13.

"Ye are my friends, if ye do whatsoever I command you." xv. 14.

"Henceforth, I call you not servants; for the servant knoweth not what the master doeth, but I have called you friends, for all things that I have heard of my Father, I have made known unto you." xv. 15.

"Ye have not chosen me, but I have chosen you." xv. 16.

"That they all may be one; as THOU, FATHER, ART IN ME, and I in thee, that they also may be one in us**." xvii. 21.

"I in them, and thou in me that they may be made perfect in one***." xvii. 23.

When I spoke of these higher aspects of Christ's teaching to a missionary, he observed to me that it only struck him lately that fellowship with God was a higher spiritual condition than fatherhood of God. Among ourselves, the Mādhwa system may be said to be pure Dāsamārga. The Rāmānujah in its popular aspects, is Dāsamārga and Satputramārga and a little more. Śaṇkara's system will be Sahamārga. But the mistake is made, in not understanding that these truths are only symbolic and then, they are apt to become dogmatic. I have seen Christian friends contend that God is our real father, as Vedāntins and Yōgis may declaim that there is no other God but the self.

A true and universal religion will combine all these various paths which are required and necessitated by the varying degrees of man's intellectual and spiritual development.

And then, we will not see the mote in our brother's eye, and will live in peace and amity for ever.

I only need quote to you one verse from the Gītā, where all these four paths are set forth.

"Therefore, with bowing and body bent, I ask grace of thee, Lord and Adorable, as father to son, as friend to friend, it is meet, O Lord, to bear with me as Lover to Loved."—I may also observe that Śaivaism of to-day, which I regard as the true modern representative of the historic religion of the Gītā and the Mahābhārata period, combines all these four paths and its great Saints Appar, Jñānasambaṇdar, Suṇdarar and Māṇikka-vāçagar are regarded as teachers of these four paths.

More than all this, I wish to emphasize the fact that love is the essence of all real Religion, and real worship of God is the worship of God's creatures and loving them one and all without distinction of caste or creed, as observed by Srī Kaṇṭha, and unless this is fully recognized and practised, no real spiritual progress is possible.

THE PERSONALITY OF GOD

ACCORDING TO THE SAIVA SIDDHANTA.*

It will be interesting to note that, it was about 12 years ago, we brought out our first work in English on the Ṣaiva Siddhāṇta Philosophy from Tiruppattūr, and we have continued ever since, to work hard at it, and, our translations of Ṣivajñānabodham.' 'Ṣivajñānasiddhiyār,' 'Tiruvaruṭpayan,' along with our contributions to the *Siddhāṇta Dīpikā*, during the last ten years, and Dr. G. U. Pope's 'Tiruvāçagam' form the only bibliography on the subject in English. And we are glad to note that, within the last few years, considerable interest in the subject has been awakened. and several European missionaries have made a special study of the subject, and have discussed it before missionary societies and in the public press. We quote the latest opinion from the *Christian College Magazine*, Vol. XX, 9, from the pen of Rev. W. Goudie.

"There is no school of thought and no system of faith or worship that come to us with anything like the claims of the Ṣaiva Siddhāṇta.

"This system possesses the merits of great antiquity. In the religious world, the Ṣaiva system is heir to all that is most ancient in South India; it is a religion of the Tamil people, by the side of which every other form is of comparatively foreign origin.

"In the largeness of its following, as well as in regard to the antiquity of some of its elements, the Ṣaiva Siddhāṇta is, beyond any other form, the religion of the Tamiḻ people and ought to be studied by all Tamiḻ missionaries.

---

* Reprinted from the *New Reformer* 1907.

"We have, however, left the greatest distinction of this system till the last. As a system of religious thought, as an expression of faith and life, the Śaiva Siddhāṇta is, by far the best that South India possesses. Indeed, it would not be rash to include the whole of India, and to maintain that, judged by its intrinsic merits, the Śaiva Siddhāṇta represents the high-water mark of Indian thought and Indian life, apart, of course, from the influences of Christian Evangel."

And we had remarked in our introduction to 'Tiruvaruṭ-payan' or 'Light of Grace': "And there can be no doubt that we have, in these works, the brightest and largest gems, picked out from the diamond-mines of the Sanskrit Vēdāṇtic works, washed and polished and arranged, in the most beautiful and symmetrical way, in the diadem of Indian thought."

Through want of active propaganda, by means of lectures and conferences, the subject is not properly brought to the notice of the English-educated public, and appreciated by them as it deserves to be; and we are, therefore, much obliged to the editor for having allowed us to contribute a paper on the subject.

Despite the opinion of a few European and Indian scholars, who would trace Śaiva Siddhāṇta to a purely South Indian source, we have all along been holding that Śaiva Siddhāṇta is nothing but the ancient Hinduism in its purest and noblest aspects; and it is not a new religion nor a new philosophy, and it can be traced from the earliest Vēdas and Upanishats. We do not hear of anyone introducing Śaivaism at any time into India, and the majority of Hindus have remained Śaivaites from before the days of the Mahābhārata.

The ideal of the Highest God has, from the beginning, been centred round the person of Rudra, or Śiva, and in the Ṛig Vēda we find him described as the "Lord of Sacrifices and Prayers," and we find this maintained, in the days of Vālmīki, when beliefs in other deities were slowly gaining ground.

Consistently with this position in the Ṛig Veda, the Yajur Vēda declares that "There is only one Rudra, they don't allow a second," "Eka-ēva-Rudrō Nadvitiyāya tasteḥ" (kāṇḍa 8, 6, 10). "He who is one is called Rudra," "Ya Ekō Rudra Uchyati." And St. Tirumūlar declares accordingly:

> ஒன்றவன் றானே யிரண்டவ னின்னருள்
> நின்றனன் மூன்றினுள் நான்குணர்ந் தைந்து
> வென்றனன் ஆறுவிரிந் தனனேழும்பர்ச்
> சென்றவன் றானிருந் தான் உணர்ந்தெட்டே.

> The only One is He; The second is His Sweet Grace (Šakti).
> He stood in the Three; He uttered the four (Dharmas).
> He conquered the five (Senses); He spread Himself out as the six (Ādhāras).
> He stood transcendent as the seventh, knowing the eighth.

> நானவ வேதாந்தம் நான் என்னும் சித்தாந்தம்
> ஆனதுரியத்த னானவன் றனைக்கண்டு
> தேனார் பராபரஞ்சேர் சிவயோகமாய்
> ஆன மலமற்றருஞ் சித்தியாதலே.

> 'Sōham' is Vēdānta; One only (without a second) is Siddhānta.
> In the imperishable Turiya, after seeing the self (Atmadaršan),
> Thou unitest with the Parabrahman in Šivayōga.
> Thou canst attain the rare Siddhi, losing mala.

"God is only one." "Siddhānta declares there is God alone without a second."

The first mantra, it will be noted, is not so well known as the mantra "Ekamēvādvitiyam Brahma", occurring in an Upanishat of the Šāma Vēda; and Max Muller has shown that the use of such words as Rudra, Hara, Šiva, to denote the Highest God, is much earlier than the use of such words as 'Brahman', 'Ātman' and 'Paramātman'; and, in fact, these words do not occur in the Ṛig Vēda at all to denote the Highest God. And we may also point out that the word 'Nadvitīyam' occurring in the Yajur Vēda is certainly a more ancient and original form of the word than 'Advitīyam', which has been obtained by the elision of the letter 'n'.

And St. Meykaṇḍān comments on this mantra in the following verse:—

> "ஒன்றென்றது ஒன்றேகாண் ஒன்றேபதி, பசுவாம்
> ஒன்றென்றநீபாசத்தோடு ளைகாண்—ஒன்றின்றால்
> அக்கரங்களின்றாம் அகரவுயிரின்றேல்
> இக்கிரமத்தென்னும் இருக்கு."

"The Vêdic text means there is only one Supreme Being without a second. And this one is the Lord. You who say 'there is one,' is the Paśu bound up in Pāśa. The word 'second-less' means that, beside God, nothing else will exist, as when we say that there will be no other letters (consonants) when the vowel is not."

No consonant sounds can possibly be formed unless the vowel sound is uttered at the same time; and this will justify us in stating that the vowel is alone, without a second; and yet the vowel is not the consonant nor the consonant the vowel. When we utter the consonant sound (மெய் எழுத்து or உடல் எழுத்து), the vowel and the consonant are linked in a peculiar, inseparable and eternal manner. This is the link or relation between our own human body and the mind (உடல் or மெய் and உயிர்). And from analogy we say there is a similar link between God and the world (including souls). And this link or relation is called, in the Śaiva Siddhānta, 'the Advaita,' and the philosophy, postulating this peculiar link between God and man, is called the 'Advaita Siddhānta Philosophy.'

But how does the One link Himself to the many, and become the many, and divide Himself among the many as it were? St. Tirumūlar postulates "ஒன்றவன்றானே இரண்டு அவன் இன்னருள்" "He is the one; the second is His Grace (Aruḷ)" This division of Him is brought about, because He is also Grace or Love. His Second is His Śakti. He is one with His Śakti or Love.

> அன்பும் சிவமும் இரண்டென்பர் அறிவிலார்
> அன்பே சிவமாவதாரு மறிந்திலார்
> அன்பேசிவமாவ தாருமறிந்தபின்
> அன்பேசிவமா யமர்ந்திருந்தாரே.

"The ignorant say, Love and God are different.
None know that Love and God are the same.
When they know that Love and God are the same,
They rest in God as Love."

And accordingly, also, St. Meykaṇḍān postulates his second Sūtra, in which he declares that God is one and different from the world and the souls, as He is one with His Ājñā-Śakti, which is all Power, all Intelligence, and all Will and all Love. And in the last argument, he shows that as God is Pure Intelligence, this one-ness, or union with the world, or omnipresence is possible. If He was not intelligent, but material or jaḍam, this could not be possible.

As such, Śivajñānabōdam contains the shortest definition of God as Śiva-Sat, or Chit-Sat, or Sat-Chit. Sat denotes God as a Pure Being, in which aspect He can never reach us; Chit or Aruḷ or Love denotes His aspect in which He can reach us, and we can know Him. Sat is the sun, which we can never comprehend. Chit is the Light, one ray of which is enough to remove our darkness and enlighten us; and but for that one ray of light, we can never know the Sun.

All other conceptions of God follow from this essential definition of God as 'Sat-Chit' and, if true, must conform to it. If not, they must be rejected as false.

From the fact that He is intelligent, it follows also that God wills and acts.

"சத்தியின்வடிவேதென்னில் தடையிலா ஞானமாகும்,
உய்த்திடுமிச்சை செய்தி யிவை ஞானத்துளவோவென்னின்,
எத்திறஞானமுள்ள தத்திறமிச்சைசெய்தி,
வைத்தலான் மறைப்பின்ஞானம் மருவிடுங்கிரியையெல்லாம்."

"The form of this Sakti is Unlimited Intelligence.
If asked, whether supreme Will and Power are also found in this Intelligence,
We answer, yes. Wherever there is intelligence, there are Will and Power,
As such, Power and Will will also be manifested by this Chit Śakti."

And He wills to create the worlds, He creates them, and resolves them, and reproduces them again and again. He could not do this purposelessly or out of His mere whim and pleasure; and, as we know He is all love, He could do it only out of such love, to help to lift up the erring and ignorant souls, by giving them their bodies and senses, so that they, themselves, may will and act, and taste the bitter fruit of the tree of knowledge of good and evil, and be chastened and purified by suffering and sorrow, and learn to submit their will to the Will of the Supreme.

And Kāḷidāsa in his 'Kumāra Sambhava' declares :—

" No selfish want e'er prompts a deed of mine :
Do not the forms—eight varied forms—I wear,
The truth of this to all the world, declare."

And these eight forms, he mentions in his invocation in 'Śākuntala.'

" Īśa' preserve you! He who is revealed,
In these eight forms, by man perceptible.—
Water of all creation's works the first ;
The *Fire* that bears on high the Sacrifice,
Presented with solemnity to Heaven ;
The *Priest*, the holy offerer of Gifts ;
The *Sun* and *Moon* those two majestic orbs,
Eternal Marshallers of day and night.
The Subtle *Ether*, vehicle of sound,
Diffused through the boundless universe,
The *Earth*, by sages called the place of birth,
Of all material essences and things,
And *Air* which giveth life to all that breathe."

St. Appar has the following verse :—

" இருநிலனுய்த் தீயாகி நீருமாகி
இயமானனு யெறியுங் காற்றுமாகி
அருநிலைய திங்களாய்ஞாயிறாகி
ஆகாசமா யட்ட மூர்த்தியாகிப்

> பெருநலமுங் குற்றமும் பெண்ணு மாணும்
> பிறருருவுந் தம்முருவுந் தாமே யாகி
> நெருநலையா யின்றாகி நாளை யாகி
> நிமிர்புன்சடையடிக ணின்றவாறே."

"As Earth, Fire, Air and Ejamān (of sacrifice), as Moon, the Sun and Ākāš, as *Ashṭamūrti*, as goodness and evil, as male and female, Himself, the form of every form, as yesterday and to-day and to-morrow, my Lord with the braided hair stands supreme."

St. Māṇikkavāçagar has the following verse :—

> "நிலம்நீர் நெருப்புயிர் நீள்விசும்பு நிலாப்பகலோன்
> புலனாய மைந்தனோ டெண்வகையாய்ப் புணர்ந்துநின்றான்.
> உலகேழெனத் திசை பத்தெனத் தானொருவனுமே
> பலவாகி நின்றவாதோ ணோக்கமாடாமோ."

Earth, Water, Air, Fire, Sky, the Sun and Moon,
The sentient man, these eight forms, He pervades
The seven worlds, Ten quarters, He the *One*
And Many, He stands so, let us sing.

He pervades these eight forms ; they form His eight bodies and hence Šiva is called Ashṭamūrti.* By this is established His Antaryāmitvam or Omnipresence, or Immanence in all nature, as He is Chit. But He is beyond all these forms and beyond all nature and man.

---

* As pervading these forms, He gets eight names also. The following verse is usually quoted but its source is not known.

"Pṛithivyō Bava, Āpah Sarvah, Agnē Rudraḥ, Vāyūr Bhīmaḥ Ākāšasya Mahadevaḥ, Sūryasya Ugraḥ, Chandrasya Somaḥ, Ātma naḥ Pašupatiḥ."

Srikaṇṭhašivāchārya comments on these names in his Bhāshya on I. i. 2. as follows:

As to Brahman being the subject of eightfold appellation: The Supreme Brahman is the Being denoted by the eight appellations of *Bhava, Sarva, Īšāna, Pašupati, Rudra, Ugra, Bhīma, Mahādēva.* Though He is denoted by all words, He is designated specially by Bhava and other like words, indicative as they are of His Highest being: it does not follow that He is not designated by other words than these eight.

The famous passage in the 7th Brāhmaṇa of the 3rd chapter in the Bṛihadāraṇyaka Upanishat deals with God being immanent in nature and in man.

Brahman is called *Bhava* because He exists everywhere at all times, the root "bhū" meaning sattā or existence. We are taught that Brahman is the Existent, running through all things. Accordingly the Sruti says:

> "Existent alone, my dear, this at first was, one only without a second." (Chhā. Up. vi, 2.)
>
> "Truth (Existence), Wisdom, Endless is Brahman." (Tait. Up. ii, 1.)
>
> "He who is existent, who delights in Prāṇa, whose joy is in manas. (Tait. Up. i, 6.)
>
> "The ineffable glory" (Mahānārāyaṇa Up. 24.)

and so on. As running through all things—as for instance "jar *existing*" cloth *existing*—it is evident that Brahman, the existent, constitutes the upādāna or material cause of all. The jar, for instance, always associated as it is with clay, is said to be made out of clay, i.e., has clay for its upādāna. Thus Brahman, the existent, is designated by the word *Bhava*.

Brahman, the all-destroyer, is designated by the word *Sarva*, derived from the root "Sri" to destroy. Brahman is spoken of as the destroyer in the following passages:

"Hail! hail! therefore, to the Destroyer, to the Great Devourer." (Atharvaśiras Up.)

"To whom the Brāhmanas and Kshatriyas (are as it were) but food" (Katha. Up. ii, 25.)

Brahman is denoted by the word "*Iśāna*," the Ruler, as endued with the unconditioned supreme sovereignty, as revealed in the passage, "Who rules these worlds with His powers of ruling." (Atharvaśiras Up.)

As the Iśvara or Ruler must have some beings to rule over, Brahman is denoted by the word *Paśupati*, Master of *Paśus* or subject beings (souls). Thus, the Sruti says:

> "Whom—the four-footed as well as two-footed souls (paśus)—Paśupati, the Lord of souls, rules." (Taittiriya Samhitā III. i, 4.)

As Paśus (souls) are so called because of pāśa (bond), Paśu stands for both Paśu and Pāśa. By this epithet, Brahman is shown to be the Ruler of *chit*, and *achit*, of matter and spirit.

Brahman is called *Rudra* as expelling the malady of samsāra, as we are told in the passage:

> "The knower of Ātman crosses beyond grief" (Chhā. Up. vii. 1.)

Beginning with the verse, "yasya pṛithivī śarīra, &c." * * "He who dwells in the earth, and within or different from the earth, whom the earth does not know, whose body (śarīra) the earth is, and who rules the earth within, He is thy Ātmā, the Ruler within, the Immortal,"[1] and giving similar statements

Brahman is called *Ugra* or Fierce, because He cannot be overpowered by other luminaries, as taught in the passage:

> "Not there the sun shines nor the moon and stars." (Sveta. Up. vi. 14.)

As the regulator and the source of fear to all sentient beings, Brahman is known by the name of *Bhīma* or Terrible. The Sruti says:

> "By fear of Him does the wind blow." (Tait. Up. ii. 8.)

As Great and Luminous, Śiva is called *Mahādeva*. So the Atharvaśiras Up. says:

> "For what then, is He called Mahādēva?—As having abandoned all things, He is adored for His Ātma-Jñāna or spiritual wisdom and for His yōgic glory; wherefore He is called Mahādēva."

That Being called Śiva, known as free from all taint of Samsāra and as the repository of all that is good, is, because He is of such a nature, the cause of the birth &c., of the whole world, Since a Being of such a greatness can be the twofold cause of the world, That (Being called Śiva), endued as He is with such a greatness, is called Brahman. He has also been proved to be the seat of Bliss and such other attributes; wherefore it is vain to raise the question whether Bliss etc., can constitute Brahman, each by itself. From the passage "one should know Māyā as Prakṛiti", it may be seen that Māyā is the Prakṛiti or cause, that Māyā being Iśvara essentially, as taught in the concluding part of the sentence:

> "And know Iśvara as the possessor or the seat of the Māyā." (Svetāśvatara Up. iv. 10.)

Brahman, associated with the sūkshma or subtle chit and achit, is the cause; and Brahman, associated with the sthūla or gross chit and achit, is the effect. Wherefore the Siddhānta or demonstrated conclusion is, that birth etc., of the universe form the distinguishing marks of Brahman.

[1] *Amṛita* a word which frequently occurs in the description of God, is a name of Rudra, in the Ṛigvēda (I. 43-9).

"Whatever beings are Thine, Amṛita, in the Highest place of the law, on its Summit, in its centre, O Sōma, cherish them, remember them, who honour Thee"!

regarding water, air, fire, &c. * * it ends with "He who dwells in Vijñāna (soul) and within or *different* from Vijñāna, whom Vijñāna does not know, whose body Vijñāna is, who rules Vijñāna within, He is thy Ātmā, the Ruler within, Immortal.

That God is different from all nature and man is further brought out by the famous 'Nēti, Neti' verse of this same Upanishat (3-9-26), which Parañjōti Munivar translates and expands in the following lines:—

அல்லையீதல்லை யீதெனவன்மைச் சொல்லினாற்றுதித்தி
ளைக்குமிச்சுந்தரன்.

"God Suṇdara who is described as 'not this' 'not this'".

"பூதங்கள் அல்ல பொறியல்லவேறு புலனல்லவுள்ளமதியின்
பேதங்கள் அல்ல விவையன்றிநின்ற பிறிதல்லவென்றுபெருநூல்
வேதங்கிடந்து தடுமாறு வஞ்சவெளியென்பகூடன்மறுகிற்
பாதங்கணோவவளை யிந்த குறிபகர்வாரையாயுமவரே."

"The Sages declare, 'He is not the five elements, not the senses, nor sensations, nor the Andakaraṇas, nor the soul;
He is the deceitful nothing [1] which the Vēdas fail to discover".

The Supreme is adored as the Creator, Hara; as Protector, Saṅkāra; as Destroyer, or Reproducer, Rudra; and as Bliss-giver, Śiva. God is called "எண்குணத்தான்" [2] as possessing

---

[1] The word '*Veḷi*' in Tamil means a 'void space' aud corresponds to the Telugu word '*Bayilu*' which sage Vēmana is very fond of using.

[2] St. Tiruvaḷḷuvar:

கோளில் பொறியிற் குணமிலவே யெண்குணத்தான்
தாளை வணங்காத் தலை.

Like the senses not enjoying the proper sensations
Is useless the head, not bowing to the Lord with eight attributes.

The Commentator Parimēlaḷagar says, these eight are defined in the Śaivāgamas. They are frequently mentioned in the Purāṇas also. Srikaṇṭha Śivāchārya comments on them as follows in his Bhāshya on I. i. 2. quoting the Vēdic sources of these attributes.

"Admitted that birth etc., as attributes inhering in the universe, do not pertain to Brahman; still, they rightly constitute the defining marks of Brahman as one closely connected with the universe. The Entity called Śiva, possessed of the attribute of omniscience and so on and

eight attributes and they are as follow:—Self-dependence, Purity, Self-knowledge, Omniscience, Being Ever Free from Sin, Supreme Graciousness, Unlimited Bliss.

---

denoted by the eight appellations, is said to be Brahman, the cause of the universe: and to that Entity alone, Bliss and all other like attributes point. The attributes referred to are Omniscience (*Sarvajñatā*), Ever-contentedness (*nityatṛiptatā*), Beginningless Wisdom (*Anādibodhata*), Independence (*Svatantratā*), Never-failing Potency (*Nityāluptaśaktita*), and Infinite Potency (*Anantaśaktita*).

Omniscience (Sarvajñata) consists in all things becoming objects of direct perception—of stainless intuitive experience—independent of all external organs of sensation. It is known to inhere in Brahman, from such passages as: "Who perceives all and who knows all, whose essence consists of knowledge." (Muṇḍaka-Upanishat. I. i. 4). Thus the cause (of the universe) is Brahman who knows the appropriate ways and means of building up the several bodies suited to all sentient beings for the reaping of the fruits of their multifarious acts.

Ever-contentedness (nityatriptata) consists in being replete with unsurpassed Bliss, wherein there is not the slightest trace of distress. Hence the revelation "Bliss is Brahman" (Tait. Up. iii. 6). That Bliss (ānanda) which—introduced in the words "There is yet another Ātman who is composed of Bliss," (Tait. Up. ii. 5), and carried to the culminating point of unsurpassed Bliss by repeated multiplication in the passages beginning with "Here follows the measuring of Bliss" and ending with "that is the unit of Brahman's Bliss" (Tait. Up. ii. 8), is the attribute of Para-Brahman is figuratively spoken of as Brahman Himself in the passage "Bliss is Brahman," because of the abundance of Bliss in Him. Brahman who delights in enjoying such a Bliss is said to be ever-contended. The enjoyment of this mighty Bliss on the part of Brahman is effected through *manas* only, not through external organs of sensation. Hence the passage,

> "There is Brahman who is *ākāśa-śarira* (whose body is light), *satyātman* (Himself the existent) *prāṇārāma* (whose joy is life), *mana-ānanda* (delighted in the mind), *śānti-samriddhā* (perfect in peace), and *amrita* (immortal)." Tait. Up. i. 6.

Here by ākāśa—literally, that which shines all round, the Light—is meant the *chit-ambara*, the ether of spirit, the spirit-light; but not the material ākāśa or ether, because the latter can mark no distinction (*i. e.*, the latter cannot serve to distinguish Brahman from other things in nature). The *chit-ambara* here referred to is that Supreme Power (Parama-Śakti), that highest cause, that ocean, as it were, from which spring up all the hosts

Then follow questions whether God should be said to possess form or no form, whether He should be regarded as Saguṇa or Nirguṇa, Personal or Impersonal, and so on.

---

of bubbles, the mundane eggs of all groups. Brahman, whose form is that supreme light, is spoken of in the śruti as "*ākāśa-sarira*." That *chid-ākāśa* is the highest cause is known from such passages as the following:

"All these beings take their rise from Ākāśa and return into Ākāśa." (Chhā. Up. III. ix. 1).

"He who is called Ākāśa is the revealer of all forms and names" (Chhā. Up. VIII. xiv. 1.)

Satyatman: He who is the Sattā or existence. *Praṇarāma*, He who delights in Prāṇa, the *chit-ambara-śakti*, the Power of Spiritual light, the Basis of all, constituting Brahman's own essential nature. *Mana-ānanda*: He whose joy is in Manas (mind), not in the external organs of sensation. Here, too, "ānanda" refers to the spirit-light, the *chit-ambara*, the Prakriti or cause. Accordingly the Śruti says:

"Who could breathe if that Bliss, that Light, exsited not." (Tait. Up. III. vii, 1.)

Sāṇti-samṛiddha: He who has attained to Śivatā, to Śiva's condition. *Amṛita*: He who has been free from time without beginning.

Thus, it is seen that Brahman who is essentially Existence, Intelligence and Bliss, and whose essential nature is the Supreme Light, enjoys the Bliss of His essential nature by mind alone, independent of external organs of sensation, as implied by the epithet "Mana-ānanda." This epithet also implies that the emancipated souls who have attained to the state of Brahman are possessed of the *antaḥ-karaṇa* or mind, the organ which acts independently of external organs, and by which they experience the unsurpassed bliss of their essential nature. Wherefore, *nityatripta* or ever-contented is Brahman, enjoying the infinite Bliss of His essential nature by manas which is pure *bodha-śakti* itself the faculty of knowledge which can act independently of external organs. That is to say, for Him there is no necessity for the slightest joy of the world (samsāra) external to Himself.

The possession of unsurpassed knowledge—which is *svātās-siddha*, self-existing or inherent,—constitutes what is called *anadibodhatva* or beginningless wisdom. Indeed, the *antaḥ-karaṇa*, jñāna or knowledge, which is the organ whereby He enjoys the Bliss of His own essential nature exists through eternity. Wherefore, Brahman is one of beginningless wisdom, inasmuch as knowledge which repels samsāra exists through

In regard to the question of form or no form, the Siddhānta is positive that God is neither Rūpi nor Arūpi nor Rūpārūpi. "சிவன் அருவுருவுமல்லன் சித்தினொடு சித்துமல்லன்" "God is neither Rūpi nor Arūpi, neither soul nor matter." It recognises that all Rūpa and Arūpa are forms only of matter which is objective to our senses, and God can never be objective to us, and cannot possess any of these material forms or bodies. The nature of matter is to limit, and God is the illimitable and can never be

---

eternity; He is ever free from the evil of samsāra and is spoken of in the Śruti as "perfect in peace and immortal."

Independence (svatantratā) consists in freedom from servitude to others and from other marks of inferiority, and in all things other than Himself being brought under his own control. Independence of Brahman as the impelling agent of the universe of matter and spirit is taught in such passages as the following:

> "There are two, one knowing (Iśvara), the other not knowing, both unborn, one strong, the other weak." (Śvetā. Up. i, 9).
>
> "By knowing the enjoyer, the enjoyed, and the ruier &c." (Śvetā. Up. i, 12).
>
> "But he who controls both knowledge and ignorance, is another." (Śvetā. Up. v, 1 1).

It is evident that because of His independence in all matters, Brahman is the author of all.

The never-failing potency (*Nityaluptasaktitva*) consists in all potencies being inherent in His own nature. Accordingly, the Śruti says "His Higher Power (Parā-sākti) is revealed as manifold, as inherent, acting as force and knowledge." (Śvetā. Up. vi, 8). From this it follows that the potencies of the universe of spirit and matter are inherent in Brahman and that He is never without these specific attributes.

The possession of unlimited potentialities is what is called Endless Potency (anantaśaktita). It is in virtue of these endless potencies that Brahman is the producer and the ruler of the world. Accordingly it is revealed to us that

> "There is one Rudra only.—they do not allow a second—who rules all the worlds by His powers"; (Atharvasiras Upanishat).
>
> "Who rules all these worlds by His supreme powers of ruling and producing." (Atharvasiras Upanishat).

As possessed of endless potencies, Brahman can be the material cause of the infinite universe.

found by any material forms. Some would say God is Arūpi, not realizing that matter is also formless as air, and nothing is gained by calling Him Arūpi. The fact to be clearly borne in mind is that God cannot be objective to us, and possess material form.

But if it is pointed out that Śaiva Siddhānta religion recognises forms of God and His appearances and acts, it is answered that these forms of His are not material but are purely spiritual forms formed of His great love and grace, and to be perceived not by the human mind but with the divine grace, 'அவன் அருளாலே அவன்றாள் வணங்கி.'' St. Aruḷnandi says:—

உருமேனி தரித்துக்கொண்ட தென்றலு முருவிறந்த
அருமேனி யதுவுங் கண்டோ மருவுரு வானபோது
திருமேனி யுபயம் பெற்றோம் செப்பிய மூன்று நந்தம்
கருமேனி கழிக்கவந்த கருணையின் வடிவுகாணே.

"All these forms of His are assumed out of His supreme grace for destroying our evil bodies." And how this is possible is shown in the following:—

"As He does not possess the defect as an object of perception, and as He is possessed of absolute intelligence and power, as He is not possessed of likes and dislikes, the Nirmala God can assume any form out of His grace." And these forms are described in the following verse. "His form is Love; His attributes and knowledge are Love; His five functions are Love; His organs like arms, feet, &c., and His ornament like the crescent moon, &c., are also Love. These things are assumed by the Nirmala God, not for His own benefit but for the benefit of mankind." With which compare the following verse from the Taittirīya Upanishat:—

"His head is surely Love; joy His right wing; delight His left,
Bliss is His Self, Brahman whereon He rests."

The following beautiful hymn from St. Appar, and the text from the Maṇḍūkya Upanishat may also be read,—

மைப்படிந்த கண்ணாளுந் தானுங் கச்சி
மயானத்தான் வார்சடையான் மாசொன்றில்லான்

ஒப்புடையனல்லன், ஒருவனல்லன்,
ஓரூரனல்லன் ஒருவம னில்லி
யப்படியன் அவ்வுருவன் அவ்வண்ணத்தன்.
அவனருளே கண்ணாகக் காண்பதல்லால்
இப்படியன் இவ்வுருவன் இவ்வண்ணத்தன்
இவனிறைவ னென்றெழுதிக் காட்டொணாதே.

"The Lord, with the braided hair, lives in the Kāñchi burial ground, with His beautiful Umā with pencilled eyebrows. He has no sin. He is not one of the mortals, and is not to be compared with any of them. He has no place, and is incomparable. We can, with His grace alone as our eye, perceive Him, His form and nature, otherwise none can paint Him, in His real form and nature."

"This Ātmā is not attainable by explanation nor yet by mental grasp, nor by hearing many times. *By Him whom He chooses*—by him is He obtained. For him, God, His proper form reveals." (Maṇḍūkya iii, 2, 3.)

It is to be noted also that the various forms in the temple are mere earthly symbols, necessary in our view for the ordinary human mind to grasp and follow the divine ideals, until the soul has advanced to a very high stage indeed. A missionary friend of ours wrote to say that as regards the use of symbolism, he found it necessary for the educated people, but as regards its salutary effect on the illiterate people, he felt not convinced. This opinion will be found opposed to the common current of opinion on the subject, but yet it is true, in so far as it postulates the necessity of the use of symbols even as regards highly educated people.

And we regard the various conceptions of God, as He, She and It, as conceptions derived from material forms, and as such not appertaining to His real essence, but the forms are necessary for our own easy conception of God:

"பெண்ணாணலியாகிப் பிறங்கொளிசேர்
மண்ணாகி விண்ணாகி யித்தனையும் வேறாகி"

"He is male, female and neuter, earth and heaven and none of these."

"பெண்ணாணலியெனும் பெற்றியன் போற்றி"

"Praise be to Him who is female and male and neuter."

Further, the words Saguṇa and Nirguṇa are usually translated as personal, and impersonal, and we have often pointed out how vaguely and loosely these words are used, and protested against this translation. We will first consider the words Saguṇa and Nirguṇa. It literally means "with guṇa," and "without guṇa." One school of people would interpret it as meaning "with *good* qualities," and "without *bad* qualities," and that this is absurd is seen from the fact that the two words are made to mean the same thing. The word "Guṇa," however does not mean any good or bad quality, but is a technical word as used by the Sāñkhya and Vēdāṇta schools and as occurring in the Upanishats, Gītā, etc. It means the three guṇas, Satva, Rajas, Tamas, the qualities of Prakṛiti or Pradhāna or matter; and as such the words would mean "with *material qualities*" or "without *material qualities*". St. Tirumūlar uses the phrase "முக்குணநிர்க்குணம், mukkuṇa-ṇirguṇam," so that no mistake may be made of the word Nirguṇam itself.

சாத்திகமெய்து நனவெனச் சாற்றுங்கால்
வாய்த்த விராசத மன்னுங்கனவென்ப
ஒய்த்திடும் தாமத முற்ற சுழுத்தியாம்
மாய்த்திடும் நிற்குண மாசில் துரியமே.

"Satva is condition of wakefulness (Jāgrata); Rajas is dream-condition (Svapna); Tamas is Sushupti; the stainless Turiyam is Nirguṇa."

So also the Gītā speaks of "Thraiguṇyo Nirguṇaha," and it stands to reason that God cannot be "Saguṇa," clothed in matter or material qualities, and must be therefore, non-material, Nirguṇa. The Supreme God is, therefore, described in the Upanishats and Gītā and Śivajñānabōdham as Nirguṇa and not as Saguṇa, as in the following passages:—

"This one God is hid in every bhūta pervading all, the inner *ātmā* of every *ātmā*, Inspector of all deeds (spectator) in whom everything dwells (supporter), the witness, the pure Intelligence and Nirguṇa Being; the Īśvara of Īśvaras, the Mahēśvara, the God Supreme of Gods, the king of kings, the supreme of supreme, the "Īśā" of the universe. (Svetāś). "Beginningless, Nirguṇa, Paramātman, Imperishable, though seated in the body, O Kaunteya, worketh not, nor is soiled (Gītā 13-31). Note Rāmānuja explains Nirguṇa as destitute of satva and other qualities.

"Will not the Lord, who is *Nirguṇa*, Nirmala, Eternal Happiness, Tatparam (transcending all things) and beyond comparison appear to the soul when it gets rid of its *tattvas* such as ākāś, etc? Will not He appear as a far transcending wonder and an inseparable light of its understanding?" (Śivajñānabōdham ix. 2. a.) But certain deities are stated to be Saguṇa, as being clothed with pure Satva or Rājasa or Tāmasa, and they should not be confounded with the Turiya mūrti or the Fourth, the chaturtha, the supreme Brahman; these Śaguṇa beings are merely certain souls from among Sakalars wielding very high powers and possessing still material bodies.

"Śāntam śivam advaitam *chaturtham*" (Rāmatāpini Up.)

The word Nirguṇa is the same as the word "guṇātīta," beyond guṇa or matter." The word, therefore, implies non-material and therefore pure chit. Christian missionaries need not, therefore, shy at this word, and they should certainly drop the word "Saguṇa," which technically means material. From the passages quoted above, especially from the verse from Śivajñānabōdham, it will be seen that God is called "Nirguṇa," "Intelligence and Rationality and Consciousness," are not denied to Him. This is made further clear in the following verses from St. Meykaṇḍān and St. Tirumūlar.

ஏகமாய் நின்றே யிணையடிகள் ஒன்றுணரப்
போகமாய்த் தான்விளைந்த பொற்பினான்—ஏகமாய்
உள்ளத்தின் கண்ணுனென் உள்குவா ருள்கிற்றை
உள்ளத்தாற் காணுனே வுற்று.

"When the soul becoming one with God and feels Him,

He becomes the Supreme Bliss, as God becomes one with the soul. So understanding Him, will he not know with the soul what is understood by the soul?."

> நானறிந் தன்றே யிருக்கின்ற தீசனை
> வானறிந்தார் அறியாது மயங்கினர்
> ஊனறிந் துள்ளே உயிர்க்கின்ற வொண்சுடர்
> தானறியான் பின்னை யாரறியாரே.

"That day I knew my God, the same was not understood by the Gods. The bright effulgence lighting the *inside* of my soul and body, it is said, does not know! Who else can know?"

Of course, it is also said in these works that God 'cannot know' 'உடியாமரியா உணராமறைவா' and it is pointed out by Śiva-jñāna Svāmigal in his Drāviḍa Mahā Bāshya that this only means that God's consciousness is not like the consciousness of the individual man, which is limited, and cannot become conscious unless it forgets, and can only understand in relation ("change is essential to consciousness"—Bain). This human consciouness is called சுட்டுணர்வு. God does not possess this limited சுட்டுணர்வு. His consciousness is what transcends all limitation and all relation and is absolute, as in His Akaṇḍākāra, there is no distinction of this and that, there is nothing out of Him "போக்கிலன் வரவிலன்."

Coming to the question of God being personal or impersonal, we are not quite sure in what sense our Indian writers use these words, but they mostly take it as meaning Saguṇa and Nirguṇa. There is some difference of opinion as regards the connotation of the words among European writers. Some use it as implying individuality and limitation; others use it as not meaning individuality, and this is the more prevalent and cultured opinion. We take the following definitions from a vocabulary of Philosophy.

Person: A being intelligent and free, every spiritual and moral agent, every cause which is in possession of responsibility and consciousness, is a person. In this sense, God considered as a creating cause is a *person*.

"The intimate relation of God, as Being, to all His attributes and to all His essence, constitutes the Divine *Personality*; which for God is His entire Being. God only exists for Himself, in a manner infinite and absolute. God has relation entirely to Himself; for there is no being out of Him to which he can have relation. His whole essence is for Himself and this relation is altogether internal. The divine consciousness or personality embraces all that is in God, all of which He is the reason. "Person as applied to Deity, expresses the definite and certain truth that *God is a living being*, and not a dead material energy."

Emerson says that personality signifies true being (Sat) both concrete and spiritual. It alone is original being. It is not limited. It is that universal element that pervades every human soul and which is at once its continent and fount of being. Distinction from others and limitation by them results from individuality (Ahaṅkāra or Āṇava) not personality (Sat). Personality pertains to the substance of the soul, and individuality to its form. Another Christian writer (Rev. J. Iverach) points out that the absolute and unconditioned Being is *Personal* is not a contradiction in terms, such as a round square, but that it will be true as when we say a white or crimson square. "When we speak of the absolute, we speak of it as a predicate of pure being; we simply mean that the Absolute Personal Being is and must be self-conscious, rational and ethical, must answer to the idea of spirit. Why may not the Absolute Being be self-conscious? To deny this to Him would be to deny to Him one of the perfections which even finite beings can possess."

St. Meykaṇḍān and St. Tirumūlar had stated the same question long ago, as we had shown. This self-consciousness, *இயற்கையுணர்வினனுதல்*, and *முற்று முணர்தல்*, as we have shown above, is not to be confounded with the limited *சுட்டுணர்வு* of the soul.

As it is, Personality clearly means Sat and Chit, and neither Saguṇa nor Nirguṇa. Personality is opposed to Achit or

Jaḍa or irrational matter and relates to the substance, Saguṇa and Nirguṇa to the form, either as individual or otherwise—God can never become individualised as man, woman or brute, the limitation of the latter class of beings arising from its union with matter or Guṇa (Saguṇa). From this view, impersonal would clearly mean irrational, unintelligent and material, and we don't believe any Indian writer would desire to use this word in relation to the Deity, if they only understood its signification.

From the statement that God is Nirguṇa and not Saguṇa, it follows that God can neither have birth nor death. This is one of the central doctrines of Śaiva Siddhānta, and in this respect it differs from all the existing forms of faith, whether Hindu or otherwise, except, perhaps, Muhammadanism and the Unitarian form of Christianity.

> பிறப்பிலி பிஞ்ஞகன் பேரரு ளாளன்
> இறப்பிலி யாவர்க்கு மின்ப மருளும்
> துறப்பிலி தன்னைத் தொழுமின் தொழுதால்
> மறப்பிலி மாயா விருத்தமு மாமே.

"The unborn, with the braided hair, supreme grace, the undying, bestowing bliss on all, O thou worship! If worshipped, thy Māyā will vanish without doubt." (Saint Tirumūlar.)

Of course, it must stand to reason that our soul itself is neither born nor can it die. What is born or what dies is the material body formed of Māyā or Guṇa associated with it from the beginning. These repeated births and deaths occur on account of the peculiar link subsisting between the soul and matter; and, therefore, the souls comprising all Sakalars are called Saguṇa. This same peculiar link does not subsist between God and matter, and hence, He is Nirguṇa. So it is, God can neither be born in the womb nor die. This peculiar doctrine of Śaiva Siddhānta is what should elevate it to the highest rank of philosophy; and the latest discoveries in science could not shake its foundation.

One other feature of Śaiva Siddhāṇta, in regard to the Godhead, we will mention, before we close this paper. And that is, that the supreme Brahman of this school called Śiva or Śivam is not to be confounded with the Hindu Trinity. God is peculiarly denoted by the words Śivam, Sankara, Sambhu, Rudra (he who removes sorrow), as they express the most spiritual nature of God as Love and All-beneficent. And that this is no sectarian conception of the Deity, and that the God of the Śaiva Siddhāṇtis is the universal God of all the nations and all religions is finally brought out by St. Aruḷnaṇḍi Śivāchāriyar in his very first verse in 'Śivajñāna Siddhiyār.'

அறுவகைச் சமயத்தோர்க்கும் அவ்வவர் பொருளாய் வேறாம்
குறியது உடைத்தாய் வேதாகமங்களின் குறியிறந்தங்
கறிவினி லருளான் மன்னியம்மையோ டப்பனாகி
செறிவொழியாது நின்ற சிவனடி சென்னிவைப்பாம்.

" Let me place on my head the feet of Śiva who stands as the goal of each of the six forms of religion, and who stands in the various forms conceived of by the various internal schools of Śaiva faith, and yet stands beyond the conception of all Vēdas and Āgamas, and fills all intelligences with His love, and becomes my Heavenly Father and Mother and fills one and all inseparably."

To sum up, according to the true Vēdāṇta Siddhāṇta Philosophy, God is Sat, Chit, Ānaṇda, not material nor enveloped in matter, Nirguṇa and Personal, ever blissful and All Love, and all His acts such as creation, &c., are prompted by such Love. He is neither He, She nor It, nor has He any material Rūpa or Arūpa, and He can reveal His grace and majesty to those who love Him. He cannot be born nor can He die, and as such, indeed, He is the Pure and Absolute and Infinite Being, able to lift up humanity wallowing in the bonds of mala, māyā, and karma. To know Him as our true Heavently Father and Mother and love Him as such is the only panacea for all the evils of erring mankind.

ADVAITA ACCORDING TO THE SAIVA SIDDHANTA.

In a former paper contributed to *The New Reformer* we dwelt on the Personality of God as understood in the Šaiva School; and we propose to dwell at length on the Advaita Philosophy, as expounded by the Siddhānta writers, and we crave the earnest attention of all students of Indian Philosophy ; and we confidently hope that as this philosophy is more and more understood, it is bound to win its way into the hearts and hopes of all sincere people of every religion. As we pointed out in our last paper, this philosophy has only been placed before the world at large without being hidden under a bushel, within a short time, and there is all the future before it, when it can shine like a beacon light from the summit of the loftiest hill.

And first we have to point out that the word 'Advaita,' pure and simple, is used to describe their philosophy by all Siddhānta writers ; and the word *Višishṭādvaita* never finds place in the Siddhānta Literature. People who for the first time hear of this philosophy put it down at once as *Višishṭādvaita*, without pausing to enquire into its real aspects. But, as we said above, all Šaiva Siddhāntis call themselves strict Advaitis. Saint Meykaṇḍān uses the word 'Advaita' in his commentary on the second Sūtra of Šivajñānabōdham in the passage "அத்துவிதமென்ற சொல்லே அந்நிய நாத்தியையுணர்த்து மாயிட்டு," and expounds his system of Advaita. In another place, "அத்துவிதமாதல் அகண்டமும்மைநவமே அத்துவிதியன்பாற்றெழு," he calls his system 'Advaita,' and addresses his pupils as 'Advaiti.'

Saint Umāpati Šivāchārya uses it in the following introductory verse in Šivaprakāšam :—

புறச்சமயத்தவர்க்கிருளாய கச்சமயத்தொளியாய்
புகலளவைக்களவாகி பொற்பணிபோலபேதப்

பிறப்பிலதாயிருள்வெளி போற்பேதமுஞ்சொற்பொருள்போற்
பேதாபேதமுமின்றிப் பெருநூல்சொன்ன
அறித்திறனல் விளைவதா யுடலுயிர்க் கண்ணருக்கண்
அறிவொளிபோற் பிறிவறு மத்துவித மாகுஞ்
சிறப்பினதாய் வேதாந்தத் தெளிவாஞ் சைவ
சித்தாந்த திறனிங்குத் தெரிக்க லுற்றாம்.

"We expound here the beauty of Śaiva Siddhānta, the cream of the Vēdānta, *whose excellent merit consists in its exposition of the Advaita,* postulating an inseparable relation like body and soul, eye and the sun, the soul and the eye, supported as it is by the Dharma of the highest authoritative books, and unlike the Bhēda and Bhēdābhēda and Abhēda relations illustrated, respectively, by light and darkness, word and meaning, gold and ornament, set forth by other schools, and which is further supported by perfectly logical methods, and is light to the truth-seekers and darkness to others."

Saint Tāyumānavar uses the word freely and has this verse in praise of his Parama Guru Saint Meykaṇḍān:

பொய்கண்டார் காணாப் புனிதமா மத்துவித
மெய்கண்ட நாதனடி மேவுநா ளெந்நாளோ.

"Oh! for the day when I can reach the feet of my lord, who found the truth of the pure *Advaita*, and which could not be comprehended by persons dwelling in untruth." There is another verse of his also in which he uses the word twice, illustrating and explaining the meaning of the word itself, and which will be discussed later on:

ஆணவத்தோ டத்துவிதமானபடி மெய்ஞ்ஞானத்
தாணுவினோ டத்துவித மாகுநா ளெந்நாளோ"

"Oh! for the day when I will be in *Advaita* relation with God, as I am now in *Advaita* relation with *Āṇava* (the world)."

Going back to the word itself, it occurs in the following passages of the Vēda and Upanishats, and in a few other places :—

"Eka eva Rudro Nadvitıyāya tasthe" (Yajur Vēda, 1. 8. 6.)

"Ekhohi Rudro Nadvitıyāya tasthe (Svetas Upanishat, 3, 2.

"Ekamevādvitīyam" (Chhāndog Upanishat, 6, 2, 1.)

"Sāntam Sivam Advaitam Chaturtham Ātmā" (Maṇḍūkya Upanishat, 7.)

"Amatras chaturtavya vakārika prapunchopasamas Śivodvaitavave." The partless fourth, incomprehensible, that ends all going out. Siva-advaitam. (Maṇḍūkya Upanishat, 12.)

The first two texts give the word in its original form, '*Nadvitīyam*,' and the word now in use has been got by elision of the initial 'n'; and 'na' is the negative prefix. The word literally means therefore no two, or not two. The word as used in the texts quoted above and as read with the context would not convey all the philosophic meaning which has been imported into it by the Āchāryas of various schools. It simply meant there was no other person except the one mentioned at the time. In the first text, it meet an that there was only one God and no second God. However this be, we have to deal with the word as brought into use by the various schools. And the negative prefix has been taken to mean variously. This prefix is said to connote (1) இன்மை or Abhava, positive negation, (2) அன்மை Sadṛisyam, and (3) மறுதலை or Virodha—or the opposite. Both in Sanskrit and in English, the same prefix or word is used to denote the first two meanings, but in Tamiḷ we have two different words இல்லை and அல்லை to denote these two different meanings. If in the word 'Advaitam,' the first meaning be taken, it would mean that one or other of the two or both would be non-existent, and it would mean one only out of the two or neither. Śivajñānasvāmigaḷ points out that almost all the Āchāryas of other schools, including Śaṅkara, Rāmānuja and Mādhva take it to mean 'one,' taking the 'Abhava' meaning. If the *Sadṛisya* meaning be taken, it would mean non-different or non-dual. This meaning is best explained and illustrated by taking the first stanza of chapter 36 of the sacred Kuṛaḷ—entitled "How to Perceive Truth."

பொருள் அல்லவற்றைப் பொருளென் றுணரும்
மருளானு மாணாப்பிறப்பு

The delusion whereby men deem *that the truth which is not*,
That is the cause of hapless birth.

Here the word used is அல்ல and the meaning is, of the two things before us, say a copy of Kuṟaḷ and a copy of Śivajñānabōdham, if one mistakes one book for the other, this would be delusion, Mityajñānam or false knowledge or Avidyā or ignorance. Here the existence of two books is not denied. But if the words used were பொருள் இல்லவற்றை instead of பொருள் அல்லவற்றை then the meaning would be altogether altered, and it would mean, there being no copy of Kuṟaḷ before us at all, we fancy there is a copy of Kuṟaḷ before us. In the former case, the reality of the objects before us is not questioned. In the latter case, the reality of the object presented before us is denied. In the familiar example of shell and silver, both objects and ideas are real, and we can never have these conceptions, unless both were real and different. The delusion arises from the fact that we mistake one thing shell, for the silver *which is not*, and this arises also because on account of the resemblance which exists between these objects, shell and silver, or the two books. when there was no shell before us, the silver would present itself before us, this would illustrate the Abhava meaning, but ordinarily no such object or idea will present itself before us. This same difference will be felt throughout in the working of the two systems. One holds the world including the body and ths soul as real, but ordinarily, we often mistake the body for the soul, and minister to its wants instead of seeking the soul's salvation. And so too, we mistake the soul for God. If we only understood the true nature of each of these, and understood the transient nature of the pleasures of the body, and gave them up for the eternal bliss of the union with God, our path would be clear. Saint Tiruvaḷḷuvar follows up this view and states in his second stanza :

இருணீங்கி இன்பம் பயக்கும் மருணீங்கி
மாசறு காட்சி யவர்க்கு.

"Darkness departs (with which we have been identifying ourselves before) and rapture springs to men who see the mystic vision pure, from all delusion free." In this view, no attempt is made to deny the reality of the world and sin and ourself and God, but one is asked to discriminate one thing from the other. In the other view, there is no world, no sin, no soul, and all these fantasies arise. But there is no reply to the question 'How?'

However, let it be premised that the Siddhāṇta writers take the negative prefix to mean not *Abhava* இன்மை but *Sadrisya* அன்மை; and we will proceed to show how they develope their system.

Count Tolstoy defines religion as "a certain relation established by man between his separate personality and the endless universe or its source; and morality as the perpetual guiding of life which flows from this relation." And Siddhāṇta writers attempt to trace alike this relation between God and man and the world, and thereby discover the means or Sādana for our guidance whereby we can get rid of all pain and sin, And the first postulate is contained in two words in the second Sūtra of Šivajñānabōdham.

"அவையே தானேயாய்"

"God is one with them, and *different*."

And Saint Aruṇaṇdi Šivāchārya adds another relation, 'one-and-different.' Here then is involved 'Abhēda,' 'Bhēda,' and 'Bhēdābhēda' relations. But other schools postulate one or other of these relations, and the similes used are 'gold and ornament' to denote the Abhēda relation, 'darkness and light' to denote Bhēda relation, and 'word and meaning' to denote the Bhēdābhēda relation. And there can be no reconciliation between these views, and no meeting place between them. The Siddhāṇta postulates all these different relations, but by other similes, such as body and soul to denote Abhēda, eye and the sun to denote Bheda, soul and the eye to denote Bhēdābhēda, as set forth above in the stanza quoted from Saint Umāpati-Šivāchārya, and yet so as not to be contradictory. There must therefore be something peculiar in this view which makes it possible to admit of all these different relationships or aspects, and yet not to be self-contradictory, and to appear as one harmonious whole. And it is this peculiar relation which cannot be easily defined or described, that is denoted by the word 'Advaita.'

And Saint Meykaṇḍān accordingly discusses this word in his first argument. "The word *Advaita* cannot mean one-ness or Ekam; no one can think of himself as one, and the very thought implies two things. The word simply denies the separateness of the two, *Anyanāsti*, and hence God is said to be one with the souls," that is to say, *Advaita* is *Ananya* or non-different. The relation is such, that though there be difference in substance, no separation is possible, and the word is used to emphasize its non-different character. And he instances the case of a man and his body. Though these are different, yet man identifies himself with the body, owing to the inseparable connexion between the two, and so practically they are one or non-different. So too, the soul identifies itself with God, though God is not the soul, and the soul is not God; and hence God is one, and not one with the soul. And in the second stanza, he develops this argument, and analyses the text 'Ekamevādvitīyam' and illustrates it.

> "ஒன்றென்றது ஒன்றேகாண் ஒன்றேபதி பசுவாம்
> ஒன்றென்ற நீபாசத்தோ டுளைகாண்—ஒன்றின்றால்
> அக்கரங்க ளின்றாம் அகரவுயி ரின்றேல்
> இக்கிரமத் தென்னு மிருக்கு."

"In the Vēdic text, 'Ekam' means that there is only one and that one is the Pati (Lord). You who say 'There is one' is the *Paśu*, bound up in *Pāśa*. The word 'Advaita' means that beside God nothing else will exist, as when we say that there will be no other letters (consonants) when the vowel 'A' is not." And the meaning will be clear when the illustration is fully understood. The illustration is that of vowel and consonants i.e., உயிர் and மெய் or உடல், meaning soul and body.

> "உடல்மேலுயிர்வந் தொன்றுவ தியல்பே."

"The vowel becoming one with the consonants is natural union," is the Nannūl sūtra.

And the illustration of body and mind or soul was what was stated in the first stanza.* So that we have two

---

* We are glad to extract the following from Mr. Armstrong's book, 'God and the Soul' wherein he brings out the same analogy.

"But I would much rather put it in this way: the relation of the physical universe to God is, within certain limits, analogous to the relation of my body to myself. The movement of my tongue as I speak, of my eyes as I glance at my friend, of my hand as I write these words, proceeds from that stream of conscious energy which you may call my mind, my soul, my spirit, my will, or myself. Instantaneously the command of my unseen self flows through my seen self and modifies its attitudes, its gestures, its several and separable parts. But the intimate connexion between myself and my body does not imply that I am my body or that my body is myself, the 'Ego.' If they are in absolute alliance they are also in absolute antithesis. Nor, even if you went on to imagine my body the absolute product of my own will, and its automatic and reflex action, the breath, the circulation of the blood, the beating of the heart, the growth of the hair and the nails to be the effect of my will, and my consciousness to be perpetually engaged in conducting these processes, would you be one step nearer identifying me, the 'Ego,' the self, with this body, but it would be other than the body, above and beyond it, transcending it, of a nature belonging to a superior order to it, in another and a higher plane than it. Press the analogy home, and you have a safeguard against Pantheism. The universe may be thought of as the body of God but as it is gross to confound the body with the man, so it is gross to confound the universe with God. The soul is in the body only in the sense that its energies flow through the body; a man's soul (that is the man) is not in the body in any physical sense. The body is its organ and its instrument.

But why do we shrink from Pantheism? Not from dread of losing the physical universe in God, but from dread of losing our own souls in God. Pantheism only becomes deadly to vigorous religion and morality when it makes the man's soul, the man's self, a portion of God. Theism claims that the human soul is a free cause, a separate island of individual will in the midst of the great ocean of the Divine Will. Leave us man confronting God, not absorbed in Him, and the conditions are preserved for the ethical life of the individual, and also for the communion of the soul with God, as another than itself, the very possibility of which is destroyed if a separate personality is wiped out. On this matter of the otherness of man from God, I hope to say more in a later chapter."

illustrations to describe the relation of God to the world, and these two illustrations going by the same name show that the relation between mind and body is what obtains between vowels and consonants.

Viśishṭādvaita writers have no doubt used the illustration of mind and body but nowhere do they discuss the nature of this relation; much less do they seem to have apprehended the analogy of vowels and consonants. Doctor Bain discusses this question in his book on "Mind and Body," and we wrote on the subject in the *Siddhānta Dīpika*, Vol. II, page 13, and this is reproduced in pp. 52-63 of this book.

So that whatever word we may use, the nature of this relationship is clear. If the Vedic texts postulate oneness, it is in a higher sense than what is understood in the current philosophies. In this position is reached a higher and truer Monism. We have shown how true it is that St. Meykaṇḍān stated that there is no other letter but 'A.' So it is, we can state 'There is nothing else but God,' 'Only one, without a second.' This comes as the result of the Highest experience or Jñāna or Svānubhava or Śivānubhava. And this is stated in the central stanza of Tiruvāçagam, its *Hṛidaya* sloka:

'இன்றெனக் கருளி இருள்கடிந் துள்ளத்
தெழுகின்ற ஞாயிறே போன்று
நின்ற நின்தன்மை நினைப்பற நினைந்தே
நீயலாற் பிறிது மற்றின்மை
சென்று சென்றணுவாய்த் தேய்ந்து தேய்ந்து ஒன்றாம்
திருப்பெருந் துறையுறை சிவனே
ஒன்று நீயல்லை யன்றி யொன்றில்லை
யாருன்னை யறியகிற் பாரே."

"This day in Thy mercy unto me Thou didst drive away the darknes and stand in my heart as the Rising Sun.
Of this Thy way of rising—there being naught else but Thou—I thought without thought.
I drew nearer and nearer to Thee, wearing away atom by atom, till I was One with Thee,
Oh Śiva, Dweller in the great Holy Shrine.

Thou art not aught in the universe, naught is there save Thou.
Who can know Thee ?

—(*from* P. A's *Translation*).

As man nears God, he wears away atom by atom, so that at the moment of union, nothing of him is left and what is left is the Presence of the Supreme One only and the feeling of His Presence; and no feeling or consciousness of feeling of himself or others. This feeling of the Presence and Bliss of God, is One and Advaita, and there is no consciousness of such oneness or Bliss, and duality will certainly arise the moment man regains consciousness. So what he is said to lose in fact atom by atom is his various conscious selves.

"வான்கெட்டு மாருதமாய்ந்து அழல்நீர்மண்கெடினும்
தான்கெட்ட லின்றிச் சலிப்பறியாத் தன்மையனுக்கு
ஊன்கெட்டு உயிர்கெட்டு உணர்வுகெட்டு என்னுள்ளமும்போய்
நான்கெட்ட வாபாடித் தெள்ளேணங் கொட்டாமோ."

"Though Ether, Wind, Fire, Water, Earth should fail
His Constant Being fails not, knows no weariness!
In Him, my body, soul, and thought and mind were merged (lost),
How all *myself* was lost, sing we and beat TELLENAM."

(*from* Rev. Doctor G. U. POPE's *Translation*).

His bodily consciousness, His life-consciousness, His mental consciousness, all these alone constitute his individuality, the feeling of I and mine. This 'I-ness', 'நான்', is what has got to be rid of. So that when this 'I-ness' or individuality is lost, 'நான் கெட்டவா'; he becomes Śivam or God, 'நான் கெட்டு சிவமானவா.' What perishes of course is the Soul's individuality or consciousness of 'I ness', inducing duality, but what subsists even in Mōksha is the soul's personality, which has Svānubhava or Śivānubhava, identifying itself with God.

The soul in union with God becomes pure object (God) as it were, which is the true Monism of Science. Hence it is Saint Meykaṇḍān states this paradox (xi. 2. c.): "when becoming one with God, if the soul perished, there will be nothing to unite with God, as it perishes. If it did not perish, it cannot become one with God. Just like the salt dissolved in water, the soul, after losing its mala, unites itself with His feet and becomes the servant of God (loses its 'I ness' or individuality). Then it will have no darkness (as separation)." The salt in its crystaline conditions constitutes its individuality. In that condition it is distinguished from water. But after it is dissolved in water, what is lost is its individual character and not itself or its substance or personality.

The following sentence from a text-book of science will show how exact is our language: "When a river enters the sea, it soon loses its *individuality*, it becomes *merged* with the body of the ocean, when it loses its current, and when therefore it has no power to keep in suspension the sediment which it had brought down from the higher lands." If re-read as follows, its application will become clear: "When the soul loses its individuality (feeling of 'I' ness, Ahaṅkāram or Āṇavam), it becomes merged in God, when it loses its Karma, and when therefore it has no power to keep in suspension its mala with which it has been associated from the beginning." And this is the exact figure and language used by St. Meykaṇḍān in viii. 4. A. This losing of self is the real sacrifice brought about by love. It is this sacrifice, பலி, we are asked to make as we enter the Temple, and the moment we make it, our பசுத்துவம் (Paśutvam) will leave us, and we will become the *Naṇdi*, the Blissful Śivam.

That the Siddhānta marks the Highest Standard of Monistic Truth is what is brought out by St. Tirumūlar also in his famous line "தானுன வேதாந்தம் தான் என்னும் சித்தாந்தம்" "Vedānta postulates 'Aham Brahmāsmi,' 'I am Brahman,' Siddhanta postulates Tat (one) alone." That is to say that the Siddhānta appeals fully and finally to only One Experience, the Bliss of God and One alone; whereas the Vedānta has reference to the Sōham-paths whereby this experience is gained. And anyone can perceive that the Sōham experience is a conscious one and a dual one or Dvaita. In this sense Siddhānta is Advaita and Vedānta is Dvaita. And what are considered as the strong-holds of Vedānta by followers of Sankara admit of easy interpretation by the Siddhāntis. The question, as pointed out by Śivajñāna Yōgi, did not arise absolutely as to whether padārthas were one or two. It arose in connection with the famous Mahāvākya texts, 'Aham Brahmāsmi,' Tatvamasi, etc. Says he:—

மற்றென்னையோ அத்துவிதமென்னும் சொற்குப் பொருளெனிற் சித்தாந்த சைவருரைக்குமாறு காட்டுதும், 'அது நீயாகின்றாய், எ-ம், அது நானாகின்றேன், எ-ம், 'அதுவிது வாகின்றது,' எ-ம், மூவிடம்பற்றி நிகழும் தத்துவமசி முதலிய மகாவாக்கியங்களைக் கேட்டவழி அதுவென்பது ஒருபொருள், நீயென்பது ஒருபொருளாகலின், ஒருபொருள் மற்றொரு பொருளாமாறி யாங்ஙனம் என்னும் ஐய நீக்குதற்கு எழுந்ததாகலின் அதுவிது வாதற் கேதுவாய், அவ்விரண்டிற்கு முளதாகிய சம்பந்த விசேட முணர்த்துதலே யத்துவிதமென்னும் சொற்குப்பொருளென்றுணர்ந்துகொள்க.

"If you ask, what then is the meaning of the word *Advaitam*, I will show how Śaiva Siddhāntis explain it. On hearing the great texts called Mahāvākya, Tatvamasi, etc., which are used in the three persons, we see that these sentences speak of 'that' as one substance and 'Thou' as another, and inquire how one can become the other. The answer is given to remove this doubt, by stating *how one can become the other and what relation subsists between these two*, and the word Advaitam is used to express this peculiar relation."

The word does not mean one or non-existence of two or more, but is used to express the peculiar relation that exists between two distinct things which can become one, and we had long ago called attention to this meaning in our very first work, and before we had any chance of seeing this luminous exposition of Śivajñāna Yōgi, and we observed, *vide* Śivajñānabōdham p. 17:

"Though in all these cases, an identity is perceived, a difference in substance is also felt. It is this *relation* which could not be easily postulated in words but which may perhaps be conceived, and which is seen as two (Dvaitam) and at the same time as not two (Advaitam); it is this relation which is called *Advaitam*, 'a unity in duality,' and the philosophy which postulates it, the Advaita philosophy."

Of all the mass of the Vedic and Theosophic literature that has come into existence during the last two or three decades, there is none that equal the writings of Professor Kunte for real insight into the nature of Hindu philosophy and critical acumen. And his summary, added at the end of the first pāda of the first Adhyāya of his translation of the Brahma Sūtras, is a most beautiful and original one. Wonderful as it may seem, both Śivajñāna Yōgi and Kunte exactly propound the same questions and give the same answer. He shows there are texts in the Upanishats which support the dualistic and monistic view, and the mainstay of the monists are the *Mahā* Vākya texts and these texts are the great stumbling block in the path of dualists, and he shows that their interpretation cannot bear an examination, because the texts evidently do not admit of it, and all that they say is simply beside the mark.

"What is to be done? There are doubtless a few texts in the Vēda which support the Pantheistic views. Most however support the Theistic principles. But so long as Pantheistic texts are not explained, the proposition that the Vēdas do not teach Pantheism cannot be accepted. Again, the adjustment and the interpretation proposed by the Theists cannot be accepted because of their being far-fetched and forced. But we do not see how the few Patheistic texts come in the way of Theism, because we believe that though they be interpreted as the Pantheists do, yet they support Theism. How can this be?" And he proceeds to show how this can only be understood in the light of Yōga. After instancing the various forms of Bhakti (Charya and Kriya), he says: "But there is a special feature of such adoration—a feature not included in any of these. It is the ecstatic condition of the spirit, a condition which can neither be explained nor understood without an illustration. Let the reader realize the love a mother has for her child. A mother or her child sometimes experiences a state of mind, an indescribable state. That which either of them expresses can alone convey an idea of their feelings when they are in the ecstatic condition. The mother directly addresses the child thus, 'Oh, my piece of Gold, Oh, my soul, Oh, my life, can I eat you up?' '*தின்பன்கடிப்பன் இருத்துவன்தானே.*' Under these circumst. nces, the mother forgets that her body is different from that of her child, which experiences the same feeling. Such an *identity* is the form of the ecstatic condition of the mind. This is a special feature of adoration. This sort of *ecstatic identity, the Yōgis feel.* Hence in the Vēda and in the Upanishats, the Pantheistic doctrine of the identity of the human spirit and the Supreme Spirit, *if enunciated, is enunciated in this way.* Again the Brahma Sūtra of Bādarāyaṇa does not inculcate it." And he explains further below. "The characteristic feature of the Indian Vēdāṇta is its recognition of spirit-power, as it is explained in the Yōga Sūtras which systematically lay down the following propositions: That the Supreme Spirit or God is *related* to the human spirit, that the human spirit has very great *potential powers* and that if certain methods of living be adopted, it can *call out its powers* and become *actually able to know the past and the future,* and that the spirit disenthralled from the flesh is ultimately *absorbed in one sense* into the Supreme Spirit. The Yōga system is properly the backbone of the Vēdānta."

And we had pointed out in another place, *Personality of God,* (pp. 223—243) that the Yōga *Pāda* is not merely the backbone of Vēdāṇta, but it is Vēdāṇta itself.

It is not well understood that the word Upanishat really means the same thing as 'Yōga.' Yōga means the Sādana required for bringing the Soul and God in Union; and the Upanishat is also the teaching of the Sādana whereby man comes nearer and nearer to God, by destroying the bonds that bind him. The root-meaning (upa = near, ni = quite, sad = to perish) is hit off to a nicety in the famous line in Tiruvāçagam quoted above. "The house of God," 7th verse, சென்று சென்று அணுவாய்த் தேய்ந்துதேய்ந்து ஒன்றாம், "*nearer* and *nearer* to Thee I drew, *wearing away* atom by atom, till I *was one with Thee.*" And in the passage in (Chandog, 1. 1. 10) and in several others, the word Upanishat is used as a synonym for Yoga. And this derivation really explains the scope of an Upanishat, a misunderstanding of which has led to no end of confusion. The Siddhāṇti takes the Upanishat as the text-book of the Yōga Pāda or School.

The higher stage or Pāda being the Jñāna Pāda, the words Upanishat, Vēdāṇta, Yōga, Saha-Mārga or Sōhamārga or Hamsa-Mārga are all synonymous; and as Vēdāṇta strictly means Yōga, the words Vēdāṇta and Siddhāṇta are contrasted, Siddhāṇta meaning the Jñāna-Mārga or *Pāda*, though it embraces all the remaining *Pādas*, Charya, Kriya, and Yōga. The practice involved in the Mahāvākya-texts is this Sōham Bhāvana or Śivōham Bhāvana, and when this practice is matured, the soul stands in complete allegiance to the Supreme One, renouncing all idea of self and self-action; then can the soul say: "I am all the world," யானே புலகென்பனின்று. (Śivajñānabōdham, 2-1-4). "In me everything originated, in me everything established, in me everything merges. That secondless-Brahman am I. (Kaival. Up. 21)."

As Professor Kunte speaks of the ***potential power of man*** by calling out which he can become one with God; Śivajñāna Yōgi dwells at great length, and too frequently, on this special characteristic or power of man whereby man can be said to become God; and this power is the power of the soul *to become that to which it is united*, அதுவதுவாதல், in the language of St. Meykaṇḍān or, சார்ந்ததன் வண்ணமாதல் and யாதொன்றுபற்றின் அதன் இயல்பாய் நிற்றல் in the language of St. Tāyumānavar, and this power is likened to that of the crystal or mirror.

Says Professor Henry Drummond:—

"All men are mirrors—that is the first law on which this formula (of sanctification or corruption) is based. One of the aptest descriptions of a human being is that he is a mirror." This illustration is to be originally found in the Upanishats and Gitā.

"As a metal disk (mirror) tarnished by dust shines bright again after it has been cleansed, so the one incarnate person satisfied and free from grief after he has seen the real nature of himself. And when by real nature of himself, he sees as by a lamp, the real nature of the Brahman, then having become the unborn eternal God who transcends all tattvas, he is freed from all pāśa." (Svetās Upanishat ii. 14, 15). "From meditating Him (abhidhyānāth), from joining Him (yojanāth), from becoming one with Him (tatvabhāvāt), there is further cessation of all Māyā in the end." (Svetās Upanishat i. 10.) "As a flame is enveloped by smoke, as a mirror *by dust*, as an embryo is wrapped by the womb, so this (soul) is enveloped by it (desire). (Gitā iii. 3.)

And St. Meykaṇḍān has this stanza (viii. 3. a.) பண்ணிறமே. The principle of it receives its exposition in the Sāṅkhya and in the Yōga Sūtras, by means of this illustration of mirrors and colours.

"Though it (soul) be unassociated, still there is a tinging (reflectionally) through non-discrimination ; [for there is not a real tinge in that which is unassociated (with tincture or anything else), still there is as it were a tinge ; hence the tinge is treated simply as reflection by those who discriminate the tinge from the soul which it delusively seems to belong to].

"As is the case with the Hibiscus and the crystal, there is not a tinge, but a fancy that there is such." Sāṅkhya aphorism vi. 27-28—Gablie's *Translation.*

In the words of Professor Max Muller, this is how the subject is treated in the Yōga Sūtras : "Now if we ask what is the result of all this, we are told in Sūtra 41, that a man who has put an end to all the motions and emotions of his mind, obtains, with regard to all objects of his senses, conformation grounded on them, or steadiness and consubstantiation, the idea being that the idea is modified or changed by the objects perceived, 'அது அதுவாதல்' (i. 41). As a crystal when placed near a red flower, becomes really red to our eyes, in the same way the mind is tinged by the objects perceived" (*Six Systems.* p. 453).

This principle of mind identifying itself with the objects perceived, is stated in the following passages of the Upanishat also.

"Now a man is like this or that, according as he acts and according as he behaves, so will he be : a man of good acts will become good, a man of bad acts bad. He becomes pure by pure deeds, bad by bad deeds.

"As is his desire, so is his will; and as is his will, so is his deed. Whatever deeds he does, that he will reap.

"Whatever object man's own mind is attached to, to that he goes strenuously with his deed.

"He who desires the Ātman, being Brahman, he goes to Brahman. That Ātma is indeed Brahman." (Brihat IV, iv. 5. 6.)

Similar passages are found in the Mahābhārata and the familiar statement of it in Sanskrit is:

'*Yat Bhāvam tat Bhavati.*'

Hebert Spencer calls this union as one of absolute identity. And this is almost the language used by St. Meykaṇḍāu 'அது அது ஆதல்'.

As the Upanishat writers, Sāṅkhyans, and Yōgins, and Siddhāṇtins state this principle and base on it their scheme of salvation, so does also Professor Henry Drummond in his remarkable address entitled "The Changed Life," based on the text from St. Paul.

"We all, with unveiled face, reflecting, as a mirror, the glory of the Lord, are transformed into the same image, from glory to glory, even as from the Lord the Spirit." He paraphrases the sentence as follows: "We, all reflecting, as a mirror, the character of Christ, are transformed into the same image from character to character—from a poor character to a better one, from a better one to one a little better still, from that to one still more complete, until by slow degrees the perfect image is attained. Here the solution of the problem of sanctification is compressed into a sentence, "reflect the character of Christ, and you will become like Christ." or, as we will say, reflect the image of God in yourself, and you will become God-like, or God.

But how is the poor character to be made better and better, or the reflecting image clearer and clearer? It is by cleansing the mirror (soul) freer and freer from dirt, and bringing it more and more in line with the effulgent light, that this can be effected;

and when the mirror is absolutely perfect and nearest, the light shines brightest, and so overpowers the mirror, that the mirror is lost to view, and the Glory and Light of the Lord are felt. For, observes the learned Professor truly, "What you are conscious of is 'the glory of the Lord.' And what the world is conscious of, if the result be a true one, is also the glory of the Lord. In looking at a mirror, one does not see the mirror or think of it, but only of what it reflects. For a mirror never calls attention to itself—except when there are flaws in it." These flaws are the colours of the Siddhāṇti who compares them to the māyā or body. In union with the body, it is the body alone that is cognized, and not the mirror-like soul. In union with God, the Glory and Light alone are perceived and not the mirror-like soul either; and the Professor declares, "All men are mirrors—that is the first law on which this formula (of sanctification or corruption) is based. One of the aptest descriptions of a human being is that he is a mirror," and we must beg our readers to go through the whole pamphlet to note how beautifully he draws out this parallel.

He notes the second principle which governs this process, namely, the law of assimilation or identification. "This law of assimilation is the second, and by far the most impressive truth which underlies the formula of sanctification—the truth that men are not only mirrors, but that these mirrors, so far from being mere reflectors of the fleeting things they see, transfer into their own inmost substance and hold in permanent preservation, the things that they reflect. No one can know how the soul can hold these things. No one knows how the miracle is done. No phenomenon in nature, no process in chemistry, no chapter in necromancy can even help us to begin to understand this amazing operation. For think of it, the past is not only focussed there in a man's soul, it is there. How could it be reflected from there if it were not there? All things he has ever seen, known, felt, believed of the surrounding world, are now within him, have become part of him, in part are him—he has been changed into their image."

These two principles in fact underlie our Maṇtra and Taṇtra, our Upāsana and Sādana, Bhāvana, and Yōga, and our books instance the case of the snake-charmer chanting the Garuḍa Maṇtra in illustration of this second principle of assimilation or identification. The Professor instances from Darwin, how in the working out of this principle of association and assimilation or identity in the human and animal evolution, persons ever associated with pigs get piggy faces, and with horses, horsey faces. In the case of husband and wife when they have been perfectly loving, it has been found to effect a complete assimilation of their features. Such is the power of the human mind, both a demerit and a merit; it can lower itself to the very depths of the brute, or it can rise to the very height of Godhood. This law is spoken of in our text books as the law of 'Garuḍadhyānam.' The writer of the book "Spiritual Law in the Natural World" (Purdy Publishing Company, Chicago) observes that all "who have made a study of the cause of all things have become so *at one with it*, as to have causing power, for it is an invariable rule, that *we become like what we study or are closely associated with.* We become so like people with whom we live constantly, that the expression of face and sound of voice grow similar, and even features grow alike. Sometimes a child will look more like its nurse than its mother." And the whole book is an exposition of this principle, and it holds out as a Sādana for spiritual elevation, that a man should firmly believe that there is no world, no untruth, no sin, no sickness, no death, and he is a child of God, that there is only 'Truth, Power, Love, and Presence in this universe and nothing but this, that he is the reflection of God, the image and likeness of God, and then he can truly conquer sickness and death, and become truly the son of God. This is exactly the Sōhambhāvana or Śivōhambhāvana. And the following verse of St. Aruṇandi Śivāchārya sums up the whole teaching :—

"கண்ட விவையல்லே னானென்ற கன்றுகாணாக்
கழிபரமு நானல்லேனெனக் கருதிக்கசிந்த
தொண்டினொடு முளத்தவன் றானின்ற கலப்பாலே
சோகமெனப் பாவிக்கத் தோன்றுவன் வேறின்றி

விண்டகலு மலங்களெல்லாங் கருடதியானத்தின்
விடமொழியு மதுபோல விமலமதையு மடையும்
பண்டை மறைகளுமது நானானே னென்று
பாவிக்கச் சொல்லுவதிப் பாவகத்தைக்காணே."—(ix. 7.)

"Say 'I am not the world, and am separate from it.' Say also 'I am not the Unknowable Supreme One.' Then unite with Him indissolubly by loving Him in all humility, and practise Sōham ('I am He'). Then will He appear to you as yourself. Your mala will all cease, just as the poison is removed by *Garuḍadhyāna*, and you will become pure. So, it is, the old Vēdas teach us to practise this maṇtra 'Aham Brahmāsmi,' 'I am Brahman'."

As this right knowledge of non-difference and difference of ourselves from God and the universe is essential for our salvation, Śrīkaṇṭha discusses these questions in his Bhāshya on the Sūtras, II, i, 21-3, and we quote the whole of these passages, and he quotes and beautifully reconciles the numerous Bhēda Srutis with the Mahāvākya texts:—

"The Sūtrakāra raises and refutes an objection to the foregoing theory:—

(Jīva) being mentioned (to be one with) the other, there follows an incongruity such as neglecting what is good. (II. i. 21.).

(Objection): Because in the words "That thou art," and "this Ātman is Brahman," Jīva, the effect, is mentioned as one with Brahman, because, it has been shown that they are not distinct from each other. In that case it would follow that the all-knowing and all-pervading Paramēśvara dissolves the Universe for his own [good] and creates it for his own [evil]. Then it may be asked, how is it that Īśvara, who is all-knowing and of unfailing will, and who knows that the pain of Jīva, who is no other than Himself, is His own pain, engages Himself in the creation of the Universe, which as leading to Samsāra is an evil, and does not abstain from creation for His own good. Accordingly, once it is proved that Jīva and Paramēśvara are one, there follows this incongruity that Paramēśvara, though all-knowing, is guilty of a want of sense in so far as he abstains from what is good to Himself and engages in what conduces to His own evil. Wherefore it does not stand to reason that Jīva and Īśvara, the cause and the effect, are one.

(Answer): In reply we say as follows:—

But the Cause is superior, because of the mention of a distinction. (II. 1. 22.)

Though the cause and effect are one, the cause is declared in the Šruti to be superior to the effect, to the sentient and insentient universe, in such passages as the following:—

"Superior to the universe is Rudra, the Mighty Sage."

So, a distinction is also made between Jīva and Paramēšvara in the following passages:—

"But he who controls both—Vidyā and Avidyā is—another."

"The one God rules the perishable (Pradhāna) and Ātman."

"Thinking that the Atman is different from the Mover (the Lord)."

"Two birds, inseparable friends, cling to the same tree."

"Two Brahmans ought to be known, the superior and the inferior."

"There are two, one knowing, the other not knowing: both unborn; one strong and the other weak."

"He is the eternal among eternals, the sentient among the sentient."

"Having entered within, He is the ruler of the creatures."

"Know then Prakṛiti is Māyā, and the great Lord the Māyin."

"From that, the Māyin sends forth all this; in that, the other is bound up through that Māyā."

"When he sees the other, the Lord is contented...then his grief passes away."

"He is the master of nature and of man, the Lord of the three qualities."

"Of these creatures, pašus, the Pašupati is the Lord."

Wherefore quite superior to the universe is Brahman, otherwise called Šiva.

(Objection): By establishing non-duality in II. i. 15, and duality in II. i. 22, you have only proved duality and non-duality of Brahman and the universe.

(Answer): No: we do not establish that sort of Visishṭādvaita which takes the form of duality and non-duality. We are not the advocates of an absolute distinction between Brahman and the universe as between a pot and a cloth, because of its opposition to the Šruti declaring that they are not quite distinct from each other. Neither are we the advocates of an absolute identity as of the mother-o'-pearl and silver, one of them being illusory; for, it is opposed to the Šruti which points to a difference in the inherent attributes of Brahman and the universe. Nor do we hold to duality and non-duality, which is opposed to the nature of things. On the other hand, we maintain that the unity of Brahman—as the cause and the effect—is like that of the body and of the embodied, or like that of the substance and its attribute. By unity of Brahman and the universe, we mean their inseparability like that of clay and the pot as cause and effect, or like that of the substance and its attribute. A pot, indeed, is not seen apart from clay, nor is the blue lotus seen apart from the colour blue. Similarly, apart from Brahman, no potentiality of the universe can exist; nor is Brahman ever known apart from something else, the former must ever be conditioned by the latter, and this latter is naturally one with the former.

Wherefore, Brahman who is in no way separable from the universe is said to be one with the other. And there is a natural distinction between the two; so that the Supreme Brahman is ever higher than the universe. As to their distinction as to the cause and the effect, it has been already explained in II. i. 9. Wherefore this theory is quite unopposed to the Srutis declaring distinction as well as non-distinction.

And as in the case of stone, etc., it is incongruous (II. i. 23,).

(Objection): Under all conditions, Jīva and Īśvara are one, because of the Śrutis declaring non-duality.

(Answer): No, because of an incongruity. Jīva and Īśvara cannot be identical, because, like the insentient stone, timber, grass, etc., the Jīva also is, on account of ignorance, etc., said to belong to quite a distinct class from the Īśvara who is possessed of such attributes as omniscience. Therefore Īśvara is a distinct entity from Jīva. Thus even the Jīva, sentient as he is, cannot be identical with Īśvara owing to this difference, that the latter is superior. Much less can the insentient existence which is essentially different be identical with Īśvara. From all standpoints of view, by Śruti, Smriti and Reasoning, we see that the omniscient and omnipotent Paramēśvara is quite superior to the whole universe, sentient and insentient though, as His own emanation, it is not altogether distinct from Him.

And he brings out the non-difference more by means of the simile of soul and body in his commentary on I. ii. 1.

"All this is Brahman, as beginning, and breathing in Him; and therefore let a man meditate on Him."

This passage may be explained as follows:— The origin, existence, and end of all this depends on Brahman. All this, both the sentient and the insentient existence, is verily Brahman, and therefore let a man meditate on Brahman, tranquil in mind. Just as water-bubbles which have their origin, existence and end in the ocean, are found to be only forms of that ocean, so, too, that which depends for its origin, etc., on Brahman associated with Śakti must be made up of Brahman and nothing else. Nothing distinct from Him is ever perceived. Accordingly in the Atharvaśiras it has been declared by Īśāna as follows:

"Alone I was at first, (alone) I am and shall be, there is none else distinct from Me."

And then was declared by Him, in the words "I am Brahman," that the whole universe is His own form. And in the words "He entered the more hidden from (or than) the hidden one" etc., His entering into universe is given as reason for the whole universe being His own form. Thus this universe having no origin, existence or end outside Brahman, it is not a quite distinct thing from Brahman. Accordingly the learned say:— "His Śaktis or energies form the whole world, and the Maheśa or the Great Lord is the energetic (Śaktimān). Never can energy exist distinct from the energetic. Unity of these two is eternal, like that of fire and heat, inasmuch as unseparateness always exists between energy and the energetic. Wherefore the supreme energy belongs to the Supreme Ātman, since the two are related to each other as substance and attribute. The energy of heat is not conceived to be distinct from fire" and so on. Vāyu-Samhita too says:

"From Śakti up to earth (the whole world) is born of the principle Śiva, by Him alone it is pervaded, as the jar, etc., by clay. His variegated Supreme Śakti, whose form is knowledge and bliss, appears as one and many, like the light of the sun."

The following passages of the Śruti speak of Para-Brahman as possessed of infinite powers of creating, ruling, and maintaining the world, all inherent in Him:

"His supreme Śakti is spoken of as manifold, inherent, endued with the activity of knowledge and life."

"One verily is Rudra—they were not for a second—who rules these worlds with the powers of ruling." In short, on the authority of Śruti, Smriti, Itihāsa, Purāṇa—and the saying of the learned, the Supreme Śakti—whose manifold manifestation, this whole universe of chit and achit is, whose being is composed of Supreme Existence, Intelligence and Bliss and is unlimited by space and time—is inherent in the nature of Śiva, the Supreme Brahman, and constitutes His own essential form and quality. Apart from Śakti, He cannot be the Omniscient, the Omnipotent, the cause of all, the all-controlling, the all-adorable, the all-gracious, the means of attaining all aspirations, and the Omnipresent; and, moreover, such grand designations as '*Maheśvara*,' the Supreme Lord, '*Mahādeva*,' the Supreme Deity, and '*Rudra*,' the expeller of pain, cannot apply to Him. Thus, it is Brahman whose body is the whole sentient and insentient universe, and who is denoted by all words. Just as the word 'blue' denotes not the blue colour only, but also the lotus which is of blue colour, so does the word 'universe' also denotes Brahman. Therefore, such passages as "All is Rudra verily" teach that Brahman is denoted by all words. Accordingly the passage "All this verily is Brahman", refers to Brahman whose body the whole of the sentient and insentient universe is. The universe being thus a form of Brahman and being therefore not an object of hatred etc., let everyone be peaceful at heart and worship Brahman. This doctrine is clearly expounded even in the purāṇic texts such as the following:—

"The body of the God of Gods is this universe, moving and unmoving. This, the Jīvas (Paśus) do not know, owing to the mighty bondage. They say sentiency is Vidyā, and insentiency Avidyā. The whole universe of Vidyā and Avidyā is no doubt the body of the Lord, the Father of all; for the whole universe is subject to Him. The word 'sat' is used by the wise to denote the real and the good, and 'asat' is used by vedic teachers to denote the contrary. The whole universe of the *sat* and the *asat* is the body of Him who is on High. Just as, by the watering of the roots of a tree, its branches are nourished, so by the worship of Śiva, the universe which is His body is nourished. Ātman is the eighth body of Śiva, the Paramēśvara pervading all other bodies. Wherefore the whole universe, if ensouled by Śiva, if any embodied being whatsoever be subjected to constraint, it will be quite repugnant to the eight-bodied Lord; as to this there is no doubt. Doing good to all, kindness to all, affording shelter to all,—this they hold, is the worshipping of Śiva." And so on.

Brahman being all-formed, it is but right to say "all is Brahman" and "let every one be peaceful and worship Brahman." Wherefore it is Brahman who in the opening passage is stated to be the object of worship, that is also spoken of as manōmaya, as partaking of the nature of manas, and so on. Neither should it be supposed that the partaking of the nature of manas is a characteristic mark of a samsārin; for Brahman may limit Himself by assuming a shape which can form an object of worship.

The slight difference there is between the way the subject is treated by Śrīkaṇṭha and that St. Meykaṇḍān has to be noted. Śrīkaṇṭha calls this relation, following Bādarāyaṇa as one of cause and effect and calls it as a peculiar *Apūrva parināma*, in which the efficient cause is not affected by the change, as in an ordinary case of causation, and yet his illustration of soul and body, would seem to bring, if not quite, within causation at all. Śivajñāna Yōgi distinguishes between two kinds of *Tādātmyam*. One thing appears as two, as Guṇi and Guṇa, substance and attribute. This is one kind. Again two things might be so connected as to be regarded as one. This is also *Tādātmyam*; and this latter relation is what is called *Advaita* and the former relation is simply known as *Tādātmyam*; and Śrīkaṇtha would seem to conform himself to *Tādātmyam* first described.

Professor Max Muller would not seem to understand the importance of the distinction between Kapila's Sāṅkhya and Patañjali's Yōga called also Sēshvara Sāṅkhya. He says, in his 'Six Systems of Philosophy,' that the Sūtra "Devotion to God" is not very important and is only one of the various means of obtaining Kaivalya. We have dwelt at length on the difference between the Nirvāṇa as postulated by Buddha, and that the Siddhānti in our notes to Śivajñāna Siddhiyār, Parapaksham, under Buddhism, and also in our paper on the 'Tree of Knowledge of good and evil.' Buddhism postulated Pāśatchaya, freedom from desire and pain; but Siddhānta postulates, in addition, Patijñāna, entering into the Brahma-Nirvāṇa or Śivānubhava, and we have shown how, with all our effort, *Pāśatchaya* will not be practicable, unless there is Patijñāna.

The thing is best illustrated by the simile of crystal or mirror and colours, used by both Sāṅkhyans and Yōgins. By the juxtaposition of a red flower with a mirror, the mirror is tinged by the reflexion of the red flower; so the soul, when in relation with the world, is affected by the world; and death and birth and pain arise. According to the Sāṅkhyan, the soul will regain its freedom when it knows that it is different from the colours reflected in itself, and it is not affected by the colours or reflexion; and the gaining of this knowledge is secured to it by the action of Pradhāna itself. But is it possible for the soul to attain this knowledge by its own effort or the effort of the

Pradhāna? If so, let us examine the illustration itself. The mirror and red flower came into juxtaposition, and the reflexion was caused on the mirror.

But did they come into juxtaposition by the effort of the mirror or the effort of the red flower? Let us take it that somehow they came into juxtaposition, and could not help coming into this position. Having been placed in juxtaposition, how could the reflexion now present on the mirror be removed? Could this be done by any effort of the mirror or by any effort of the red flower? There being nothing but the Soul and Pradhāna or mirror and red flower according to the Sāṅkhyan, how could this release be effected? It is clear that, under the circumstances stated by the Sāṅkhyans, there is possibly no way out of the difficulty, and the juxtaposition must for ever remain fixed, and there can be no release and no freedom and no Mōksha, unless it be in name. The ever recurring cycle of births and deaths should go on for ever and ever. But it being noted that the Yōgins use the same figure, is there really no way by which the mirror can get rid of this reflexion? Yes, there is. But this will require a slight examination as to how the reflexion itself was caused. Suppose the position between the mirror and flower remained fixed as ever, could we see the reflexion at night? No. Why not? Because the essential condition of the reflexion itself being thrown on the mirror is the presence of light or the Sun. And it is the essential presence of the Sun that we had forgotten all the time we were using the figure of the crystal and flower. Well, at night-time, when there is no reflexion and no knowledge of tingeing, this is the kēvala condition of the Soul. In this condition of the Soul, it is devoid of all *ichcha* and *kriya* and it is not even conscious that it is undergoing pain, without knowing how to get rid of the pain. As the Sun dawns the reflexion is felt on the mirror, and by means of this conjunction, the Soul's *ichcha* and *kriya* are aroused and it experiences both pleasure and pain, sins and suffers, and by suffering, gains experience and freedom. As the *Sun travels* over and over, and nearer and nearer the crystal, the shadow of the red flower will grow less and less till, at noon-time when the Sun is at the nearest point to the crystal, it will be covered with a blaze of light that you cannot see, and the image of the flower will be lost. In the former position, the mirror was one with the red flower (Bhanda-one or Advaita in Āṇava,) and in the latter condition, the mirror was one with the Sun (Mōksha-one or Advaita in God). This is the position of the Yōgi or the Theistic Sāṅkhya, and the importance of the doctrine of 'Devotion to God' will now be manifest, Though 'Chitta Nirodha' * should necessarily precede it. [Cf. Dēvāram]: the Soul by its own effort or that of Pradhāna cannot get rid of its mala. Neither of them could be energized by their own will and power unless the Supreme Will and Power thought "may I become many" and so willed all creation and evolution. And the freedom from the world and desire and from the thirst after birth and death cannot be gained, unless the Soul rests its desire in God, or becomes devoted to Him. That this is the only way of securing freedom from mala is set forth distinctly in the tenth and eleventh sūtras of Śivajñānabodha, treating as they do of Pāśatchaya and Patijñāna. These sādhanas are, becoming one with God, dedicating one's acts to God and unceasing love and devotion to God. By such dedication and devotion, it brings itself in harmony with the Divine Law and loses its pride of self and self-knowledge; karma and ignorance cease to operate, the man's whole being becomes covered with the flood of His Grace.

This love and devotion to God who is Love Himself begets joy and bliss which completely fulfils our highest desire, unlike the joys of the world, which ever and anon create a gnawing desire, a thirst after such more and more, like the unquenched

---

* "அகனமர்ந்து அன்பினராய் அறுபகைச்செற்று ஐம்புலனுமடக்கி ஞானப் புகழுடையோர் தம்முள்ளப் புண்டரிகத் துள்ளிருக்கும் புராணர்."

"The Ancient one who dwells in the heart-lotus of Jñānis who had controlled the five senses and killed the six foes, and whose heart blossoms with Love."

thirst of the confirmed drunkard. This supreme Bliss Rest and Joy fill our hearts like the flood brooking not its banks, when in all humility and love, our body and soul are devoted to His service.

When this joy fills him, then does he revel in God, delight in God and rest in God as the Muṇḍaka Up. (III. i. 4) puts it; then does he love God, delight in God, revel in God and rejoice in God, and become a Svarāj, and Lord and master in all the worlds, as the Chāndōgya Up. (VII. 25. 2) puts it.

In this condition of Svarāj, when he is fully God-filled, even when he moves about there laughing or eating, playing or rejoicing, be it with women, carriages or relations (Chāndōg. Up. VIII. 12. 3.), these actions will not affect him as fire cannot burn a man skilled in agni-stambha (See principle stated in Śivajñāna Siddhiyār X. 5 and 6).

This position has therefore to be clearly distinguished from the ethics and psychology of both Buddhists and Sāṅkhyans. The Yōgi and the Siddhānti believe that true salvation can be secured only by such Self-renunciation and Love to God.

That it is only possible to get rid of our mala by attaching ourselves to the Supreme Paramēśvara is brought out also by St. Tiruvalluvar:

"பற்றுக பற்றற்றான் பற்றினைப் பற்றினைப்
பற்றுக பற்று விடற்கு".

"Desire the desire of Him who is desireless.
Desire His Desire so as desire may leave you."

"சார்புணர்ந்து சார்புகெட வொழுகின் மற்றழித்து
சார்தரா சார்தரு நோய்."

"The true support who knows, rejects support he sought before,
Sorrow that clings shall cease and cling to him no more."

"இருள்சேர் இருவினையும் சேரா இறைவன்
பொருள்சேர் புகழ்புரிந்தார் மாட்டு."

"The two kinds of dark karma will cease from one,
whose praise is, he is devoted to God."

Compare this with the Christian aspiration after Divine joy.

'If, to any, the tumult of the flesh were hushed, hushed the images of earth, and waters, and air, hushed also the poles of heaven, yea the very soul be hushed to herself, and by not thinking on self, surmount self, hushed all dreams and imaginary revelations, every tongue and every sign, and whatsoever exists only in transition, since if any could hear, all these say, 'we made not ourselves, but He made us that abideth for ever.' If then, having uttered this, they too should be hushed, having roused only our ears to Him Who made them, and He alone speak, not by them, but by Himself, that we may hear His Word, not through any tongue of flesh, nor Angel's voice, nor sound of thunder, nor in the dark riddle of a similitude, but, might hear Whom in these things we love, might hear His very self without these (as we too now strained ourselves, and in swift thought touched on that Eternal Wisdom, which abideth over all); could this be continued on, and other visions of kind far unlike be withdrawn, and this one ravish, and absorb, and wrap up its beholder amid these inward joys, so that life might be for ever like that one moment of understanding which now we sighed after; were not this, enter into thy Master's joy? (*St. Augustine*).'

We have used above the illustration of crystal and colours whether that of the red flower or the variegated clouds. Pure water is crystalline in its nature and it reflects and refracts light just as a prism does*. This water is discoloured and affected by the dirt in it, and when our ahaṅkāra and the dirt subside, the water regains its own pure clear nature, and then the reflexion of the Supreme One fills it with His glory and this is the truth contained in the famous central verse (Hridaya Ślôka) in St. Tirumūlar's Tirumaṇtiram.

* In the famous spring at Mahāṇaṇdi near Naṇdyal (Kurnool District), you can see the actual phenomena of the refraction of light; just as the water ripples in sunlight, all the colours of the rainbow can be seen on the bottom of the spring.

உரையற்ற தொன்றை யுரைசெய்யு மூமர்காள்
கரையற்ற தொன்றை கரைகாண லாகுமோ
திரையற்ற நீர்போல் சிந்தை தெளிவார்க்கு
புரையற்றிருந்தான் புரிசடை யோனே.

O ye fools that speak of the unspeakable,
Can ye see the limits of the limitless one ?
To one whose mind gains clearness as the waveless sea,
Will appear faultless the Lord with the braided Hair.

THE SAIVA RELIGION

AND

SAIVA ADVAITA SIDDHANTA PHILOSOPHY.*

Professor Max Müller, in his last great work on the "Six Systems of Hindu Philosophy", has remarked as follows :—

"The longer I have studied the various systems, the more have I become impressed with the view taken by Vijñāna Bikshu and others that there is behind the variety of the Six Systems, a common fund of what may be called National or Popular Philosophy, a large Mānasa lake of philosophical thought and language, far away in the distant north and in the distant past, from which each thinker was allowed to draw for his own purposes."

And it would have certainly surprised him if one had told him that one need not go neither to the distant north nor to the distant past to discover what this National or Popular Philosophy was, from which each thinker drew his own inspiration, and a study of the two popular Hindu Religions of Modern India—we mean Śaivaism and Vaishṇavism—will convince any one that they inherit to-day all the thought and traditions of by-gone ages, as the Modern Hindus themselves represent lineally their old ancestors who were settled in Bharata Khaṇḍa, since the days of the Ṛig Vēda ; and their religion of to-day is as much a living faith, suited to all sorts and conditions of men, whether peasant or paṇḍit, sinner or saved.

ŚAIVAISM IS BASED ON THE VEDAS AND ĀGAMAS.

Śaivaism comprising in its fold Śāktaism and Gāṇāpatyam and worshippers of God Subrahmaṇya &c., counts among its followers, the majority of Hindus, and it accordingly claims to

* A paper read before the Convention of Religions, at Calcutta, 1909.

represent the old traditional and parent religion of the days of the Vêdas and Upanishats, Āgamas or Taṇtras, and Itihāsas and Purāṇas, and bases its authority on these ancient revealed books and histories. It claims God Śiva to be the author of the Vêdas and Āgamas. Says Śrī Nīlakaṇta Śivāchārya in his Sūtra Bāshya:

"We see no difference between the Vêda and the Śivāgama. Even the Vêdas may properly be called Śivāgama, Śiva being the author thereof. Accordingly Śivāgama is twofold, one being intended for the three higher castes, the other being intended for all. The Vêdas are intended for people of the three castes, and the other for all. Śiva, alone as the author of the Vêda, is declared in the following passages of Śruti and Smriti." *

"He is the Lord of all Vidyās,"
"(The Vêda) is the breath of the Mighty Being."

"Of these eighteen Vidyās of various paths, the original author is the wise Śūlapāṇi Himself. So says the Śruti."

It will be therefore important to trace Modern Śaivaism from the traditions and thought and language of the past.

ITS ANTIQUITY.

The Supreme polity of the Vêda is Sacrifice. Various Gods, Iṇdra, Vāyu, Varuṇa, Agni, Hiraṇyagarbha, Sôma, the Sun, the Moon, Vishṇu and Rudra, are worshipped. Each is addressed as a most powerful deity, and his aid is invoked for all kinds of earthly blessing and freedom from evil. They are all supposed to represent various powers of nature, and to idealize man's aspiration after the Supreme. Then we meet the text, "Ekam Sat Viprā Bahudhā Vadanti"; and who is this one? Was any one God recognised, above all others, as the Chief, as the

---

* वयन्तुवेदशिवागमयोर्भेदं नपश्यामः । वेदोपिशिवागमः इतिव्यवहारोयुक्तः । तस्यतत्कर्तृकत्वात् । अतः शिवागमोद्विविधः त्रैवर्णिकविषयः सर्वविषयश्चेति । वेदस्त्रैवर्णिकविषयः सर्वविषयश्चान्यः । उभयोरेकएवशिवःकर्ता 'ईशानस्सर्वविद्यानां' 'अस्यमहतोभूतस्य निश्वसितमित्यादि श्रुत्या' 'अष्टादशानांविद्याना मेतासांभिन्नवर्त्मनां । आदिकर्त्ताकविस्साक्षात् शूलपाणिरितिश्रुतिः'

God of Sacrifices, as the Pati? And we have the following texts from the Ṛig Vêda.

"Tasmāt Rudraḥ Paśunāmadhipatiḥ" * (Ṛig Vêda).

"Gāthapatim Mêdhapatim Rudram Jalāsha bhêshajam Tat Samyôḥ Sumnamīmahê." † (Ṛig. 1 Ashṭa, 1 Maṇḍ, 26 Anu.)

"We seek from Rudra, the Lord of Songs, the Lord of Sacrifices, who possesses healing remedies, his auspicious favour (Ṛig Vêda I. 43. 4.)

As the Pati of all sacrifices, He is the fulfiller of sacrifices, "Yajña Sādham" ‡ (1. 114-4) and 'Rudram yajñānam sadhadishṭim abasam' (111-2-5). As the God of gods, He is said to "derive His renown from Himself" 'Rudrāya *Svayasase*'. His glory is said to be inherent, independent, or self-dependant God, 'Svadhavane' (Ṛig. VII. 46-1). He is also called *Svapivata*, which is variously explained as meaning 'readily understanding' 'accessible,' 'gracious,' 'He by whom life is conquered,' 'He whose command cannot be transgressed,' 'Thou by whom prayers (words) are readily received.' He is called the 'father of the worlds,' '*Bhuvanasya Pitaram*,' § VI. 49-10, and the Ṛik story of His becoming the Father of the fatherless Maruts can be recalled in many a Purāṇic story, local legend, and common folklore.

He is referred to in the text "*anter ichchanti*"—(VIII. 61-3). His form as described in the Ṛig Vêda is almost the same as the Image of later days. He is called the Kapardin, with 'spirally braided hair.' He is of 'Hiraṇya' 'golden formed' and 'brilliant like the sun,' and 'shining like gold' 'Yaḥśukra

* तस्मात्रुद्रःपशुनामधिपतिः

† गाथपतिं मेधपतिं रुद्रं जालाषभेषजम् तच्छंयोस्सुम्नमीमहे ।

‡ त्वेषंत्र्यंरुद्रंयज्ञसाधंवंकुंकविमवसेनिह्वयामहे ।

—Ṛig, 1 Ashṭaka, 1 Maṇḍala, 16 Anuvāka.

§ भुवनस्यपितरंगोर्भिराभीरुद्रंदिवावर्धयारुद्रमुक्तौ ।

बृहंतमृष्वमजरंसुषुम्नमृधग्घुवेमकविनेषितासः ॥

—Ṛig, 4 Ashṭaka, 6 Maṇḍala, 4 Anuvāka.

iva Sūryō hiraṇyam ivarōchati' (1-43-5.) And in Ṛig Vêda, X. 136-1 to 7, He is the 'long-haired being who sustains the fire, water and the two worlds; who is, to the view, the entire sky; and who is called this 'Light.' He is *Wind-clad* (naked) and drinks *Visha* (water or poison) and a Muni is identified with Rudra in this aspect.

Rudra is derived by Sāyana from the roots, Rut drāvayita,* meaning 'he who drives away sorrow.' And consistent with this derivation, Rudra is called in the Ṛig Vêda itself, as the 'bountiful' and the 'Healer' possessed of various remedies (the later Vaidyanāth) 'benign' and 'gracious.' And the term *Śiva* clearly appears in the following text of the Ṛig Vêda (X. 92-9): "Stôman *va* adya Rudrāya śikvase kshyad-viraya namasā didishṭāna yêbhiḥ Śivaḥ † svavan êvayavabhir divaḥ śikshati svayaśaḥ nikāmabhiḥ."

(With reverence present your Hymn to-day to the mighty Rudra, the ruler of heroes, (and to the Maruts) those rapid and ardent deities with whom the gracious (Śivaḥ) and opulent (Rudra) who derives his renown from himself, protects us from the sky.)

If the Gods, Iṇdra, etc., personified individually the different powers of nature, in the supreme Personality of Rudra will be found combined all these different powers. He is a thunderer and storm-God, the father of the Maruts. He is Agni. He is Vāyu. He is Varuṇa. He is Sōma. He is the Sun and Moon. We have the high authority of Sāyana that Sōma means Sa-Umā. He deduces the story of Tripuradahana

---

* रुद्दुःखंदुःखहेतुर्वातद्द्रावयतियःप्रभुः रुद्रइत्युच्यतेसद्भिः शिवः परमकारणम् ।

—Vāyu-Samhitā, I. Chap. 28, vv. 35-36, (Bombay Ed.)

Śrikaṇṭha says in the Bhāshya:

संसाररुग्द्रावकत्वाद्रुद्रशब्दवाच्यंब्रह्म ।

Haradatta says:

रुग्द्रावणेनभवन्तमवैमिरुद्रम् ।

† Sāyana in his great Bhāshya takes Śivaḥ as a noun and not as an adjective as translated by most oriental Scholars.

and Vishapāna from two texts in the Ṛig Vêda. We have in the Ṛig Vêda also the germ of the later Hindu Cosmology, in the famous Nasadasaya sūktam; and this is also the central text of Śiva Śakti worship.

> "In the beginning there was neither sat nor asat;
> Then there was neither sky nor atmosphere above.
> What then enshrouded all this teeming universe?
> In the receptacle of what, was it contained?
> Was it enveloped in the gulf profound of water?
> Then was there neither death nor immortality;
> Then there was neither day, nor night, nor light,
> Nor darkness, only the Existent One breathed without breath self-contained.
> Nought else but he there was, nought else above, beyond.
> Then first came darkness, hid in darkness, gloom in gloom;
> Next all was water, all a chaos indiscrete.
> In which the one lay void, shrouded in nothingness.
> Then turning inwards, he, by self-developed force
> Of inner fervour and intense abstraction, grew.
> First in his mind was formed Desire, (Ichchā-śakti) the primal germ,
> Productive, which, the Wise profoundly searching say,
> Is the first subtle bond, connecting Sat with Asat."

In the Ṛig Vêda also, we find the famous text which is repeated in the Atharva Vêda and subsequently in the Śvetāśvatara Upanishat and also in the Kaṭha and Muṇḍaka Upanishats, and which forms the chief stronghold of Indian Theism against Idealism. "Two birds, inseparable friends cling to the same tree. One of them eats the sweet fruits, the other 'Anya' looks on without eating".

YAJUR VEDA.

In the Yajur Vêda the position of Rudra becomes more established as Paśupati and Lord of sacrifices and as The One without a second.

"Paśunām sarma asi sarma yajamānasya sarma me yacha *Eka Eva Rudro Na Dvitīyāya Tasthe Ākhusthe Rudra Paśuḥ Tam Jushasva.* Esha tê Rudra Bhāgaḥ *Saha Svasra Ambikāya* tam Jushasva Bheshajam Gave Asvāya Purushāya Bheshajam." This text is repeated in the Śvetāśvatara Upanishat and is the original of the famous text in the Chhāndōgya Upanishat 'Ekamevādvitīyam Brahma'. Nadvitīyam is more ancient form than Advitīyam or Advaitam. And we know this is the central text of the Advaita philosophy. In this vêda, His supreme Majesty is fully developed, and He is expressly called Śiva by name 'Śivo namaśi' (Yaj. S. 3-63) and the famous mantra, the *Pañchākshara,* is said to be placed in the very heart of the three Vêdas (the name occurs in Tait. S. IV. 5, 1-41 "*namah śāmbhave cha mayobave cha namah Śaṅkarāya cha mayāskarāya cha* NAMAHŚIVĀYA *cha Śivatarāya cha*"). And the famous Śatarudrīyam which is praised in the Upanishats and in the Mahābhārat forms also the central portion of this central Vêda. And this is a description of God as the all, the all in all, and transcending all, 'Viśvadevo, Viśvasvarūpo, Viśvādhiko'; and anybody can see that the famous passage in the Gītā in chapters 10 and 11 merely parodies this other passage and these two chapters are respectively called *Vibhūti Vistāra Yoga* and *Viśvarūpa Sandarśana Yoga* which is exactly the character of the Śatarudriya. The Yōgi who has reached the highest state "Sees all in God and God in all." In the Śatarudriya and in the whole Vêda, Rudra is called Śiva, Śaṅkara, Śambhu, Iśāna, Iśa, Bhagavān, Bhava, Sarva, Ugra, Sōma, Paśupati, Nilagrīva, Giriśa, Mahādeva and Maheśvara.

The word 'Pura'* in the Upanishat technically mean 'the body.' Tripura means the triple bond (of the soul) and Tripura samhāra means the destruction of our human bondage by the grace of God.

"The fools say the ancient of days with the braided hair

---

* पुरत्रयेक्रीडतियश्चजीवः । —Kaivalyōpanishat.

नवद्वारेपुरेदेहीहंसोलीलायतेबाहिः । —Śveta Upanishat Chap. 3.

and the Gaṅgā destroyed the three cities. The three Pura are the result of the three mala; who knows what happened after (pāśatchaya)?"—Tirumantiram.

The story of Tripurasamhāra is much more fully set forth in the Yajur Veda (6th Kaṇḍa, 2nd Praśna, 3rd Anuvāka and 12th Maṇtra).

Mahāpuram Jayantiti ta ishum Samas Kurva to gnium anikan Soman Salyam Vishum Tejanam the bruvan ka imam asishatita Rudra iti aleruvan rudro vai Kruru; Somya twiti, sobravit Varam Vrina aham eva Paśunām Adhipatirasāniti tasmāt rudraḥ Paśunām aḍhipatishṭam rudrova Sṛijat Satisra Puro bhitva ebhyo: lokebhys Suran pranudata.

"There were the three cities of iron, silver, and gold (belonging) to Asuras. The gods not being able to win them (by fight) wished to win them by siege. (The great) say that He (the Brahmin &c.), who knows (what ought to be known) and he (the non-Brahmin &c.), who does not know—they are able to win by seige the great city which cannot be overtaken by fight: (then) the gods made an arrow composed of Agni as (the bottom hilt) Soma as (the middle) iron and Vishṇu as (the top) and declared (consulted) who will discharge it, and determined Rudra, (was) able: He (the Rudra) said the boon was made over, I am the Lord of Paśus (both the two-footed and four-footed); So Rudra the Lord of Paśus discharged it, broke up these three cities, and blew them up all from these worlds." *

---

* It is clear from the Yajur Vêda that there is a closer link between the Lord's aspect as Tripurasamhāra, as the burner of the three cities, and His other aspect as Paśupati, the Lord of the Paśus. In fact it is from the Lord's aspect as Tripurasamhāra, we come to know of His other aspect as Paśupati. The whole story of Tripurasamhāra, with the earth becoming a chariot, the Sun and Moon forming its wheels, the four Vêdas becoming its horses, the Kshêtrajña Brahma its driver, the Vishṇu, Agni and Sōma becoming the portions of the arrow held in the hands of the Lord etc., is on the face of it symbolic. That this story is symbolic can be further gleaned from an earlier portion

The importance of this lies in the fact that in the chief festival in each temple, called the Brahmotsava, the important event is the car-feast in which the charioteer is the four-headed Brahma, recalling and representing this old old story referred to in the Ṛig Veda and Yajur Veda.

The Yajur Veda is the Central Veda and is a most important one and as such more than ninety per cent of the Brahmins of to-day are Yajur Vedies. The occurrence of the words Pati, Paśu and Pāśam should be noted as their significance will be referred to later on.

---

of the Yajus-Samhitā. The following texts occur in the 5th Kaṇḍa of the Yajur-Vêda:

रुद्रोवाएपयर्दमिः तस्यतिस्वः शरव्याः प्रतीची, तिरश्ची, अनूची, etc., यत् तेपुरः धनुः तद्वातः अनुवातुते तस्मै ते रुद्रसंवत्सरेण नमः करोमियत्ते रुद्रदक्षिणाधनुः तत् वातः अनुवातुतेतस्मैते रुद्रपरिवत्सरेणनमःकरोमि । यत्तेरुद्रपश्चात्धनुः तत्वातःअनुवातुते । तस्मैतेरुद्रइदावत्सरेणनमः करोमि । यत्तेरुद्र उत्तरात् धनुः तत् वातः अनुवातु ते तस्मै ते रुद्रइदुवत्सरेणनमः करोमि । यत्तेरुद्रउपरिधनुः तत्वातः अनुवातुतेतस्मै ते रुद्रवत्सरेण नमः करोमि.

Here all the quarters (i.e., space) are said to be the arrows of Rudra, and the bows are the various periods of time, i.e., Eternity, and the Rudra Himself is the Spirit inhering in all things, bound by Space and Time,

योरुद्रो अग्नौ य अंसुय ओषधिषु योरुद्रोविश्वा भुवनाविवेश तस्मैरुद्रायनमोअस्तु ।

(Yajus, Kaṇḍa 5). In the Karṇaparva, Mahābhārata, we are expressly told that, that Time is represented by the Bow of the Tripuraghna.

त्रिचित्रंऋतुभिः षड्भिःकृत्वासंवत्सरंधनुः ।

And what is Eternity! It is that which transcends the periods of past, future and present.

यच्चान्यत्त्रिकालातीतं तदप्योंकारएव ।

Hence the same Bow is described as OMKĀRA सकृत्वाधनुरोंकारं सावित्रींज्यां महेश्वरः The Supreme God made a bow of Omkara and a string of Sāvitri.

As to what the grant of boon means, the following text makes it clear:

स्वतस्सिद्धंपतित्वं मे युष्माकंपशुतापिच ।
तदेतद्दर्शयाम्यद्य वरवन्धविनोदने ॥

"The Patitvam or the Lordship of mine is as natural to Me as that of dependence or Paśutvam to you all, and it is this fact that is shown by my playing with you regarding the grant of boon." It is like a Father playing with his children requiring them to say "call me father". It is the acknowledgment of the utter dependence upon the Lord.

THE UPANISHATS AND ĀGAMAS.

As we noted above, the polity of the vēdas was the performance of sacrifices. This was continued in the Upanishat period and the Brāhmaṇas elaborated the Rituals. But at the same time, the worship of the many Gods was being given up in favour of the one God, and the efficacy of sacrifices in general was being doubted, and a more spiritual form of worship was being substituted in its place, and the first departure is noted in the story given in the Kēna Upanishat.

KENA UPANISHAT.

"Brahman obtained the victory for the Dēvas. The Dēvas became elated by the victory of Brahman, and they thought, 'this victory is ours only'. Brahman perceived this and appeared to them. But they did not know it, and said: "'What yaksha is this?' They said to Agni (fire): 'O Jātavēdas, find out what sprite this is.' 'Yes,' he said. He ran towards it, and Brahman said to him: 'Who are you?' He replied: 'I am Agni, I am Jātavēdas.' Brahman said: 'What power is in you?' Agni replied: 'I could burn all whatever there is on earth.' Brahman put a straw before him, saying: 'Burn this.' He went towards it with all his might, but he could not burn it. Then he returned thence and said: 'I could not find out what sprite this is.' Then they said to Vāyu (air): 'O Vāyu, find out what sprite this is.' 'Yes,' he said. He ran towards it, and Brahman said to him: 'Who are you?' He replied: 'I am Vāyu, I am Mātariśvan.' Brahman said: 'What power is in you?' Vāyu replied: 'I could take up all whatever there is on earth.' Brahman put a straw before him, saying: 'Take it up.' He went towards it with all his might, but he could not take it up. Then he returned thence and said: 'I could not find out what sprite this is.' Then they said to Iṇdra: 'O Bhagavān, find out what sprite this is.' He went towards it, but it disappeared from before him. Then in the same Ākāś, ether, he came towards a woman, highly adorned: it was Umā, the daughter of Himavat. He said to her: 'Who is that sprite?' She replied: 'It is Brahman. It is through the victory of Brahman that you have thus become great.' After that he knew that it was Brahman."

This is a further step than the position in the Ṛig Vêda where the Ekam Sat or Rudra Paśupati is identified in a manner with all the Gods. Here, he is not Iṇdra or Varuṇa, Vāyu or Agni. He cannot be comprehended of the Gods, though He is before them, and it was left to *Umā Haimavati* to point out the Supreme Brahman, as her consort. This story is frequently repeated in the Purāṇas * and the person of Rudra-Śiva is introduced as Umā's Lord.

This is called the Brahami Upanishat, and it introduces the grand thought "he by whom Brahman is not thought, by him it is thought; he by whom it is thought, knows it not."

This departure from the old polity of the Vêdas to the worship of the One Supreme Brahman, Umā's Lord, will be found illustrated further in the Purāṇas by the stories of the Daksha's sacrifice and the Dārukavana Ṛishis. Daksha, son of Brahma (Śabda Brahma or Vedas), simply means sacrifice and Dākshāyaṇi meant the spirit of sacrifice. And so long as this spirit of sacrifice was devoted to the One Supreme Brahman, Śiva, it was beneficial. But once this sacrifice was divorced from the worship of the One Supreme Brahman, represented in the person of Śiva, the consort of Dākshāyaṇi, as Daksha tried to do, then this sacrifice was of no avail. When the spirit of sacrifice was divorced from the word, then Dākshāyaṇi died and was reborn as Umā Haimavati, the bearer of Brahma Jñāna and was reunited to Śiva. This reunion or rebirth of the old jñāna is what is celebrated in every temple, in the important feast of Tirukkalyāṇa, and is figured in the oldest sculptures in the Elephanta and Ellora cave-temples. In the Dārukāvana story, the Vêdic sacrifice was also divorced from the worship of the One Supreme Brahman. The Vedas represented the

* Vide *Vāyu Samhitā* II Chap. 3 and *Suta Samhitā.*

Śabda Brahman, and the Ṛishis thought that no God was required, and the worship of the Śabda Brahman was alone sufficient for securing salvation. The bleating of the Śabda Brahman represented by the deer (மான்மறை) was found in no way to reach God.

The Śvetāśvatara Upanishat, the greatest authority of the Śaiva School, repeats the text of the Yajur Vêda "Eka Eva Rudrō Nadvitīyāya Taste", and the philosophy of Advaita Siddhāṉta is fully expounded in this Upanishat. This Advaita is neither the Śāṅkhya nor the Yōga, neither Dvaita nor Advaita, as ordinarily understood. Hence, Oriental Scholars like Monier Williams, Professor Macdonnel and Garbe regard this Upanishat as the oldest representative of the ancient *eclectic* * school of Hindu philosophy. With this book they couple the Bhagavat Gītā.

The highest conception of the one God, 'Eko Dêva' is, given here which, as Max Müller says, corresponds to the conception of God in the Christian theology. "He is the one God hidden in all beings, all pervading, the Antar Ātmā of all things, watching over all works, dwelling in all beings, the witness, the perceiver, the only One Nirguṇa." "He is the eternal and infinite, unborn being, partless, actionless, tranquil, without taint, without fault, the highest bridge to immortality."

"He is the causeless first cause, the all-knower, the all-pervader; the creator, sustainer and liberator of the world, the end and aim of all religion, and of all philosophy. He is the Īśvara of Īśvaras, Mahêśvara, the God Supreme of Gods, the king of kings, the supreme of the supreme, the Īśa of the Universe. The sun does not shine there, nor the moon and the stars, nor these lightnings, and much less this fire, everything shines after Him; by His light all this is lightened." God is nirguṇa; and as I have shown elsewhere, nirguṇa does not mean impersonal,

* Of the eclectic movement combining Śāṅkhya, Yōga and Vêdāṉta doctrines, the oldest representative is the Śvêtāśvatara Upanishat, more famous is the Bhagavat Gītā (Macdonnell's *History of Sanskrit Lit.* p. 405).

and Saguṇa is not to be translated personal. Nirguṇa simply means beyond the three Guṇas, Satva, Rajas, and Tamas, and Saguṇa means united to these three. Personality means, as Emerson and other Christian writers interpreted, 'pure spiritual being,' 'Sat' and God can be personal and Nirguṇa, absolute. It follows also that God cannot be born as He is not united to matter. The meaning of the Ṛig Vēda Sūkta we quoted above is brought out in the following verse. "When there was no darkness nor day nor night nor Sat nor Asat then Śiva alone existed (Śiva Eva Kevalaḥ). That is the absolute, that is the adorable condition of the Lord. From that too had come forth the wisdom of old (Jñānāśakti)."* After repeating the text about the two birds, this is how it proceeds. "On the same tree man (Anīśa) sits grieving, immersed, bewildered by his own impotence. But when he sees the other Īśa, contented and knows His glory, then his grief passes away." † That this is the highest teaching of the Ṛig Vēda is pointed out in the next verse. "He who does not know that Indestructible Being (Akshara) of the Ṛig Vēda, that highest Ether (Parama Vyōmam) wherein all the Gods reside, of what use is Ṛig Vēda to him? Those only who know It rest contented." ‡ The otherness of God (Anyatā) referred to in the Ṛig Veda Mantra is brought out fully also in the following verses. "Aye, that one unborn (Aja-soul) sleeps in the arms of one unborn (nature Pradhāna) enjoying (her of nature, red, white and black), who brings forth multitudinous progeny like herself. But when her charms have been enjoyed, he (soul) quits her (prakṛiti) side (for) the unborn other, (Anyatā) (Lord)."

---

* यदातमस्तन्नदिवानरात्रिः नसन्नचासच्छिवएवकेवलः ।
तदक्षरंतत्सवितुर्वरेण्यं प्रज्ञाचतस्मात्प्रसृतापुराणी ॥ (Śvēta.)

† समानेवृक्षेपुरुषोनिमग्नोऽनीशयाशोचतिमुह्यमानः ।
जुष्टंयदापश्यत्यन्यमीशमस्य महिमानमितिवीतशोकः ॥ (Śvēta 4—7)

‡ ऋचोऽक्षरेपरमेव्योमन् यस्मिन्देवाअधिविश्वेनिषेदुः ।
यस्तन्नवेदकिमृचाकरिष्यति य इत्तद्विदुस्तइमेसमासते ॥
—(Ṛig Vēda 2nd Ashṭaka, 3rd Adhyāya)

"In the imperishable, and infinite highest Brahman, wherein the two, Vidyā, (Vijñāna-Ātmā) and Avidyā are hidden, the one, Avidyā, perishes; the other Vidyā, is immortal; but He who controls both Vidyā and Avidyā, is another (Anyatā)." * And in the subsequent verses, this another is clearly pointed out to be the "only one God, without a second, the ruler of all, the generator of all and the supporter (ripener) of all." This forms the subject of discussion in the hands of Bādarāyaṇa in I. ii, 21. And the famous passage in Bṛihadāraṇyaka is referred to. "He who dwells in Ātmā (Vijñāna) and *different from Ātmā*, whom the Ātmā does not know, whose body *Ātmā* is and who pulls (rules) Ātmā within, He is thy Ātmā, the puller within, the immortal" (III. 7, 22).

(3) The Supreme Mantra of the Vêda or the Šabda Brahma is the Praṇava or Omkāra. It is ordinarily known that Om is a compound of the three letters A, U, and M, and that they represent the deities Brahma, Vishṇu, and Rudra. What is not known is that there is a fourth part of this § Omkāra called its Ardha Mātra sound, this is called the Chaturtam or Turīyam, and represents the supreme Brahman or Šiva. This is brought out in several of the Upanishats and in the following verses it is coupled with Šivam and Šambhu.

"Šivam Šāntam Advaitam Chaturtam Manyaṇte".

—(Māṇḍūkya.)

"Dhyāyêtīšānam pradhyāyitavyam, Sarvamidam, Brahma Vishṇu Rudrêndrasthe, Samprasūyante, Sarvāṇi chêndriyāṇi Sahabhūtaiḥ; Nakaraṇam Karaṇānām Dhāta Dhyāta; Kara-

---

* द्वेअक्षरेब्रह्मपरेत्वनन्ते विद्याऽविद्येनिहितेयत्रगूढे ।
क्षरेत्वविद्याह्यमृतंतुविद्या विद्याऽविद्येईशतेयस्तुसोन्य: ॥ (Šveta 5—1).

§ एवंत्रिसमिरेवेदं मात्राभिर्निखिलंत्रिधा ।
अभिधायशिवात्मानं बोधयत्यर्धमात्रया ॥

"Thus knowing all these things to be denoted by the Tri-mātras, understand that Šiva, the Ātman of all, is denoted by the Ardha-mātra," (Vāyu-Samhitā IV Chap. 7, vide also Chap. 27 of Vāyu-Samhitā II in the Mahāliṅga Prādarbhavadhyāya.)

ṇantu Dhêyêyaḥ Sarvaiśvarya sampannaḥ Sarvêśvaraḥ Śambhurākāśa Madhye. Śiva êkô Dhyāyat Śivaṅkara Sarvam Anyat Parityaja.—(Atharva Śikha).

The more popular Hymn in the Mahimnastôtra addressed to Śiva brings out this idea. "The mystical and immutable one which, being composed of the three letters 'A', 'U', 'M', signify successively the three Vêdas, the three states of Life (Jāgra, Svapna and Sushupti), the three worlds (earth, heaven and hell), the three Gods (Brahma, Vishṇu and Rudra), and which by its ardha-mātra is indicative of thy Fourth office, as Paramеśvara."

(4) * The Supreme Upāsana of the Upanishat is the Dahara Upāsana in the *Hṛid Puṇḍarika*, in the ākāś, Vyōma Paramālaya. The Yōgi has to think of the Supreme Brahman in the cave of the heart, in the midst of the Chidākāśa. The Taittiriya Upanishat speaks of this Brahman as of the form of Krishṇa Piṅgala. This Krishṇa Piṅgala † is identified as Umāsahāya or Pārvati Paramêśvara, in several of the Upanishats.

This again is described as Jyōtir (the supreme light; (the jyōtir Liṅga).

(5) When the polity of the sacrifice was given up in favour of the worship of this Jyōtir Liṅga, and the Symbolism of the sacrificial ground was invested with a more spiritual meaning, then we would seem to have arrived at the period of the Āgamas, and our modern temple worship would seem to have been started. The Āgamas brought into use the very

---

* कदुद्राचप्रर्चतसेमोदुष्टमायतीव्यसेवोचेमशंन्तमंहृदे ॥

(—1st Ashtaka, 1st Maṇḍala, 8th Anuvāka. 1 Repeated in Mahopanishat.)

† अर्धान्तकमनग्नार्ध मस्थ्युत्पलदलशाजम् ।
अर्धपुल्लक्षणंतन्दे पुरुषंकृष्णपिङ्गलम् ॥

Half with locks of long hair (female) half without dress (Digambara male) half with garland of bones (male) and other half with garland of the Nilōtpala (female)—such a form of half male and female is called Krishṇapiṅgaḷa—Bhavishyat Purāṇa,

same maṇtras, as pointed out by Svāmi Vivêkānaṇda,* in his famous address before the Chicago parliament of Religions, used in the old sacrificial worship, into the new system of worship, and the offer of the self as a sacrificial oblation was made in the place of animal sacrifice. The Pašu was the animal in man and when it was offered as sacrifice in Jñāna Agni, it became the Naṇdi or Šiva.

PURĀṆAS.

The Purāṇas are the earliest interpreters of the Vêda and the Upanishats. Whole passages from the Upanishats are quoted and explained. The principles are illustrated by stories and parables, and the Vêdic stories themselves are more elaborated. All these explain the difference between the old and new system of worship and thought, bring out fully the difference and distinction between the Supreme Brahman Šiva and man, and illustrate the paths to salvation. These stories are the Daksha sacrifice, the churning of the milky ocean, and Tripura Samhāra, Durga Pūja etc. The Linga Purāṇa specially deals with the birth of the Jyōtir Linga. The largest number of Purāṇas are Šaivaite, and the oldest of them is the Vāyu or Šiva Purāṇa, as pointed out by Wilson. The Chhāndōgya Upanishat traces the wisdom of old from Skaṇda Sanatkumāra (तपसस्यारंदर्शयतिभगवान् सनत्कुमारस्तगुं स्कन्दइत्याचक्षते—तंस्कन्दइत्याचक्षते—Chānd. 26th Kaṇḍa,) and Skāṇda Purāṇa accordingly deals with the same subject. The Uttara portions of some of the purāṇas are clearly later interpolations showing the rise of new sects and faiths.

---

* "The Taṇtras as we have said represent Vêdic rituals in a manifold form, and before any one jumps to the most absurd conclusions about them, I will advise him to read the Taṇtras in connexion with the Brāhmaṇas, especially the adhvarya portion. And most of the Maṇtras used in the Taṇtras will be found taken verbatim from these Brāhmaṇas. As to their influence, apart from the Šrauta and Smārta rituals, all other forms of ritual observed from the Himalayas to the Comorin have been taken from the Taṇtras and they direct the worship of the Šāktas, Šaivas and Vaishṇavas alike."

ITIHĀSA.

The only worship universal in the days of Mahābhārata was that of Śiva and Śiva Liṅga, and we refer to the stories of Krishṇa's and Arjuna's Tapas, and the discussion between Aśvatthāma and Vyāsa. Most of the temples mentioned in the Āraṇya Parva are temples dedicated to Śiva.

MAHĀBHĀRATA.

Oriental Scholars point out that the superior castes in the days of Mahābhārata were following the worship of Śiva, and we quote the following passage from Anuśāsana Parva, which explains at the same time Rudra's different aspects, the beneficient and apparently terrible forms, as the Creator, Protector, and Destroyer.

Lord Krishṇa says "Large armed Yudhishṭira, understand from me the greatness of the glorious, *multiform*, many-named Rudra. They call Mahādêva, Agni, Iśāna, Mahêśvara, one-eyed, Tryambaka, the *Universal-formed* and Śiva. Brāhmans versed *in the Vêda* know two bodies of this God, one awful, one auspicious, and these two bodies have again many forms. The dire and awful body is fire, lightning, the sun; the auspicious and beautiful body is virtue, water and the moon. The Half of His essence is fire and the other half is called the moon. The one which is His auspicious body practises chastity, while the other which is His most dreadful body, destroys the world. From His being Lord and Great, He is called Mahêśvara. Since He consumes, since He is fiery, fierce, glorious, an eater of flesh, blood and marrow, He is called Rudra. As He is the greatest of the Gods, as His domain is wide and as He preserves the vast Universe, He is called Mahādeva. From His smoky colour He is called Dhūrjaṭi. Since He constantly prospers all men in all their acts seeking their welfare (Śiva), He is therefore called Śiva."

And it can be shown that the picture of God as the fierce and the terrible is not altogether an un-Christian idea. The following paras, we cull from a book called "The woodlands in

Europe" intended for Christian Readers and we could not produce better arguments for the truth of our conception of the Supreme Śiva, the Destroyer, and the Creator and the Preserver (vide p. 6. *Śivajñānabōdham*, English Edition.)

"And how about the dead leaves which season after season strew the ground beneath the trees? Is their work done because when their bright summer life is over, they lie softly down to rest under the wintry boughs? Is it only death and nothing beyond? Nay, if it is death, it is death giving place to life. Let us call it rather change, progress, transformation. It must be progress when the last year's leaves make the soil for the next year's flowers, and in so doing serve a set purpose and fulfil a given mission. *It must be transformation when one thing passes into another, and instead of being annihilated, begins life again in a new shape and form.*

"It is interesting to remember that the same snow which weighs down and breaks those fir branches is the nursing mother of the flowers. Softly it comes down upon the tiny seeds and the tender buds and covers them up lovingly, so that from all the stern vigour of the world without, they are safely sheltered. Thus they are getting forward, as it were, and life is already swelling within them. So that when the sun shines and the snow melts, they are ready to burst forth with a rapidity which seems almost miraculous.

"*It is not the only force gifted with both preserving and destroying power, according to the aspect in which we view it.* The fire refines and purifies but it also destroys, and the same water which rushes down in the cataract with such overwhelming power, falls in the gentlest of drops upon the thirsty flower-cup, and fills the hollow of the leaf with just the quantity of dew which it needs for its refreshment and sustenance. And in those higher things of which nature is but the type and shadow, the same grand truth holds good, and from our Bibles we learn that the *consuming fire and the love that passeth knowledge are two different sides of the same*

37

God. Just and yet merciful, that will by no means clear the guilty, yet showing mercy unto thousands."

Bādarāyaṇa also touches upon this subject in I. iii. 40 and we quote below the Pūrvapaksha and Siddhānta views on this question from the commentary of Śrīkaṇṭha.

"Because of trembling (I. iii. 40).

"In the Kaṭhavallīs, in the section treating of the thumb-sized purusha, it is said as follows:

'Whatever there is, the whole world when given forth (from the Brahman) trembles in the *breath*. (It is) a great terror, the thunderbolts uplifted, those who know it become immortal' (Cit. 6, 2).

"Here a doubt arises as to whether the cause of trembling is the Paramēšvara or some other being.

"(Pūrvapaksha):—Here the Sruti speaks of the trembling of the whole universe by fear caused by the entity denoted by the word *breath*. It is not right to say that the Paramēš-vara, who is so sweet-natured as to afford refuge to the whole Universe and who is supremely gracious, is the cause of the trembling of the whole Universe. Therefore, as the word thunderbolt occurs here, it is the thunderbolt that is the cause of trembling. Or it is the vital air which is the cause of trembling because the word breath occurs here. Since the vital air causes the motion of the body, this whole world which is the body, as it were, moves on account of the vital air. Then we can explain the passage, 'whatever there is, the whole world, when given forth (from the Brahman) trembles in the *breath*.' Then we can also explain the statement that it is a great terror, the thunderbolt uplifted, inasmuch as lightning, cloud and rain, the thunderbolt which is the source of great terror are produced by action of the air itself. It is also possible to attain immortality by a knowledge of the air as the following Śruti says:

'Air is everything itself and the air is all things together. He who knows this conquers death.' (Bri. Up. 5. 3. 2).

"(Siddhāṇta): As against the foregoing, we say that Paramēśvara himself is the cause of the trembling. It is possible that as the Ruler, Paramēśvara is the cause of trembling of the whole Universe and by the fear of His command, all of us abstain from prohibited actions and engage in the prescribed duties and it is by the fear of the command that Vāyu and others perform their respective duties as may be learned from such passages as the following:

'By fear of Him, Vāyu (the wind) blows' (Tait. 14. 2. 8).

"Though gracious in appearance, Paramešvara becomes awful as the Ruler of all. Hence the Sruti.

'Hence the King's face has to be awful' (Tait. Bra, 3. 8. 23).

"Wherefore as the master, Īśvara himself is the cause of the trembling of the whole Universe."

THE GĪTĀ.

The Bhagavat Gītā epitomises the philosophy of the Śvētāśvatara Upanishat. Oriental scholars link both together as expounding an eclectic school of Hindu Philosophy. In it, the words Īśvara, Īśa, Mahēśvara, Paramešvara, are used and in the Uttara Gītā*, the word Śiva is used not to denote the lower Brahman but the Supreme Brahman.

THE RĀMĀYANA.

In the Rāmāyaṇa, Rudra's position as the Lord of sacrifices is affirmed in spite of some dissentients, showing the rise of new faiths. The worship of Śiva and Śiva-Linga was

---

*In the Anu Gītā, Śrī Krishṇa was asked by Arjuna to tell him the Knowledge of Brahm as was given before—during the war. Śrī Krishna replied; "सहिधर्मस्सु पर्याप्तोब्रह्मण: पदर्थंदनेनशक्यंतन्मयात्वक्तुं तथाभूयोप्यशेषत: । परंहिधर्मंकथितं योगयुक्तेनतन्मया । I did exhaust all ways of knowing the Brahman and I am not able to recount to you all these again. I was then in deep-yoga and I then told you the knowledge." And the real position of Krishṇa in reference to Arjuna is that of Guru to disciple. अहंगुरुर्महाबाहोमन: शिष्योहिदिविद्वीमे. In the Uttara Gītā, the Lord is certainly styled as the fourth; तुर्यंचतुर्थातीतं च शिवस्थानमनामयम्.

Universal as shown by the establishment of the temple at Rāmeśvaram.

THE SŪTRAS.

All the Sūtrakāras recognise Īśvara as the Supreme God and Purusha. Śrī Nīlakaṇṭha's Bhāshyam * on the Brahma Sūtras is the earliest commentary now extant; as such it is entitled to the greatest weight and will be found to be the most accurate and reliable interpreter of the Vedāṇta Sūtras, and Śrī Nīlakaṇṭha is the accepted authority by the Southern Śaiva School.

It is now proved by Thibaut and admitted by Max Muller that the interpretation of Śaṅkara is not correct. Says Doctor Thibaut.

"If now, I am to sum up the results of the preceding enquiry, as to the teaching of the Sūtras, I must give it as my opinion that they do not set forth the distinction of a higher and lower knowledge of Brahman; that they do not acknowledge the distinction of Brahman and Īśvara in Śaṅkara's sense; that they do not hold the doctrine of the unreality of the world; and that they do not, with Śaṅkara, proclaim the absolute identity of the Individual and the Highest Self."

"The Upanishats no doubt teach emphatically that the material world does not owe its existence to any principle independent from the Lord, like the Pradhāna of the Sāṅkhyas; the world is nothing but a manifestation of the Lord's wonderful power and hence is unsubstantial (Asat) if we take the term substance (Sat) in its strict sense. And again everything material (Achit) is immeasurably inferior in nature to the highest spiritual principle from which it has emanated and which it now hides from the individual Soul. But neither unsubstantiality nor inferiority of the kind mentioned constitutes unreality in the sense in which the Māyā of Śaṅkara is unreal. According to the latter the whole world is nothing but an erroneous appearance as unreal as the snake for which a piece of rope is mistaken by the belated traveller, and

* English Translation published in vols. I to VII *Siddhānta Dīpikā.*

disappearing just as the imagined snake does as soon as the light of true knowledge has risen. But this is certainly not the impression left on the mind by a comprehensive review of the Upanishats which dwells on their general scope, and does not confine itself to the undue urging of what may be implied in some detached passages &c."

Says Professor Max Muller in his Life of Rāmakrishṇa Parama Hamsa : 'It is difficult to say which of the two schools was the more ancient and I am bound to acknowledge after Professor Thibaut's luminous exposition that Viśisṭādvaita interpretation is more in keeping with the Sūtras of Bādarāyaṇa."

Śrī Nīlakaṇṭha Śivāchārya in his Bhāshya quotes, with approval, this beautiful text from the Upanishats. "Apivāyas chaṇḍālaḥ Śiva iti vācham vadēt tēna saha samvadēt, tēna saha samvasēt, tena saha bhuñjīt" * which means :—"A chaṇḍāḷa though a person is, if he utters the name Śiva, converse with him, live with him, dine with him".

"Wherefore the whole universe is ensouled by Śiva. If any embodied being whatsoever be subjected to constraint, it will be quite repugnant to the eight-bodied Lord ; as to this there is no doubt. Doing good to all, kindness to all, affording shelter to all, this they hold as the worshipping of Śiva,"

During the Buddhist and Jaina period, it was Śaivaism that was able to rise above the onslaught of these two creeds and vanquish them. The rise of the great Āchāryas, St. Jñāna-Sambandar, St. Appar, St. Sundarar and St. Māṇikkavāçagar was in this period. By the close of the ninth century, both Buddhism and Jainism had become inert and dead.

The next few centuries saw the rise of the great teachers Śri Śaṅkara, Śri Rāmānuja and Śri Madhvāchārya. Following them close, came the great Santāna Āchāryas, St. Meykaṇḍān ‡

---

* अपिवायश्चण्डालः शिवइतिवाचं वदेत् तेन सह संवदेत् तेन सह संवसेत् तेन सह भुंजीत्.

‡ The author of *Śivajñānabodham*.

St. Aruṇaṇdi,* St. Maṟai-Jñāna-Sambaṇdar and St. Umāpati Śivāchāryar § and modern Śaivaism may be said to commence from that time.

We will now begin the study of Modern Śaivaism. Its form of ritualism and philosophy is determined in the South by the Āgamas or Taṇtras, 28 in number, from Kāmika to Vātuḷa, called the Dakshiṇa or Right-handed; and the different temples in Southern India follow the rules prescribed in one Āgama or another, though there are still some temples like the one at Chidambaram where the pure Vêdic Rituals † are followed. This Āgama Philosophy has also been greatly developed and systematised in Tamiḷ by a line of Teachers beginning with St. Tirumūlar, ‡ St. Meykaṇḍān, St. Aruṇaṇdi Śivāchāriyar, St. Maṟai-Jñāna-Sambaṇdar and St. Umāpati Śivāchāriyar. Both in the rituals and in the philosophy, the same maṇtras, forms and words derived from the old Vedic Times are used. For instance, the temple represents the old Yajña-śālā symbolising the human body. The Śiva Liṅga,¶ (it is due to Svāmi Vivekānaṇda to point out that this was no Phallic Symbol $ and this view was reiterated by

---

* The authour of *Śivajñāna Siddhiyār.*

§ The author of *Light of Grace* and *Śivaprakāśam.*

† The pūjās done in the Chidambaram are according to the paddhati of Patañjali; who takes the one from Śaivāgamas and the Maṇtras from the Vêdas,

‡ The author of *Tirumantiram.*

¶ See the full subject discussed with all the authorities in *Siddhānta Dipikā* Vols. VI and VII.

$ The Svāmi said that the worship of the Śiva Liṅga originated from the famous liṅgam in the Atharva Vêda Samhitā sung in praise of the Yūpastambha, the sacrificial post. In that hymn a description is found of the beginningless and endless Stambha or skhamba and it is shown that the said Skhamba is put in place of the eternal Brahman. As, afterwards, the sacrificial fire, its smoke, ashes and flames, the soma plant and the ox that used to carry on its back the wood for the Vêdic sacrifice, gave place to Śiva's body, his yellow-matted hair, his blue throat, and bull, the Yūpastambha gave place to the Śiva Liṅgam and was raised to

Dr. Ānaṇda K. Kumārasvāmi in his paper read before the Historical Congress of Oriental Religions in which he shows that it is the least anthropomorphic of symbols,) takes the place of Rudra Paśupati and its form is that of the Praṇava* and there is the Balipīṭha at the entrance to the temple with the Yūpastambha † and the Paśu or animal offered in sacrifice in the form of the Bull. Every Brahmōtsava still commences with a sacrifice, (the blood sacrifice is altogether given up in the South Indian Temples) and the Paśu, in effigy in cloth, is tied up to the Yūpastambha and after the festival is taken down. The position of the bull or Paśu will be found to be on the other side (God side) of the Balipīṭha and Stambha, and it is not called Paśu but Naṇdi (Blissful), God. Because, according to the phraseology of Śaivaism, the Jīva or soul, once it had become freed, is no more called Jīva but Śiva or Brahman. What had to be offered in sacrifice was not an animal but the Jīva; the soul called also the Ejaman of the sacrifice, had to offer his Jīvtavam, his animal part of himself, his individuality or Ahaṅkāra or Avidyā or Ignorance, and the Naivedyam in all temples is now interpreted as this Paśutvam, or Paśubhōdham as it is called. As soon as he enters the temple, he is asked to prostrate in front of the Yūpastambha. This is his

---

the High Devahood of Śrī Śaṅkara. In the Atharva Vēda Samhitā, the sacrificial cows are also praised with the attributes of the Brahman. In the Liṅga Purāṇa, the same hymn is expanded in the shape of stories meant to establish the glory of the great Stambha and superiority of Mahādēva. Later on, he says, the explanation of the Śiva Liṅgam as a Phallic emblem began in India in her most thoughtless and degraded times.

* "The whole Linga is the Omkāra filled by Nāda and Biṇdu. The base is Akāra. The Kaṇṭa is Makāra, and the round form Ukāra". *Tirumantiram.*

† पतिस्तंयइतिप्रोक्तो पशुःस्तगइतिस्मृतः ।

रज्जुःपाशइत्तिप्रोक्तः त्रिविधास्तेचर्मन्तिच ॥ —Ajitāgama.

The standard pole represents Pati. The flag or piece of cloth that is being raised to the top represents Paśu and the cord (made of grass) represents Pāśa,

offer of his self as sacrifice; and self-sacrifice thus becomes the centre of Hindu and Šaivaite Philosophy, on which the whole process of salvation depends. This is the Arpaṇa or Šivārpaṇa referred to in Verse 57, Chap. 18 of Gītā.

The philosophy also retains the old language for its technical terms. Whereas the newer systems have such technical terms as 'Chit, Achit, Išvara,' 'Jagat, Jīva, and Para;' the Šaiva-Siddhānta technical terms to denote these Padārthas or categories are Pati (God), Pašu (soul), and Pāša (bondage).¶

¶ In the hymn to the unknown God in the tenth Maṇḍala of the Rig Vêda, God is termed the Pati—which means Protector or Saviour coming from the root Pā, to protect. It strictly corresponds to the English term Providence. Even the term Īša or Īšvara which simply means Ruler, does nor bring out the Inner Narure of the Lord which is Love. Vide also the Brahma Sūtra text पत्यादिशब्देभ्यः because of the term Pati and others: Pašu, as Šrīkaṇṭha Yogi explains, involves bondage in Pāša— "पाशसंबन्धेन पशुत्वव्यवहारात्" and Pāsa in its root meaning simply means "that which binds". It means a noose or a cord only in its extended meaning of imagery. A man bound to a pole by means of cords, his hands and feet, neck and back being tied to it, can have no liberty and he is said to undergo *pain*. Pāša therefore does not simply mean "limitation" but is limitation which involves pain or pain to the core. The Āgamas explain the noose or a cord held in one of the ten hands of Sadāsiva's form as पाशंमायास्वरुपकं and "मलमाया कर्मपाशश्च".

In Šaivaism the soul is symbolised as a cattle tied by means of a rope to a pole. This supposes the existence of a master to it. The Vāyu-Sambitā has.

ब्रह्माद्याःस्थावरान्ताश्च पशवःपरिकीर्तिताः ।
पशूनामेवसर्वेषां प्रोक्तमेतन्निदर्शनम् ।
यएषबध्यतेपाशैः सुखदुःखाशनःपशुः ।
लीलासाधनभूतोय मीश्वरस्यनिसूरयः ।
अजोजन्तुरनीशोय मात्मनःसुखदुःखया ।
ईश्वरप्रेरितोगच्छेत् स्वर्गंवाश्वभ्रमेववा ।

Beings from Brahma to immovable things are termed Pašus. These are the characteristics of all Pašus (i.e.,) that it is bound or tied by means of ropes that it chews the cud of Šukha and Duḥkha (pleasure and pain) arising out of its own acts, that it forms an instrument for the Lords to

Pāśa is the rope with which the Paśu is tied to the sacrificial stake and this is the word mostly used in the Upanishats also to describe Man's bondage or Mala. "Pāśam dahati Paṇḍitaḥ" (*Kaivalya Upanishat*).

The Pati is accordingly described in the text-books as follows:

This Pati is Param, neither Rūpa nor Arūpa, Nirguṇa without mark, Nirmala, Eka, Eternal, Chit of Chit, Achala, Infinite, Ānaṇda, the unapproachable, the Goal, the least of the least, and the greatest of the great, Tat and Śiva (*Śivaprakāśa* I.)

ŚAIVA IS NIRGUNA AND PERSONAL.

We have only to notice that the God postulated by Śaiva Siddhāṇta is not Saguṇa, but Nirguṇa,* which as we have pointed out above means only above the three guṇas, Satva, Rajas and Tamas, i.e., above Prakṛiti i.e., non-material or Chit.

NIRGUṆA NOT TO BE TRANSLATED IMPERSONAL.

We have condemned ever so often the translation of the words Nirguṇa and Saguṇa into Impersonal and Personal and

---

play with in His Pañchakrityas, just as a cow is tied or released, that it has no wider vision (Agam) and is not master of its self (Anisa) and it is laid by *a master*, or Īśvara, to heavenly regions or other places."—Hence is the soul symbolised as a Paśu. Śri Haradatta says;

आत्मान्तराणिपशव: परतन्त्रभावात् ।
स्वातन्त्र्यत:पशुपते: पतिरीश्वरत्वम् ॥

"Owing to dependence upon *its master*, the Ātmans are Paśus and independence is the mark of thyself—the Pati and Isvara". The term Mala applied to corrupting element has been more in vogue in classic works. Thus Pataṅjali has in his Yoga sūtras "तदासर्वावरणमलापेतस्य ज्ञानस्य" and, in the Manu-smriti we have पूर्वांसन्ध्यांजपान्तिष्ठेन्नैशमेनोव्यपोहति । पश्चिमान्तुसमासीनो मलंहन्तिदिवाकृतम् ॥ (Manu Chap. 2). And what is Mala? "मलविच्छरकोनेजो." Mala is what intrinsically covers the Chit or the intelligence of the soul.

* These three guṇas stand for the three states Jāgra, Svapna and Sushupti, and Nirguṇa therefore means Turiya or Chaturta. "Jāgra is Satva, Rajas is Svapna, Tamas is Sushupti. Nirguṇa is therefore Turiya." *Tirumantiram.*

thus scare away the Christians from the Highest Conception of the Supreme. Personal is explained to mean 'Pure Being,' the absolute, by Emerson and Lotze and other Christian writers and would correspond to our word Sat. And I have shown therefore that God can be both Nirguṇa and Personal.

God neither has form nor is formless as air, ideas all derived from matter, but He can assume any form suited to the conception of his Bhakta and these Forms are not material but as the text says, "His Form is produced out of Divine Grace or Love." God is therefore not to be called Saguṇa simply because He is spoken of as Umā-sahāya, Nilakaṇṭha, Sambhu, Umāpati, Ambikā-Pati &c., Lord of Kailās, as Śiva, Hara, Rudra.*

God is neither he, nor she, nor it, but He can be thought of in all these forms, as male, female and neuter; and all specific names of Śiva are declinable in all the three genders without

* "It has been said, for instance, that the *Śvetāśvatara Upanishat* is a sectarian Upanishat, because, when speaking of the Highest Self or the Highest Brahman, it applies such names to Him as Hara (I, 10), Rudra (II, 17. III, 2, 4. IV, 12, 21), Śiva (III, 14. IV, 10) Bhagavat (III, 14), Agni, Āditya, Vāyu &c., (IV 2). But here it is simply taken for granted that the idea of the Highest Self was developed first, and after it had reached its highest purity was lowered again by an identification with mythological and personal deities. The question whether the conception of the Highest Self was formed once and once only, whether it was formed after all the personal and mythological deities had been merged into one Lord (Prajāpati), or whether it was discovered behind the veil of any other names in the mythological pantheon of the past, have never been mooted. Why would not an ancient Rishi have said; what we have hitherto called Rudra and what we worship as Agni, or Śiva, is in reality the Highest Self, thus leaving much of the ancient mythological phraseology to be used with a new meaning? Why should we at once conclude that the late sectarian worshippers of mythological gods replaced again the highest Self, after their fathers had discovered it, by their own sectarian names? If we adopt the former view, the Upanishats which still show these *Rudras* of the ancient temples, would have to be considered as more primitive even than those in which the idea of the Brahman of the Highest Self has reached its utmost purity."—*Max Muller.*

change of meaning Śiva, Śivaḥ and Śivam,* Śambhu, Sāmbhavi and Sāmbhavam, Īśa, Īśaḥ and Īśānam &c.

ŚIVA IS NOT ONE OF THE TRINITY.

The Pati or Śiva of the Śaiva Religion is not one of the Trimūrtis, Brahma, Vishṇu and Rudra and scores of texts could be quoted from the popular Tamiḻ Hymn-books conveying the same idea as in the hymn of *Mahimna Stōtra* quoted above. God is 'Śivam Advaitam Sāntam Chaturtam.'

GOD CANNOT BE BORN IN MAN.

As Śiva is Nirguṇa and Turīya, the Supreme absolute Brahman, it follows that God cannot be born as a man through the womb of the woman. That Śiva had no avatāras or births is generally known.† This is the greatest distinction of the ancient Hindu Philosophy and of the Śaiva School, making it a purely transcendental Religion, freed of all anthropomorphic conceptions. It was the late Mr. T. Subba Rao who in his "Notes on Bhagavat Gītā" entered a vigorous protest against the conception of the Supreme Brahman having human avatārās and we regret that, in all the mass of current writings, no writer has thought fit to bring this view to prominence. But this absolute nature of Śiva does not prevent Him from His being personal at the same time and appearing as Guru and Saviour, in the form of man, out of His Great Love and feeling for the sin and sorrow of mankind, and helping them to get rid of their bondage.

REASON FOR CREATION.

And this is the reason as shown in Sūtra I., of *Śivajñāna-bōdham*, why God creates the Universe, and resolves it for the purpose of making the souls eat the fruit of the "Tree of Knowledge of Good and Evil" § (good and bad karma) and attain salvation.

---

* This noun form occurs rarely in Sanskrit, but in Tamiḻ, it is very commonly used as synonymous with the masculine form 'Śiva'.

† नजन्ममरणेतस्यनकांक्षितमकांक्षितम् । He has neither birth nor death neither likes nor dislikes.—*Vāyu-Samhitā.*

§ Vide pp. 185-201 *ante.*

THE NECESSITY FOR A GURU.

The necessity for human effort is postulated, but without God's appearance as the Divine Guru, in human form, and His Divine Grace, the final salvation is not possible. Man can but try and get rid of the cataract covering his eye, but that he shall enjoy the light of the Sun (Śiva Sūrya) is independent of his effort; and without the hope of reaching this Light (Śivānubhūti) a man can have but poor inducement to get rid of his cataract (Desire, trishṇa, the seed of birth), which veils him by making him undergo all the trouble and expense (tapas etc.), if the Doctor were to forbid him to see the Light after he regained his sight; and darkness could not vanish unless Light entered.*

DOCTRINE OF GRACE.

The doctrine of Grace and Love ‡ is the distinguishing feature of Śaivaism, and God is accordingly defined by St. Tirumūlar in the following terms:

GOD IS LOVE.

"The ignorant think that Love and Śiva are different; none know that Love and Śiva are the same; when every one knows that Love and Śiva are the same, they will rest in Śiva as Love."—*Tirumantiram.*

GOD'S IMMANENCE.

As God ensouls the Universe of Nature and of Man, Śiva is called the Ashṭamūrti, the eight-bodied Lord, and He gets a name as He dwells in earth, water, air, fire, ākāś, sun and moon and ātman.

---

* To those who would deny this Śivānubhūti, Svāmi Vivēkānanda replied by saying 'He jests at scars that never felt a wound'.

‡ परिपूर्णस्यसर्गाद्यैनात्मनोस्तिप्रयोजनम् ।
परानुग्रहएवास्यफलं सर्वस्यकर्मण: ॥

All His actions are the out-come of His love towards the souls wallowing in sin. Of what avail will the acts of creation and others be to Him Who is Paripūrṇa, eternally contented, except for these who are in need of them?—*Vāyu-Saṃhitā.*

"Pṛithivyōbhavaḥ, āpassarvaḥ, Agnērudraḥ, Vāyōr Bhīmaḥ, Ākāšasya Mahādēvaḥ, Sūryasyōgraḥ, Chaṇdrasya Sōmaḥ, Ātmanaḥ Pašupatiḥ."*

The famous passage in the 7th Brāhmaṇa of the 3rd Chapter in the Bṛihadāraṇya Upanishat gives more forms than these as the *Šarira* of the Brahman, but in the Āgamas and Purāṇas, these are reduced to eight, as comprising all other forms.

GOD'S TRANSCENDENCE.

As God is immanent in the Chētana and Achētana Prapañcha as the soul of all, He is identified with the Universe as the *All*, and yet His transcendency is also brought out by such statements as 'Antas', 'Antara', 'Anyata', 'Nēti' 'Nēti.' 'They are in me, not I in them.' "Thou art not aught in the Universe, naught is there save Thou."

GOD IS SATCHIDĀNANDA.

Šiva is Sat Chit Ānanda,† Sōmāskaṇda (Sa-Umāskaṇda); ‡ Being, Light and Love. As Pure Being, the absolute, God is unknowable; $ and as Light and Love. He links himself to Man; and it is possible to Man to approach Him through Love.

GOD'S ŠAKTI IS LIGHT AND LOVE.

This Light and this Love are therefore called His Šakti,§ and

---

* शर्वोभवस्तथारुद्रउग्रोभीमः पशोःपतिः ।
ईशानश्चमहादेवो मूर्तयश्चाष्टविश्रुताः ।
भूम्यंभोग्निमरुत्व्योम क्षेत्रज्ञार्कनिशाकराः ।
अधिष्ठितामहेशस्य शर्वाद्यैरष्टमूर्तिभिः ।
चराचरात्मकंविश्वं धत्तेविश्वंचरात्मिका ॥ Vāyu-Samhitaā Chap. 3).

† *Vide* Bishop Westcot's definition, God, the Holy Ghost and Christ, as Spirit, Light, and Love.

‡ Umā literally means Light or Wisdom.

$ ज्ञानक्रियाचिकीर्षाभिः तिसृभिःस्वात्मशक्तिभिः ।
शक्तिमानीश्वरः शत्वाद्विश्वंव्यात्याधितिष्ठति ॥

§ *Vide* Brahma sūtra सर्वोपेताचतद्दर्शनात् and also Svēt. text
परास्यशक्तिर्विविधैव श्रूयतेस्वभावकीज्ञानबलक्रियाच । ......
कल्यापरमाशक्तिः कथितापरमात्मनः ॥

as our Mother is all these. This Śakti of God becomes the Mother of the Universe (Bhuvanasya Mātaram) as Śiva is the Bhuvanasya Pitaram.*

St. Aruṇaṇdi accordingly describes Her as follows:—

THIS LIGHT AND THIS LOVE ARE THE MOTHER.

"She, who is Īśa's Kṛipāśakti (Love and Grace), Ichchā-Śakti, Kriyā-Śakti, Jñānā-Śakti, § and Tirōpava-Śakti, who actuates all creation, sustentation and resolution, who is Rûpa and Arûpa and neither, who is the consort of Īsa in these forms, who is all this world and all this wealth, who begets the whole world and sustains them; the Gracious Feet of this *our mother*, who imparts blissful immortality to souls, removes their bonds of birth and remains seated with *our Father* in the hearts of the Freed, let me lift up on my head."

ŚAKTI IS NOT MĀYĀ. $

This Chit-Śakti (Umā, Durga)† Nirguṇa, is sharply distinguished from Māyā (Saguṇa) also a Śakti of the Lord; and inasmuch as God is in a sense identified with His creation, as the Upādāna Kāraṇa ‡ of the Universe, inasmuch as it is His

---

* यथानजायतेपुत्रः पितरंमातरंविना ।
तथाभवंभवानींच विनानेतच्चराचरम् ॥ Vāyu-Samhitā II.

§ The description of Her as Ichchā and Kriyā-Śakti follow from the first definition of Her as Chit, Jñānā-Śakti. Says Arupandi: "The form of this Śakti is unlimited Intelligence. If asked whether Supreme Will and Power are also found in this Intelligence, we answer yes. Wherever there is Intelligence, there is Will and Power. As such, Power and Will will also be manifested by this Chit-Śakti."

$ सैकापराचचिद्रूपाशक्तिः प्रसवधर्म्मिणी। She, the transcending One, the Chidrūpa, the causer of all things: अथासैकापराशक्तिः चिन्मयीशिवसंश्रयां। She the Parāśakti, the ancient One, the Chinmayī, and inhering the Lord Śiva.

† Literally, deliverer from evil, Mahishāsura Mardhani; Mahisha meaning buffalo, is a symbol of Ignorance.

‡ The words Upādāna does not occur in the Upanishats. The word Pariṇāma occurs in the Śvêtāśvatara Upanishat: "यच्चस्वभावंपचति विश्वयोनिःपाच्यांश्चसर्वान् परिणामयेद्यः"). The 'Pariṇāma' is also found in the

Light that illumines all this world, so Our Mother is also identified with Māyā, as Mahāmāyā.*

This Māyā is matter, the 'object' of Western philosophy, and comprises Tanu (the body), Karaṇa (the sense, internal) Bhuvana (the world) and Bhōga (sensation) and is defined as follows:

MĀYĀ DEFINED.¶

" Indestructible, formless One, seed of all the worlds, Achit, all-pervasive, a Śakti of the Perfect One, cause of the souls, bodies, senses and worlds, one of the three Malas (impurities,) cause also of delusion, is Māyā."

COMPOSED OF THIRTY-SIX TATTVAS.

This Māyā or Prakriti, or Pradhāna of most Indian Schools comprise the 24 tattvas from earth to Buddhi or 25 with Mūlaprakriti, but the Śaiva School † postulates 11 more tattvas above this 25; which are Kālam (Time), Niyati (order), Kalā, Vidyā, Rāga or Ichchā, Asuddha-Māya, Śuddha-Vidyā, Sādākyam, Īśvaram, Bindu or Śakti, and Nāda or Śiva (Śuddha Māyā).

---

text Badarāyaṇa Sūtra I. 4, 27 and, Śrikaṇṭha Śivāchārya in his Bhāshya distinguishes it from the ordinary conception of Pariṇāma by calling it 'Apūrva Pariṇāma.'

* शिवेच्छयापराशक्तिः शिवतत्वैकतांगतः ।
ततः परिस्फुरत्याद्यौसर्गे तैलंतिलादिव ॥

By the will of the Lord (Śiva) Parāśakti became one with Śiva-tattva (a nonsentient primordial substance), and thence, in the original creation is produced all as oil from sesamum.

¶ मयत्यस्मात् जगत्सर्वं माया तेनसमीरिता ॥
मायात्रभुनंज्ञानं ॥ ......
माययासततंविंति प्राणिनंश्शुभाशुभम् ॥

All beings always know good and bad by means of Māyā.

† See for a full discussion of the 36 tattvas, Śri Kāsivāsi Seṉtinātha Aiyar's 'Śaiva Siddhānta Tattva Prakāśa Catechism', published in the Siddhāṉta Dipikā, Vol III, p. 205 *et seq.* Vide Authorities for 36 Tattvas.

कालःस्वभावोनियतिर्यदृच्छाभूतानियोनिः पुरुषइतिचिन्त्यम् । Śvet. Up.
कलासर्गकरं देवं येविदुस्तेजहुस्तनुम् । Śvet. Up.

This Šuddha Māyā is the Kuṭila or Kuṇḍalinī Sakti of the Yōgis, of which Mūlaprakṛiti called also Kuṇḍalinī is the grossest form. These higher tattvas, and their Powers can alone be perceived and realized by the Highest Šiva Rāja Yōgis; and they are so subtle as to be mistaken for the Light of the Mother Herself, as they reflect Her Light most perfectly.

MĀYĀ DISTINGUISHED FROM AVIDYĀ.

This Māyā is again to be distinguished from *Aṇava* Mala (the technical * term in the Āgamas for Ahaṅkāra, or Avidyā or Ajñāna or ignorance), and the definition and distinction are stated in the following verses by St. Aruṇaṇḍi:

AVIDYĀ OR ĀṆAVA MALA DEFINED.

"Āṇava Mala, with its many Šaktis, is One, pervading through the numberless Jīvas, as the dirt in copper †; it binds them from jñāna and kriyā. It also affords them the capacity for experience and is ever the source of ignorance."

DISTINCTION.

"Do you say 'there is no other entity as Mala (Āṇava); it is only the effect of Māyā'? Understand well, that Māyā causes Ichcha, Jñāna and Kriyā to arise in the Jīvas, but Āṇava causes the same to disappear. Āṇava is inherent in Jīvas, but Māyā is separate from them (as one's ignorance and body can be called inseparable and separate), and besides manifesting itself as the Universe, forms the body, senses, worlds and enjoyments."

KEVALA, SAKALA AND SUDDHA OR NIRVĀṆA CONDITION OF THE SOUL.

According to the Pūrvapakshin, Māyā is the cloud that hides the light of the Sun. But the Siddhāṇtin answers, "You

---

* The technical term to denote the Mala called Āṇava.

पशुत्वपशुनीहारमृत्युमूर्च्छामलंजनैः ।
अविद्याऽवृतिप्रत्तग्लानिपापमूलक्षयादिभिः Mṛigêndrāgama.

† नीहारोनादिरेकोमखुज सहभवस्ताम्रकाकालिकेव ।
स्वाधीकारान्तनाशी प्रतिपुरुषदृगावारकोऽनेकशक्तिः ॥ Siddhānta Sārāvaḷi.

cannot speak of the sun being hid by the clouds, unless there is a seer. The cloud has no capacity to hide the sun but it has power to hide the seer's eye. This sun is Śiva. The cloud or cataract in one's eye is the Āṇava Mala; the seer or his eye is the Jīva or Ātmā or soul. When the soul is enshrouded by Āṇava Mala and is without action will and intelligence, it is its night —the Kēvala State.* When God, out of His great love, sets him in evolution giving it the body and the worlds out of *Māyā* for his enjoyment and experience, whereby his kriyā śakti etc., are aroused, this is called its sakaḷa condition. Āṇava Mala is night and darkness, and Māyā acts as the lamp-light—the power of million arcs is the Śuddha Māyā—in darkness. But when the sun rises, all darkness and night vanish and there is no need of any lamp, however powerful, and the soul is fully enveloped in that Supreme Splendour, that "Light of Truth, that, entering body and soul, has melted all faults and driven away the false darkness." This is the soul's Śuddha or Nirvāṇa condition.

> "This day in Thy mercy unto me Thou didst drive away the darkness, and stand as the Rising Sun:
> Of this, Thy way of rising—there being naught else but Thou—I thought without thought.
> I drew nearer and nearer to Thee, wearing away atom by atom, till I was one with Thee.
> O Śiva, dweller in the great Holy Shrine,
> Though art not aught in the Universe, naught is there save Thou.
> Who can know Thee?" ¶

The above expresses the kernel of Śaiva Advaita Siddhānta. This leads us naturally to the discussion of the nature of *Advaita* postulated by the Śaiva School, and before we do so,

---

* From start to finish, life consists of series of awakenings till the final goal is reached. Accordingly existence itself is five-fold.

अबुद्धश्चैवबुद्धश्च बुध्यमानस्तथैवच ।
प्रबुद्धस्सुप्रबुद्धश्च पंचापिकथयामिते ॥

Abuddha, Buddha, Budhyamāna, Prabuddha and Suprabuddha.

¶ From St. Māṇikkavāçagar's Tiruvāchakam.

we will glance at the nature of the Jīvātmā or soul itself, as this is essential to the understanding of the *Advaita*.

SOUL DISTINGUISHED FROM SAT AND ASAT.

The Sāṅkhyans, Yōgins, and Vēdāṇtins admit that the Purusha or Ātmā or soul is other than Prakṛiti and above Buddhi and 23 tattvas. There is confusion in trying to establish its relation to God. The soul is not a reflection nor a particle nor a spark of the Partless and Changeless Brahman,* nor one with Him. God is *other* than the soul. Even where the Sūtrakāra postulates Pariṇāma, he does it only in reference to Māyā, but he postulates the difference of the Human Soul and the Supreme Soul: no harm would arise if we regard Māyā as One with the Brahman as His inseparable Śakti, but all religion and morality are sure to die, when we regard the soul the same as God.† There will be no way to account for the Presence of evil or ignorance in the world, and even when we try to whittle it

---

* पृथगात्मानंप्ररितारंचमत्वा । जुष्टस्ततस्तेनामृतत्वमेति ॥ Śvēt. Up.

विद्याविद्यईशतेयस्तुसोन्यः । (Śvēt. Up.)

जुष्टंयदापश्यत्यन्यमीशम् । (Śvēt. Up.)

द्वासुपर्णासयुजासखाया समानंवृक्षंपरिषस्वजाते ।

तयोरन्यःपिप्पलंस्वाद्वत्य नश्नन्नन्योऽभिचाकशीति ॥

(Ṛig-Veda 1st Maṇḍala 22nd Anuvāka.)

आत्मानंचपृथङ्मत्वा प्रेरितारंततःपृथक् । ।

असौजुष्टस्ततस्तेन ह्यमृतत्वायकल्पते ॥ (Vāyu-Samhitā.)

† This is pointed out by a Christian writer in the following words:

"But why do we shrink from Pantheism? Not from dread of losing the physical universe in God, but from dread of losing our own soul in God. Pantheism only becomes deadly to vigorous religion and morality when it makes the man's soul, the man's self, a portion of God. Theism claims that the human soul is a free cause, a separate island of individual will, in the midst of the greatest ocean of the Divine Will. Leave us man confronting God, not absorbed in Him and the conditions are preserved for the ethical life of the individual and also for the communion of the soul with God as ANOTHER than itself, the very possibility of which is destroyed if a separate personality is wiped out. On this matter of the OTHERNESS of man from God, I hope to say more in a later chapter." (*'God and Soul'* by Rev. Mr. Armstrong).

away as an illusion, delusion or myth, the presence of this delusion has itself to be accounted for. Delusion is a conscious experience and the question, who is under delusion? will arise. If the soul is other than God, other than Māyā and is in baṇdha or bondage, then the necessity for the creation of the world becomes intelligible. We therefore postulate three Padārthas, three planes of existence, or three centres, the plane of matter, the plane of souls and the plane of God. In the language of Euclid, God is the point, that which hath no parts, nor magnitude; that which is everywhere, in and out, above and below; the soul is the centre of the circle, and the circumference is the Māyā that bounds. When this centre can rise up to the Point, then its Nirvāṇa is possible.

MAHĀVĀKYA TEXTS.*

But what are we to do with the Mahāvākya texts 'That Thou art,' 'I become that,' I am that' etc? It will be noted that these texts are not discussed by the Sūtrakāra Bādarāyaṇa in the First Adhyāya relating to Pramāṇa or Proof of the nature of the Padārthas, where he distinctly postulated the difference, but they are in the chapter on *Sādana* relating to the means of salvation. The Teacher tells the pupil to practise the Sādana, telling him that he is God (Tattvamasi), and the pupil accordingly practises Soham bhāvana or Śivohambhāvana, by repeating the maṇtra 'Aham Brahmāsmi'; there is consciousness, and consciousness of duality, of two Padārthas—Aham and Brahma. This is Dvaitam, the Yōga or Upanishat or Vēdāṇta Pāda. When by this practice of Śivoham, the consciousness can disappear then the soul can become One with God, Jñāthru, Jñāna and Jñēya all disappearing (the Jñāna or Siddhāṇta Pāda). And the question arises how can this oneness be reached, how can the two become one? This becomes possible on account of

---

* अहमात्माशिवोऽन्यः परमात्मेतियःस्मृतः ।
एवंयोमासतेमोहात् नशिवत्वमाप्नुयात् ॥
यश्शिवस्सोहमेवेति अद्वयंभावयेत्सदा ।
अद्वैतभावनायुक्ताः सर्वसात्मनिसंस्थिताः ॥ (Sarvajñānottarāgama.)

the peculiar nature of the soul and its relation to God. This peculiar nature of the soul is alone discussed in the Yôga Sûtras and in Śaiva Siddhāṇta Text-books. And the peculiar relation between God and the Soul is called Advaita.

NATURE OF THE SOUL.

This nature of the soul consists in its becoming one with whatever it is united to, losing its own individuality, and its not being able to exist independently, except in union with one or the other. It can only be united to the world or to God. It can reach God only when it leaves the world. It cannot serve God and Mammon at the same time. It is the caterpillar of the Upanishats, which leaves one leaf-stalk to gain another. And when it is united to one thing or the other like the mimicking caterpillar again, it is indistinguishable from the one or the other. It is the shadow of the one (Māyā) or the light of the other (God) that completely hides its (Soul's) individuality. So when in union with matter, with the body, it is so lost in the nerve-centres and so on, that the Scientific Agnostic fails to discover the soul, by the closest analysis. In union with God, the Pure Idealist finds no soul there. The soul identifies itself absolutely with the body or God, and its individuality or identity disappears but not its personality or being (Sat).

MAN IS A MIRROR OR A CRYSTAL.

This law of the Human mind called The Law of Garuḍa-dhyāna is stated in the terms that *we become like what we are associated with*, and may be called the Law of Association or Identity, and Professor Henry Drummond calls it the Law of Reflection and of Assimilation, and likens man to a mirror or a crystal. "*All men are mirrors*. That is the first law on which this formula (of sanctification or corruption) is based. One of the aptest description of a human being is that he is a mirror."

And we will find this is exactly the simile used by the Upanishats and the Siddhāṇta writers and the following extracts contain the illustration and the formula of sanctification.

THE FORMULA OF SANCTIFICATION.

"As a metal disk (mirror) tarnished by dust shines bright again after it has been cleansed, so is the one incarnate person satisfied and freed from grief after he has seen the real nature of himself; and when by the nature of himself, he sees, as by a lamp, the real nature of the Brahman, then having known the unborn eternal God who transcends all tattvas, he is freed from all pāśa." (*Śvētaś Up.* ii. 14, 15).

"From meditating (abhidyānāth) on Him, from joining (yojanāth) Him, from becoming (tattvabhāvāt) one with Him, there is further cessation of all māyā in the end." (*Śvētāś. Up.* i. 10).

And St. Meykaṇḍān has this stanza (viii. 3. a.)

"The soul, who reflecting that the knowledge derived from the senses is only material *like the colours reflected on a mirror*, and that these colour-like sensations are different from itself, and, after perceiving next false knowledge as false, understands the Truth, will become one with God Who is different from itself."

The formula stated in plain terms would read: "I see God, I reflect God, I become Godlike, Godly, God, I am God."

The crystal or the diamond, unlike the Sun's Light which it reflects though in its inner core it is pure, possesses the defect of being covered by dirt, mala, (Māyā) and it is luminous (Chit) in a sense but unlike the Self-Luminous Sun, (Para-Chit); and either in darkness or the full blaze of the Sun, the identity of the mirror cannot be perceived,

ADVAITA DEFINED.*

We now come to the definition of Advaita. And we may say at once, all the Śaiva Siddhānta writers describe their system as 'Advaita' pure and simple, yet people who hear it casually described call it Viśishtādvaita and fail to note its

* See pp. 244-272 *ante*.

special features. Advaita is defined by St. Meykaṇḍān as meaning *Anyō nāsti* or *Ananya* * or inseparable; and his disciple calls the relation 'as neither one nor two.' Advaita †, literally meaning not two, simply denies the separability or duality of God and soul and matter, but does not postulate Oneness by denying the existence of one or other Padārtha or by postulating their mutual convertibility as in causation &c. Mind (unextended) is not matter (the extended); yet they are ever inseparable and found as one; how the unextended is present in the extended is the puzzle and the contradiction as stated by Doctor Alexander Bain. And the illustrations of mind and body, vowels and consonants ‡ are used to denote their Advaita relation of God to the Universe of nature and of man. God is the Soul, whose body (Śarīra) is the Universe of nature and man, as so well and forcibly put in the *Bṛihad-āraṇya Upanishat* texts referred to above, beginning from Earth to Ātmā.

'He who dwells in the earth, other than the earth, whom the earth does not know, whose Śarīra (body) the earth is, who rules the earth within, He is thy Ātmā, the puller within, the immortal.'

"He who dwells in Ātmā (Vijñāna), *other* than Ātmā, whom

---

* अद्वैतमागमशिरोभिरुपासनायां उक्तंतवेतिपरमार्थतयानवाच्यम् ।
भेदःस्पुटीगरुडमानिकथैरिवालीकं तादात्म्यभावनमयापिविषंप्रमार्ष्टि ॥
ब्रह्मोच्यतेपरमसोपरमंचतत्वंज्योतिः परंचपरमेश्वरपद्मनाभः ।
त्वद्भावनैकविषयः त्वदनन्यभावात् मान्त्रीयथागरुडभावनया गरुत्मान् ॥ (Haradatta.)
अनन्येनैवयोगेणमां ध्यायन्तउपासते । (Bhagavad Gītā.)

M. N. Dvivedi in his 'Monism or Advaitism' points out also that advaita does not mean Eka or Abhinna or Abhinna but Ananya and that this is the view of the Sūtrakāra.

† Vide Śrīkaṇṭha's Bāshya on Vēdānta Sūtrās II, i. and 22.

‡ Dr. Bain complains that there is not even an analogy to illustrate this unique union of mind and body, but Śaiva Siddhāntins have this analogy of vowels and consonants to illustrate this union from the very beginning of their letters.

Ātmā does not know, whose Śarīra the Ātmā is, who rules Ātmā within, He is thy Ātmā, the ruler within, immortal." (III. vii. 22).

Here 'He is thy Ātmā', simply means 'He is the Soul's Soul.'

And the analogy of vowel and consonant explains this relation fully. In Tamil Grammar, the words used to denote vowels and consonants are the same as the words meaning mind and body. And we find the following text to our surprise in the *Taittirīya Upanishat* (II. iv. 1.)

'Its consonants form its body; its vowels, the soul (Ātmā).'

The vowels are those that can be sounded by themselves but the consonants cannot be pronounced without the aid of the vowel.* The consonants cannot be brought into being unless the vowel supports it; and in union, the two are inseparable; and *One* is the word used in the oldest Tamil Grammar to denote the union of the two. A vowel short has one mātrai, a consonant (pure) half a mātrai; and yet a vowel-consonant has only one mātrai, instead of one and a half. But the vowel is not the consonant nor the consonant the vowel. God is not one with the soul and the Universe, and yet without God, where is the Universe?

"Thou art not aught in the universe, yet naught is there save Thou."

He is not one, nor different from the Universe, and this relation is called Ananya, Advaita. The Sūtrakāra brings out the nature of this relation which is neither one nor different in II. i. 15 and 22. The Śaiva Advaita Siddhānta accordingly postulates that God is neither Abhēda with the world, nor Bhēda, nor Bhēdābhēda, as these terms are ordinarily under-stood, and yet He is one with the world, and different from the world, and Bhēdā-bhēda.

---

* शिवस्थितःसर्वजन्तूनां अक्षराणामकारवत् ।
Śiva is situate with reference to all, as the letter *A* stands with reference to the letters.

(*Šivajñānabōdham* Sūtra 2, *Šiva-jñānasiddhiyār* II. 1.) And St. Meykaṇḍān declares accordingly: "You can indeed say God is One, without a Second, as when you say without the vowel '*A*' no other letters exist." This is a view of Advaitam or Monism, which is not ordinarily met with, which must appeal to the hearts and intelligence of the people of every nation and every religion and which I commend to your earnest consideration.

PRACTICAL RELIGION AND FOUR PATHS.

I will just glance at the practical aspect of Šaiva Religion. It holds out four paths or mārgas for the spiritual aspirant, called Charyā, Kriyā, Yōga and Jñāna,* or otherwise called Dāsa-mārga, Satputra-mārga, Saha-mārga and San-mārga. When you want to approach God, you can approach Him as your Lord and Master, you can approach Him as your Father, or as your Friend or as your Beloved. The last is no mārga at all but where the One-ness is reached fully and finally. There is return to birth, while one is in the first three paths. And these paths are so adjusted in an ascending scale to suit the intellectual, moral and spiritual development of the aspirant. The lowest and the highest have equally a place in this scheme and are given room for their development and progress. No one path is put in opposition to the other. It will be noticed this scheme differs from the so-called Karma-mārga, Bhakti-mārga, Yōga mārga, and Jñāna-mārga, and the latter is no logical scheme at all but involves cross division. For it may be easily perceived that when one approaches his Maker, he must know Him as such (Jñāna) and must love Him as such (Bhakti) and must adjust

---

* चर्य्यांक्रियाचयोगश्च ज्ञानश्चेतिसुरेश्वरी ।
चतुष्पादस्समाख्यातः ममधर्म्मस्सनातनः ॥ (Vāyu-Samhitā.)

"Charyā, Kriyā, Yōga and Jñāna—these are styled the 'four paths' and these are eternal dharmas whereby one attains Me."

"तत्रोक्तःपरमोधर्मः चर्य्याद्यात्मश्चतुर्विधः" (Vāyu-Samhitā I.)

The higher dharmas, which are of four kinds viz: Charyā and others, are enumerated in the Saivāgamas.

his conduct accordingly (Karma). In each condition therefore, Karma, Bhakti and Jñāna are all together essential, and from the Dāsa to the Sanmārgi this Karma, Bhakti and Jñāna are progressive. There is no opposition, there is no parting away with one to follow another. So the practical Religion offered by Śaivaism is all in all and for all.

ŚAIVAISM IS AN ECLECTIC PHILOSOPHY AND AN UNIVERSAL RELIGION.

Śaiva Siddhānta, as representing the old Hinduism and with its chief scripture the *Śvētāśvatara Upanishat* and the *Gitā*, claims to be an eclectic philosophy and an universal Religion; and the various points I have brought out above will show how it brings itself into agreement with every shade of opinion, Religion and Philosophy. It describes Philosophy accordingly by such terms as 'Sāra', 'Samarasa', 'Siddhānta' meaning 'essence of all,' 'true end,' 'the Truth'. And we invite the kind attention of every religionist assembled here to the definition of an Universal Religion given by St. Aruḷ Naṇdi several centuries ago.

"Religions, postulates and text books are various and conflict one with another. It is asked: which is the true religion, which the true postulate and which the true book? *That is the True Religion and postulate and book, which not possessing the fault of calling this false and this true and not conflicting with them, comprises reasonably every thing within its fold.* Hence all these are comprised in the Vedas and Āgamas. And these are embedded in the Sacred Foot of Hara."

And we will close this paper with culling a few opinions of European Students of Śaiva Siddhānta.

The late Rev. Dr. G. U. Pope remarks: "It is the choicest product of the Dravidian (Indian) intellect." "The Śaiva Siddhānta is the most elaborate, influential and undoubtedly the most intrinsically valuable of all the religions of India."

Rev. Mr. F. Goodwill follows with the remark: "Those who have studied the system unanimously agree that this eulogy is not a whit too enthusiastic or free-worded. That the system is *eclectic* is at once apparent."

Rev. W. F. Goudie writes in the *Christian College Magazine* (xx. 9) as follows:—

"There is no school of thought and no system of faith or worship that comes to us with anything like the claims of the Śaiva Siddhāṇta."

"This system possesses the merits of a great antiquity. In the Religious world, the Śaiva system is heir to all that is most ancient in South India, it is the Religion of the Tamiḷ people by the side of which every other form is of comparatively foreign origin."

"In the largeness of its following, as well as in regard to the antiquity of some of its elements, the Śaiva Siddhāṇta is, bey nd any other form, the religion of the Tamiḷ people and ought to be studied by all Tamiḷ Missionaries."

"We have, however, left the greatest distinction of this system till last. As a system of religious thought, as an expression of faith and life, the Śaiva Siddhāṇta is by far the best that South India possesses. Indeed it would not be rash to include the whole of India, and to maintain that, judged by its intrinsic merits, the Śaiva Siddhāṇta represents the high water mark of Indian Thought and Indian life, apart, of course, from the influences of Christian Evangel."

ITS ETHICAL BASIS

Śaivaism is based on the Highest morality. As a course in ethics usually precedes the study of Religion, the subject of ethics is not usually discussed in text-books on Religion. The greatest authority in Tamiḷ is the sacred *Kuṛaḷ* by St. Tiruvaḷḷuvar translated into many European languages and pronounced by Rev. Dr. G. U. Pope as a book unparallcled in any language of the world. The Śaivaism of the South holds to the ahimsa * doctrines as its chief pillar.

---

* The eight flowers which the yōgins are required to offer to Śiva in their hearts are thus enumerated :

अहिंसाप्रथमंपुष्पं इन्द्रियाणांचनिग्रहः ।
क्षान्तिपुष्पंदयापुष्पं ज्ञानपुष्पंअतःपरम् ।
तपःपुष्पंतथ्यपुष्पं भावपुष्पमथाष्टकम् ॥

Ahimsā (abstention from killing), Indriya-Nigraha or Dharma (control of the senses), Kshama (forbearance), Dayā (compassion), Jñāna (Wisdom), Tapas (Austere life) and Satya (Veracity)—These are the eight flowers and of these Ahimsā or abstention from killing is the first ; Vide also Tirumūlar's *Tirumantiram* under the chapter Aṭṭapushpam.

The eight characteristic marks of a Śaivite are enumerated thus :

शिवेभक्तिस्सदाशान्तिरहिंसासर्वदादमः ।
संतोषस्सत्यमस्तेयं ब्रह्मचर्ययथाष्टकम् ॥

Love to God, peace of mind for ever, abstention from killing, control of the senses, gladness of the heart, veracity, abstention from stealing, and the leading of a pious life (Brahmachārya).........

It is the settled principle of the Śaivites that the abstention from killing conduces to the highest possible good. The Śaivāgamas persistently puts this question.

कमद्यःकशिवेभक्तिः कमांसंकशिवार्चनम् ।
मद्यमांसप्रतिष्ठानां दूरेतिष्टतिशंकरः ॥

Where is intoxicating drink and where is love to God (Śivabhakti) ?

Where is the flesh-food and where is the propitiation of the Lord (Śivārchana) ?

Indeed, Śaṅkara stands far away from those who are addicted to drink and flesh-eating.

The *Vāyu-Samhitā* says that a Śaivite is distinguished from the ordinary ignorant people by certain marks and acts and of these, abstention even from the smell of Madya (drink) and Māmsa (flesh) are reckoned as the chief.

मद्यस्यमद्यगन्धस्य मांसस्यापिचवर्जनात् ॥

The *Śivadharmōttara Āgama* says :

पर्वताग्रोग्रतपसा अश्वमेधस्ययत्फलम् ।
फलंप्राप्नोत्यन्तेन मधुमांसविवर्जनात् ॥

What merit a man does attain by severe penance on the summits of mountains, and also by Asvamēdha, that merit he attains without any the least labour and difficulty by simply abstaining from drink and flesh-diet.

THE NATURE OF THE JĪVA.*

The subject on which I propose to address you this evening is the nature of the Jīva, but coming as I do at the fag-end of the day, with the atmosphere at the burning point, I do not wish to inflict on you a long speech. The importance of the question admits of no doubt; and at any rate, this should engage our first attention before we attempt to solve problems as to the existence and the nature of God which are beyond our cognition in a sense. And as I will show, the subject is so important that when we had solved the riddle about man himself, we would have solved the riddle about the universe. The subject is treated under Sūtra III of Śivajṇānabodham, and in that masterly treatise of St. Aruḷ Naṇdi Śivāchāriyar, in all its pros and cons, but I will confine myself to the true position of the Siddhāṇtins as regards the nature of the Soul. There are two characteristics of it elaborated in our system. The first is called அது அது ஆதல் by St. Meykaṇḍān, and is paraphrased as *யாதொன்று பற்றின் அதன் இயல்பாய் நிற்றல்* by St. Tāyumānavar, which all mean that the soul becomes one with whatever it is attached to or associated with. That is to say, whatever its own nature or individuality may be, when it becomes united to another, it loses its own characteristics and individuality and partakes of the nature of the thing united to, and completely merges itself in the other. As illustrated in the proverb, "Youth and white paper take all impressions", the human mind is a *tabula Rasā* in which are imbedded the impressions which are received from out-side. Children catch the manners, habits and the peculiarities of their parents. Their very voice is imitated. Pupils copy many of the peculiarities of their teachers also. A Madras Tamilian settling in Tinnevely

* A paper read before the Śaiva Samayābhivriddhi Sabhā, Palamcotta, 1910.

would readily copy the very intonation in speech of the people around him.

> நல்லாரைக் காண்பதுவும் நன்றே நலமிக்க
> * * *
> தீயாரைக் காண்பதுவும் தீதே
> * * *

The principle of this is stated by St. Tiruvaḷḷuvar also in the oft-quoted verse.

> "நிலத்தியல்பால் நீர்திரிந் தற்றாகும் மாந்தர்க்கு
> இனத்தியல்ப தாகு மறிவு."

"The waters' virtue changes with the soil over which they flow, so man's mind changes with the company he keeps." The water falling from heaven is colourless and tasteless, but as it touches the earth, it becomes sweet or brackish, dirty or discoloured, according to the nature of the soil, losing thereby its individuality and purity. So does a man become good or bad according to the association he forms. The law of association is stated in the words 'we become like what we study or are closely associated with.' In Biology the working out of this law is fully illustrated.* Darwin instances how

---

* As analogous to this, I might instance the case of mimicry in plants and animals. Mostly for purposes of protection, insects and birds and animals assume the colour of their environment. Worms and insects feeding on green plants would assume the colour of the leaves or the wood of the plants and even assume the shape of leaf-stalks and twigs. The stick cater-pillars, the larvae of several species of moths, stand perpendicularly on twigs, and are indistinguishable from the short twigs in the same branch. In the case of the stick-insects which popularly are called 'praying insects or spectres' (Māntidœ) which being unable to move about, assume the size and shape of leaves, birds, and flowers, dried twigs, stalks of grass, according to the respective habitat, so as to deceive and catch their prey which consist of butterflies and other insects &c., which hop about these plants. I have seen specimens of walking-leaf insects, one resembling the leaves, stalks of the Vāgai tree, one resembling exactly a stalk of ariali grass, the resemblance extending even to the dried ends of the blades of grass. These are called நெட்டைப்பூச்சி or மழைப்பூச்சி by the Tamiḻs.

As a plant changes colour from green to yellow, even so these insects change their colour. The most remarkable case is that of the

persons ever associated with pigs, get piggy faces, and with horses, horsey faces. In the case of a husband and a wife when they have been perfectly loving, it has been found to effect a complete assimilation of their features. They might have started life with perfectly distinct facial features, yet their souls become one through love, and through the power of the soul, their bodies are also become one. The writer of the book *Spiritual law in the natural world* (Purdy Publishing Company, Chicago.) observes "all who have made a study of the cause of all things have become so at one with it as to have causing power, for it is an invariable rule that we become like what we study or are closely associated with. We become so-like people with whom we live constantly that

---

chameleon. It does not change colour from fright. When left in confinement, it rarely changes colour. But as it runs about, it changes colour according to the colour of the surface over which it runs. As it runs over the bare soil, if the colour of the soil be red, it will become red; if black it will become black. As it runs over the brown trunk of a tree, it changes into brown; and when it reaches the green leafage, it changes into green. In the case of birds, their colour is determined from the colour of the soil &c., wherein they build their nests. It is to protect themselves from birds of prey. In the case of lions, their grey colour is due to their habitat. In the African wilds, where there is little or no vegetation, these lions generally find their lair amidst small pieces of gray rocks, and while they stand beside these pieces of rock, the hunter could hardly distinguish them from the pieces of rock. Artists in their pictures even produce this effect. With regard to tigers which usually haunt thick forest glades, their black and yellow stripes are the result of their environment. These stripes imitate the alternate light and shade which falls slantingly through the leafage and the animal becomes indistinguishable thereby. If one observes closely the leaves of the orange tree, he would find things there which imitate closely the excreta of birds, black with a white tip. These are really live caterpillars which seek their mimicry to escape even the keen eyes of the birds that feed on them. There are flowers especially those of orchids which resemble butterflies (I have seen in the conservatories at Ooty and Peradeniya gardens orchid flowers resembling butterflies) and doves and pigeons. (See for a treatment of the protective resemblances or mimicry in insects, Chapters VI & VII in *Romance of the Insect world* by L. M. Badenoch).

often the expression of the face and sound of voice grow similar, and even the features grow alike. Sometimes a child will look more like its nurse than its mother ?." This causing power of the mind or as Professor Kunte calls it, the ***potential power*** of the man is its அது அது ஆதற்றன்மை, and lies at the root of all Upāsanas and sanctification, and it explains also how we got at our bondage. If we were perfect, pure and free, how is it, we became imperfect, impure and bound? To say that we did not bocome so, would be against all experience and common sense. To meet the question by saying that we do not know, would be begging the question and would be illogical. Have we evidence that the perfect became the imperfect? How do we know then? Āptavachanam and Śruti would be the last resort of philosophers of this school. Siddhāṇtins could quote text for text from the Śruti also to show that man is not God, and the few texts that alone can be counted in favour of the other school would be found explained below. The Theory of the soul herein set forth would be found to explain how man got bound and impotent. The soul, different from the body, five senses etc., identified itself with the body, five senses &c., and on this mistaken identity, its actions flowed. He cared for the body. He did whatever gave pleasure to the body and the five senses, and avoided what gave him pain. In seeking these transitory pleasures of the body, he forgot his duties to others and to God, and he committed sins, Karma, good and bad. Desire—*Tanha Trishṇa*—possessed his soul and man is dragged down,* as by force constrained.

---

* Cf. *Gitā* III 36, 37, 38, where the classical simile of crystal and colour is also brought out to explain the subject. "But dragged on by what, does a man commit sin reluctantly indeed, O Vārshṇêya, by force constrained?"

"The beloved Lord said: It is desire, begotten by the rajas energy all consuming, all polluting. Know thou this our foe here on earth."

"As a flame is enveloped by smoke, or *a mirror by dust*, as an embryo is wrapped by the womb. so this (man) is enveloped by it."

This desire gives rise to births innumerable. St. Tiruvaḷḷuvar sums up them in the two verses.

" காமம் வெகுளி மயக்க மிவைமூன்றின்
நாமம் கெடக்கெடும் நோய்."

When desire, aversion and error's name are lost, then the disease shall cease.*

" அவாவென்ப வெல்லாவுயிர்க்கு மெஞ்ஞான்றுந்
தவாஅப்பிறப்பீனும் வித்து."

" The wise declare through all the days, to every living thing,
That ceaseless round of birth from seed of strong desire doth spring."

This காமம் is desire of pleasurable things (to the senses) and வெகுளி is aversion to the things that do not give pleasure and மயக்கம் is error as defined in the first verse of the same chapter.

" பொருளல் லவற்றைப் பொருளென் றுணரும்
மருளானு மாணாப் பிறப்பு."

" Men desire that as a thing when it is not. From this delusion does birth arise," This மயக்கம், மருள் error or delusion is the Āṇava or Ahaṅkāra or Avidyā and we have elsewhere shown also its real nature. This delusion consists in not mistaking a thing to be existing when it is not, but in mistaking one thing for another. When no shell is really seen, a man fancies he sees silver, this will be delusion of one sort. When what he sees before him is really a shell, and he fancies it to be a silver, this will be another kind of delusion. When there is no world, no body, and he fancies this to be his all, his whole soul, this will belong to the first category. When there is a world and a body, and he identifies his soul with this body and world, this belongs to the second category. The first kind of delusion is what is called Mityāvādam. The second theory is the true theory of Avidyā as set forth by

* The commentator observes that Sanskritists note faults as five, Avidyā, Ahaṅkāra, Desire, Aversion, and Attachment. This is stated in Yōga sūtras 11, 3.

St. Tiruvaḷḷuvar and accepted by Advaita Siddhāṇtins. In this theory, there is no necessity to call anything Mityā or unreal, but we show how by mistaking one for the other which it is not, the error is started, and how all other things flow therefrom. This error or ignorance will not receive play but for the power of the mind above set forth.

If a man does not possess this power of identifying himself with whatever he is united to, then, he could not mistake his body for his soul. Readers of Dr. Bain's masterly treatise on *Mind and body* would notice how he shows that mind though not exactly the same as the brain and body, though there is a correspondence and concomitance of both mental and bodily phenomena along the whole line, can in its objective condition become thoroughly identified with and lost in the body or brain centres. The mind is lost in the body, and yet without the mind, there could be no object. This power of mind in becoming one with the united object is also spoken of as its power of losing self. It loses its self, soul, and becomes the body. It loses its self and becomes God.

And this brings us to the question how by this power whereby he degrades himself to the very depths of the brute, he can rise to the very height of God-hood. This power of man becomes therefore a demerit and a merit at the same time.

In considering this aspect of the case, it has to be noted that almost every religion, theistic or atheistic, prescribes certain code of religious and moral duties for attaining salvation and betterment, but no religion attempts to prove how the following of this or that religious practice elevates one. How Sādhana Chatushṭayam, Guru-upadēsam, Tapas and Yoga can free one from sins and Avidyā, is not explained. This is, however, explained in the older yōga and sānkhya treatises and is elaborated in the Siddhāṇta Śāstras. Both these older schools admitted the essential individuality of man and had to explain the real nature of jiva, so as to lay down the

41

steps by which men can ascend up. They form, thus, the essential foundation for Vēdānta and Siddhānta. Without this foundation, the higher schools cannot be explained. To dissociate Vēdānta from Yōga would be to build on sand. As I have elsewhere explained, Vēdānta strictly so called, and as distinguished from Siddhānta, is really the Yōga mārga (the words Upanishat and Yōga being synonymous) and Siddhānta is jñāna mārga. However as I said, both the Yōgins and Sāṅkhyans define man by this power of identifying oneself with the associated object, becoming Sārūpya; and their classical simile * is that of crystal and hibiscus flower, about which more anon. In regard to the process of sanctification, the power by which man came down has to be reversed. Man identified himself with the body and became bound. This should cease. But how is he to cut himself from the eternal association with the body and the world from this pāśa, as cucumber is severed from its vine? He became low because he became associated with low things. Let him associate with high things and he can become high. † He became mortal because he associated himself with mortal and transitory things like the body &c. Let him become one by the same power with the immortal, the amṛita. § By associating with the body, he loved the

* See Yōga sūtras 1—41 and commentary thereon, Śāṅkhya sūtras VI 27, 28.

† Rudra is called Amrita in *Ṛig Vēda* (I. 43. 9)

" Whatever beings are thine, Amrita (Rudra) in the highest place of the law on its summit, O Sōma, cherish them, remember them who honour thee."

§ Cf. *Gītā* "They who with mind fixed on me, ever harmonised worship me with faith supreme endowed, these, in my opinion, are best in yoga." (xii. 2.) "Renouncing and subduing the sense, regarding everything equally, (இருவினைஒப்பு) in the welfare of all rejoicing, these also come unto me." (xii. 4.) " Those verily who renouncing all actions in me and intent on me, worship meditating on Me, with whole hearted yoga," (xii. 6.) " These I speedily lift up from the ocean of death and existence, O Pārtha, their minds being fixed on me." (xii. 7.) " Place thy mind in me, in me let thy reason enter; then without doubt thou shalt abide in me hereafter." (xii. 8.)

bodily pleasures. Let him cut asunder this desire and aversion, love and hate, like and dislike, then will he lose this birth. But is it possible for him to cut off this desire by merely desiring the desirelessness? Some philosophers opine that this is possible, but they speak without their book. Here it is, that the second characteristic of man which we spoke of before is brought into play, namely, பற்றுக்கோடின்றி நில்லாமை, not being able to exist without a support. It must support itself by clinging to the body and the world or to the Lord. If it must give up the world, it must cling to the Lord. If there is no God, the soul must go back to the world and again resume its round of births. It is a noteworthy feature of all systems which do not postulate the existence of a soul that they do not postulate God either. It will be seen how subtly Gautama Buddha avoids the question of the existence of the soul. This was so, inasmuch as he denied the existence of God. His followers followed the system to its logical conclusion, and denied the existence of the soul or at any rate postulated its utter annihilation. What existed after? Nirvāṇa nothing, however much some scholars might try to prove to the contrary. The one exception was the Nirīśvara Sāṅkhyan who thought he denied God, the author of the universe, yet affirmed the separate existence of a soul. However as I said, the soul must exist in the world or in the Lord and all the religious and moral practices are prescribed for bringing about the clinging to the Lord, after the soul frees itself from the attachment to the world.* This latter attachment is by itself the means whereby he can effect his severance from the old attachment.

> "பற்றுக பற்றற்றான் பற்றினை யப்பற்றை
> பற்றுக பற்று விடற்கு." (*Kuṟaḷ* 350.)

* We know how difficult it is to give up some of our habits and often one is advised to take to some other habit less serious to cure oneself of the old habit. People take to chewing tobacco or smoking to get rid of the habit of snuffing. I know a doctor who advised one to take to opium to cure himself of the vice of drunkenness.

"Desire the desire of Him who is desireless.
Desire His desire so as desire may leave thee."

"சார்புணர்ந்து சார்புகெட வொழுகின் மற்றழித்து
சார்தரா சார்தரு நோய்." (*Kuraḷ*. 359.)

"The true 'support' who knows—rejects 'supports' he sought before—
Sorrow that clings and all destroys, shall cling to him no more."

The commentator explains that the "ஒழுக்கம்" required for getting rid of the old desire for the world are the Ashṭāṅga-yōga. The author had set forth in the preceding three verses Sravaṇa, Manana or Dhyāna, and Bhāvana (பாவனை) as he calls it, as the three means of effecting freedom and union with God, and St. Tiruvaḷḷuvar describes God by the terms செம் பொருள் (Good being), உள்ளது (The existent), மெய்ப்பொருள் (True being). And the commentator's explanation of the world is also noteworthy, and he brings out the reason for the Bhāvana.

தோற்றக்கேடுகளின்மையின் நித்தமாய், நோன்மையாற்றன்னை யொன்றும் கலத்த லின்மையின் தூய்தாய், தான் எல்லாவற்றையும் கலந்து நிற்கின்ற முதற்பொருள் விகாரமின்றி எஞ்ஞான்றும் ஒருதன்மைத்தாதல்பற்றி அதனைச் செம்பொருள் என்றார். மேல் மெய்ப்பொருளெனவும் உள்ளதெனவும் கூறியதூஉம் இதுபற்றியென வுணர்க. அதனைக்காண்கையாவது, உயிர் தன்னவிச்சை கெட்டு அதனோடு ஒற்றுமை யுற இடைவிடாது பாவித்தல். இதனைச்சமாதி யெனவும் சுக்கிலத்தியான மெனவும் கூறுப. உடம்பின் னீங்குங் காலத்து அதனால் யாதொன்று பாவிக்கப்பட்டது, அஃது அதுவாய்த்தோன்று மென்பது எல்லா ஆகமங்கட்குந் துணிபாதலின், வீடெய்துவார்க்கு அக்காலத்து பிறப்பிற் கேதுவாய பாவனை கெடுதற் பொருட்டு, கேவலப்பொருளையே பாவித்தல் வேண்டும்." (*Kuraḷ note* 358.)

It is called செம்பொருள் (Good being), because it is eternal having no birth and no death; it is pure on account of its subtle nature and nothing can taint it by attachment; and yet it is the first cause that pervading all, yet remains one, without change. Hence, God is called மெய்ப்பொருள் and உள்ளது, True Being and Existent. To see it, is the Bhāvana to become one with it, so that Avidyā may be lost. As it is held as true by followers of all the different Āgamas, that the soul when leaving the body at death, is re-born as that which it was thinking upon, those who desired Mōksha, should place their Bhāvana on the Highest Truth, so that the Bhāvana which is the cause of birth may be lost. This power of becoming one with the other is really great and lies at the root of all. Tapas or Upāsana or Bhāvana is set forth by our author in two other places. In the chapter (XXVII) on 'Tapas,' he has this verse (5).

வேண்டிய வேண்டியாங் கெய்தலாற் செய்தவ
மீண்டு முயலப் படும். (*Kuṟaḷ* 265.)

" That what they wish may, as they.wish, be won,
By men on earth are works of painful 'penance' done."

In chapter (LXVII) on 'Power of Action,' we have this verse:

எண்ணிய வெண்ணியாங் கெய்துப வெண்ணியார்
திண்ணிய ராகப் பெறின். (*ibid.* 666.)

" Whtever we think, ev'n as they think, men may obtain,
If those who think can steadfastness of will retain."

I now go back to the point where I started from, namely, that by the very nature of this other characteristic of the soul, the necessity for a supreme Lord is manifest. I always use a simile to illustrate as what would happen if there were no God. At fairs and festivals, a greasy pole with a hook at the top and a prize tied to it is one of the attractions. Of hundreds who attempt, rarely one gets to the top and takes the prize. Even he who had climbed to the top could not have retained his hold there for long, if there had not been the hook or பற்றுக்கோடு to hold by; otherwise he would have slipped down by the pole again.*

So if a religion or philosophy, however dignified it may be, offers us no God, there can be no real salvation nor nirvāṇa nor freedom from births. After the mighty efforts made to purify and perfect oneself by desirelessness etc., he must sink back into the abyss of birth and death, again and again, must try and climb the greasy pole. To them, Iśvara and men are

* I might instance the Upanishat caterpillar which, by its power of mimicry (அது அது ஆதல்) concealing itself effectively in one leaf, catches hold of another before it gives up the other leaf to which it has been clinging already.

ever evolving and evolving, gaining experience ever and anon and the oft-repeated words of the Upanishat, "There is no return, There is no return" have no meaning. These people though they might speak of a God, could not really mean God in the proper conception of the word. The ignorance of these two characteristics of the soul lies at the difficulty of both agnostics and idealists. In union with the body, the soul has become one with the body and its individuality is lost and it could not be discovered by any amount of physical and anatomical analysis. In union with God, it has become one with God and no trace of its individuality could be found there. So both declare there is no soul, and the latter declare that the soul we were cognizant of was God Himself. To them, of course, all talk of anubhava and svānubhava will be unmeaning also. To the Buddhist and Idealist, there is simply the tearing asunder of Pāša, and lo and behold! there is nirvāṇa and annihilation to the one, and God regains its own self to the other. But in either case, there is nothing to prevent that which arose from nothing or from God, from arising again and undergoing the never-ending round of samsāra. To the latter, the only possible explanation for this evolution of God into man would be that furnished by Dr. Paul Deussen—necessity connected with the doctrine of Samsāra. This would eventually strike at the root of all necessity for bettering ourselves and weaken, at any rate, the moral and religious sanction. If, after all our effort to better ourselves, we should sink back again, why all this bother—Guru-upadēšam and tapas etc.? Our glory is in God and we delight in His glory. He is our Redeemer and the fruit of redemption. But for our enjoyment in Him, there is no need for redemption at all. Our final consummation is in Him. As the Chhāṇdōgya Upanishat puts it, "He who sees, perceives and understands this, loves God, delights in God, revels in God, rejoices in God, He becomes svarāj; He is Lord and master in all the worlds."

I will now proceed to show how this conception of the soul as herein set forth affects our view of Dvaita, Advaita and

Višishṭādvaita. I have dwelt at length on this question on "Advaita according to the Šaiva Siddhānta" (pp. 244-272 *ante*). The question is, is the soul different from God or one with Him? If different, what is the meaning of those Mahāvākya texts, Ahambrahmāsmi etc.? The word Advaita, as I have shown, does not mean one, does not deny the existence of the other entities, but it simply denies the separability of the two, ananya or anyōnāsti. It postulates a peculiar relation between the two, that, though different, they can become one. How is this possible? St. Meykaṇḍān suggests the puzzle; if they are two, they cannot become one; if one, there can be no Svānubhōgam. How is this puzzle to be solved? The question is only possible when we bear in mind this peculiar characteristic of the soul we have been considering. Though the soul and God are different, yet inasmuch as the soul becomes one with whatever it is attached to, losing its individuality and consciousness of self, so the soul when in union with God becomes one with It. This one is the God but not the soul. The subject is illustrated with the similes of mind and body, the vowel and the consonant.

"உடல்மேல் உயிர்வந்தொன்றுவ தியல்பே".

"It is a natural union when the vowel unites with the consonant as one" is the *Nannūl* sūtram (204). The word one has been used to describe this union of the vowel with the consonant. They are distinct and yet inseparable. No consonant can be thought of without the vowel. This is the meaning of the famous Hṛidaya šlōka in Tiruvāçagam.

இன்றெனக்கருளி இருள்கடிந்துள்ளத் தெழுகின்ற ஞாயிறே போன்று
நின்ற நின்றன்மை நினைப்பற நினைந்தே னீயலாற் பிறிதுமற்றின்மை
சென்று சென்று அணுவாய் தேய்ந்து தேய்ந்து ஒன்றாம் திருப்பெருந்
[துறையுறை சிவனே
ஒன்று நீயல்லையன்றி யொன்றில்லை யாருன்னை யறிகிற்பாரே.

"When the soul loses its various sheaths—body, senses, intelligence and consciousness of self (நான் கெட்டு)—then, what stands forth as the Lord of the Heaven of Peace is the one Supreme but not the soul." I quote here our learned Šivajñānayōgi from his *Drāviḍa Bhāshya* where he puts the whole question so pithily:

"If you ask, what then is the meaning of the word '*Advaitam*'? I will show how Ṣaiva Siddhāṇtins explain it. On hearing the great texts called Mahāvākya Tatvamasi etc., which are used in the three persons, we see that these sentences speak of 'that' as one substance and 'thou' as another and enquire how one can become the other. The answer is given to remove the doubt by stating *how one can become the other* and *what relation subsists between the two* and the word *advaitam* is used to explain the relation." St. Umāpati Śivāchārya queries, "are there not objects in this world which become dark in darkness and light in light?" (*Tiruvaruḷpayan* II. 3.) And the answer usually returned is, these are the eye, the mirror, the crystal and the Ākāšam. The eye loses its power of seeing in darkness and recovers it in light. The others become dark or light as darkness or light surrounds it. They are not lost in either case, but their individuality is lost and merged in one thing or the other. To these we may add also water, clear as crystal. But the classic simile I have stated in the beginning is the crystal or the mirror. This is brought out in Šāṅkhya sūtra (VI. 28) and yōga sūtra (I. 4).* Now let us inquire into the nature of the crystal or the mirror or the glass. There is before you, a picture of our late Sovereign Lord and King-Emperor (Blessed be his name)

* I bring together here all the texts bearing on the subject.

"Now a man is like this or that according as he behaves and so will he be. A man of good acts will become good, a man of bad habits bad. He becomes pure by pure deeds, and bad by bad deeds.

"As is his desire, so is his will; and as is his will, so is his deed. Whatever deeds he does, that will he reap.

"To whatever object man's own mind is attached, to that he goes strenuously with his deed.

"He who desires the Ātman, being Brahman, he goes to Brahman. That ātman is indeed Brahman (*Brihad. Up.* IV. 5, 6).

"As a metal disk (mirror) tarnished by dust shines bright again after it has been cleansed, so is the one incarnate person satisfied and freed from grief, after he has seen the real nature of himself.

"And when by the real nature of himself, he sees, as by a lamp, the real nature of the Brahman, then having known the unborn eternal God, who transcends all tattvas, he is freed from all pāša" (*Šveta. Up.* II. 14, 15).

EDWARD VII. As you see it, you fail to see the glass that covers the picture. An ignorant rustic who had never seen

---

" From meditating (abhidyānāt) on him, from joining (yōjanāt) Him, from becoming one with Him (tatbhavāt), there is further cessation of all māyā in the end." (*Śveta. Up.* I. 10).

" A person becomes like those with whom he dwells and like those whom he reverences, and like to what he wishes to be." (*Mahābhārata.* Sāṇti Parva ccc. 32)

" As a flame is enveloped by smoke, *as a mirror by dust*, as an embryo is wrapped by the womb, so this (soul) is enveloped by it (desire)." (Gītā III. 38.)

" Though it (soul) be unassociated, still there is a tinging (reflectionally) through non-discrimination, for there is not a real tinge in that which is unassociated (with tincture or anything else), still there is, as it were a tinge; hence the tinge is treated as simply a reflection, by those who discriminate the tinge from the soul which it delusively seems to belong to.

"As in the case with the Hibiscus and the crystal, there is not a tinge but a fancy there is such." (*Sāṅkhya aphorisms* VI. 27, 28, Garbe's translation.)

" In the case of one the transformations of whose mind have been annihilated, there is entire identity with and complete absorption in, the cogniser, the cognition and the cognised, as in the case of a clear gem (crystal)." (*Yōga sūtras* I. 41),

பன்னிற மேகாட்டும் பளிங்கேபோல் இந்திரியத்
தன்னிறமே காட்டும் தகைநினைந்து—பன்னிறத்தும்
பொய்ப்புலனை வேறுணர்ந்து பொய்பொய்யா மெய்கண்டான்
மெய்ப்பொருட்குத் தொண்டுமாம் வேறு.

" The soul which after reflecting that the knowledge derived from the senses is only material, *like the colours reflected on a mirror*, and that these colour-like sensations are different from itself, and after perceiving false knowledge as false understands the Truth, will become the servant of God Who is different from Asat." (4 Meykaṇḍān. VIII. 3. a.)

வந்தேனுடல் பொருளாவி மூன்றுந்தன்கை
வசமெனவே யத்துவா மார்க்க நோக்கி
ஐந்து புலனைம்பூதங் கரணமாதி
அடுத்தகுண மத்தனையு மல்லை
இந்த உடலறிவறியாமையு நீயல்லை
யாதொன்று பற்றினதன் இயல்பாய் நின்று
பந்தமறும் பளிங்கனைய சித்து நீயுன்
பக்குவம் கண்டறிவிக்கும் பான்மையேம்யாம்.

glass before or a picture framed in glass would positively deny that any glass-plate was there. But with all his denial born of his own direct perception (Svānubhūti), we know he is wrong. Why is it so? Because the glass once brought into conjunction with the many-coloured picture has lost its form, has lost itself so to speak; lost its individuality but not its substance. Remove the picture, you can see it by itself. But bring it into strong sun-light; even then, you cannot see the glass but a strong blaze of light will dazzle your eyes.* So, the nature of a crystal or a mirror is, it becomes one with the form of whatever comes in contact with it, losing its own form. When covered with colour or dirt, it is indistinguishable from either the colour or the dirt. When flooded by light, it is indistinguishable from the light. Take the crystal by itself. It is pure and in a sense luminous, but its purity and luminosity do not prevent its being covered by dirt and becoming dark in darkness. This is its defect. And this purity and luminosity have to be distinguished from the purity and luminosity of the blazing sun and its light. Take a very large-sized pure diamond, the so-called brilliant.† Is this brilliance its own? If so, you must find it shining in utter darkness. But you will not be able to find it in darkness; it will be utterly lost. This brilliance is not its own, and it is derived from the sun-light or the lamp-light. This is the difference between man and God. We are the crystals and He is the light reflected in the crystal. How well is this brought out by St. Appar in his phrase "வெண்பளிங்கின் உட்பதித்த சோதியோனே", "O thou light imbedded in the white crystal!" How well does Tennyson grasp the situation when he says "we are but broken lights of thee!" Nay, not exactly so. "We are only shining

* As you drive about in the road between 11 and 12 forenoon, if you look at one of the Municipal lanterns, you will realize this.

† The facets of the cut-diamond act as a prism and so refract the different colours of the sun's rays. Crystal water has the same power and I have seen the water refracting the different colours in the famous spring at the Mahāṇaṇdi (Naṇdiyal, in Kurnool District.).

from borrowed light from thee." Whatever good is in man is all derived from God's light. In our Kēvala condition, we are like the diamond buried in dirt and darkness. When brought to light, it is still covered by dirt and the more and more we cleanse it by turning it on the diamond cutter's lathe, the more and more we let light into it. This is our Šakala condition, where we are able to exercise our will and intelligence with the grace of the Lord. When the whole diamond is polished and rounded, the full blaze of light will shine on it, and the diamond will be lost in the brilliance. This is the Šuddha or Mōksha condition. Bhaṇda results when this dirt covers it, and Moksha, when the dirt is removed. Nay, the latter condition is not the mere removal of dirt alone. There is the flooding of light—Anubhūti, Šivānubhūti or Svānubhōgam. Would anybody appreciate a polished diamond if it will not reflect the light. See how well *St. Aruṇagiri* puts it:

தாசாமணியும் துகிலும் புனைவாள்
நேசா முருகா நினதன்பருளால்
ஆசாநிகளம் துகளாயினபின்
பேசா அநுபூதி பிறந்ததுவே.

"O! Thou lover of the well adorned Dēvasēna,
O Muruga! with Thy kindly grace,
The chains of desire are sundered in twain,
And lo! that unspeakable joy was born."

And consider the divine words of St. Tirumūlar.

உரையற்ற தொன்றை யுரைசெய்யு மூமர்காள்
கரையற்ற தொன்றைக் கரைகாணலாகுமோ
திரையற்ற நீர்போல் சிந்தை தெளிவார்க்குப்
புரையற்றிருந்தான் புரிசடையோனே.

"O Ye fools! who speak of the unspeakable,
Can ye find the limits of the limitless one?
When as waveless sea, ye attain clearness of mind,
Then will the Lord with braided hair appear bright."

Why do we desire the purity of the crystal and the clearness of water? Why do we love all that is loveable in nature? Why do we love one another? Why does a husband love his wife, a father his children, and so on? Is it because of these things themselves that we love them and ought to love them? When we do, our bhandam is assured; we begin to gather precious stones, lovely objects and beautiful women all round us and strive hard to gather more and more. But when we recognize that it is not for these that we love them but for the Lord imbedded in them (வெண்பளிங்கின் உட்பதித்த சோதியான்) who gives them their life and light and love, then will our thoughts be turned away from them, be fixed in the Light Adorable, and our Mōksha will be realized.* It has also to be noted how this attachment of dirt to the crystal or the man is not one that goes to its core. If so, this dirt or defect could never be removed. It is not that man is by nature unintelligent and impure, and he grows more intelligent and better by education and evolution. But all the purity and perfection, all his powers are in him to the full: only they are veiled and covered by dirt, and once the veil is removed, he regains himself and sees his true form (Ātma Darśan) just for a moment when he feels in his Vibhūtitvam (expanded nature) he is all that, and then merges himself in the Feet of the Lord. This distinction is important, as this marks the fundamental difference between Indian Philosophy and Western philosophy. This is why the Western philosophy of Evolution has been found to fail. The superstructure is all right but the foundation is all wrong. According to the theory of evolution, everything, every power of man is acquired by evolution, adaptation and survival of the fittest. But according to us,

* Few understand that this is the real meaning of the famous passage in the *Brihadāranyaka Upanishat* II (IV. 5).

"Verily, a husband is not dear that you may love the husband; but that you may love God, the husband is dear.

"Verily, a wife is not dear that you may love the wife; but that you may love God, therefore a wife is dear.

"Verily, sons are not dear, that you may love the sons; but that you may love God, therefore sons are dear.

"Verily, wealth is not dear that you may love wealth; but that you may love God, therefore wealth is dear."

everything is there—all his powers of Ichchā, Kriyā and Jñāna. He is also Satchidānaṇda, but the powers are veiled and all the Pañchakṛitya and evolutionary powers are required to rid him of his veils. And when this veil is removed, his original form is attained.* Here again another caution is required to be borne in mind.

The soul no doubt regains its full powers of Ichchā, Kriyā and Jñāna and becomes Satchidānaṇda. But these have to be distinguished from those of the Supreme. And here it is where the Upanishat and other writings speak of the Freed soul and its greatness, the passages there are misunderstood, and identity of soul with God is sought to be made out. No doubt the identity of God-and soul has been reached, and no doubt what is perceived in the freed soul is not the soul itself but the full Light of the Lord and the soul itself becomes merged in the overpowering Śivānubhōga, on account of the characteristic of the soul we have all along been considering. There is joy inseparable to the soul no doubt, but it is not conscious of such joy. It sees then without seeing; it hears then without hearing; it smells there without smelling; it tastes there without tasting: it thinks there without thinking. Once its consciousness enters into its feeling, there will be duality, and the Bliss will be lost: †

---

* This will explain the phenomena of Kāḷidāsa, Kamban and Shakespeare breaking out into song and poetry, and not the theory of evolution.

† This then is the meaning of the famous passage in *Bṛihad. Up.* IV. 3. 23. "And when there he does not see, yet he is seeing, though he does not see. For sight is inseparable from the seer, because it cannot perish. But there is then no second, nothing else different from him that he could see."

Professor Max Muller takes this avasta as sushupti, and he does not think that there is a condition transcending all the Avasthās—Turiyam and Turiyātitam. The statement in this Maṇtra that he sees, is made so as to remove any misconception that may arise in the statement in maṇtra 21, when he is said to know nothing that is without, nothing that is within. This would end in sūnyam, but not so. There is enjoyment, feeling, and seeing but without seeing i.e., without consciousness. The figure given

These phrases therefore கேளாது கேட்டல், நோக்காது நோக்கல் நினையாது நினைத்தல் (hearing without hearing etc.,) have reference to what is called சுட்டறவுணர்தல் (non-objective knowledge). Our ordinary knowledge involves the dual conception of object and subject. In this சுட்டறவுணர்தல் there is no duality, the distinction between object and subject, Jñāthru but Jñēya is lost, and there is knowledge or pleasure alone but no consciousness. And it is not possible either to know God as we know an object (சுட்டறிவு), for as the Upanishat puts it and all our Advaita Siddhāntins declare: "How should he know him by whom he knows all this? How should he know the knower?" (*Bṛhad Upanishat* II, IV. 13).

" Thou couldst not see the (true) seer of sight, thou couldst not hear the (true) hearer of hearing, nor perceive the perceiver of perception, nor know the knower of knowledge. This is thy God (Ātmā) who is within all." (*Bṛihad Up.* IIIi, v. 2).*

there that of a man embracing his wife, is a favourite one with all mystics. Says Uyyavaṇḍa Dēva in *Tiruvuṇḍiyār*, 33.

> பெற்ற சிற்றின்பமே பேரின்பமாயங்கே
> முற்றவரும் பரிசுந்தீபற
> முளையாதுமாயை யென்றுந்தீபற
> Turn lower pleasure into one supreme,
> Then was the consummation reached,
> Then will māyā sprout no more.

* See how well the philosophy of this is brought out in Sūtra VI. 8, by St Aruṇandi :—

> அன்னிய மிலாமையானும் அறிவினுள் நிற்றலானும்
> முன்னிய வெல்லா முண்ணின் றுணர்த்து வருதலாலும்
> என்னது யானென்றோது மிருஞ் செருக் கறுத்தலானும்
> தன்னறி வதனாற் காணுந் தகைமையன் அல்லன் ஈசன்.

The principle involved is this. In the lower pleasure also, the highest pleasure is reached when in the enjoyment thereof, all his senses and consciousness are hushed and there is bare enjoyment alone. Our Hindu writers thus explain the case of idiocy, imbecility and viciousness of children of healthy and highly intelligent and pious parents. Their minds were not at one, so their characteristics were not transmitted to the offspring. This happens also in the case of drunken parents. The same mode

"As God is ananya with the soul, as He resides within the soul and as He, from within, enables you to know all that you know; and in Him there is no distinction of I and mine, He cannot be perceived by the soul's own intelligence."

It only remains for me to point out how this doctrine of the nature of Jiva or Paśu should commend itself to all intelligent minds. At any rate we are able to quote below the authority of the late Professor Henry Drummond who is said to have revolutionised Christian thought during the last forty years. His remarkable address entitled "*The changed Life*" is based on the famous text from St. Paul.

"We all, with face unveiled, reflecting as a mirror the glory of the Lord, are transformed into the same image from Glory to glory even as from the Lord the spirit" is a veritable varthikam on the அது அது ஆதல் of St. Meykaṇḍān.

He paraphrases the sentence as follows: "We all reflecting as a mirror the character of Christ are transformed into the same image from character to character—from a poor character to a better one, from a better one to one a little better still, from that to one still more complete, until by slow degrees the perfect image is obtained. Here the solution of the

---

is prescribed for the higher enjoyment also, as in the mantra before us. There too you have to hush up all your senses and thinking and consciousness, and then you become overpowered with the Bliss of the Lord alone. I quote below Mantra 21 also.

"This indeed is his (true) form, free from desires, free from evil, free from fear. Now as a man when embraced by a beloved wife knows nothing that is without, nothing that is within; thus this person when embraced by the intelligent God knows nothing that is without, knows nothing within. This indeed is his form in which his wishes are fulfilled in which God is his wish and in which no wish is left, free from sorrow"

The subject is treated in Tamil Literature under *Agapporuḷ*, and *Tirukkôvaiyār* of St. Māṇikkavāçagar is the highest expression of the Higher feelings. Read in this connection also St. Tāyumānavar's *Revel in Bliss* (translated into beautiful English by the Hon'ble Mr. P. Aruṇāchalam of Colombo in Vol. 1. page 145. *The Siddhānta Dipikā*, which brings out every one of the points discussed in this paper.

problem of sanctification is comprised into a sentence, reflect the character of Christ, and you will become like Christ," or as you will say, reflect the image of God in yourself, and you will become Godlike or God.

But how is the poor character to be made better and better or the reflecting image clearer and clearer? It is, by cleansing the mirror (soul) freer and freer from dirt and bringing it more and more in line with the effulgent light, that this can be effected; and when the mirror is absolutely perfect and nearest the light shines the brightest, and so overpowers the mirror that the mirror is lost to view, and the glory and the light of the Lord are felt. For, observes the learned Professor truly, "What you are conscious of, if the result be a true one, is also the glory of the Lord. In looking at a mirror one does not see the mirror or think of it, but only of what it reflects. For a mirror never calls attention to itself—except when there are flaws in it". These flaws are the colours of the Siddhāṇtin who compares them to the māyā or the body. In union with the body, it is the body alone that is cognised, and not the mirror-like soul. In union with God, the glory and light alone are perceived and not the mirror-like soul either! And the Professor declares, "All men are mirrors—that is the first law on which this formula of sanctification or corruption is based. One of the aptest descriptions of a human being is that he is a mirror," and we must beg our readers to go through the whole pamphlet to note how beautifully he draws out this parallel.

He notes the second principle which governs this process, namely, the law of assimilation or identification. "The law of assimilation is the second and by far the most impressive truth which underlies the formula of sanctification—the truth that men are not only mirrors, but that these mirrors, so far from being mere reflectors of the reflecting thing they see, transfer into their own inmost substance and hold in permanent preservation the thing that they reflect. No one can know how the soul can hold these things. No one knows how the miracle is done. No phenomenon in nature, no process in chemistry, no chapter in Necromancy can even help us to begin to understand this amazing operation. For think of it, the past is not only focussed there in a man's soul, it is there. How could it be reflected from there if it were not there? All things he has ever seen, known, felt, believed of the sorrounding world, are now within him, have become part of him, in part are him—he has been changed into their image."

Following the language of Professor Henry Drummond, the formula of sanctification would read as follows.

"I see God, I reflect God, I become God-like, Godly, I am God." I close with only one quotation from St. Aruṇaṇdi Śivāchāriyar which sums up the whole teaching.

கண்டவி வையல் லேனானென்ற கன்றுகாணாக்
கழிபரமு நானல் லேனெனக் கருதிக் கசிந்த
தொண்டினொடு முளத்தவன்றனின்றகலப்பாலே
சோக மெனப்பாவிக் கத்தோன்றுவன் வேறின்றி

விண்டகலு மலங் களெல்லாம் கருடதியானத்தின்
விடமொழியு மதுபோல விமலதையு மடையும்
பண்டைமறை களுமதுநானானேனென்று
பாவிக்கச் சொல்லு வதிப்பாவகத் தைக்காணே.

"Say, 'I am not the world and am separate from it.' Say also, 'I am not the unknowable Supreme One.' Then as He is ananya with you, melt in love in all humility, and practise sōham (I am He); and He will appear as yourself, and your mala will all cease, and you will become pure, just as the poison is removed by *Garuḍadhyāna*. So it is the old Vedas teach us to practise this mantra 'Aham Brahmāsmi'."

PRAISE BE TO MEYKANDA DEVA.

SRI PARVATAM.

"'Oh Yes! when I reach the Alps', he hath said to me 'I always pray.' He would betake himself to some quiet corner, among that grand scenery, and fall on his knees. He was praising God in the work of His creation, the Alps, and bowed in simple praise of it."

This is what is reported of the saintly Ruskin, and the noble feeling given expression to above, clearly explains the wide-spread system of worship obtaining among the Hindus, We refer, of course, to the system of setting up places of worship to the Most High on the highest mountain-peaks and most magnificent hills. And the more inaccessible and difficult of reach these hills are, the more sacred do they become in the eyes of the people. And there can be no possible doubt that some of these pilgrimages call forth no small amount of endurance, toil, patience and expense, which the people will never show, unless they are animated by an equal amount of fervid piety. There can be no doubt whatever also about the elevating influence of Nature in her grandest and magnificent aspects. The sense of elevation and freedom, purity and beauty, awe and reverence, one feels when one reaches one of these mountain-tops must be felt and not told, yet writers have holden forth about the marvels of a sunrise or sunset on Mount Blanc or on the Himālayas, and one cannot but cry out at such sights from his heart of hearts.

"சோதியே சுடரே சூழொளிவிளக்கே * சுரிகுழற்பணை முலைமடந்தை
பாதியே, பரனேபால்கொள் வெண்ணீற்றாய் பங்கயத்தயனுமாலறியா
நீதியே—
தீதிலா நன்மைத் திருவருட்குன்றே."

* A friend of ours mentioned to us how the picture at Tiruvaṇṇāmalai, with the setting sun, the flaming hill top and myriad lights, called to him at once these lines. Yōgis have a different explanation of the triple light.

In fact, the Śiva Liṅga is nothing but the hill-top in its origin, and the custom of worshipping God on mountain-tops was current among the Jews and the Romans. And to Moses, God appeared as fire and light on mountain-tops, accompanied with thunder, clouds and lightning, the true picture of Śiva, as *Giriśa* and *Kapardin*. And the highest peaks in India had, from the beginning, been dedicated to the worship of Śiva and Pārvati, on Himāvat, on the Vindhya, on the Western Ghats, on the Central Ranges, on the Eastern Ghats and on Maināka, etc. Of these, the most sacred, of course, is Kailāśa, and when we find that even St. Appar did not succeed in finding this Mountain Abode on earth, we will be correct in stating that this Mount Kailāśa does not represent any material plane, but certainly means the Highest Summit of Man's spiritual, moral and intellectual elevation, reaching which, after leaving his sense of his own greatness (Ahaṅkāra), he will surely unite in that Abode of Eternal Peace, Beauty and Bliss. But mortals identify this Supreme Abode with this and that mountain-peak, in particular, with Maināka in Ceylon, with the Rock at Trichy, with the Hill of Kālahasti, with Śrī Parvatam, with Himāvat, &c., and there is a purpose in view. Man cannot reach up to the Highest Ideal all at once. He must climb, must be made to understand by slow degrees, mark each as the highest, and then ascend higher and higher, not condemning what he has already reached, but always looking up higher and higher, until he shall have reached the highest of these hills.

Of these hill-shrines, none is more sacred than the hill called Śrī Śaila, Śrī Parvata, Śrī Mallikārjuna and Mahānandi. Its importance may be guessed from its appellation itself "Parvata", "The Mountain." It is so called by its pre-eminence, whereas all other hills are distinguished by peculiar names. And for one thing, this hill is much more difficult of approach, and presents a much grander scenery than those below in the south. The people and princes of ages gone by have expended their wealth and labour in building and beautifying this Holy Shrine, though their degenerate descendants simply sit with folded hands and see the disintegration of this noble edifice.

To southerners generally, a temple is sacred, if it had been visited by the Śaiva Saints or Āḷvārs; and Śrī Śailam has been visited by all the three Saints Appar, Sambhaṇdar and Suṇdarar, and their separate Hymns appear in the *Dēvāra* Collections; and the place is called Śrī Paruppatam, Tamiḷ reading of Śrī Parvatam, and the hill is locally known by this name more than by the name of Śrī Śailam or Mallikārjunam.

Now to describe briefly our journey to the place. From Madras, we reach Naṇdyal, by the M. and S. M. R. lines, and from Naṇdyal, we go by cart to Ātmakūr, a distance of 28 miles. The road is wretchedly bad for the greater part, and does not reflect much credit on the Board in charge of it. In fact, cart-men avoided the High Road for nearly 10 miles and preferred to go by the country roads. Ātmakūr is a small town and is the seat of the Deputy Tahsildar, Police Inspector and a Local Fund Hospital. From here to the foot of the Hill (Nāgalūṭi) is a distance of 12 miles. This road, too, except for a few miles, is of the worst description. The situation of Nāgalūṭi is very pleasant, surrounded by shady groves, in which there is a nice and cool spring, the water flowing into a small tub from the mouth of a bull. There is here a small Temple dedicated to Śiva and Vīrabhadrasvāmi. From Nāgalūṭi we commence the ascent, and it is a steep one for over 2 or 3 miles. The chief difficulty of the ascent is due to the flight of steps that have been constructed over this distance. After we go up two or three hills, the road is not bad and it is slightly up and down, and as we reach Pedda-cheruvu, we get into a big plateau, a valley surrounded on all sides by the hills. Peddacheruvu is our halt for the day, and its distance is reported to be about 16 miles. There is a fine tank here and it is edged with tall growing bamboos, which give it a most picturesque appearance. In the tank itself, beautiful white lotuses, water lilies and tall cuscus, grasses grow and the water actually tastes sweet with the smell of the cuscus, grass. Early next morning we resumed our journey, and after some distance the way was rough but not difficult, having to go over several small hills; and nearing Bhīmani Kollum, we descend into a deep ravine which cuts off Śrī Parvata proper from the surrounding hills. And both the descent into this ravine and the ascent from it are both difficult, but not so bad as it was reported to be. The view from above into the ravine, and far below is very grand. The ravine cuts through these rocks to a considerable depth, and the cut sides look more like fort walls, so steep and straight and brown they are. The bed of the Ravine is one slaty bed, there are no loose stones or sand. From the bottom of the Ravine at this spot, called Bhīmani Kollum, commences the ascent of Śrī Parvatī, or Mount Kailāś; and as we go up, vista after vista of hills and ranges of hills present themselves before us, the distant peaks and the line of trees on them become silhouetted like our Temple Vimānas and the row of Kalasams on them. One view specially seemed a remarkable likeness of the Śiva-Liṅga, with the pedestal. It stood between two ravines, the highest Peak and another small one forming Śiva and Pārvati, and the Pedestal was a table-like rock in front. Our artist has taken a view of this beautiful picture and has named it Śiva-Pārvati, and it is not unlikely that similar views had given rise to the symbol of the Śiva-Liṅga itself. We ascend higher and higher, our toil and trouble seem to burden us, untill, at last, we reach the Top, where is situated what is aptly called the Kailāśa Vākkili, the "gate to Heaven". As the wearied traveller feels the refreshing breeze under the cool shade of this tower, the feeling of rest and pleasure one feels is simply thrilling. Indeed, in this world, at least half the pleasure we feel will be lost to us if it is not that, in seeking and securing this, it entails any amount of pain and trouble. From the gate of Kailāś, we travel over more or less level ground slightly falling, and rising till we reach the Temple, of which we catch a glimpse from some distance and which is situated in a dip of Mount Kailāś. Mount Kailāś is surrounded on all sides by deep ravines and by the Kistṇā, so that on any side it is steep and inaccessible, the ravine at Bhimani Kollum joining the Kistṇā below. Its situation is also central, and any way, you have to go 30 or 40 miles to reach the low country.

The temple proper is surrounded by castellated walls, longest sides being 1500 feet each, and the shortest being nearly 1000 feet each and the height is 21 feet and thickness 4 feet. Nearly the whole outer face of these walls (fancy such a dimension of 5000 × 21 feet) is fully sculptured with the figures of animals, men and Gods. There are hunting pictures of all kinds, there are horses and elephants in every pose, Purāṇic representations of episodes, Rishis doing tapas in all kinds of postures; and there are animals and reptiles in every grotesque form, athletes wrestling with each other, &c.* These pictures show that the race of men who cut them were a warlike and manly race. There are three towers, one of which is the highest, and will compare favourably with the highest in Southern India.

Passing within, the whole space is intersected into 3 squares, one below the other and the sides are filled with innumerable maṇṭapams and shrines, the shrines mostly without any images and in the worst of repairs. There are large number of wells with small towers or domes above, the only source of supply to all the pilgrims who resort to the place. Some one or two of the tanks altogether dry and filled up more or less.

The central shrine is that of Mallikēśvara and is the most costly structure. The principal Vimānam is covered from top to bottom with plated gold, unlike any other Temple in Southern India, and all the images of Naṇdis and Dakshaṇāmūrti placed over the terrace in the maṇṭapam fronting the Vimāna are also similarly covered with gold. It is reported that of old these images contained inside untold wealth, and the Rohillas who once plundered the whole Temple have left their marks in the mutilated condition of most of these images. The style of the principal structures is quite dissimilar to those in Southern India, the Chōḷa and Pāṇḍiyan styles, but there is a remarkable resemblance between these and the shore temple at Mahāmalaipuram (corrupted into

* There is one picture in which two men hold each other by their legs, stretched at full length, and withal making a regular ball. We have witnessed many an Indian and European circus performance, but never saw any such pose before.

Mahābalipuram) and the traditions in connection with the latter Temple show that priests from Śrī Śailam were brought to the Mahāmalaipuram Pagoda, which in itself proves the great antiquity of Śrī Śailam Temple. The structure is clearly Chālukyan, and the Coñjīvaram Pagodas and the seven Pagodas were also constructed by the Rulers of the Chālukyan Dynasty, when they held sway over those parts. The rock-cut Temple at Ellora, also called Mount Kailāśa, was also their work, and it speaks volumes for the great religious zeal and piety of these noble sovereigns who adorned this ancient line of Kings, and yet to-day, the student of South Indian History knows hardly anything about them.

The Temple of Śri Pārvati is a very small one at present, but it is reported that the original image was stolen or mutilated and its place has also been changed. The Principal Amman Shrine is occupied by a Goddess called Brahmarāmbā, in whose name a big feast is held in the month of Chitrai when bloody sacrifices are also offered. This is clearly an image of Kāḷi, and this shrine stands apart and is shut up after sometime in the night, even when other shrines are open. Evidently, the image was set up sometime after the Temple had come into the hands of the Pushpagiri Muṭṭ. Perhaps the image which had remained outside the Temple was set up in the place of Śri Pārvati when the image of the latter had been was lost. Anyhow the worship of this Brahmarāmbā is not to be confounded with the principal worship of the shrine itself.

The Temple-tree is a fig tree, and it must be a very ancient one. It towers far above the tallest tower and at its base, it measures more than 55 feet. Under its shade are seated Sanyāsins and Yōgis, and a good picture of this was photographed by our artist. The tree on the right-hand side of the principal picture is the fig tree we have mentioned above. Such an old tree we have not seen anywhere else.

There is one liberty allowed in this Temple and other Temples in this District, namely the right of free worship allowed to every caste Hindu, a right which. we dare say, as obtaining at one time everywhere in the South, as it is still to-day in the north,

And we had then the satisfaction of worshipping God with our own hands at our own leisure and our abhisheka and archanā were performed with the accompaniment of *Dêvāra* and *Tiruvāçaga* Hymns. One has necessarily to attain to that calm, resigned and reverent attitude of mind and body, forgetting all self, which is necessary in a worship of this kind, before one can expect to feel any soul-elevation.

A visit to the Kistṇā which cuts through the Nalla Malais at this point and a bath in it are held very sacred; and this is a pretty stiff job. It is one steep journey, down and down you go, till at the very bottom lies the perfectly blue and placid waters of Pātāḷa Gaṅgā or Nīl-Gaṅgā. The scene hereabouts can only be matched by the Nerbudda at the marble rocks. Our artist has taken 2 or 3 views of the bathing-ghat and the winding river. The distance between Peddacheruvu and mount Kailāś is about 15 miles and from Mount Kailāś to Pātāḷa Gaṅgā (Kistṇā) is about 5 miles.

For the greater part, the hills are covered with bamboos and various valuable forest trees, but at the time we went, owing to the drought and other causes the trees were more or less bare and the bamboos presented a withered appearance. The forest produce are all enjoyed by the Cheñchus, the native inhabitants of these jungles and hills. On the route to Śrī Śailam, these Chenchus occupy three settlements, called Gūdems, one near Nāgalūṭi, one near Peddacheruvu, one near Śrī Śailam. They levy from the pilgrims a kind of poll-tax at these different points, at one anna per head; and this is said to be in consideration of their protecting the property and person of the pilgrims in these wild regions, and the Police Inspector himself told us that they are, so far, remarkable for their honesty. These hill-men do not differ much from other natives of the low country, but they are almost naked except in the piece-cloth (laṅgōṭi) which they wear. One big cloth besides they wear with which they cover their upper part of the body or lay it losely over their shoulders. They have a peculiar way of tying their hair, in the style known as *Koṇḍai Muḍichu*, which kind of dressing may also be perceived in some of the ancient Sculptures in Madura and elsewhere. By no means, are these savages or aborigines, but they must certainly have belonged to a very ancient and civilized race, but from the circumstance of having been confined to a residence in these hills, had gradually degenerated more or less. The females are better dressed and they could not be very much distinguished from the people of the plains. As residents of *Kuriñji*, the marriage which usually obtains amongst them is what may be called the Gaṇdharva form. As a Cheñchu put it, boys and girls roam about and get acquainted with each other, and choose for themselves, and after a time, the marriage is published by the inviting and feeding of a few guests; just in the same way as we read of in *Kuriñjippāṭṭu*. Of course the environments favour them so much, and the people are so few, and the liberty of movement is so great, that you cannot but expect such kind of marriages in such a community. Of course our poets and lawyers put it as though such and such a kind of marriage is required for such a kind of land (*Tiṇai*, திணை), and our friend Mr. T. Vīrabadra Mudaliyār wonders why our poets should of necessity people 'மருதம்' with prostitutes and dancing girls. Of course there is no necessity, but as in their view 'மருதம்' (*Marudam*) the land covered with paddy fields represented the seat of wealth and luxury, and civilized activity and prostitution clearly follow in their wake, the poets always lay down as a law that whenever 'civilized towns' are spoken of, prostitution should also be maintained. In a sense this rule appears rigid, but ample scope is given when they usually speak of 'திணை மயக்கம்.'

An account of the trip cannot be complete without a special description of the famous spring and Temple at Mahāṇaṇdi; and usually all pilgrims to Śrī Śailam pass through Mahāṇaṇdi on their return. It is about 9 miles from Naṇdyal and the Temple is situated at the foot of the same range. Our artist has also photographed the beautiful Temple with the whole Tank. The chief interest lies in the Tank which is a perennial spring, and there are two big outlets which carry off with great force the ever-bubbling water. The water is slightly tepid, and it is of remarkable purity and clearness. Light is refracted as in a perfect crystal, and you could see all the colours of the rainbow on the bottom of the tank. The depth is about 5 feet all round, and once you get into it, you are reluctant to get out of it. You can see a pin at the bottom clearly, and however you may dirty the water, it becomes clear in no time. There is not a speck of dirt in the water or at the bottom, and any leaves or other matter that may fall into it are all lifted up and carried out. Visitors marvel, generally failing to account for the clearness and pellucid character of the water, but if one places his eye in level with the surface of the water, he would easily perceive that all over the tank, there are streaks rising above the water, as in a tumbler of soda water, and this cannot be anything else than compressed air rising out with the water. Bigger bubbles can also be perceived here and there. The force of the spring and this compressed air both combine together to lift up all dirt and rubbish, and they are carried outside by means of the flowing outlets. The waters running from this spring serve to keep hundreds of acres under permanent cultivation, and here in fact may be seen an instance of what our poets are fond of delineating, the commingling of forest and hill and country scenery, of what is called திணைமயக்கம், of *Kuriñji*, and *Mullai*, and *Marudam* all in one place, and the scenery about this place is accordingly very enchanting.

SAIVAISM IN ITS RELATION TO OTHER SYSTEMS.*

It was the *Statesman* of Calcutta who in reviewing the work of the last convention suggested that, in an assembly like this, it is the point of contact between the different religions that should be brought out rather than the points which distinguish one from the other. As I think the suggestion is good, and as I have dwelt on the distinguishing marks of Śaiva religion and philosophy in my former paper,‡ I address myself to the question of the elements common to the Śaiva religion and other systems of faith.

This aspect of the question is familiar to our religious writers and I quoted a dictum of one of our Āchāryas who is at least 8 centuries old, in my last address, and it could bear repetition and should in my opinion form the plank on which we should all meet. It is to this effect. "Religions, postulates and text-books conflict one with another. It is asked: which is the true religion, which the true postulate and which the true book? That is the true religion, that the true postulate and that the true book which, not possessing the fault of calling this false and that true, and not conflicting with them, comprises reasonably everything within its fold." But how is this possible? Where can the meeting ground be, between a religion which acknowledges no soul and no God, and a religion which bases its faith on the immortality of the soul and a Redeemer? They seem to be poles apart. There are such differences innumerable between one religion and another and no amount of argument and explanation could minimise the differences. Argument would lead to acrimonious debate and heated controversy.

* The first paper that was read before the Convention of Religions, Allahabad 1911.

‡ *Vide* page 273 *ante*.

It will not do for one to try to convert the other. We are yet to see persons who have been converted by argument. There must be a predisposing state of the mind in all conversions. For argument also to be useful, there must be a pure heart and an unprejudiced mind. If one enters into a controversy with prepossessions of all kinds, and each is convinced of his own truth, no agreement will be ever possible. Even in my private talks, I avoid discussing with any person whose mind, I know is prejudiced. With this one element absent, I have talked to persons of all persuasions, free-thinkers included, and by the time we parted, we had become dearer to each other.

However, our scheme is this. It takes stock of the fact that there are essential differences between man and man. Owing to differences of heridity and environment, facilities for acquiring knowledge and their absence, and a hundred other similar causes, people differ in their intellectual, moral and spiritual equipments. If in a single family of half a dozen children, fostered under the loving care of the same parents, one should turn out to be an idiot and another an intellectual giant, one a vagabond and another a saint, it is not merely heridity alone that seems to count. There seems to be something behind all these to account for the disparity. Our Hindu writers try to account for it by the law of Karma and past experience or *Pūrva Puṇya*. Be this as it may, the differences in the moral and intellectual calibre of people are a fact and no amount of education or correction seems to be of any use in such cases. Apart from cases of physical and mental deformities, one cannot minimise the difficulties of the mind itself. Man must think. You cannot shut out his mind. As we imbibe knowledge and acquire learning, our minds begin to think and ponder over the same problems which have agitated men's minds from the very beginning of time. And with all the guides and mentors and correctives we possess, we take to particular lines of thought which, in the end, are all limited. But it is never too late to mend. We can outgrow our thoughts and can change; and we do change, both consciously and, in most cases, unconsciously. Even in the case of a single individual, with a little introspection, it might be perceived, how he had been changing from time to time, though he never changed his outward observances, his attendance at Church on Sundays so to speak. Thoughts about the reality of the world, his own individuality and the existence of a Supreme Being, have assailed him from time to time, yet he has emerged from all these triumphantly in the end, and he had become a Godly man.

Hence we arrived at the truth that all religions are necessary so as to serve the cause of progress of man in all stages of moral, intellectual and spiritual development. What will serve one will not serve another equally well. One could not be easily hustled from one stage to another with profit. One of our Āchāryas instances the case of a tree and its produce. One cares for the leaves alone and does not care for the flowers or the fruit, however tempting the latter may be. Another cares for the flowers alone; another, the raw-fruit; and another the mature fruit; and yet another rejects such parts of the ripe fruit as the skin and stone &c., and drinks the rare sweet juice alone. Yet the tree had its uses for all, and each derived benefit from it according to his need. One writer puts it in another way also. To reach a city or a hill top, there may be any number of ways, some shortcuts and some circuitous, some dangerous and rough, and some smooth; yet each is filled with a desire to reach the goal, to climb the hill-top. Yet there is a third mode in which they present it by the simile of the ladder. It is called the *Sōpānamārga*—Sōpānam meaning ladder. As there are so many rungs to the ladder and each has to be climbed in order, before one can get to the top, each different religion forms one rung or other of the ladder. Each rung is necessary, and one cannot reject each as false or untrue. And our Śāstras proclaim that all religions are from God and all are acceptable to God, whether these religions may be said to have a divine origin or a human origin.

"If people without *broadness of mind* promulgate new religions, even out of jealousy, even such are acceptable to our Lord". This explains, by the way, how even man-made movements are doomed to disintegration and division by two potent factors, narrowness of mind and jealousy.

God is the father of all, in every age and in every clime. He has not been partial to any one people nor to any one age nor to any one country. He has revealed Himself at all times in all countries and to all races. Nay, in every thinking and loving heart, He is revealing Himself. If there is truth anywhere, it is God's truth, and as the Rev. G. M. Cobban puts it, all truth is authoritative and inspired and all truth is from God.

"Wherever you find God, there it is our own Lord the God that is present." So it is the accepted canon of the Śaiva religion that its God is the God and Father of all religions, and every religion is acceptable to Him, and that no religion should be derided or rejected as false.

Of course, it is an essential requisite and condition of all religions that they reveal a desire to reach the goal, or to climb to the top, a desire after truth and righteousness, a desire for a higher life. If this condition is fulfilled, it does not matter whether they are theistic or atheistic systems, God-made or man-made. The searcher after truth is sure to proceed onward and onward, till he one-day reaches the goal. It is in this sense, one of our Tamiḷ Saints, St. Appar, who before his conversion was a Jain, says that he never ceased worshipping Śiva any time with water and flowers, water representing purity and sincerity, and flowers love.

Having made this preliminary statement, I may now be allowed to compare Śaivaism with some only of the world religions of to-day. Among them, the first that claims our attention is Buddhism. It has two forms, northern and southern. Northern Buddhism, if not in origin, had assumed a Śaivite form in its final shape. The famous *Lipika* symbol traced in the pages of the Secret Doctrine, by Madame Blavatsky is nothlng but the Śiva Liṅga. There are stories scattered about in the pages of the Bhuddhist Scriptures that it was Śiva himself who taught the Buddhist Religion, just as Tuḷasi Dās makes Śiva communicate the narrative of Rāma's life to Goddess-Umā, and just as it is believed that it is Lord Viśvanāth that communicates Rāmatāraka-mantra to every one dying in Benares. I, however, believe that the southern form, deprived of its more dogmatic teaching of anātmā &c., is the true form, which is of greater value to us. Of course, even Oriental Scholars have pointed it to us that Buddha was a Hindu, a Hindu of Hindus and the best of Hindus. His positive teaching emphasising the importance of moral greatness was already in Hinduism and formed part of it. And yet Buddhism was of great value then and is of value for all time to come. In our search after man and God, and in putting on cloaks of holiness and piety, and in indulging in all sorts of ceremonials, we are apt to neglect and ignore one part of our duty, which is, after all, the foundation of all religions. In our desire for religious purity, we are apt to neglect moral purity as though that were a minor matter. But as our religion teaches us, it is an absolute *sine qua non*. The gulf between man and God cannot be crossed unless moral purity is attained. Of the importance of this Sākya Gautama reminded us, by his great personality and his teaching. We require such reminders every day. He is said to have incarnated several times, but even to-day is ripe for a fresh incarnation of him, in the troublous time we are passing through. For what is this new spirit that is said to be leavening us and creating all this unrest and all the misery in its train? This spirit is the spirit of Mammon, the materialism of the West, which is dazzling our eyes and captivating our minds. The West stands to us for untold wealth, untold power and untold enjoyment. This new spirit is the desire to share in the wealth, power and enjoyment. But what does the story of Sākya Gautama teach us? He was not a pauper who was turned into a sannyāsi as most of the modern-day holy-men are manufactured. He was the heir to the throne of a great Empire. He was in the prime of life and manhood, and in the enjoyment of all that wealth and luxury could bring. Yet he turned from them all, by seeing a few instances of death. He feared death and yet he was not a moral coward. He would have been glad to die if that had ended all. He feared death simply because to him, it simply spelled another birth. As his Tamiḷ Prototype puts it, "Death is like sleep and birth is but the awakening." Our holy men have always desired to die but prayed to be saved from re-birth. It was the great cycle of births and deaths that was feared. This birth is spoken of as the great ocean of birth. He believed in the law of Karma which is at the same time the foundation of all Hindu theistic Systems. This cycle of the law is the wheel or circle, which is the chief symbol of Buddhism. Proceeding a step further, he enquired as to the cause of this birth and death. It was the desire for enjoyment, the thirst after power and pelf, *Tanha*; as the author of the Sacred Kuṟaḷ puts it, "It is the desire that is the seed of birth at all times and for all mankind." It was this desire in its two forms—desire of good things (Kāma) and avoidance of bad things (Krōdha) in the train of ignorance—that is the cause of all Karma, all our sin and sorrow, our birth and death. If we can cut off this *desire* we can cut off the seed of birth and become deathless and attain *Nirvāṇa*.

" Desire and aversion and ignorance, their name destroyed, disease is gone." (*Kuṟaḷ*. 360.)

We are quoting these texts from the sacred *Kuṟaḷ* of Tiruvaḷḷuvar, the sage of Mylāpūr who is claimed as an orthodox Śaiva and is worshipped as such, just to show how far the two systems proceed together. Kāshi is claimed by all Śaivites as the true burning ground as distinguished from all other burning grounds, and the meaning is this. Where we ordinarily die and are burnt, we simply sow the seeds of a fresh birth. It becomes a new planting ground merely. The true *shmāshaṇa* will be where we will be burnt up truly and really without a chance of rebirth. There is real annihilation as is intended by the word Nirvāṇa, but there is deathlessness also. What is it that dies and that which does not die? It is man's individuality, the " I-ness ", the egoism that is formed of Karma, the shadow that always dogs his foot-steps, the bundle of his desires, passions and numerous enjoyments, the tree of knowledge of good and evil; it is this that is annihilated. What is not destroyed and, by the annihilation of the former, becomes freed of its fetters and becomes immortal, is the real spirit, the soul or ātmā (the tree of life). Buddha would not postulate the other side of death, the real annihilation. Because he thought it only complicated matters. The thing was clear, desire was the ultimate cause of the disease of birth and sorrow, and, if by any herculean effort, we could remove the cause, the object would attained. As such he laid great stress on Desirelessness, or becoming balanced in pleasure and pain, in sinlessness and self-sacrifice; and this teaching is priceless to all and every one; and as I said, I wish even now a fresh avatār of Buddha would incarnate to carry home to every one this teaching, not only on the Holy land of his birth, but to the West also, which also sorely needs an avatār of his type, to turn them away from the thought of mere material aggrandizement.

In the scheme of salvation as framed in Śaivite theology, this forms the first of the four rungs, namely Karma Sāmyam, (becoming balanced in pleasure and pain), the other three being Malaparipākam and Sadgurudarśanam and Sattinipādam. Before I leave this part of the subject, I wish to draw the special attention of the Convention to the existence in the Tamiḷ language of the Sacred *Kuṟaḷ* by Śaivite Sage Tiruvaḷḷuvar, who lived about 2000 years ago. It is an ethical treatise which has profoundly influenced the Tamiḷ people for the last 2000 years, and in the words of its English translator the late Rev. Dr. G. U. Pope, "it is not surpassed by any thing of the kind in any literature." The same learned doctor further remarks that "it is evident from what has been said above, we have in Southern India an ethical treatise which in a Christian point of view is nearly unexceptionable." I will quote another observation of his also before I address myself to the next subject, namely, Christianity.

"To meet thoughtful Hindus in a spirit of dogmatic antagonism or to treat them with contempt or to speak of them as the perishing heathen, is absolutely unfitting. We have even to learn something from Hinduism."

The Rev. G. M. Cobban was a missionary gentleman who was a prominent and popular figure in Madras in my College days. He was a good student of Tamiḷ and of Śaiva Siddhānta. Writing to the *Contemporary Review* he wrote, "First, I think, we should insist on the cordial recognition of these truths and cheerfully acknowledge their kinship to Christianity, for all truth is akin. The Hindu poet knows what to say of it. He says 'the heart is made pure by the truth.' If I am asked whence these truths came, I would say from heaven, from Him who is the Truth. But whether they are the direct gifts of God to the Hindus, or whether like boulders, they have drifted and travelled to India, I cannot tell; the evidence on this point is incomplete. If any urge that, although Hindus recognize their authority, they are un-inspired and not really authoritative, I would say truth is authoritative, because it is truth, not because it came in a particular way. And all truth is from God." He also remarks "we find much truth both in books and men, so much as to surprise the student and delight the wise Christian teacher."

These observations were all made in reference to the truths contained in Šaiva and Vaishṇava works in Tamiḻ. And I have given other estimates of Śaiva Siddhāṇta from Christian writers in my last address. The resemblance which struck them most between Christianity and Šaivaism, and which I wish to emphasize here, relates to the ideal of Godhead, God's relation to man, the doctrine of Love and Grace, and the necessity for a divine teacher. I have defined the terms 'Personal and Impersonal', 'Saguṇa and Nirguṇa' in my last address and I have shown that, according to Šaiva religion, God is personal in the true acceptation of the word, according to Christian writers. God is Sat, Chit, and Āṇanda, Nirguṇa, absolute and personal at the same time. He is our Lord and Master, our heavenly Father, our intimate Friend and Beloved One. He loves us and we can love him. He understands our helplessness and is ever intent on our good, and if we only could respond to His Love which, in the words of one of our Saints, is "limitless and is ever rising and flowing over", and which, in the words of another, is "a flood brooking not its banks rushest into the cavity of my heart," our salvation would be assured. 'God is love' and every Christian missionary who knows anything of Tamiḻ knows by heart the famous verse in St. Tirumūlar's *Tirumaṇtiram* "Sivam and Love are different, say the fools. No one knows that Šivam and Love are the same. When one knows that Šivam and Love are the same, then he rests in Šivam as Love."

I have urged Christians to drop the word "Saguṇa" (meaning clothed in the three guṇas, Satva, Rajas and Tamas), and to drop their prejudice against the word Nirguṇa, which means non-material or Pure Intelligence and spirit. Our Idea of God is Sat-chit-ānaṇda, symbolised in the form of Sōmā-skaṇda (Sa-umā-skaṇda) and this is the same as God the father, God the mother or Holy ghost, and God the son, and I have quoted in some other place the definition of these terms from Bishop Westcott, God as pure being or spirit, God as light that links to him all humanity, and God as Love.

I have referred to the Doctrine of Grace as a special feature of Śaiva Siddhāṇta in my last address; and in this respect also, it differs in no respect from that of the Christian Doctrine. Christian Theologians have fought over the question of desert and grace, and there is a similar divergence in Śaiva Siddhāṇta schools also. The doctrine of *Nirhetukaruṇa* is well set forth by Śaiva sages also, and all schools recognize that even where you deserve the grace, it is God that helps you to deserve it. Our Skaṇda is Kumāra Skaṇda, son of God, the first teacher and Parama Guru, and I have shown that unless God comes down to us as the son of man, our redemption is not possible. Christianity speaks of only one revelation for all time to come. But in the Śaiva Siddhāṇta, God reveals Himself as the son and Guru to each in his own fulness of time.

What repels most Christians in Hinduism is its idealism and Pantheism. But in the manner in which '*advaita*' is defined by the Śaivite school and hence called Śuddha Advaita Siddhāṇta, the doctrine is without any reproach. "Thou art not aught in the universe; Naught is there save Thou; (God) Who can know Thee?' is our postulate. We distinguish clearly between the plane of God, the plane of man and the plane of the universe, just in the same way as Professor Henry Drummond does, and we postulate a unity at the same time. 'God is all and not all' is one of our axioms. Even in regard to the doctrine of atonement, there is considerable agreement. We equally say with Christians, that where we can do His will, atoning ourselves with God, then He takes upon Himself all our burdens, and all our burdens fall off. (Vide *Śivjñāna-*

bōdham, Sūtra. 10.) As man falls away from God, by not doing His Will, so the final act of Sanctification consists in doing His will, and the moment we do this, we will be re-united to our Father in Heaven. I only hope that the day, the Christian world realizes the beauty of Śaiva Siddhāṇta in all its aspects, much of the prejudice against Hinduism will fall off, and we will be united to each other in bonds of fraternal love as, we should be, children of the same Father. One learned Jesuit Father blessed us after hearing of our idea of Śivam as Love, saying, 'Yes, this is the truth and I wish God would give you grace to preach it."

In the scheme of practical religion, consisting of *Charyā*, *Kriyā*, *Yōga*, and *Jñāna*, otherwise called Dāsamārga, Satputramārga, Sahamārga, and Sanmārga, Christianity brings to the foreground Satputramārga or the Doctrine of Father-hood of God, though as I have shown elsewhere, it comprises other mārgas also.

In regard to our relation to Mahomedanism, I am only sorry to say that mutual ignorance of each other's truths has kept them from recognition of their closest kinship, much closer in fact, than any other Hindu school even. We are like passengers entering a Railway carriage, and one who gets in first tries to prevent the other getting in. But once both get in and fall to talk, their kinship for generations is discovered, and they fall on each other's necks, kiss and embrace. I will give you a story to illustrate. There was once a quarrel between the Śaivites and their other Hindu brethren in a certain place. They went before the Nabob with their complaints. He promised to decide if each would show his God on the morrow. The Śaivites went home dejected; for, how could they hope to show the Nabob their God? They fell to fasting and prayer, and at night, God appeared in a vision and told them to rise in the morning and after proper ablutions, to divide their cadjan Holy Hymn Book with a thread at random, and the Hymn which was found should be taken and shown to the Nabob. The other party was jubilant, for in their wealth and power to decorate their God, they had no equals. They brought out their God gaily adorned with costly crowns and sparkling gems to the presence of the Nabob. The Śaivites took their old browned palm-leaf and read out the verse which was to this effect. "The Lord with braided hair and His spouse with pencilled brows, live in the burning ground of Kañchi. He knows no sin. He is not one of the mortals. He has no one as His equal. No town claims Him as its citizen. He is beyond compare; unless we with the eye of His Grace perceive His true nature, we can't paint Him, and show Him as of such form and figure."

The Nabob nodded his head and said to the other party, "Sabash! This is a great Rājā"; but told the Śaivites, "Yours is God." My Mahomedan friend to whom I related the story said, "True, if the Nabob did not know the nature of God, would he have recognized yours as God." And that is the moral I am trying to bring out by means of the story. The God of the Śaivites who form the bulk of the Hindu people and whose doctrine is the most ancient form of Hinduism, is not an anthropomorphic conception. That they hold strictly with Mahomedans that God cannot be born, as a man, through the womb of the woman, attests this truth. Śiva, (Śivam, Sāntam, Advaitam, Chaturtam) who by the way is not one of the trinity, in all His revelations to man, never was born and could never be born. He is therefore called birthless (Aja) and deathless (Amṛita) 'immortal,' even in the Ṛig Vêda. In the higher regions of philosophy and mysticism, there is very close approximation. We believe also that the famous *Kaaba* of Mecca is nothing but a Śiva Linga. I quote very frequently from Shaik Sāḍi and other writers to illustrate the higher truths of Śaiva philosophy. Here is a rose picked from the Gulistan. "A certain person took his basket and told his friends that he would go into his garden and bring them fine flowers. He went in and the moment he came amidst the flowers, he was so overpowered by the strong scent, he fell down unconscious. He forgot himself, he forgot the promise given to his friends, and the basket slipped from his hands unnoticed." This is the condition of the Jivan Mukta according to Śaiva philosophy. There is joy in heaven and endless bliss but one will not be conscious he is so enjoying. This is pure advaita bliss. There is no return from there, 'no return' is the refrain of the Upanishats. One of our sages sings: "we have not heard, nor learnt from those who had cast their eyes on

Thee." All our religious practices, ceremonies, forms and Shibboleths fall off from us, as the basket from the sleeper's hand, and they are of no consequence when we reach His seat. I will appeal to my own religionists to try and study Mahomedanism as it deserves to be studied, and I would appeal to my Mahomedan brethren to come out of their seclusion and know something of us; for as I may say with truth with my valued Christian friend, "you have even something to learn from Hinduism." In the scheme of practical religion, the popular form of Mahomadanism is Dāsa Mārga, though, as I have shown, the Mahomedan mystics have reached the highest experience of religion. Amongst the Tamiḻ people, Christians address God usually as Pitā, "Father" and the Mahomedans as "Āṇḍavan, Lord and Master."

Coming now to the Hindu Schools, Śaivaism includes the school of Gāṇapatyas, Śāktas and Vēdāṇtins of Śaṅkara's School. So far as the practical religion is concerned, Vēdāṇtins and Śaivites are indistinguishable in form, and they follow the Charyā, Kriyā and Yōga paths together. It is only in regard to the doctrinal part they differ. Vēdāṇtins interpret "Advaitam" as 'Ekam,' 'Abhēda,' 'Abhinna.' But if as Maṇilal Dvivedi in his *Monism*, shows, 'Advaita' does not mean all this, but 'Ananya' or Anyōnāsti, as our Āchāryas, Śri Nīlakaṇṭha Śivāchārya and St. Meykaṇḍān take it to be, even the slight difference vanishes. There may be a purpose in emphasizing the one-ness of all things, by reason of God's immanence, as against gross dualism, but still an one-sided picture is always not safe. As regards its relation to Vaishṇavism, there is much greater doctrinal harmony between Śaivaism and Vaishṇavism of Śrī Rāmānuja's school than between these and Vēdāṇtism, of Śaṅkara's School, though in the forms of religion they differ. I presented a copy of my *Śivajñānabōdham* to the late P. Śrīnivāsa Rao, Judge, City Civil Court, Madras, a prominent Madhva; and when I next met him, he said he thought I was an advaiti, but the reading of my book showed that there was no difference between his philosophy and mine. I am proud to call mysef an advaiti still. But there was a meeting-ground possible between my Advaitam and his Dvaitam whereas, there was no union possible between his Dvaitam and what he fancied to be *advaitam*. A Śrīvaishṇava friend of mine had written a key to my Śivajñānabodham. However I am glad to say the leaders on both sides are giving up their narrow prejudices and in the last Śaiva Siddhānta conference* held at Rāmnād, we had several Vaishṇava friends lecturing on the platform, and on Śrī Pañchākshararn itself. However the value of Vaishṇavism is in emphasizing the importance of Dāsa Mārga or Bhakti Mārga, though Vaishṇava saints have belonged to all the four Mārgas. One of my Calcutta friends told me that Śaivaism is not so popular a Bhakti Mārga as Vaishṇavism. And I spent a whole night in speaking to one who is considered as a great teacher now in Calcutta, in the presence of my friend, and the great man was kind enough to acknowledge his entire agreement with my views. In fact, the foundation of Śaivaism is built solely on *love*. Usually the more exuberant form of Dāsa Mārga is alone mistaken for Bhakti Mārga. The Deeper the river, the more silently does it flow. As love grows more and more, it grows silent. Outward manifestation is only in the lower stages. There is the deep-seated love of heart to heart, the secret of which no one outside could know. With Hindus, it is only to strangers that, open words of welcome and salutation are extended. To close and intimate friends, if they are offered, they are regarded as insult. So it is, one of our saints says: "how he could even raise his hands in praise when his heart was full and as in whatever act he did, he recognized God's fulness." The two and only two means of Sanctification according to Śaivaism are Karma Sāmya or self-sacrifice, Dedication or Śivārpaṇam and undying love to God (*vide* Sūtras 10, 11 of *Śivajñānabodham*). As I have shown in the scheme of the fourmārgas, it is not in Dāsa-Mārga alone that there is Bhakti, but Karma, Bhakti.and Jñāna grow deeper and higher, as we ascend from Dāsa-Mārga through Satputra-Mārga and Saha-Mārga to San-Mārga.

* The fifth conference held on 26th, 27th & 28th December 1910.

We love a child. We deck it with precious jewels and costly clothes. The child does not want them. It can hardly distinguish between a piece of glass and a diamond. But yet our acts mark our love. The same love induces a Christian to build the most costly Churches with the richest ornamentation. The London correspondent of 'the Hindu' of Madras once gave us an idea as to what amount of money is spent in Europe in decorating the Churches with flowers during Easter and Christmas. Even the most iconoclastic Mahomedans have spent millions in marble, gems and richest brocades in ornamenting their places of worship. If this be the mark of Bhakti or love, the thousands of Śaivite temples from Mount Himāvat to Cape Comorin and beyond, a hundred times more than that of any other faith, attest the Bhakti side of Śaivaism.

The number of canonised saints as given in the Agastya Bhakta Vilāsa and Upamanya Bhakta Vilāsa in Sanskrit, corresponding to the Periya Purāṇa in Tamiḻ, is more than sixty three, whereas the list of canonised Vaishṇava Saints (Āḻvārs) contains only eighteen. The out-pourings of love of the Śaivite Saints comprise twelve collections, the chief of which are called "*Dēvāram*" or garland of God, and *Tiruvāçagam* or 'the holy utterence', the latter of which has been translated into excellent English by Rev. Dr. G. U. Pope. Says he: "These remarkable poems are full of a simple fervour, which Tamiḻ people find absolutely irresistible; and hence with Śaivas, they quite take the place occupied among Christians by the book of Psalms." These collections are several times larger than the similar collections among Tamiḻ Vaishṇavas.

However, I hope I have succeeded in showing that Śaivaism is in harmony with each and every one of the living faiths of the world, and I pray to Lord Śiva, the Source of all Power, all Light and all Love, to speed the work of this Convention.

PRAISE BE TO MEYKANDA DEVA.
